The Friendly
Shakespeare

N O R R I E   E P S T E I N

The Friendly
Shakespeare

A Thoroughly Painless Guide
to the
Best of the Bard

A Winokur/Boates Book
V I K I N G

VIKING
Published by the Penguin Group
Viking Penguin, a division of Penguin Books USA Inc.,
375 Hudson Street, New York, New York 10014, U.S.A.
Penguin Books Ltd, 27 Wrights Lane, London W8 5TZ, England
Penguin Books Australia Ltd, Ringwood, Victoria, Australia
Penguin Books Canada Ltd, 10 Alcorn Avenue, Suite 300,
Toronto, Ontario, Canada M4V 3B2
Penguin Books (N.Z.) Ltd, 182–190 Wairau Road,
Auckland 10, New Zealand

Penguin Books Ltd, Registered Offices:
Harmondsworth, Middlesex, England

First published in 1993 by Viking Penguin,
a division of Penguin Books USA Inc.

1 3 5 7 9 10 8 6 4 2

A Winokur/Boates Book

Grateful acknowledgment is made for permission to use the following copyrighted works:
An excerpt from "Too Much Hamlet," by P. G. Wodehouse. By permission of A. P. Watt
Ltd., on behalf of the Trustees of the Wodehouse Estate.
Photograph of Mel Gibson from the motion picture *Hamlet*.
© 1990 World Icon N.V. All rights reserved.
Photograph of Olivia Hussey and Leonard Whiting from the motion picture *Romeo and Juliet*.
Copyright © 1968 by Paramount Pictures. All rights reserved.
Courtesy of Paramount Pictures.

LIBRARY OF CONGRESS CATALOGING-IN-PUBLICATION DATA
Epstein, Norrie.
The friendly Shakespeare / Norrie Epstein.
p.   cm.
Includes bibliographical references and index.
ISBN 0-670-84447-0
1. Shakespeare, William, 1564–1616—Outlines, syllabi, etc.
2. Shakespeare, William, 1564–1616—Study and teaching.   I. Title.
PR2987.E6   1992
822.3'3—dc20   92-54080

Printed in the United States of America
Set in Century O.S., Centaur, and Gill Sans
Designed by Amy Hill

*F*or my father,
Henry David Epstein,
with love

৵

❧ *I rejoice to concur with the common reader, for by the common sense of reader, uncorrupted by literary prejudices, after all the refinements of subtlety and the dogmatism of learning, must be generally decided all claim to poetical honors.*

——*DR. JOHNSON*

Acknowledgments

*P*eople have been enormously gracious with their time, ideas, and research. In writing this book, I found that those who love Shakespeare also love to talk about him, and I've spent many happy hours gossiping about Hamlet's sexuality or Lear's insanity with people I had never met before, as though these fictitious characters were mutual friends. I've acknowledged my specific debts—which are considerable—in the text and bibliography, but I am particularly indebted to Larry Bender, Reid Boates, Tony Church, Georgia Davis, Stephen Dickey, Pam Dorman, Charles Dutton, Andrew Gurr, Kathryn Harrison, Steve Hunter, Tom Kavanaugh, Bernice Kliman, Jan Kott, Alisa Kramer, Carol Sue Lipman, Louis Marder, Charles Marowitz, Ralph MacPhail, Jr., Ib Melchior, Peggy O'Brien, Charlton Ogburn, Stan Osher, Regina Pally, Martha, Joel, Katharine, Caroline, Meredith, and Mariana Pierce, Roger Pringle, Nicky Rathbone, Eva Resnikova, Theodora Rosenbaum, Kenneth Rothwell, J. Wynn Rousuck, Sam Schoenbaum, Shakespeare Authorship Roundtable, Gillian, Chris, and Chandra Speeth, Cindy Stern, David Suchet, John C. Thomas, Paris Wald, John Waller, Elinor Winokur, and most especially, Cyrus Hoy, Stephen Wigler, and Barbara Epstein. My greatest debt, however, is to Jon Winokur, without whom this book would not exist: *Il miglior fabbro.*

Preface

When I began to write this book I had three rules:

1. I would never call Shakespeare "the Bard."
2. I would keep a firm grip on my enthusiasm.
3. I would make no unsupported claims of Shakespeare's greatness.

I have broken them all.

I wanted to write a book that remained respectful of Shakespeare while making him accessible and intelligible. The epithet "the Bard" suggested the glib idolatry I wanted to avoid. Unfortunately, it was impossible to keep writing "Shakespeare" or "the dramatist" without sounding repetitious. I have tried, however, to use the term ironically whenever possible. Incidentally, the "Friendly" of the title isn't intended to presume a chumminess that would turn Shakespeare into a "household pet" (to use Shaw's expression)—he can on occasion be shockingly brutal. What I wanted to convey was the *real* Shakespeare—not the academic, the watered-down, or the airbrushed one presented to tourists and students but the man himself and the people who spend their lives studying him and practicing his art.

As for rule number two, most introductory books on Shakespeare mistakenly assume that their readers share their author's passion. When the writer goes into ecstasies, the reader feels suddenly abandoned, as if everyone else is having a fabulous time at a party while he or she's alone in a corner. Moreover, I wanted to see for myself if Shakespeare was really all that great. In that regard, I can't do better than repeat Robert Graves's remark, "A remarkable thing about Shakespeare is that he is really very good in spite of all the people who say he is very good."

And rule number three: although I've tried to explain what makes a line or a speech so wonderful, I soon discovered that this is truly impossible. Sometimes, as with Ariel's songs in *The Tempest,* Shakespeare is so profound that he doesn't lend himself to a literal explication. Sometimes he's good simply because he moves us. Above all, I didn't want to take the scalpel to him. To analyze and dissect would pluck the heart out of his mystery.

But I'll say here that Shakespeare is good because he is true. When I first began to read the plays and poems, certain lines would evoke poignant memories and images. But gradually over the years the reverse began to happen. For instance, as I walked in Hyde Park last August, the air already had the sad, burnt smell of approaching autumn, and immediately I thought, "And summer's lease hath all too short a date." I wasn't quoting; I was merely thinking what I felt. We can still put Shakespeare's words in our mouths and be true to our own experience.

A Note to the Reader

*T*o quote Laurence Olivier on his movie of *Henry V,* I wrote this book for people who think Shakespeare is "not for the likes of them." It's for everyone who has ever felt that overwhelming sense of oppression as they got into their seats at yet another Shakespeare play knowing that they probably wouldn't like or understand what was going to happen; it's for the reader whose only contact with Shakespeare was through Cliffs Notes, and the reader who wonders what the Shakespeare fuss is all about. Even the reader who already likes Shakespeare but would be interested in some of the less familiar Shakespearean lore might find the book useful. Above all, however, it's addressed to the intelligent common reader who is tired of academic jargon and the patronizing tone of the student handbook.

While working on this book I often felt compelled to justify why I was adding yet another item to the Shakespeare bibliography. *The Friendly Shakespeare* differs from other books on Shakespeare in that it is not a work of academic criticism, a handbook to help students write term papers, or a coffee-table book extolling the beauties of the Bard with glossy pictures of Anne Hathaway's cottage. Its aim is to introduce the reader to the Shakespearean spirit in all its forms, from the commercialism of Stratford to the lyricism of *Romeo and Juliet.*

Obviously, my own likes and dislikes prejudice the book. For instance, I've omitted what I consider extraneous details, such as textual distinctions between quarto and Folio readings—not because they're unimportant, but because they aren't relevant to enjoyment of the plays. For the most part I avoid plot summaries, because they are boring to read and tedious to write. (And besides, plot summaries are rarely helpful in understanding Shakespeare's genius, since for the most part he didn't invent his own plots.) For reasons of space, I couldn't include all of Shakespeare's plays or give them all equal attention—naturally, the *Hamlet* section is fuller than others, and the minor plays receive more cursory treatment. I wanted to whet the reader's appetite for Shakespeare, not satiate it. Deciding which plays to include was difficult, but I tried to select a representative sampling that would illustrate the range of Shakespeare's work, from the little-known *Troilus and Cressida* to the more standard *Macbeth* and *King Lear,* plays that readers could expect to encounter regularly in classes, on television, in the movies, and on stage. Again, my own preferences guided my selection. I omitted *Julius Caesar* because I don't like it and felt it was time to give the play a rest. On the other hand, I chose some of the more obscure plays to show that Shakespeare is more than *Hamlet.* For instance, *Titus Andronicus* is rarely taught and even more rarely performed, but it shows Shakespeare as a purveyor of popular taste, a glimpse rarely viewed in the classroom. I find that people are fascinated by the play's gaudy violence and by the fact that it's considered "bad Shakespeare." I also included some "sleepers," such as *Love's Labour's Lost,* one of my favorites, but since it, too, is rarely included in the curriculum, the reader might not have encountered it. Most of all, I chose plays that gave me pleasure, and hoped that others would agree.

Finally, I make no assumptions concerning your feelings about Shakespeare. You don't even have to believe Shakespeare *was* Shakespeare. Don't feel compelled to read this book from cover to cover: it's meant to be dipped into and browsed through at your leisure, because Shakespeare should never be a duty.

ॐ

NOTE: Most quotations are keyed to the New Penguin editions of the plays. Pelican editions were used for *Titus Andronicus, Romeo and Juliet, Timon of Athens,* and *Cymbeline.*

Contents

Shakespearean Romantic Comedy 76

The Histories 156

The Problem Plays 236

Shakespearean Tragedy 302

The Tragicomic Romances 450

The Spin-offs 464

The Friendly
Shakespeare

I'll bet Shakespeare compromised himself a lot: anybody who's in the entertainment industry does to some extent.

—CHRISTOPHER ISHERWOOD

*R*eading Shakespeare is sometimes like looking through a window into a dark room. You don't see in. You see nothing but a reflection of yourself, unable to get in. An unflattering image of yourself blind.

—ANTONY SHER

SHAKESPEARE

*I*f the public likes you, you're good. Shakespeare was a common down-to-earth writer in his day.

—MICKEY SPILLANE

*D*esmond McCarthy . . . said somewhere that trying to work out Shakespeare's personality was like looking at a very dark glazed picture in the National Portrait Gallery: at first you see nothing, then you begin to recognize features, and then you realize that they are your own.

—SAM SCHOENBAUM

I read Shakespeare directly I have finished writing. When my mind is agape and red hot. Then it is astonishing. I never yet knew how amazing his stretch and speed and word coining power is, until I felt it utterly outpace and outrace my own. . . . Even the less known plays are written at a speed that is quicker than anybody else's quickest. . . . Why then should anyone else attempt to write?

—VIRGINIA WOOLF

*O*ne must, I think, assume that Shakespeare is at least in the mind, if not in the writing, of all dramatists writing in English, and probably of all modern dramatists in the Western world.

—JACOB H. ADLER

*T*he trouble with Shakespeare is that you never get to sit down unless you're a king.

—GEORGE S. KAUFMAN

*T*o know the force of human genius we should read Shakespeare; to see the insignificance of human learning we may study his commentators.

—WILLIAM HAZLITT

*P*rofessors spend a lifetime analyzing one metaphor that Shakespeare probably unthinkingly scribbled and whose significance completely bypasses an audience. Neither the professor nor the actor has a monopoly on Shakespeare. His genius is that he wrote texts to be studied *and* scripts to be performed.

—LEONORA EYRE

*P*eople simply do not read Shakespeare anymore, nor the Bible either. They read *about* Shakespeare. The critical literature that has built up about his name and works is vastly more fruitful and stimulating than Shakespeare himself.

—HENRY MILLER

I believe he was a genius.

—MEL GIBSON

First Encounters with Shakespeare

I began to act the tragedies for the benefit of my father and mother. Unfortunately I was an only child, which meant that I had to play all the parts, so I leapt in and out of the door at the end of our sitting room duelling with myself, forcing myself to drink from my own poisoned chalice, and furiously upbraiding myself as my own mother. They were productions which must have been far more enjoyable to perform than to watch. When I was 13 and played Richard II at school, I was astonished to have an actual Queen to kiss, and a murderer to assault me in the gaol. As I died on the speech room platform I thought that life would never provide me with a more glorious moment; nor has it.

—JOHN MORTIMER

*L*ike most schoolboys, I had been sickened of Shakespeare by education. I was wearied almost to revolt by this examination business of commenting and annotating. All too well did I know and was able to repeat on paper what the Rialto was; I could define an argosy to any teacher's delight and could be profound about Arden, Ducdame, and the Symbolic Value of Ariel and Caliban. Hour after hour I had estimated significances, contrasted characters, explained allusions. By the age of eighteen I was allergic almost beyond hope of therapy.

—IVOR BROWN

*T*his goes back to 1943, when I was a senior in high school and I had read in *The New York Times* of a production that had just opened on Broadway and it was of *Othello*. The cast included Paul Robeson as

Othello and a young unknown actor named José Ferrer as Iago. I saw that production almost forty years ago, and I remember it as vividly, more vividly, than the things I saw on TV this past week. I remember Iago drawing the audience into his web, and I remember his hand gestures when he indicated what his plans were. I remember Brabantio's white beard. I remember the drums beating and Robeson's extraordinary voice and physique. And my reaction then—and my reaction now—is wowsers!

—SAM SCHOENBAUM

I saw [Olivier's movie of *Henry V*] twenty-seven times and labored for a time under the delusion that [it] was the greatest play ever written. I committed to memory every word of Shakespeare's text and every bar of William Walton's score. I knew the names of every actor and the behavior of every performance, including the four subsidiary characters Olivier anonymously played in addition to Henry. Like many young actors of the time, I was persuaded by this film to make a career on the stage, and my own performances were apish imitations of Olivier's stirring cadences and Robert Newton's extravagant eye-popping Pistol.

—ROBERT BRUSTEIN

*O*ne morning I received the following charmingly worded communication:

2ND APRIL 1924

Dear Mr. Gielgud,
   If you would like to play the finest lead among the plays by the late William Shakespeare, will you please call upon Mr. Peacock and Mr. Ayliff at the Regent Theatre on Friday at 2:30 p.m. Here is an opportunity to become a London Star in a night.
   Please confirm.

Yours very truly,
Akerman May

[The part was Romeo, the nineteen-year-old Gielgud's first major London success.]

—JOHN GIELGUD

I remember our teacher sent us to see a local production at the university of *King Lear* and I just made out with my girlfriend and then we left.

—KEVIN KLINE

I know the house lights have gone to half, then to black. The opening music for *Romeo and Juliet*. The curtain rises, the audience applauds the set, the Duke of Verona speaks. It is happening. I feel slightly sick and have to remind myself just how many years I have wanted this. I want to weep and go home. . . . I hear my cue. I have to force myself into action as though I am to plunge into a freezing sea. I run across the stage toward my mother and my nurse. I am distracted for a moment by the brief applause that greets my appearance, then everything begins to fade except the reality of the play. I feel that I have a wonderful story to tell.

—CLAIRE BLOOM

Why Is Shakespeare So Popular?

*W*hen Shakespeare died in 1616 the event was barely noticed. Today he is the cultural icon of the English-speaking world. Here two Shakespeareans, one an iconoclast, the other a conservative, offer responses to the question: Why is Shakespeare so popular?

Gary Taylor

*G*ary Taylor infuriates most orthodox Shakespeareans because to him Shakespeare is just another writer—better than most, but certainly not the greatest one who ever lived. Taylor challenges the inherited assumption of Shakespeare's greatness, preferring to see his current status as the fruit of centuries of public relations on the part of British imperialism, "which propagated the English language on every continent." His irreverent study of Shakespeare's reputation, Reinventing Shakespeare, dispassionately analyzes how successive generations recreate Shakespeare according to their own preoccupations, anxieties, and beliefs.

Shakespeare is popular now because he has been popular. If we could rewind the tape of the past and erase from 1650 to the present and simply go back on our own to the literature of the fifteenth and sixteenth centuries, I'm not sure Shakespeare would be the one we would choose to elevate. His status in our time is a reflection of inertia as much as anything else.

Shakespeare became popular in the eighteenth century because he represented a return to the safety of the past before all the upheavals of the revolutions, both English and French. Shakespeare began to get popular during the French Revolution, when he was seized upon as the champion of solid English values such as the monarchy.

In the eighteenth century, the actor David Garrick used Shakespeare to make theatre respectable. Shakespeare was a classic, and if actors performed his works, then theatre would be high culture rather than crude entertainment for the masses.

The period of Shakespeare's greatest power and cultural influence began in the late eighteenth century and lasted through most of the nineteenth century, when the university system for the study of literature began. So the study of Shakespeare was culturally locked in place at that time. Shakespeare and the Bible were the two books everybody knew, but making the Bible compulsory is controversial today, while Shakespeare courses are still required. Shakespeare is our last cultural stronghold. His works have become our secular Bible.

Roger Pringle

*A*s *director of the Shakespeare Birthplace Trust, Roger Pringle is the custodian of Shakespeare's reputation. Here, he offers a more conservative view.*

I appreciate Gary Taylor's point, but surely Shakespeare's popularity is due to his extraordinary facility for language, his memorable characters, and his wonderful stories. There's always an element in the appreciation of Shakespeare which is linked to social behavior and cultural ideals, but in the end an artist only endures if people recognize his genius.

Why Is Shakespeare Boring?

*I am more easily bored with
Shakespeare, and have suffered
more ghastly evenings with him,
than with any dramatist I know.*

—PETER BROOK
(who calls these evenings
"Deadly Theatre")

*B*rook points out that Shakespeare's plays contain everything: "duels, battles, storms, coronations, trials, suicides, feasts and funerals." To this one could add lovemaking, murder, betrayals, marriages, revenge, and lust. Why, then, do so many of us find him boring? Perhaps because so many directors insist on doing "Shakespeare by numbers."

*M*any directors have a sense of automatic Shakespeare. They think you can just push a button and have a play unwind. You have to rethink and, to a large extent, reinterpret and reconstruct a play, even if you're doing a traditional version. If you think, "This is a great play, it's been around for over four hundred fifty years and it's a classic, and all we have to do is put it in costume and put it onstage," well, of course it's going to be boring. This sort of thing is always a product of people who love Shakespeare too much. The people who revere him always do the worst work. Shakespeare should grab you by the throat.

—CHARLES MAROWITZ

*W*e find Shakespeare boring because we're lazy. We're not willing to get through the language. That's the only barrier. If a play is performed right by those who are properly trained, after about twenty minutes you won't be aware of the language because the human story is so strong.

—DAVID SUCHET

*P*eople tend to think that Shakespeare wrote these highfalutin metaphors. But the metaphors are very simple. We know what it means when Lear says "Sharper than a serpent's tooth it is to have an ungrateful child." Every parent who has experienced hardships with his kid knows what *that* means. My God! These plays are supposed to be passionate! *Macbeth* is about murder! It's about what happens when we contemplate murder. It's not about going to the supermarket and renting a video; it's about blood on one's hands! The actress who plays Lady Macbeth shouldn't be concerned with getting the speech technically correct, she should be concerned that her husband is going to kill the king. And there's nothing nice about Richard III: he walks out and right away says, I am going to kill everybody in town. Standing on stage and speaking well is all very nice, but you can buy the album if you want that. An actor has to keep it exciting, and not let the audience get ahead of him. It's the task of the actor, the *new* Shakespearean actor, to be the Othello that might *not* kill Desdemona, to be the Lear that may *not* go mad. To be the honest Iago!

—CHARLES "ROC" DUTTON

On Teaching Shakespeare: What Went Wrong?

To this day I can't read King Lear, *having had the advantage of studying it accurately in school.*

—*ALFRED NORTH WHITEHEAD*

Peggy O'Brien

*P*eggy *O'Brien is director of education at the Folger Shakespeare Library. In addition to teaching students, she also teaches teachers how to teach Shakespeare.*

NE: *Everyone blames their teachers. Is it the teacher's fault most people hate Shakespeare?*

PO: No one wants to bore a whole class to death. But probably one of the reasons we don't like Shakespeare is because we sat in class and somebody droned on and on and said, "This is the world's greatest playwright blah blah blah." And then, of course, teachers don't know how to teach him because they may also have sat in classes and listened to the same thing.

When they clapped, I almost felt like crying.

—DAVID DILEO,
STUDENT, AGE NINE,
ON PLAYING MALVOLIO
IN HIS GRAMMAR
SCHOOL PRODUCTION
OF *TWELFTH NIGHT*

NE: *Why is Shakespeare so hard for American students?*

PO: He's hard because they believe he's hard. Also, there's no readily available version of any Shakespeare on video- or audiocassette that's done by American actors. So American kids only hear Shakespeare spoken with an English accent. They don't hear him spoken by people who sound like them.

NE: *How soon can children start with Shakespeare?*

PO: You can read them the stories at a very young age. *Macbeth* is a hot favorite in the fourth grade. They don't know they're not supposed to like Shakespeare, so they don't have that resistance yet. And they're already learning new words all the time, so Shakespeare isn't different from anything else.

NE: *What are some good plays for teenagers?*

PO: *Henry IV, Part I,* is a great play for high school kids because you have the old king saying to his son, "You should do this," and you have the kid saying, "Yeah? Watch me." High school students just love that play.

NE: *What about the verse? Don't they find that difficult?*

PO: Look, if kids can remember the lyrics and rhythm to rap music, then they can figure out iambic pentameter.

Why Julius Caesar?

*J*ulius *Caesar* bears the stigma of being the play that's routinely forced upon students in school. One of the most austere and static of all Shakespeare's plays, *Julius Caesar* probably has the distinction of turning away more students from Shakespeare than any other play. Why, then, *Julius Caesar,* when any of the comedies would be more pleasurable? In the nineteenth century, when Latin was still part of the curriculum, high school teachers thought it would be helpful to assign Caesar's *Commentaries* along with Shakespeare's play. Although few schools today teach Latin, *Julius Caesar* remains embedded in the curriculum like a fly in amber. According to O'Brien, there are two reasons for this: it's short, and it has no sex. Not one sexy pun or allusion in the entire play—not one word that would cause a class to disintegrate into giggles and nudges. No wonder we grow up hating Shakespeare.

Forget the Footnotes!
And Other Advice

*S*ome experts advise not to start reading Shakespeare until you're at least sixty-five; others say the sooner the better. Some suggest reading the plays before seeing them; others suggest seeing them first. To read footnotes, or not to? And so on. People tend to procrastinate because they think there's a right way of "doing" Shakespeare. But just plunge in. See a play, read it aloud, rent a video, listen to a tape. It's up to you. When you look at Shakespeare close up, he's not as intimidating as when he's seen from afar.

To help you get started, experts offer the following suggestions:

*T*he worst way of interpreting Shakespeare is to say he meant this, and just this, and to give a formula. As David Hare said, "Shakespeare was thinking while he was working through the plot," and this is the right way to approach Shakespeare. . . . But don't ask for simple answers from Shakespeare! Just believe in Shakespeare—in his greatness, in his wide outlook, in his ability to put into one play a whole world with all its contradictions, contrasts, and problems.

—ALEXANDER ANIKST

*F*irst of all, you should read the play aloud. Don't read one scene today and then another tomorrow. It doesn't work that way. Read a whole scene without looking anything up. You'll be surprised by how much you know. We tend to fall into the trap of looking at every single footnote, and then we start looking at footnotes of words that we know, words like "ye" and "thee."

If there's a production near you, see it. If you're bored at the halfway point, leave. But don't blame Shakespeare for that production. Don't think that because you're bored, he's boring.

—MICHAEL TOLAYDO

*L*isten to Shakespeare and don't listen to the critics. You don't need to understand every word, and if you don't, you can go back to the footnotes later.

—LOUIS MARDER

*D*on't read the play; see it first. It was Olivier's *Henry V* that made me realize that Shakespeare was about real people and that his language wasn't simply beautiful poetry, but that it carried the vein of action. So I would advise someone to see the Branagh and the Olivier *Henry*s—or even the Olivier *Hamlet,* which is actually not all that good.

—ROBERT BRUSTEIN

*M*y advice to anybody going to the theatre: don't worry too much. Just make sure your ears are clean and your eyes are sharp. Listen and look and watch. Look at the distances people stand from each other; look at the relationships being developed. Don't be put off if during the first ten minutes you can't understand what's being said. Stay with it. Don't negate the move that Shakespeare will make toward your gut, toward your soul—because he *will* touch you there, if you allow yourself to be touched.

—DAVID SUCHET

*T*he video series *Playing Shakespeare* is a superb introduction to the study of Shakespeare. Actors such as Patrick Stewart, Ben Kingsley, David Suchet, and Ian McKellen illustrate rather than talk about the essence of Shakespeare. The series demystifies Shakespeare, because instead of having an eminent professor hold forth and tell viewers what to think, it depicts actors in a casual workshop setting grappling with and arguing about various interpretations.

If you can't see a play or rent a video, you can always buy an audiocassette of any play. They are inexpensive, easy to listen to, and available at most record stores.

*D*on't choose something you already did in school. *Othello* would be a good place to begin because it has only one plot to deal with. And it really moves: in the first eighty-five lines it's already going a hundred

TO READ OR TO SEE THE PLAYS?

—————◆————

*T*he printed word can't convey the undertone and nuances of speech. For that, you need to hear a gifted actor. Inflection reveals at once whether a speaker is ironic, genuine, sad, or funny. Irony, for instance, is mainly conveyed through inflection and facial expression. Take that masterpiece of political irony, Marc Antony's funeral speech. To the novice, "But Brutus is an honorable man" seems pretty straightforward. But when you *hear* the lines, an entirely new meaning emerges. What we hear is not a superficial bit of flattery or an honest assessment, but a brilliant stroke of rhetoric in which Antony means precisely the reverse of what he says.

On the other hand, reading a play alone allows you to proceed at your own pace, giving you the time to dwell on poetry and the complex images that might fly right by you if they were only heard.

miles a hour. It's also very gripping. It has the parent-child theme, the racial issue, and there's Iago! There are a lot of adult emotions in the play. *Hamlet* can wait.

—PEGGY O'BRIEN

*T*here are some parts of the plays you'll never understand. But excuse me, I thought that's what great art was supposed to be about. Don't freak out over it. . . . Keep reading.

—PETER SELLARS

Academics Versus Actors

*B*ut you don't have to choose between literary analysis or theatrical representation. Each complements the other. Most non-Shakespeareans tend to imagine the Shakespeare scholar as Charles Dickens's Mr. Curdle, with his "pamphlet of sixty-four pages, post octavo, on the character of the Nurse's deceased husband in *Romeo and Juliet.*" Such scholarship tends to wither the flesh-and-blood vitality of drama, which, after all, is meant to be enjoyed, not probed to death. But a play is also a text, and in the hands of a gifted teacher and critic it can be suddenly illuminated, revealing unsuspected and surprising meanings. For some scholars, the plays are dramatic poems, and what excites them is not necessarily the human situation the plays depict, but Shakespeare's subtle use of language and how one word or image resonates throughout a play and reflects its underlying meaning. Professors devote years to studying one image in *Hamlet* which a director might cut or an actor ignore. Linguistic analysis reveals that in addition to being a powerful dramatist, Shakespeare was also a very great poet. As an example of how Shakespeare "unpacks" a word, allowing its various meanings to resonate throughout a play, Professor Marjorie Garber of Harvard University cites the significance of ear imagery and poison in *Hamlet*—images that might be lost on a modern audience. (Claudius kills old King Hamlet by pouring poison in his ear.) "You can trace the poison metaphor or ear imagery throughout the play. Then think of all the spying and the eavesdropping that goes on in *Hamlet*. Or the way in which words can poison the listener." This is only one example, but in all of Shakespeare's mature plays he rarely uses an idea or an image in isolation, but allows it to accumulate meaning, gathering depth and richness, so that a play is not just plot with events, but a unified work of art in which language, themes, and plot are woven together.

Y ou can't get a sense of anything when you just read a play because you can't see the character who is on stage but who doesn't speak. For instance, you won't be able to understand Antonio in *The Merchant of Venice* because in that play Shakespeare created a dramatic situation where the main character rarely speaks. Get another person to be the silent character while you read a part aloud, and you'll discover why and what's being said.

—TONY CHURCH

T he bastion that protects William Shakespeare has been established by scholars, critics, teachers, litterateurs—people with a vested interest in language and the furtherance of a literary tradition. It's in their interest that the texts remain sacrosanct—that they're handed down from generation to generation, each providing new insights and new refinements like so many new glosses on an old painting. A process which, judging from the past two hundred years, can go on for at least another five hundred because there will never be a shortage of scholars to point out the semiotic significance of the ass's head in *A Midsummer Night's Dream* or the tallow candle in *Macbeth* or the implications of the syllabus of Wittenberg during the years Hamlet was supposed to have been enrolled there.

—CHARLES MAROWITZ

W_{HO} I_S

Conservatives cite speeches from Shakespeare's plays and claim him as one of their own. But he's also cited by liberals to uphold *their* beliefs. The plays themselves, however, offer no clues as to what Shakespeare himself believed. He created a teeming world, yet he had the discipline to submerge his own personality to it. There's not one line you can point to and confidently assert, "Ah, that's Shakespeare there," without finding another

SHAKESPEARE?

line to contradict it. His doctrines, political and social, remain dark and elusive, and he fascinates partly because he represents the mystery behind creation itself—the wizard who disappears in a cloud of smoke after conjuring wonderful creations that are more real than himself.

*I*f the playwright is blessed with infinite generosity, if he is not obsessed with his own ideas, he will give the impression that he is in total sympathy with everyone. Beyond that, if there are twenty characters and the playwright manages to invest each one with the same power of conviction, we come to the miracle of Shakespeare. A computer would have difficulty in programming all the points of view his plays contain.

—PETER BROOK

Some Biographical Bones

*M*ark Twain compared the creation of Shakespeare's biography to the reconstruction of a dinosaur from a few bits of bone stuck together with plaster. The facts in this case are few and far between, and require a great deal of conjecture.

Parentage

*T*he playwright's father, John Shakespeare, was an established Stratford glove maker and leather dresser who also dealt in other commodities, such as wool and grain. John is first mentioned in 1552, when he was fined for keeping a dunghill in front of his house. For the next twenty years his position in Stratford steadily rose, from chamberlain to burgess to alderman, until finally he became high bailiff, a position equivalent to the modern mayor. Beginning in 1572, his fortunes began to decline, though no one knows exactly why. He stopped attending council meetings and church, lost most of his holdings, and his application for a coat of arms was turned down.

Shakespeare's mother, Mary Arden, came from a prominent Catholic family, a fact that leads some to conclude that Shakespeare was secretly a Catholic, or at the very least had papist sympathies. While providing no evidence for the assertion, Richard Davies, one of Shakespeare's first biographers, wrote, "He died a papist." In 1757, a handwritten booklet containing a Catholic avowal of faith was found in the rafters of John Shakespeare's Henley Street house. The document's authenticity has been the subject of debate, but recently it was discovered that identical documents had been circulated throughout England via the Catholic underground during that period. Nevertheless, the Elizabethan persecution made Catholicism a dangerous religion to practice, and Shakespeare was a prudent man. Given his desire to rise in the world, he probably chose the expedient course and adopted the Anglican faith.

Birth

Shakespeare most likely was born at one of his father's two houses on Henley Street, in Stratford-upon-Avon. He was christened on April 26, 1664, in Holy Trinity Church in Stratford. Since it was the custom to baptize a child three days after his birth, Shakespeare's birthday is recognized as April 23, the same day as his burial fifty-two years later.

Early Life

There's no record that Shakespeare attended school, but since such records were not maintained, there isn't any evidence against it either. Shakespeare's early biographers wrote that before becoming a playwright, he took up his father's trade. John Aubrey, the seventeenth-century author of *Lives of the Poets,* a delightfully compulsive and anarchic assortment of fact, rumor, and half-truth, wrote, "His father was a Butcher, & I have been told heretofore by some of the neighbours, that when he was a boy he exercised his fathers Trade, but when he kill'd a Calfe, he would doe it in a *high style,* & make a Speech." It should be noted that Aubrey's love of a gossip outweighed his allegiance to truth.

Marriage

The Episcopal register of the diocese of Worcester records the marriage of Willelmum Shaxpere, in 1582. The groom was eighteen; the bride, Anne Hathaway, twenty-six. As a minor, the groom required his father's permission, and it was traditional in such cases for the bride's kin to appoint bondsmen to protect her legal interests. Evidence suggests that the marriage was hastily arranged. Normally, the banns, or the public announcement of a couple's intention to wed, were read in church for three consecutive Sundays before the wedding took place. In Shakespeare's case, they were announced only once. Banns were forbidden during Advent, and the young groom probably didn't want to wait until January 13, so two friends of the bride's family rode to the Bishop's Court in Worcester to obtain a special license. They then had to give a bond of forty pounds to assure that no impediments to the union would come to light and that Shakespeare would be financially responsible for any legal actions as a result of the marriage. Obviously, the Hathaways were anxious to protect their daughter's interests.

Some discrepancy exists concerning the recording of the bride's name. The entry in the church register reads "Annam Whateley de Temple Grafton." But the bond for the marriage, issued the next day, lists the bride as "Anne Hathwey of Stratford." Through the years the Whateley/Hathaway confusion has inspired much romantic speculation: Did Shakespeare try to elope with an Anne Whateley before he was entrapped by Anne Hathaway? Russell Fraser, in *Young Shakespeare,* notes that Whateley for Hathaway "seems more than a slip of the pen," but it is unlikely that Shakespeare intended to marry another woman. Shakespearean biographers Sam Schoenbaum and Peter Levi concede that "Whateley" is probably a scribal error for Hathaway, while Fraser suggests that the vicar might have had someone else, another Anne, on his mind. Despite the fanciful conjectures of novelists such as Anthony Burgess, conventional wisdom asserts that Anne Whateley of Temple Grafton and Anne Hathaway of Stratford are one and the same.

It is the next official entry concerning Shakespeare that explains the rush to the altar: On May 26, six months after the marriage of William and Anne, Susanna Shakespeare was christened. Two years later, on February 2, 1585, the twins Judith and Hamnet were born.

The Lost Years

*F*rom 1585 to 1592, there are no official records of Shakespeare. Based on the wide range of knowledge revealed in the plays, people have variously speculated that Shakespeare was at one time or another a moneylender, gardener, sailor, scrivener, tutor, coachman, soldier, printer, schoolmaster, lawyer, and clerk. One theorist even maintained that Shakespeare joined the Franciscans and was buried in the habit of the order.

The most persistent legend concerning Shakespeare, the celebrated deer-poaching incident, explains why he abandoned his family for London. One year after his marriage, Shakespeare, consorting with some low companions, was caught poaching deer on Sir Thomas Lucy's estate, Charlecote Park. After being prosecuted by Lucy, Shakespeare retaliated by writing an insulting ballad about the Lucy family in which he puns upon Lucy, "Lowse," and "Lowsey"—similar-sounding words in the Stratfordian dialect. It was this bit of doggerel (Shakespeare's first attempt at poetry, according to the legend) that forced him out of Stratford and on to London and fame. During the early years of Shakespeare scholarship, the deer-poaching legend regularly turned up, each time with an individual twist. In one version Shakespeare is found poaching rabbits; in another, he boldly nails the ballad to the gates of the Lucy estate. Similarly, the ballad changes with each chronicler. Sam Schoenbaum, in *Shakespeare's Lives,* cites an early version recorded by one of Shakespeare's first biographers, Thomas Jones, in 1703: "A Parliamente member a Justice of Peace, / at Home a poore Scarecrow at London an Asse. / If Lowsie is Lucy as some Volke Miscalle it / Then Lucy is Lowsie whatever befalle it." (Jones's sole claim to authenticity is that he happened to live in the same village as Mary Hart, Shakespeare's granddaughter's niece.)

Since the legend was independently cited by several sources, it may contain an element of truth.

The London Years

No one knows exactly when Shakespeare moved to London or how he supported himself when he first got there. Some say he held horses for a living, but we do know that before he became a playwright he was an actor, and even as a thriving playwright he continued to perform in his own and others' plays, appearing in the parts of Adam in *As You Like It* and the Ghost in *Hamlet.*

What follows is a brief chronology of highlights in Shakespeare's life.

1592: Shakespeare is first mentioned as being in London when he is singled out by the rival dramatist Robert Greene in his bitter deathbed pamphlet entitled *A Groats-worth of Wit*:

> Yes, trust them not; for there is an upstart crow, beautified with our feathers, that with his *Tiger's heart wrapped in a player's hide,* supposes he is as well able to bombast out a blank verse as the best of you: and being an absolute *Johannes fac totum,* is in his own conceit the only Shake-scene in a country.

The "tiger's heart" is an allusion to *Henry VI, Part 3* (I.4.137). Henry Chettle, who edited—some say wrote—*Groats-worth,* later issued a formal retraction in which he admitted that Shakespeare was civil, upright, and honest.

1589–94: Shakespeare's first plays, *Henry VI, Titus Andronicus,* and *The Comedy of Errors,* are the hits of the London season.

The plague in London leads to the closing of the theatres, thus giving Shakespeare time to write poetry.

1593: "Venus and Adonis," Shakespeare's highly erotic and ornate mythological poem, is published and dedicated to the Earl of Southampton.

1593?–94?: Shakespeare begins writing the Sonnets.

1594: "The Rape of Lucrece," a long narrative poem, is published, with an extremely warm dedication to the Earl of Southampton, leading some scholars to speculate that while the theatres were closed Shakespeare lived at the Southampton estate.

1594: The Lord Chamberlain's Men is formed, and for the next ten years it is London's premier acting company. A warrant for payment records that Shakespeare is a full-fledged professional in the company, which he serves as both actor and playwright.

Official documents, such as tax assessments, court records, and land titles, reveal Shakespeare's desire to establish himself as a man of property. Through the years he steadily amasses a small fortune in real estate.

1596: Shakespeare applies for and is granted a coat of arms, the Elizabethan status symbol, on behalf of his father, whose request was denied years earlier. Father and son are now permitted to write "Gentleman" after their names. The family motto is *Non sanz droit* ("Not Without Right"); their crest is of a falcon shaking a spear.

Shakespeare's son Hamnet, the sole male heir of the Shakespeare line, dies.

1597: Shakespeare purchases New Place, the second largest house in Stratford. Unlike other London dramatists, Shakespeare maintains his connections to his hometown, and according to tradition, he pays regular visits to his wife and children.

1599: Shakespeare is made a principal shareholder in the Globe playhouse (rare for a playwright), thus establishing himself as a successful businessman. He is now involved in all aspects of the theatre.

1599–1608: Shakespeare's greatest period, during which he writes *Twelfth Night, Troilus and Cressida, Hamlet, Othello, Measure for Measure, King Lear, Macbeth, Coriolanus,* and *Antony and Cleopatra.*

1603: With the succession of James I, Shakespeare's company is given the royal patent and is now known as the King's Men. It performs about twelve times a year at court.

1607–13: Shakespeare's final period, during which he writes the romances *Pericles, Cymbeline, The Winter's Tale,* and *The Tempest.*

1610–11?: Shakespeare permanently leaves the London stage and retires to his home in Stratford, where he is an important member of the local gentry.

1613: Shakespeare collaborates with John Fletcher on *Henry VIII, The Two Noble Kinsmen,* and the lost play *Cardenio.*

1616: Shakespeare dies.

1623: The First Folio is published by Shakespeare's fellow actors Heminge and Condell.

The Shakespeare Who Makes Some of Us Uncomfortable

Neither a sensitive consumptive like Keats nor a "man's man" like Hemingway, Shakespeare does not readily lend himself to romantic mythmaking. In his infinite complexity, he resembles one of his own ambiguous creations. From generation to generation, the image of the playwright changes according to current tastes, ideals, and values. Yet the biographical facts, scant as they may be, do not always fit the idealized portrait. This is a problem with which biographers, critics, and editors have grappled since Shakespeare became an industry in the middle of the eighteenth century. Rather than confront certain facts, bardolaters tend to ignore them or to resort to elaborate evasions.

While eighteenth-century biographers ignored certain details of Shakespeare's life, Victorians felt the need to explain away his "antenuptial fornication," his homoeroticism, and his sordid affair with the Dark Lady, a married person of questionable repute. They willingly acknowledged that the Sonnets contain some of the greatest love lyrics ever written; what they found harder to admit was that most of them were addressed to a man, and that some are frankly erotic. The undeniable fact that Susanna Shakespeare was born just six months after her parents' marriage presented a vexing problem, but some nineteenth-century critics fell gratefully upon the "troth-plight," an Elizabethan contract which asserted that once a couple were engaged they were as good as married and thus could do anything they liked. According to Sam Schoenbaum, one nineteenth-century bardolater even claimed that God speeded up the gestation process for his favorite son.

The Victorians were also perturbed that Shakespeare apparently spent little time with his wife and children, choosing instead the seedy theatre district outside London. To compensate for this unfortunate image, one artist drew a sentimental picture of the Shakespeare clan gathered around Papa Shakespeare as he read aloud from his latest endeavor.

*H*onigmann provides substantial evidence suggesting that Shakespeare was a moneylender. He cites the only surviving letter ever written to Shakespeare, a business letter from Richard Quiney asking if he can borrow thirty pounds. Quiney's father advised him that Shakespeare will obtain the money "*at a price.*" "If you bargain with Mr. Shakespeare," he adds, "bring your money home if you may." For more evidence, see Honigmann's "There Is a World Elsewhere" in *Images of Shakespeare.*

In contrast to the Victorians, some modern bardolaters and scholars find Shakespeare too conservative. Unfortunately, there's little of the bohemian about Shakespeare. He's much too prudent and financially savvy for those who seek a subversive rebel. There's nothing they can do about the smug demeanor of the burgher depicted in the Droeshout Engraving, the angling for an aristocratic patron, the desire for a coat of arms. He liked—probably loved—money and was a very shrewd investor. He took people to court to collect paltry sums, never forgot a debt, and, according to some, hoarded grain during a famine. The critic E. A. J. Honigmann asserts that Shakespeare might have been a moneylender. A bisexual moneylender who dabbled in real estate is not how many people imagine the Bard, but it's probably close to the truth. Even today, with our supposedly enlightened attitudes, and when tell-all biographies reveal the most private details of an artist's life—which, after all, is *supposed* to be unconventional—many still need to see Shakespeare as a monolith rather than a man.

The man William Shakespeare is overshadowed by the power of his genius. Yet we need to see a face behind the works, and our desire uncomfortably recalls that scene in *The Wizard of Oz* in which Toto whisks aside a curtain to reveal a tiny man fiddling with controls, desperately struggling to create an illusion. If somehow we could unveil the real William Shakespeare, we'd probably find him disappointingly ordinary, neither as impassioned as Antony nor as witty as the Fool. We want the man, not just the works; but shouldn't the plays and poems be enough?

If Dr. Gall the craniologist's assertion is to be believed, the organ of robbery (covetiveness) and the organ for forming good dramatic plots, are one and the same; he certainly proved himself a great adept in the latter, and no doubt was so in the former.

—W. T. MONTCRIEFF

Shakespeare's Likeness

*T*he image that we have come to know as Shakespeare's is the Droeshout Engraving, which first appeared on the title page of the First Folio and now graces everything from twenty-pound notes to pub signs. A symbol, an icon, a logo; for most of the world it represents, in the words of W. H. Auden, "The Top Bard." The picture of the bald man with vacant eyes stands for Western culture and civilization at its peak. With slight variations, based on the fashion of the age and the individual artist, most cartoons, caricatures, and likenesses derive from this one engraving. In the four and a half centuries since Shakespeare's death, over two hundred fifty "authentic" portraits of Shakespeare have turned up in attics, pubs, and warehouses, but unfortunately, only the Droeshout Engraving and the Janssen Bust over the Stratford monument have a strong claim to being authentic likenesses.

Still, Shakespeare may have looked nothing like Droeshout's rendering. Since Martin Droeshout was fifteen when Shakespeare died, it is highly unlikely that the portrait was done from life. More likely, it was based on an earlier portrait, which may or may not have been of Shakespeare. The poet's colleague Ben Jonson must have thought it a fairly good likeness, for in his commendatory poem in the First Folio he wrote: "It was for Gentle Shakespeare cut; / Wherein the Graver had a strife / With Nature, to out-do the life."

The Janssen Bust that adorns Shakespeare's Monument in Stratford is even more disappointing, revealing an older, fatter Bard than the Droeshout. Nevertheless, as it was commissioned by Shakespeare's family, it has the best claim to authenticity. One can assume that the family found it a fair likeness, since it was never removed.

The Folger Shakespeare Library

Above: *The* Droeshout Engraving.

❧

Right: *The* Janssen Bust, over-
looking Shakespeare's grave in
Holy Trinity Church, reveals an
uncharacteristically bloated Bard.
Some say that the likeness was
taken from Shakespeare's death
mask and that the puffy features
are the result of a final illness.
Writer Charles Hamilton cites the
"Bloated Bust" as evidence that
Shakespeare was murdered, since
arsenic tends to puff up the features whereas a simple fever
makes them gaunt and drawn.

❧

The Folger Shakespeare Library

The Chandos Portrait

*T*he Chandos Portrait, or "the one with the earring," offers an idealized image of the Bard. Here he seems sensuous and Byronic, the gold earring adding a particularly dashing and modern touch. According to legend, the Chandos was painted by Richard Burbage, the leading man in Shakespeare's company. It was then bequeathed to the playwright and theatre manager Sir William Davenant, Shakespeare's self-appointed godson (as years went by, he would insinuate that he was Shakespeare's illegitimate son). It is called the Chandos Portrait because after a long chain of bequests and purchases it ended up in the possession of the Duke of Chandos. Then, in 1856, the Duke of Ellsmere donated it to the National Portrait Gallery, where it remained until 1833, when it was removed after doubts arose concerning its authenticity. It was reinstated in 1961, not because doubts were resolved but because of its role in the history of Shakespeareana—and because it makes Shakespeare so intriguingly romantic.

*P*icasso's interpretation of Shakespeare.

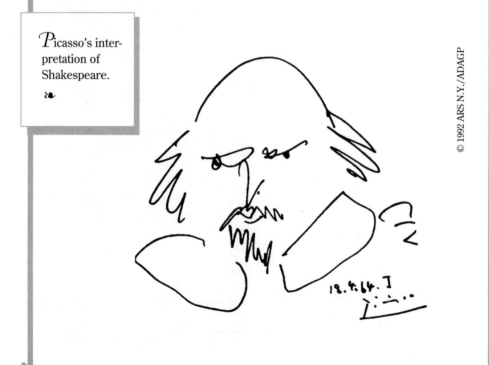

❖ Through the years, numerous portraits have turned up which at one time or another were hailed as authentic likenesses, but they all turned out to be derivative or doubtful. In 1940 researchers subjected the so-called Ashbourne Portrait of Shakespeare to X-ray and infrared photographic analysis and discovered that underneath the portrait of Shakespeare was another painting, that of Edward de Vere, the Earl of Oxford, the man some people claim wrote the plays attributed to Shakespeare.

❖ Computer analysis conducted by Lillian F. Schwartz, a consultant at Bell Laboratories, reveals an astonishing match between the Droeshout Engraving and a portrait of Queen Elizabeth. After comparing the Droeshout to that of several Elizabethan notables, Schwartz discovered that Shakespeare's features and those in the Gower Portrait of Elizabeth were perfectly aligned and, even more striking, the distance between them was identical. Schwartz arrived at the startling conclusion that the Gower Elizabeth and the Droeshout Shakespeare are portraits of the same face. The implications of this finding are unclear (Schwartz suggests that perhaps this is a veiled hint that Elizabeth is the true author of the plays), but proponents of the theory that Shakespeare isn't Shakespeare assert that this is just one more piece of evidence that the image is just as imaginary as the man.

*T*he Chandos Portrait, or "The Romantic Shakespeare."

Shakespeare's Name

*T*hroughout Shakespeare's lifetime, his name was variously spelled as Shagsbere, Shakespeare, Shaxpere, Shackespere, Shaxpeare, Shakesspeare, and Shakspeare. In 1869, George Wise published *The Autograph of William Shakespeare . . . together with 4000 Ways of Spelling the name according to English Orthography* (Scheackespyrr and Schaeaxspierre being two such possibilities).

Of Graves, Wills, and Epitaphs

No one knows how Shakespeare died. Even the exact day is uncertain. The registers of Holy Trinity Church record that William Shakespeare was buried on April 25, so it's assumed that he died two days earlier, on April 23, an attractive—and thus suspect—date, since it couples Shakespeare's date of birth and death with the Feast of Saint George, England's *other* patron saint. The church record is all we have on Shakespeare's death and burial, yet out of slim facts great theories grow.

Medical Shakespeareans are fond of speculating on the manner and cause of Shakespeare's death. The Shakespeare Data Bank, an ongoing project to computerize all information about Shakespeare's life and works, currently lists over twenty possible causes of death, including Bright's disease (a diagnosis based on the deterioration of Shakespeare's handwriting in his will), shock over his daughter Judith's marriage, writer's cramp, apoplexy, and "intolerable entrails."

As with the death of many cult figures, Shakespeare's demise is shrouded in secrecy and rumors of conspiracy. With an intensity partly romantic, partly forensic, enthusiasts scour his final years for any detail that would suggest his end to be mysteriously sudden. Shakespeare begins his will with the formulaic preamble declaring himself in "perfect health and memorie." But since he died one month later, romantics cite this statement as evidence that he died abruptly under strange circumstances.

Fifty years after Shakespeare's death, the Reverend John Ward of Stratford confidently wrote in his diary: "Shakespear, Drayton, and Ben Jhonson [*sic*], had a merry meeting, and it seems drank too hard, for Shakespear died of a feavour there contracted." Ward goes on to remind himself, "Remember to peruse Shakespeare's plays, and be much versed in them, that I may not be ignorant in that matter."

This legend spawned numerous variations. In 1897, the president of the Mersey Bowman, a club devoted to shooting the long bow, attributed Shakespeare's death to congestion following a strenuous day of shooting—obviously the Bard's favorite pastime.

Was Shakespeare Murdered?

*C*harles Hamilton, the forensic handwriting expert who exposed the "Hitler Diaries," suspects a far more sinister end for Shakespeare than indulgence in shooting or drinking. His bizarre theory involves wills, arsenic, and threats of disinheritance: the classic elements of an English murder mystery.

According to Hamilton's book *In Search of Shakespeare,* the inquiry began innocently at a quiet dinner with Dr. Michael Baden, a former chief medical examiner of New York City. When the talk turned to Shakespeare's death, Hamilton's interest was piqued, and he decided to examine Shakespeare's will, which most experts believe was written by the playwright's lawyer. Beginning with "I William Shackspeare [*sic*]" and concluding with the customary formula "By me William Shakspeare [*sic*]," the will is a perfectly businesslike document, except for one detail: it contains an inordinate number of scratches, errors, and ink blots.

Upon examining the document, Hamilton claimed to have found something unusual: Shakespeare's final signature is in the same hand as the interlineated notes. He then realized that the entire document was written in Shakespeare's hand: "All of the contradictions and irregularities that have been attributed to ineptitude on the part of Collins [Shakespeare's lawyer] or his scrivener can be explained with no difficulty if you accept Shakespeare as the unaided writer of the will," writes Hamilton. "By me William Shakspeare" means precisely that: Shakespeare penned his own will.

The will is dated in March, one month after Judith Shakespeare's marriage. As Judith was a thirty-two-year-old spinster who lived at home, Shakespeare should have been happy to see her married, but the man she chose was hardly someone to make a father proud. Her husband, the twenty-seven-year-old Thomas Quiney, was a tavern keep-er with an unsavory past. Like her parents' marriage, Judith's seems to have been a hasty affair, since it took place during Lent, a time when marriage was prohibited. But unlike William and Anne, neither Judith nor Thomas bothered to get a special license—an offense for which they were twice summoned before the consistory court. After failing to appear on both occasions, they were summarily excommunicated. Then, one month after their wedding, Quiney confessed to having "carnal intercourse" with one Margaret Wheeler, a crime for which he was sentenced to do public penance.

Some believe that Shakespeare rewrote his will to alter his bequest to Judith and thus prevent Quiney from inheriting any of her portion. As Hamilton studied the early section of the revised will, he realized that all the errors occurred from the midway point on page one to the top of page two. At that point, according to Hamilton, Shakespeare's hand grows increasingly more incoherent, "spastic and meandering." The writer angrily slashes out the words "sonne in L[aw]" and curtly refers to his daughter as "Judith," avoiding her married name. Then there are the memory lapses: Shakespeare forgot his nephew's name, and his friend Hamnet is referred to as "Hamlet." The other pages, written earlier, remain perfect. It was obvious to Hamilton that something was happening to Shakespeare while he wrote his will.

*T*he Quiney family history is a sad one. Thomas was almost prosecuted for selling bad wine, and on numerous occasions he was fined for swearing. All of the couple's offspring died young. In 1652, Thomas deserted his family for good and left for London. But the story has a suitable ending. As Sam Schoenbaum describes it in *Shakespeare's Lives*: "During the present century The Cage [Quiney's tavern] has been restored; in the very house where Thomas Quiney once dispensed his questionable wines, hungry tourists today consume Wimpy hamburgers."

Hamilton showed the document to Dr. Baden, who commented that it looked as if the writer had suffered a stroke and casually noted that the writing resembled that of suicide notes written by those who had just taken poison. Hamilton seized upon the idea. After all, Quiney had motive; by all accounts, he was an attractive bounder who had married Judith for her money. "If Shakespeare were allowed to finish that will, Quiney stood to lose everything," writes Hamilton, who speculates that Quiney tried to murder Shakespeare before the bequest could be altered. Arsenic was the ideal murder weapon: colorless, odorless, and tasteless, it was so foolproof that it came to be known as "inheritance powder." As a vintner who needed it to keep vermin out of his storeroom, Quiney could get as much arsenic as he liked—enough to kill a rich father-in-law.

*P*urists and scholars tend to throw a wet blanket on all romantic theories concerning Shakespeare. Unfortunately for conspiracy buffs, Shakespeare probably wasn't murdered by his son-in-law. Shakespearean biographer Peter Levi notes that by 1616 Shakespeare was probably exhausted. He had had a long and intense career, and like many Stratfordians that spring, he probably succumbed to a fever or a chill.

Is Hamilton's notion about Shakespeare's will merely the wishful thinking of a man determined to discover a lost manuscript? The London Public Records Office, where the will is housed, officially maintains that it was written by Shakespeare's lawyer, and a spokesman at Somerset House, the current-records office, said, "The most we can say is that the signature is authentic. Whether he wrote the whole will himself or not is another matter." Hamilton, for his part, insists that the will is holographic: "Maybe I'm jaundiced; there's always opposition to any new ideas about Shakespeare. Any Shakespearean who has based his work on the fact that there is no handwriting other than that of those six signatures would have to revise their work and nobody wants to do that."

According to Hamilton the will is in "deplorable condition. For over a hundred years," he says, his voice filled with disgust, "that will was available to everybody and anybody who wanted to come and press a greasy kiss on Shakespeare's signature. Now it's all faded and smeared."

The "Second-Best Bed" Controversy

*T*hat Shakespeare's will is the subject of intense scrutiny should not be surprising, since it's as close to a personal statement from Shakespeare as we'll ever get. Some people are disappointed by its impersonal tone, as if they expected the Bard suddenly to break into blank verse in the middle of a bequest. Any hint of an intimate revelation, no matter how remote, is immediately seized upon and magnified. Hence the "second-best bed" controversy.

Item: I gyve unto my wief my second best bed with the furniture.

With this terse statement, Shakespeare set off a debate that has lasted for centuries. This bequest—the only time Anne Hathaway Shakespeare is mentioned in the will—has been used to bolster any number of theories about Shakespeare, from the anti-Stratfordian argument that he was a meanspirited wretch and not the divine author of the plays and poems to speculation about the Bard's connubial intimacies.

That Shakespeare specifically singled out "second-best" leads naturally to the assumption that Anne herself was second-best. A more generous view is that the bequest was a sentimental gesture, the bed being the one they had shared as a couple. Be that as it may, in all likelihood Anne spent most of her nights in it alone, since her husband spent twenty-five out of their thirty-three years of marriage in London. Apologists for Shakespeare cite Elizabethan law, which entitled a wife to one-third of her husband's estate, thus leaving no need for Shakespeare to be more specific in his will. The bulk of the estate, however, including the enormous house, New Place, was left to their elder daughter, Susanna Hall, with whom Anne went to live after her husband died. There, in all likelihood, Susanna and her husband, Dr. Hall, slept in Shakespeare's best bed.

The Epitaph

Good Frend for Iesus SAKE forbeare
To diGG ⱦE Duſt EncloAſed HE.Re.
Bleſe be ⱦE Man ᵀ͟ᵧ ſpares ⱦEs Stones
And curſt, be He ᵀ͟ᵧ moves my Bones

*T*his is Shakespeare's voice from beyond the grave. When a burial ground became overcrowded, gravediggers would empty the old graves and dump the remains in the charnel houses to make way for fresh ones. If there was a Last Judgment, Shakespeare obviously wanted to arrive intact, and this bit of doggerel may be taken as a No Trespassing sign. Until now, it's worked. But that doesn't mean people haven't tried to get at Shakespeare's dust, in the interests of scientific research.

In 1849, a death mask believed to be Shakespeare's turned up at a junk shop in Mainz, Germany. It had once been in the possession of a Count Kesselstadt who lived in Cologne; hence, it became known as the Kesselstadt Death Mask. The evidence for believing it to be Shakespeare's rested on an inscription on the back that read "WS/1616." The mask still had bits of auburn hair clinging to it—a detail that made the find seem all the more thrilling and authentic—and to many bardolaters it was the literary equivalent of the Shroud of Turin. To determine its authenticity, scholars compared it with the dimensions of the Janssen Bust—also of dubious origin—but no records remain of their findings. The mask was exhibited in the British Museum as Shakespeare's Death Mask in 1849, but gradually the furor over the mask died, and it was soon forgotten.

Enthusiasm over the mask led to public interest in exhuming Shakespeare's grave—an obsession that stemmed from the desire to find out what Shakespeare looked like. In the *American Bibliopolist* of April 1876, the Shakespearean J. Parker Norris wrote: "If we could even get a photograph of Shakespeare's skull, it would be a great thing, and would help us to make a better portrait of him." He even offered instructions: "Open the grave reverently, have the photographers ready, and the moment the coffin lid is removed . . . expose the plates, and see what will be the results." In 1883, C. M. Ingleby, an opponent of the plan to unearth Shakespeare's grave, wrote a pamphlet with the daunting title *Shakespeare's Bones. The Proposal to Disinter Them, Considered in Relation to Their Possible Bearing on His Portraiture: Illustrated by Instances of Visits of the Living to the Dead.*

The American writer Washington Irving relates in *The Sketch Book of Geoffrey Crayon* that he was once told that Shakespeare's grave caved in as diggers worked on an adjacent grave: The old sexton took a peek inside, but could find nothing but dust. Still, Irving concludes, "It was something, I thought, to have seen the dust of Shakespeare."

A Look at the

Modern audiences passively *attend* Shakespearean plays, and for many of us, going to the theatre is a thankfully brief excursion into the realm of Culture. In the semidarkness of the theatre we sit in deferential silence. If the performance is good, we watch with quiet interest; if it is bad, we become suddenly taken by the advertisements in the playbill.

ELIZABETHAN STAGE

Playgoing was an entirely different experience for the Elizabethans. They actually participated in the experience. Since their stage was round, actors and audience enjoyed an intimate relationship. Without the imaginary "fourth wall," actors directly addressed the audience through solilouqies and asides, and sometimes the audience answered back. The average Elizabethan yelled, hooted, snacked, and chatted throughout the performance as he followed the action on stage. During the Renaissance, says Peggy O'Brien, playgoing was "a cross between the NCAA finals and a Madonna concert."

A Brief History

*I*n 1576, a carpenter named James Burbage built the first theatre in England, which he called, simply, the Theatre, the first time the word was used to refer to a building specifically designed for the staging of plays. Up to this time, plays had been performed in inn yards and bearbaiting arenas. Arguments with the Theatre's landlord led to the early expiration of its lease in 1597, and Burbage bought the old Blackfriars monastery as a replacement. Objecting to the proximity of the theatre with its raucous crowds, neighbors petitioned the Privy Council, and the project came to a halt. After James Burbage's death in 1597, his sons continued to try to find a replacement for the Theatre. Learning that the landlord planned to dismantle the Theatre, they assembled on the night of December 28, 1598, to demolish it and ferry across the Thames the timber that they later reused to build the Globe, the playhouse that would become synonymous with Shakespeare.

But it was not only politicians who were opposed to theatre. Puritan clergy denounced playgoing as a dangerous diversion from religious worship and a stimulus to "whorish lust." The most vociferous among them was Philip Stubbs, who grimly concluded that all acting companies were "secret conclaves" of sodomy. Finally, bowing to Puritan pressure, London aldermen banned all playhouses in the city proper, and the theatre district was confined to an area in the suburbs known as Southwark (pronounced "Sutherk"). There patrons could choose among nine theatres, and, like Broadway today, the area possessed a seedy kind of glamour.

Scattered throughout the district were arenas where patrons could watch cockfights or chained bears being baited by dogs. Several bears, such as Harry Hunks and Sackerson, attracted their own following, enjoying a celebrity rivaling that of the actors next door. In fact, Harry Hunks in his arena was considered as worthy a spectacle as Richard Burbage playing Hamlet in *his* arena. The distinction between high art and popular taste was less explicit, and bear gardens and playhouses competed for the same trade.

Near the theatres, bawdyhouses, pubs, and taverns did a booming business; pimps and prostitutes plied their trade; vendors hawked their wares; and pickpockets, thieves, and swindlers thrived. Since all of Southwark's property belonged to the bishop of Winchester, the church profited, pocketing the revenues from pimps and brothels.

✤ According to recent discoveries made at the Globe excavation site, the playhouse may have had as many as twenty sides, giving it a circular appearance. It was an open-air theatre that held about three thousand spectators.

✤ Performances were given every day but Sunday, and plays ran from two to five in the afternoon, so that sunlight wouldn't bother the audience and the players.

✤ Since the city fathers considered playgoing immoral, they prohibited theatre managers from luring customers through advertising. But the managers ingeniously triumphed over Puritan strictures: as two o'clock neared, a raised flag and a trumpet fanfare proclaimed that the performance was about to begin. The flag indicated the day's feature: black signified tragedy; white, comedy; and red, history.

✤ Patrons were transported across the Thames to Southwark by wherry boats. Shrewdly, the wherryman would withhold the price of transport until the patron was halfway across the river and was therefore unable to escape paying the fare. At one time over two thousand wherries made their way to and from the theatre district.

✤ As people entered the theatre they would drop their admission into a box (hence "box office"). Ticket prices depended on the location of the seat, or lack of one. Spectators could sit on cushions with the gentry in the cockpit or stand elbow-to-elbow with the mob in the back. The most exclusive patrons sat on the stage.

✤ Vendors offered beer, water, oranges, nuts, gingerbread, and apples, all of which were occasionally thrown at the actors. Hazelnuts were the most popular theatre snack, the Elizabethan equivalent of Raisinets.

SHAKESPEARE AND THE GLOBE

*N*o playwright has ever had more intimate knowledge of the playhouse for which he wrote his greatest plays. He helped to finance it and every working day he acted on its stage. As a "sharer" in the company he performed in early Globe productions such as Jonson's "Humours" plays, and performed kingly roles—including, so legend declares, the ghost in *Hamlet*—in his own plays. Shakespeare wrote, therefore, for a highly specific stage . . . not for any theatre in the abstract nor for the printed page. . . . The Globe's stage was the sole means of publication he expected.

—ANDREW GURR

*H*e was one of the first to put his money where his mouth was.

—MICHAEL CAINE

❖ There was not one rest room for all three thousand spectators. Nor were there any intermissions. The playhouses thus smelled of urine as well as of ginger, garlic, beer, tobacco, and sweat (few Elizabethans bathed).

❖ There was no producer or director; the actors were in complete control of the production.

❖ There were three tiers to the stage, corresponding to earth, heaven, and hell. Villains fell through a trapdoor, called the hell mouth, into the pits of damnation. A canopy, representing the heavens, extended across the stage to the back wall. The heavens were painted gold with starry spangles in the shape of the zodiac. (When Hamlet describes the heavens "fretted with golden fire" he is pointing to such a canopy.)

❖ Behind the stage were the tiring (attiring), or dressing, rooms. This was also where apprentices manned elaborate stage machinery. The Elizabethans loved spectacular stage effects, and characters like Ariel in *The Tempest* would be whisked up to the heavens in a breathtaking ascent.

❖ Scenery and props were minimal. Actors described the setting through dialogue called "scene painting." (Horatio's "But look, the morn in russet mantle clad . . ." lets us know that it is dawn.)

❖ Costumes were extravagant, spangled affairs of gold, lace, silk, and velvet, often the castoffs of the aristocratic patron. Actors also wore makeup, an abomination to the Puritans.

❖ Since women were forbidden to act on the public stage, female roles were played by prepubescent boys—one reason why there's so little actual sex in the plays. Shakespeare turned this restriction into an advantage, evoking desirability through language and dramatic action. Furthermore, bawdy puns, sexual allusions, and sensuous poetry were often used as substitutes

SHAKESPEARE'S AUDIENCE

*A*ndrew Gurr, an authority on the Elizabethan stage, asserts that Elizabethan playgoers represented "the whole spectrum" of London society, from the aristocrats who sat on special seats to the groundlings who paid a penny for admission. In the audience for one play "there might have been apprentices and the unemployed from the lowest financial levels, house servants, unskilled labourers. . . . With a little more affluence there were artisans [skilled handicraft workers], and further up the scale of wealth citizen employers, merchants, law students . . ., military officers, gentry and lords. Women were a major presence, and included a range from whores through citizen wives to Court ladies."

Like spectators at a baseball game today, the Elizabethan theatre crowd represented a good cross-section of society. It's estimated that 10 percent of London's population regularly attended the theatre—far more than in most major cities today.

for the real thing. Unable to rely on authentic female beauty, Shakespeare made his heroines interesting, witty, and intelligent. There are, however, a few allusions to onstage kissing, or "bussing," and it's likely that the adolescent boy who played Cleopatra appeared in a state of semi-undress—adding a fillip of eroticism to theatregoing.

✤ Rehearsal time was minimal. Actors learned their parts in about a week; a leading man might have to memorize eight hundred lines a day. According to one theatre historian, a leading man would learn and retain over seventy different roles in three years.

✤ The Elizabethan audience craved variety, so the repertory was made up almost entirely of new plays. According to theatre historian Bernard Beckerman, in one six-month season, from August 1595 to the end of February 1596, a single company gave one hundred fifty performances of thirty different plays. There was also a quick turnover: some plays had only one or two performances, while a hit could run intermittently for six months.

✤ Like all the other playhouses, the Globe had its own company, which was under the patronage of a nobleman. The patron system grew out of the Puritan city fathers' decision to revive an ancient statute prohibiting "masterless men," which stated that every man without a master was regarded as unemployed and a threat to law and order. To protect themselves from imprisonment, the companies found noble patrons who were willing to offer their names and financial support. Thus each company had a noble "master." Shakespeare's company was initially the Lord Chamberlain's Men, but with the accession of James I in 1603 they became the prestigious King's Men, the premier company in London.

✤ Plays belonged to the acting company and not to the playwright. Shakespeare didn't own or have any right to publish his own plays.

❖ After 1608, the King's Men began to use the old Blackfriars monastery as their winter playhouse. An enclosed private theatre with a capacity of seven hundred, the Blackfriars catered to a select audience who could afford its higher admission price (the cheapest seat there was the price of the most expensive one at the Globe). Some scholars detect a change in Shakespeare's style during this period, which they attribute to his desire to take advantage of the acoustics of indoor theatre and its fashionable clientele. Illuminated by candlelight, the indoor playhouse was ideal for such claustrophobic interior dramas as *Macbeth*. Although Shakespeare's later plays were also performed at the Globe, they are more refined and effete than those written for the boisterous audience at the public playhouse.

❖ The Globe burned down in 1613, when a prop cannon exploded during the first-night performance of *Henry VIII*. One man's breeches were set afire—and were doused with beer. The only other casualty was the playhouse itself. Needless to say, the play had a short run.

❖ After seventy years, the Puritans at last triumphed. In August 1642 Parliament passed an ordinance that shut down all the theatres.

Transvestite Theatre and Boy Actors

*E*lizabethan England was unique among the nations of Europe in forbidding women to appear on the public stage. Marjorie Garber, a professor of English at Harvard University and author of *Vested Interests: Cross-Dressing and Cultural Anxiety,* points out that transvestite theatre was the norm during periods when drama was of very high quality, such as the Kabuki theatre of Japan or classical Greek drama.

Boy actors lived with the adult members of the company and received rigorous training in dancing, music, singing, elocution, memorization, weaponry, and, as an acting manual stated, "pregnancie in wit." Very little is known about individual boys; not one portrait and very few references survive, since the boys were not considered stars like the adults. There were far fewer boys than men in the company, which is one reason that there are so few parts for women in the plays.

Transvestite theatre ended with the Restoration in 1660. As Professor Garber notes: "Because there had been an interregnum when there had been no theatre, the actors who played the parts were now too old for them. And there was no training to continue that tradition." When women began appearing in female parts, old-timers would fondly recall a boy Juliet as having been the definitive portrayal of the role; no woman, they insisted, could possibly play Juliet as well.

The Globe Excavation

*T*he year 1989 was an *annus mirabilis* for Shakespeareans. In February, archaeologists found what they are certain are the remains of the Rose playhouse, Shakespeare's original theatre. Then, on October 12, at 9:30 A.M., the real prize was unearthed: Shakespeare's beloved Globe. The historic ruins are not very prepossessing. There is little to indicate this was the site of the first performances of *King Lear, Macbeth,* and *Othello.* Could this vast field of dirt and chalk really have once held the "wooden O?"

Andrew Gurr

*A*ndrew Gurr is the leading expert on the Shakespearean stage and has been writing about the excavations since work began in 1989.

NE: *Do we know what the Globe playhouse looked like?*

AG: Contemporary illustrations from Shakespeare's time are almost all inaccurate. The typical picture of the octagonal Globe is certainly a mistaken image. This idea originated with an artist named Claes Jan Visscher, who never even went to London but who drew a conventional design of a theatre. In fact, it was discredited back in 1948, but it's still used today as a replica and is sold in gift shops. People need a fixed image, and this will do as well as any.

NE: *How does the newly discovered Globe differ from this standard portrait?*

AG: The idea was that a theatre should be round, but the Elizabethans couldn't build circles with timber, and they couldn't afford to use brick, so the Globe was a many-sided polygon. This is why the early illustrations showed the playhouses as octagons and hexagons. The Globe looks like it might have had twenty sides, because it took that many to make the theatre look circular.

NE: *The original Globe was built in 1599, burned down in 1613, and then was rebuilt. Which one was found?*

AG: We think that the Globe that was found is actually both theatres, the one that burned down and the rebuilt one. According to contemporary documents, they were built on the same site. The second Globe was pulled down in 1644 when all the theatres closed, and it was forgotten. In fact, it had a brewery on top of it until 1984. When the bottling plant of the brewery was pulled down, they used the concrete floor of the brewery as a parking lot.

NE: *When the Rose was discovered, the press compared it to a literary Pompeii, claiming that it would change the textbooks of the future. Did scholars actually learn anything new?*

AG: The Rose was a revelation. The only information we had had was a picture showing a six-sided figure, and we discovered that the playhouse had fourteen sides. So far, only 60 percent of the surface is done, so we'll get confirmation of the theatre's exact dimensions. If we dig down to bare rock, we'll know about the drainage that was used. We might also learn more about the stage area and its design.

NE: *Do you think you'll find any artifacts?*

AG: Very unlikely. The Rose site was absolutely stripped. But a few remains were found: a scabbard, a sword, shoes, a bear's skull—and a human skull.

NE: *A human skull? A prop?*

AG: Actually, it was found lodged in one of the walls of the stage area. It may have been part of a primitive building ritual. Macabre, I think.

Sam Wanamaker

F or more than twenty years, Sam Wanamaker, one of America's most distinguished actors, has been battling for the right to rebuild the Globe playhouse near its original Southwark site. Over the years his struggles have resembled those of Shakespeare's original company, involving fights with hostile city fathers, prejudices against actors, and restrictions over land use.

NE: *You got the idea to rebuild the Globe over twenty years ago, and everybody thought it was a quixotic vision of a young actor. What made you persevere?*

SW: If you had said to someone then, Show me something important about Shakespeare in London, no one would have known where to go. Ninety percent of the cabbies, who are the most knowledgeable people about London, didn't know where the Globe playhouse had been located. Extraordinary! Close to the site of the Globe there was a plaque, and on the other side of the river there's a bust of Shakespeare. There's also a statue in Westminster. But that isn't very much.

NE: *Where is the spirit of Shakespeare located, in Stratford or in London?*

SW: Stratford became the shrine for Shakespeare. His body is buried there, and he was presumably born there. The church where he was baptized is there, and supposedly the house where he lived (which is not true; it was rebuilt, but that's okay . . .). The town has a great deal of charm for overseas visitors. You've got the Avon River, and for years it was where people went if they wanted to know anything about Shakespeare. So Stratford became Shakespeare, and people forgot that the real Shakespeareland is in London, where he wrote all his plays, where all the other playwrights of the period lived and worked, and where the Rose, the Swan, the Hope, the Fortune, and all the other Elizabethan theatres existed.

NE: *Why was there so much opposition to rebuilding the Globe?*

SW: I was an American and an actor—and not a Shakespearean actor— so the Brits assumed that the only thing I could possibly have in mind was something like Disneyland. History in England is so much a part of people's lives, so the idea of *rebuilding* something could only be considered as something cheap and superficial. They thought, Isn't there enough Shakespeare? Who needs another theatre? They could only see it in real estate terms or as shallow entertainment.

NE: *What did the controversy involve?*

SW: The press reduced the debate to a conflict between Marxist populist views and elitist artists. A socialist Marxist group was in power on the local city council in Southwark, a working-class area. They thought that Shakespeare was "posh" and that culture was overrated. They wanted the land for a housing project. The debate was very much like a Shakespearean drama in which the mob is opposed to the poets.

Traditionally in Europe, an area was designated as either upper-class or lower-class, and you couldn't change that. For centuries the South Bank of the Thames had been the back alley of London, where they put car parks and cement-mixing plants. But it has the most incredible view! I remember the first time I parked there, and thinking, "My God, this is a wonderful view—from my car!" I felt that they could not take the most expensive land and put government housing on it. The debate became a bitter public argument. We had a lease on the site, but the local council took the land away from us, so we sued them. We got back the land in the courts, and it cost them nine million *pounds*!—which they could have used to build public housing on a nearby site that *was* available. It's unbelievable.

The International Shakespeare Globe Centre will be a huge complex consisting of numerous exhibits and a reconstruction of the Globe Playhouse, an actual theatre where modern audiences can temporarily experience what playgoing must have been like for the Elizabethans.

After numerous delays, the Centre is tentatively scheduled to open in April 1994, just in time to celebrate the 430th anniversary of Shakespeare's birth.

Chronology

*I*t's impossible to say with certainty when a Shakespeare play was written or first performed. The best that scholars can hope for is to narrow the date down to the limits of a particular year. Since the account books for Shakespeare's acting company are lost, scholars rely on internal and external evidence. External evidence, the more reliable, consists of personal correspondence, allusions

The Plays

to Shakespeare in other works, and entries in the Stationer's Register, which lists the date of a play's publication. These documents help to establish roughly a time *after* which a play could not have been written (*terminus ad quem*), or when it was performed, if not its actual opening day. Another source is

Henslowe's *Diary,* an account book kept by the theatrical entrepreneur Philip Henslowe from 1592 to 1603, which lists performances at the Rose theatre, where Shakespeare's earliest plays were performed. With its copious listing of props, revenues, and costumes (such as a robe to make its wearer invisible) the *Diary* provides a fascinating glimpse into early stagecraft.

Internal evidence—style, literary echoes of other works, versification, and imagery—helps to determine at what point in the playwright's career a play was written. For instance, the linguistic and thematic affinities between *Romeo and Juliet* and *A Midsummer Night's Dream* suggest that the plays were written at about the same time. Sometimes this line of reasoning leads scholars astray. Unable to believe that the loosely plotted and often incoherent *Pericles* was a product of the mature Shakespeare, some concluded that it must have been written early in the playwright's career. Despite its flaws, however, most scholars now agree that *Pericles,* which is close in sensibility to the other romances, is late Shakespeare. A topical allusion to an event also helps to establish a rough date for a play. Titania's description of the torrential summer weather in *A Midsummer Night's Dream* presumably refers to the notoriously wet summers of 1594 to 1596. This reference establishes a date *before* which the work could not have been written (*terminus a quo*). Sometimes the precision of the allusion, such as the Chorus's anticipation of the Earl of Essex's return from Ireland in *Henry V,* dates a play with gratifying neatness. Since Essex left for Ireland in March 1599 and returned in September, scholars can narrow the play's composition to those intervening six months.

Since the publication of the first edition of Shakespeare's works, the First Folio of 1623, it's been customary to arrange the plays into four tidy categories: histories, comedies, tragedies, and romances. These roughly correspond to the four phases of Shakespeare's career: his apprenticeship (1588–93), during which he wrote the rambunctious comedies and early history plays; the second phase (1593–1600), when he mastered the comic and historical forms, giving them richness and psychological depth; the tragic period (1600–09), during which he wrote his greatest, and blackest, plays; and the last phase (1609–11), when he wrote the tender and magical romances. The following table is a rough chronology of Shakespeare's plays generally accepted by most scholars.

Titus Andronicus, 1588–94

The Comedy of Errors, 1588–94

Henry VI, Part 1, 1590–91

Henry VI, Part 2, 1590–91

Henry VI, Part 3, 1590–91

The Taming of the Shrew, 1590

The Two Gentlemen of Verona, 1590–95

King John, 1591

Richard III, 1592

Love's Labour's Lost, 1593

Romeo and Juliet, 1593–96

A Midsummer Night's Dream, 1595–96

The Merchant of Venice, 1596–98

Richard II, 1595–96

Henry IV, Part 1, 1596–97

Henry IV, Part 2, 1597–98

The Merry Wives of Windsor, 1597

Much Ado about Nothing, 1598

Henry V, 1599

Julius Caesar, 1599

As You Like It, 1600

Twelfth Night, 1599–1601

Hamlet, 1600

Troilus and Cressida, 1602

All's Well That Ends Well, 1602–4

Measure for Measure, 1603–4

Othello, 1604

King Lear, 1606

Macbeth, 1606

Timon of Athens, 1606

Antony and Cleopatra, 1608

Coriolanus, 1609

Pericles, Prince of Tyre, 1607–8 (probably written with an inferior collaborator)

Cymbeline, 1609–10

The Winter's Tale, 1610–11

The Tempest, 1611

The Two Noble Kinsmen, 1613 (with John Fletcher)

Henry VIII, 1613 (with Fletcher)

Useful Shakespearean Terms

While by no means complete, the following is a list of standard terms found in Shakespearean criticism. For a fuller listing, see Stanley Wells's *Shakespearean Glossary.*

Aside: A speech in which the speaker turns away from the other characters and reveals his true feelings to the audience. The *aside* is based on the premise that although the speaker stands but a few inches away from the others, they nevertheless are unable to hear what he's saying. Often used by devious characters such as Iago and Richard III, it heightens the ironic contrast between the smiling public mask and the covert evil it hides. For instance, upon being introduced to Antonio, Shylock turns aside and mutters: "How like a fawning publican he looks./I hate him for he is a Christian." He then returns to his conversation with his Christian enemies, having provided us with pertinent information about the true dramatic situation.

Bed trick: Derived from folklore, the *bed trick* is the furtive substitution of a virgin wife for another woman who is sinfully desired. It occurs in the "problem plays" *Measure for Measure* and *All's Well That Ends Well*, and is suggestive of the sexual and moral ambiguity inherent in these plays. The bed trick is a cynical dramatization of the proverb "All cats are gray in the dark."

Blank verse: Unrhymed iambic pentameter, a form that is ideal for drama because it gives the speaker greater freedom of tone and expression; more than any other verse form, blank verse comes closest to sounding like the natural speaking voice, while possessing a formality and weight lacking in prose utterances.

Braggart soldier or **miles gloriosis:** A standard comic figure dating from antique Roman comedy, the braggart soldier talks a lot, but his actions are mostly confined to words. Falstaff (*Henry IV, Part 1* and *Part 2*), Pistol (*Henry V*), and Don Armado (*Love's Labour's Lost*) are Shakespearean descendants of this stock character.

Concordance: A reference book that alphabetically lists every word and where it occurs in an author's works. The authoritative concordance to Shakespeare, now produced by computer, is *The Harvard Concordance.*

Foil: The term literally refers to a sheet of metal placed under a precious stone to heighten its luster. In drama, a foil is a character who by contrast illuminates the hero's qualities. For example, next to his foil, the stolidly pragmatic Horatio, Hamlet, with his quicksilver intellect and visionary idealism, shines all the brighter. Actually, most of the characters in *Hamlet* are foils for the hero, as Hamlet, who is continually comparing himself with others, bitterly acknowledges ("How all occasions do inform against me . . ."). The *foils* Laertes and Fortinbras, unlike the reluctant Hamlet, have no difficulty avenging the death of their fathers.

Folio: See pages 72–73.

Great Chain of Being: A term that refers to the elaborate system of parallels and correspondences that governed the orthodox Renaissance view of the cosmos. The underlying principle of the universe is harmony. Everything—the revolutions of the spheres, the ebb and flow of the tides, the structure of society, and the civic laws, domestic affairs, and psyche of man—works according to the principle of hierarchical order. The various elements of the universe, from the celestial to the vegetative, are links in a vast chain. At the top of the chain is God, the Prime Mover, who presides over the universe, and in the middle is the earth,

 around which the spheres revolve. There are nine angelic orders, arranged in groups of three, ranking from seraphim to angels. In the terrestrial realm, each of the four elements has its own status: fire is the lightest and purest; air is more noble than the next element, water; and earth is the heaviest. In political affairs, the king parallels God in heaven and serves as His deputy on earth. Beneath the king are the various ranks and orders of nobility and gentry, corresponding to the angelic orders in the celestial realm. In domestic affairs, man occupies a higher position than woman, for whom he is king of the hearth. The lion presides over the animal kingdom, as does the oak in the vegetative world. Occupying a central point in the chain is man, who alone of all God's creatures has the freedom to choose between angelic virtue or degenerate bestiality. Within the human psyche there is also a chain corresponding to that of the outer world. The monarch of the mind, human reason, parallels God's role in the universe, which in a well-governed disposition rules over animal passions. Man thus constitutes a little world, or microcosm, which is a tiny replica of the outer world, or macrocosm.

This entire system is based on what Shakespeare and Renaissance writers and philosophers called "degree," the rightful rank or position of each link in the chain. To disturb degree in any way unleashes anarchy, the utter dissolution of the entire system. Without degree, as Shakespeare's Ulysses says, "What plagues and what portents, what mutiny,/What raging of the sea, shaking of earth,/Commotion in the winds, frights, changes, horrors,/Divert and crack, rend and deracinate/The unity and married calm of states/Quite from their fixture!" (*Troilus and Cressida,* I.3.96–101). Chaos, whether expressed through mob violence, civil war, storm, or madness, presented a terrifying picture of the universe run amok.

Shakespeare's plays, particularly his tragedies and histories, offer numerous examples of this principle. Lear's abdication, a violation of succession, turns the natural, domestic, political, and psychological orders upside down, a state of affairs manifested in storms, unruly daughters, civil wars, and insanity.

For many years this idea of the Elizabethan World Picture dominated criticism of the plays and poems. Recent scholars, however, are skeptical of attributing a homogeneous belief system to an age known for its diversity. For a complete discussion, see E. M. W. Tillyard's *The Elizabethan World Picture* and Theodore Spenser's *Shakespeare and the Nature of Man.*

Iambic pentameter: The standard metrical form that Shakespeare, and most English poets, use, most notably in sonnets and dramatic verse, because its easy inflection and rhythm closely mimic the natural speaking voice. Each line contains ten syllables, or five feet (a foot is a unit of poetic rhythm) consisting of an unaccented syllable followed by an accented one: "Shall I compare thee to a summer's day?" is an example of verse in iambic pentameter.

Humors: According to Elizabethan physiology, a humor was one of four elemental bodily fluids—phlegm, black bile, blood, and yellow bile—each relating to a specific temperament or mood. Diseases and emotions were determined by the balance of the humors, the ideal state occurring when all four were in proper proportion to the others (what we would call "homeostasis" today). When one humor dominates, a person is unbalanced, exhibiting one mood or quirk to the exclusion of others. A person suffering from an excess of phlegm is sluggish, pale, and slow; the splenetic or choleric person is quick to anger and unmerciful; the sanguine person is excessively jovial and lusty; and the melancholic person is maudlin, lovesick, and languid. The doctrine of the humors was an obvious influence on Shakespeare in creating character, most notably the malcontent Jaques in *As You Like It.*

Problem play or bitter comedy: See pages 236–301.

Quarto: See pages 70–72.

Setpiece: A poetical passage, usually quite elaborate, which follows the conventions of dramatic oratory. It differs from other dramatic speeches in that it makes no pretense to spontaneity, nor does it necessarily move the dramatic action forward. The classic setpiece, Hamlet's soliloquy "To be, or not to be," has a static, rehearsed quality; unlike the earlier "O, what a rogue and peasant slave am I!," which sounds like an outburst from Hamlet's soul, it is a crafted piece of rhetoric whose studied artistry sets it apart from the action. Setpieces are often filled with memorable quotes that can be cited by those who don't even know the play—for instance, Henry V's stirring "Once more unto the breach." It has a rhapsodic quality, and it can contain magnificent flourishes that some, perhaps unkindly, might call purple patches.

Soliloquy: A speech in which the speaker is alone with his private thoughts (*solus* means "alone"). It is designed to inform the audience what he is really thinking. When a character delivers his soliloquy, we may assume he's speaking the truth; he may lie to the other characters, but never to himself (or to us). Modern plays rarely use the soliloquy, but it was standard practice on the Elizabethan stage, where there was greater intimacy between the audience and the actors. Hamlet's "O, what a rogue and peasant slave am I!" is one of the many famous soliloquies in the play.

Stationer's Guild and Register: Upon acquiring a manuscript, honest publishers registered them with the Register, a record kept by the Stationer's Guild. The Register's purpose was to protect a work from being printed by publishers, and though it did nothing to prevent theft, the Register represents the beginnings of copyright. The Register is an invaluable scholarly resource for establishing a play's printing history.

Variant (or Collation): The various readings of the standard text. A list of the variants for most words is generally included at the back of major Shakespeare editions.

Variorum: The term, an abbreviation from the Latin *cum notis variorum* ("with notes of various persons"), refers to an edition of an author's works containing copious notes and commentary by critics and editors since the work was first published. It also includes every possible variant reading from the major editions. Begun in 1912, the *New Variorum Shakespeare* was completed in 1953.

Vice: An allegorical personification of evil and temptation, the Vice was a prominent character in medieval morality plays. The manner in which he ingeniously ensnared his victims, as well as the way they succumbed to his blandishments, was often hilarious. Iago, Richard III, and Falstaff were influenced by the Vice and attest to his continuing vitality well into the Renaissance.

War of the Theatres: A term used to describe the bitter rivalry among major Elizabethan playwrights from 1598 to 1602. The major cause of the war concerned the keen competition between the private enclosed theatres, which catered to an exclusive clientele, and the less expensive public outdoor playhouses. Rosencrantz alludes to this rivalry when he sneers at the lisping boy actors in companies composed solely of children, whose faddish popularity threatened that of the popular theatre for which Shakespeare wrote.

Shakespeare's Plots

*It is assumed by most of us that Shake-
speare is the greatest dramatist in the
world. . . . But take the poetry and the
incredible psychological insight away and
you have artificial plots that were not
Shakespeare's own to start with, full of
improbable coincidences and carelessly
hurried fifth-act denouements.*

—ANTHONY BURGESS

*I*f, as T. S. Eliot said, "Bad poets borrow, good poets steal," Shakespeare was the prince of thieves. Casting his eye over world literature,
from epics of the Greeks to contemporary prose romances, he liberally
helped himself to whatever he liked and made use of it in fashioning his
plots. With the exception of *Love's Labour's Lost, A Midsummer Night's
Dream,* and *The Tempest,* not one plot is completely of Shakespeare's
own invention. Today such "borrowing" is considered plagiarism; an
artist's work, no matter how bad, is sacrosanct, a unique expression of
his or her individuality. The canonization of artistic genius is a relatively

modern idea that originated with the Romantics, such as Beethoven, Keats, and Shelley in the nineteenth century. In the seventeenth century, however, many artists didn't bother to sign their paintings, poems were published anonymously, and Shakespeare's plays weren't his but his company's. Art was not so much an expression of private feelings as a formal and anonymous artifact mirroring the taste and style of the age.

Some of the writers from whom Shakespeare borrowed had themselves borrowed from yet another source, and scholars can sometimes trace his version through centuries of variations. Hollywood's notion of the "high concept" would not have been foreign to the Elizabethan playwright. Shakespeare had a keen eye for a good story and knew what would work. Sometimes he entwined different sources, such as the Gloucester and Lear stories in *King Lear,* whose main plot existed in at least forty different incarnations. The Roman plays, such as *Julius Caesar, Antony and Cleopatra,* and *Coriolanus,* are primarily derived from Plutarch's *Lives,* which had been translated into English by Sir Thomas North in 1579. The plot of *Othello* derives from Cinthio's *Hecatommithi,* but in transforming this minor Italian tale into his own drama of evil, Shakespeare added shrewd psychological awareness, glorious poetry, and the beguiling villainy of Iago with his enigma of motive. All this has made the play, and Shakespeare, immortal, while Cinthio's name, when remembered at all, is a footnote.

Shakespeare lifted most of the plot of *As You Like It* from the popular romance *Rosalynde* (1590) by Thomas Lodge. But among other touches, he added the malcontent Jaques, providing the necessary salt to what would otherwise be a cloying tale of love. Lodge's story is a straightforward prose romance, delightful at first reading but unmemorable. Shakespeare's play is a multilayered composition in which he takes one theme—love—and plays several variations on it, intertwining them all at the end. At first glance, *As You Like It* is as light and frothy as its source, but Shakespeare's froth is like sea foam covering hidden depths.

Shakespeare not only stole plots; at times he lifted whole passages from other works. One of his most famous speeches, the astonishingly beautiful description of Cleopatra in *Antony and Cleopatra,* derives from North's translation of Plutarch's *Lives.* By comparing the two versions, you can get a glimpse into Shakespeare's genius at work.

Here is North's translation:

[She would] take her barge in the river Cydnus, the poop whereof
was of gold, the sails of purple, and the oars of silver, which kept
stroke in rowing after the sound of the music of flutes, hautboys,
citherns, viols, and such other instruments as they played upon
the barge. And now for the person of her selfe: she was laid under
a pavilion of cloth of gold of tissue, apparelled and attired like the
goddess Venus, commonly drawn in picture; and hard by her, on
either hand of her, pretty fair boys apparelled as painters do set
forth god Cupide, with little fans in their hands, with the which
they fanned wind upon her. Her ladies and gentlewomen also, the
fairest of them were apparelled like the nymphs.

Here is Shakespeare:

> The barge she sat in, like a burnished throne,
> Burned on the water. The poop was beaten gold;
> Purple the sails, and so perfumèd that
> The winds were lovesick with them. The oars were silver,
> Which to the tune of flutes kept stroke and made
> The water which they beat to follow faster,
> As amorous of their strokes. For her own person,
> It beggared all description. She did lie
> In her pavilion, cloth-of-gold of tissue,
> O'erpicturing that Venus where we see
> The fancy outwork nature. On each side her
> Stood pretty dimpled boys, like smiling cupids,
> With divers-coloured fans, whose wind did seem
> To glow the delicate cheeks which they did cool,
> And what they undid did.
>
> (II.2.196–210)

To compare the two passages is to see the alchemy of art that trans-
forms prosy fact into poetic gold.

Editing
Shakespeare

Whose Text Is It, Anyway?

*H*ow do we know that the words we read or hear are actually Shakespeare's? Frankly, we don't. When we read a book today, we automatically assume that the words on the page are the author's. We don't have this guarantee with Shakespeare. As Kenneth Branagh said, "So much literary criticism has been the result of a printer putting down a jam sandwich in the middle of one of Will Shakespeare's works." We pay homage to words we aren't even certain Shakespeare wrote. Often what we think is pure Shakespeare is the collective effort of centuries of editors. Even today there's no definitive edition of the works—each differs in some way, from the placement of a comma to the meaning of an entire speech. An editor often has several versions to choose from, and uses the one that makes the most sense and seems the most authentic.

It is difficult to reconstruct the process a play went through before it was performed or published, and each play has its own textual history, some of which is extremely complicated. Shakespeare probably first wrote a rough draft, or "foul paper," none of which exists today. After that, any number of things could happen to the manuscript. Shakespeare would either polish it himself or turn it over to a scribe, and the new clean version would be known as the fair copy, which, when it existed, became the basis for the promptbook used to cue the actors. The prompter would regularize speeches and add stage directions, and often new additions and revisions were added all the way through rehearsal, up to and during the run of the performance itself. Finally, every play had to be submitted to the Master of the Revels, who reviewed it for anything that smacked of political or religious heresy; before it could be performed, a play had to receive his official license.

Shakespeare's Stage Directions

*I*f the stage directions are in brackets in your text, they were added by the editor, not the author. Many of the original stage directions were written by the prompter, or bookkeeper. Since his task was to get the actors on and off the stage as efficiently as possible, his directions were usually terse, no-nonsense directives, such as *"enter"* and *"exeunt with alarums."* Stage directions that describe a character's emotional state, such as that in the second quarto of *Hamlet*: *"Enter Ophelia with her hair downe,"* or more elaborate, descriptive ones, such as *"Thunder and lightning. Enter Ariel, like a harpy; claps his wings upon the table; and with a quaint device the banquet vanishes,"* were probably written by Shakespeare. The most famous stage direction in Shakespeare, *"Exit, pursued by a Bear"* (*The Winter's Tale*) has probably presented more problems to stage designers and directors than any other.

Quartos, Good and Bad

*T*he earliest published editions of Shakespeare's plays are called quartos, a printer's term that refers to the format in which the publication appears. In a quarto, each page was folded twice to provide four leaves, or eight pages. The average quarto was about half the size of a modern magazine. But just because a play is printed doesn't mean that the published version is necessarily a reliable text. By the time the manuscript reached the printer, it had passed through many hands, each contributing its own share of mistakes. Once a play was printed, Shakespeare seemed not to care about it particularly, and he probably never proofread it. Thus all errors were allowed to stand.

There are three types of quartos: good, bad, and doubtful. A good quarto was printed from a trustworthy manuscript and published with the acting company's permission. An acting company would often be forced to publish a popular play when an unauthorized version had already appeared—the bad quarto of *Romeo and Juliet,* printed in 1597, was followed by a good quarto in 1599 that bore the advertiser's boast, "Newly corrected, augmented and amended."

A bad quarto is based on memorial reconstruction, the memory of an actor who took part in the production. Usually his part was small—a major player wouldn't want to sell a play and thus cut into his revenue—and the only part he could recount with any authority would be his own minor role. Thus bad quarto texts are often incoherent, "corrupt," and garbled. A shadow of illegitimacy hangs over bad quartos, and many of them are spurious, pirated versions. Some bad quartos may also be based on eyewitness accounts of the plays: a publisher who wanted to publish a play illegally would plant a scribe, or what scholars call a reporter, in the playhouse to transcribe every word in shorthand. Often the reporter couldn't write fast enough or hear everything; occasionally his handwriting was bad, or he would forget to listen at crucial points. (A guide in a "Shakespeare's London" tour relates the tale of a scribe who did his job all too well: during the performance of *Henry VIII* when the Globe caught on fire, the reporter duly wrote down "Cardinal Wolsey"'s cry, "The theatre's afire!" This anecdote, like so many concerning Shakespeare, is pure fiction.) What all bad quartos have in common is that they have no manuscript authority behind them.

If the bad quarto of *Hamlet* were the only text available, modern actors would be reciting this:

> *To be, or not to be, Ay, there's the point,*
> *To Die, to sleepe, is that all? Ay all:*
> *No, to sleep to dreame, I marry there it goes.*

instead of these immortal lines:

> To be, or not to be—that is the question:
> Whether 'tis nobler in the mind to suffer
> The slings and arrows of outrageous fortune
> Or to take arms against a sea of troubles
> And by opposing end them. To die, to sleep—
> No more—
>
> (III.1.56–61)

Still, bad quartos were—and are—useful. If, for instance, the printer of *Romeo and Juliet* couldn't make out Shakespeare's handwriting, he would look to the early bad quarto to fill in the gaps, and modern editors will resort to a bad quarto when certain lines of a good text are garbled.

"Doubtful quartos," a term coined by the textual scholar W. W. Greg, refers to such quartos as *Othello, Troilus and Cressida,* and *King Lear,* which are probably based on memorial reconstruction and the author's manuscripts.

The distinction between good and bad quartos is currently being challenged. One view is that some bad quartos aren't inaccurate texts but acting editions, and the garbled sections represent cuts made by actors who wanted to shorten the play or make it more dramatic in places. Still other scholars maintain that the "errors" of a bad quarto are part of Shakespeare's creative process; in other words, a bad quarto is an early draft of a play. For instance, the version of the "To be, or not to be" speech quoted above may have been a rough sketch written by Shakespeare on a bad day and not by an actor with a bad memory, while the good quarto of *Hamlet* is a later draft. A few scholars maintain that *Hamlet* is an unfinished masterpiece that Shakespeare continued to revise throughout his career.

What Is a Folio?

*I*n 1623, seven years after Shakespeare's death, two of his fellow actors, John Heminge and Henry Condell, edited and assembled the first complete edition of all the plays. It was called the First Folio, so named because its leaves (*folio* means "leaf" in Latin), or sheets, were folded only once, thus producing a very large book—twice the size of a quarto, about fifteen inches high. The first printing consisted of about 1,000 copies, of which about 240 are still in existence. The original Folio sold for about a pound, which in spending power is the equivalent of about fifty dollars today. A Folio in mint condition would now cost over a million dollars. Eighteen of Shakespeare's plays appeared in print for the first time, and the title page contained the printers' boast: "The Workes of William Shakespeare, containing all his Comedies, Histories, and Tragedies: Truely set forth, according to their first Originall."

Many of the plays that first appeared in the Folio were probably based on Shakespeare's manuscripts or promptbooks that were still in the possession of the acting company. Most likely, a scribe copied them out for the printer. Yet due to carelessness on his part or that of the printer, the Folio edition still contains many errors. When a printed quarto was in existence, the printers used it for the basis of their text, so in many instances the Folio text is a curious combination of prompt-book, drafts, and quarto versions of a play, while at the same time it included many new errors. Of course, this makes an editor's work all the more difficult.

Some people believe that the Folio text might have been the original acting edition. It presented the plays with act and scene divisions, and in places, its punctuation, changed by most editors, sounds more fluent, more responsive to the spoken, rather than the written word. Which *sounds* better?

> When the hurly-burly's done,
> When the battle's lost, and won

Or:

> When the hurly-burly's done
> When the battle's lost and won.

Macbeth (I.1.3–4)

The first is the Folio. The Shakespearean critic and director John Russell Brown prefers it because it highlights the antithesis between winning and losing. And although the pause sounds more satisfying, every modern editor had taken it out. For the most part, editors are scholars who edit the plays as texts to be read rather than scripts to be performed; the acting edition of a play is usually different from the standard text available in most bookstores.

The biggest controversy in Shakespeare scholarship today concerns the Folio and the 1608 quarto texts of *King Lear:* the Folio *Lear* contains one hundred lines not in the quarto, which in itself contains about three hundred lines not in the Folio. Until fifteen years ago, editors traditionally regarded the Folio version as the definitive text, and all modern editions of the plays were a combination of the Folio and quarto texts. For the past ten years, a group of scholars (dubbed the Lear Mafia) have maintained that the two versions are independent plays, and that the quarto has its own integrity as a text. The debate has split the Shakespeare establishment into two camps, each of which argues its case through articles, conferences, and letter-writing campaigns to scholarly journals.

What a Shakespearean Editor Does

A Shakespearean editor's task is especially laborious because, since there's no authoritative manuscript behind a play, he or she has to choose among various intermediary sources, each with its own strengths and weaknesses. Some plays, like *Hamlet,* which has several versions (a bad and a good quarto, and the Folio) can be an editorial nightmare. *Macbeth,* for instance, is easier than most since there's only one version of the play. In this case, an editor need only amend words that don't make sense within a particular context. Take for example, Macbeth's hesitation to kill the king. In the First Folio the line reads:

> I dare do all that may become a man,
> Who dares no more, is none.

> (I.7.46–47)

For two centuries editors have assumed that "no" is a misprint for "do," and simply have changed it. But such uniformity of agreement is rare. Usually an editor's task is much more ambiguous. If a play has more than one text, as in the case of *Hamlet,* the editor must choose a "copytext," the version he believes is the most definitive. Nonetheless he rarely adheres solely to the copytext, and the task of editing involves laboriously comparing every word of the copytext against all the existing versions of a play—its quartos, the Folio, and various later editions. Using these various sources, an editor must try to reconstruct what one genius wrote more than four hundred years ago.

Whenever the editor deviates from his copytext and uses another, he will note the alternate reading in a section called Variants, Collations, or Alternate Readings, which usually appears at the back of the book. Some Variants list other editors' decisions, thus enabling the reader to compare the numerous ways one word appears in most of the major texts.

An editor's decision has an enormous effect on the text we read, its meaning, sound, and sense. For instance, where Shakespeare left punctuation ambiguous, it's up to the editor to choose: did Shakespeare intend "No!," "no?," or "No?" Should a word be on a line by itself or should it start a new one? What about italics and capital letters? The good quarto of *Hamlet* reads "the fat weed that roots itself in ease" (I.5.33), whereas the Folio has "rots itself in ease." Whatever word an editor chooses must be based on the context and the pattern of imagery that runs through the play.

Shakespearean editors make things easier in a variety of ways: they delete unnecessary capital letters that Elizabethan printers used, modernize spellings, and change the Elizabethan long *s* (which looks like our *f*) to the modern one.

ON FOOTNOTES

"Let's you and me go over to my pad, cop out, smoke a joint, and hide away from the fuzz." Four hundred years from now, people will need footnotes to figure out what *that* means.

—LOUIS MARDER

[Reading footnotes is] like having to run downstairs to answer the doorbell during the first night of the honeymoon.

—JOHN BARRYMORE

SHAKESPEAREAN ROMANTIC COMEDY

Shakespeare's romantic comedies can be summed up in one word: love—its trials, torments, confusions, and delights. And it's always love that begins at first sight and ends with marriage. In the comedies, Shakespeare, as always, adopts a complex perspective. He's dedicated to the idea that love is serious and essential to human happi-

ness. But at the same time, he enjoys mocking young lovers—pointing out their antics, their extravagant posturings, and, above all, the arrogance of their belief that no one else has ever felt the way they do. He examines the madness and delusions of love even as he celebrates its enchantment.

A comedy is distinguished from a tragedy in that it ends happily and no one dies. Comedies begin as potential tragedies, but through the pluck of the heroine or the grace of the gods, disaster is always averted. Shakespeare's romantic comedies begin with feuding, misunderstandings, and obstacles and end with dancing, music, and marriage. To the Elizabethans, song and dance were symbols of cosmic harmony, and marriage represented the ideal balance between the sexes. *As You Like It* ends with four marriages, *A Midsummer Night's Dream* with three weddings, and *The Taming of the Shrew* with feasting and the nuptial bed.

Comedies thus end with beginnings, and so they express the cycle of life, in which winter and decay are inevitably followed by spring and renewal. In comedies, mutability is seen as a larger part of life's continuity; in tragedies, we are confronted with mortality and time's inevitable advance.

A tragedy's focus is narrow and intense, concentrating on a solitary figure and his struggles within himself and with society. The titles of the tragedies bear this out: *Hamlet, Othello, King Lear, Coriolanus,* and *Timon* are all individual names. As the titles

ON ENJOYING COMEDIES

*B*ecause comedies rely on "fancy-meeting-you-here" coincidences and unrealistic plot devices, people tend to dismiss them as frothy confections inferior in depth and substance to tragedy. You indulge in comedy but suffer with tragedy. Shakespearean comedy, however, raises the same issues as tragedy, only in a different key and, of course, with a different conclusion. Lear is exiled on the heath, just as Rosalind and Celia are banished to the Forest of Arden. The tragic tale of *Romeo and Juliet* becomes a comedy in *A Midsummer Night's Dream*. Appreciation depends upon entering the comic world and accepting its artifice, no matter how improbable. On one level, you can uncritically accept the comedies, simply enjoying them for their silliness; on another, you can look further and see how Shakespeare uses comic absurdities to suggest profound human values and concerns. The comic world, with its fortuitous encounters, is a well-orchestrated community where everyone is potentially a brother or a sister. Similarly, their concluding marriages are not simply forced happy endings but a reflection of the human need to solemnize experience.

of comedies suggest, the comic perspective is expansive, capturing a fleeting mood and a holiday spirit: *Twelfth Night; or, "What You Will," A Midsummer Night's Dream, As You Like It.* They are about human nature, about us—what *we* like and as *we* like it.

The comic landscape is wide and teeming, capturing an enormous range of people from all levels of society. It extends, in *A Midsummer Night's Dream,* for instance, from the fairy kingdom and the nobility all the way down to ordinary mortals and the working class. Like us, the Elizabethans were interested in relationships, and comedy is about human beings in groups and in pairs. Its action always brings couples together: as Feste in *Twelfth Night* sings, "Journeys end in lovers meeting." And with comedy there's always an ingenious solution at hand; there's freedom, playfulness, surprise, and discovery. A character in a comedy can don many masks and roles without suffering serious consequences. Hero, in *Much Ado about Nothing,* pretends to be dead, and it really *is* much ado about nothing: at the end she is "revived" and happily restored to her lover. With Juliet in *Romeo and Juliet* the outcome is tragic. In tragedy, characters must endure the responsibility of their choices; in comedy, there's always another chance.

Finally, with comedy, as in a dream, any transformation is suddenly possible, and the rules of logic are temporarily suspended: girls turn into boys, servants become their masters, a shrew can be tamed, enemies turn into friends, and villains undergo miraculous conversions.

But transformations are also the stuff of nightmares: Shakespeare's comedies weave uneasily between two worlds, the ideal and the grotesque. They depict a holiday atmosphere, but like Mardi Gras or a carnival sideshow, they can quickly turn strange and disturbing. The lovers of *A Midsummer Night's Dream* flee to the Athenian woods (and "wood" meant "mad" in Elizabethan English), a place of enchantment. But it's also a labyrinth of confusion where they lose their way—and themselves—and where the line between sanity and madness, waking and sleep, is increasingly blurred. Shakespeare in all his great comedies peers into the abyss, and then quickly draws back.

Comedies give a dual perspective: life can be menacing, but along with the danger there's also a sense that everything will be safely restored to normal. We, along with the characters, enter an extraordinary world and return without harm.

Humor in Shakespeare

*Y*ou're at the theatre, watching, say, *As You Like It,* when suddenly it seems the entire audience is laughing uproariously over what seems to you, and only you, a completely unintelligible remark. Don't despair. Others probably don't get it either. People sometimes laugh not because Shakespeare is funny but because he's *supposed* to be funny. It would be nice if everyone could read the play before seeing a performance, but since a director can't depend upon this, he has the problem of how to get centuries-old jokes across to a modern audience. The director Michael Tolaydo says, "Sometimes you make verbal jokes physical; sometimes you have to cut them. Sometimes it's not important that the audience actually understand the joke so long as they understand that something *was* funny. That doesn't mean that the actors stop for a moment, guffaw like crazy, and slap their thighs, but it's possible to convey humor without the audience understanding everything specifically."

Verbal Humor

*T*he Elizabethans loved wordplay such as puns and quibbles, and they went to the theatre just as much to hear the words as to see the action. Shakespeare especially loved puns—the worse the better. According to the literary anecdotalist Robert Hendrickson, there are more than one hundred fourteen puns in *Macbeth* alone, and a list of Shakespearean puns takes up eighty-nine pages in Helge Kokeretz's

Bettman/Hulton

One of the funniest scenes in Shakespeare: Launce the clown and Crab the dog do a routine that's straight out of Abbott and Costello, with Launce playing straight man to Crab, who's oblivious to all the trouble he's caused his master:

He thrusts me himself into the company of three or four gentlemanlike dogs under the Duke's table; he had not been there, bless the mark!, a pissing while, but all the chamber smelt him. "Out with the dog!" says one; "What cur is that?" says another; "Whip him out," says the third; "Hang him up," says the Duke. I, having been acquainted with the smell before, knew it was Crab. . . .

(*The Two Gentlemen of Verona*, IV.4.15–22)

As the critic Stanley Wells points out, Crab is the greatest nonspeaking part in Shakespeare.

Shakespeare's Pronunciation. The opening pun in *Julius Caesar* is the stuff that groans are made on:

> COBBLER. . . . I am but, as you would say, a cobbler.
> MARULLUS. But what trade are thou? Answer me directly.
> COBBLER. A trade, sir, that I hope I may use with a safe
>   conscience; which is, indeed, sir, a mender of bad
>   soles.
>
> (I.1.10–14)

Shakespeare finds puns so irresistible that he even slips one in during a tragic moment: as Mercutio lies dying, he gasps, "Ask for me tomorrow, and you shall find me a grave man."

Running Gags

Cuckolds and cuckoldom were far and away the most popular subjects of jest, the Elizabethan equivalent of "Take my wife. . . ." A cuckold is a man whose wife is unfaithful; hence he is a sexual loser, a wimp, a man who can't satisfy a woman. The word derives from the cuckoo, a bird that lays its eggs in another's nest; and according to folklore, cuckolds grew horns on their brows. Thus, even a casual reference to that part of the anatomy, horns, or anything even remotely connected with them, such as goats, deer (which led to a quibble on "dear"), rams, and bulls, apparently elicited wild laughter. *Love's Labour's Lost* offers a good example of how extended and exhaustive the cuckoldry jest could become:

> BOYET. My lady goes to kill horns, but, if thou marry,
>   Hang me by the neck if horns that year miscarry.
>   Finely put on!
> ROSALINE. Well then, I am the shooter.
> BOYET. And who is your deer?
> ROSALINE. If we choose by the horns, yourself. . . .
>
> (IV.1.112–17)

Another favorite pun was on "travail," the Elizabethan word for physical labor or hardship. But it also meant labor pains, which made for many tiresome jests about a woman's travail walking through the streets, which in turn led to the other form of travail.

Quibbles

*P*atrons in Elizabethan pubs and taverns often engaged in word quibbling, a form of verbal arm wrestling in which each opponent tries to squeeze as many meanings as possible out of one word. This example from *The Two Gentlemen of Verona* is typical: it seems to go on forever, and it even smuggles in that favorite bit about a cuckold's horns. It also exploits the fact that "shipped" and "sheep" sound alike in Elizabethan English.

SPEED. Sir Proteus, save you! Saw you my master?

PROTEUS. But now he parted hence to embark for Milan.

SPEED. Twenty to one then he is shipped already,
    And I have played the sheep in losing him.

PROTEUS. Indeed, a sheep doth very often stray,
    An if the shepherd be a while away.

SPEED. You conclude that my master is a shepherd then,
    and I a sheep?

PROTEUS. I do.

SPEED. Why then, my horns are his horns, whether I wake
    or sleep.

PROTEUS. A silly answer, and fitting well a sheep.

SPEED. This proves me still a sheep.

PROTEUS. True; and thy master a shepherd.

SPEED. Nay, that I can deny by a circumstance.

PROTEUS. It shall go hard but I'll prove it by another.

SPEED. The shepherd seeks the sheep, and not the sheep the shepherd; but I seek my master, and my master seeks not me. Therefore I am no sheep.

(I.1.70–88)

Twenty-two lines later they're still at it, with the humor getting progressively more racy with plenty of bad jokes about "laced mutton" (prostitutes) whom Speed will "stick" ("slaughter," but with an obvious quibble on sexual intercourse). Notice how one word leads to another through a stream of free associations: "ship" to "sheep" to "straying" to "shepherd," finally leading to "laced mutton" and "stick[ing] her." As Samuel Johnson said, "A quibble is to Shakespeare, what luminous vapours are to the traveller; he follows it at all adventures, it is sure to lead him out of his way, and sure to engulf him in the mire." Just as all eyes at a tennis match intently follow every serve and rally, so the Elizabethan spectator followed the volley of words and the tortuous arguments issuing from each opponent's mouth.

Topical Humor

*O*f his first encounter with *Love's Labour's Lost,* the British critic John Trewin wrote: "What on earth did the jokes mean? 'If sore be sore, then L to sore makes fifty sores of sorel.'" Sixty years later, the learned Shakespearean probably still hasn't figured out what it all means. Shakespeare, like comics today, relied on topical jokes, such as puns that depend on archaic pronunciations, in-jokes, and hidden allusions to celebrities now long forgotten. Think about Johnny Carson's nightly monologue: how much of it will be comprehensible four hundred fifty years from today?

Love's Labour's Lost is Shakespeare's most topical play, filled with arcane allusions to popular fads and follies. It's commonly held that the schoolmaster Holofernes is based on the pedant Gabriel Harvey, whom everyone in the courtly audience would have recognized. Holofernes, along with his companion Dull, utters such unintelligible phrases as: "The deer was, as you know, in *sanguis,* blood; ripe as the pomewater, who now hangeth like a jewel in the ear of *caelum,* the sky, the welkin, the heaven, and anon falleth like a crab on the face of *terra,* the soil, the land, the earth." He was just the sort of pretentious nerd that the elitist would have loved to mock.

Love's Labour's Lost also pokes fun at the fashionable courtier's disease of melancholy. In a scene that could have come right out of an old vaudeville turn, Don Armado, who considers himself quite *au courant,* turns to Moth, his page and sidekick, and asks, "Boy, what sign is it when a man of great spirit grows melancholy?" Moth's deadpan reply, "A great sign, sir, that he will look sad," is worthy of the best comic straight man.

The Taming of the Shrew

Many know the plot, but few know how the play actually begins. *The Taming of the Shrew* opens with an "Induction," a story that introduces the main drama of Kate and Petruchio. The Induction tells the tale of the drunken tinker Christopher Sly, who is picked up off the streets by a group of callous young noblemen for a lark. To amuse themselves, they trick Sly into believing he's an aristocrat with amnesia. He is then taken to a sumptuous manor house where, along with his "wife" (a young page dressed as a girl), he watches the play called *The Taming of the Shrew*. Once the story of Kate and Petruchio begins, Shakespeare abandons the whole device, and we never hear anything more about Sly.

Kate is what some people today would call a bitch. While she seems unhappy with her own belligerence and would like to be loved, she does little to make herself lovable.

Kate is also fed up with being compared to her docile sister, Bianca. But Shakespeare refuses to hold Bianca up as an ideal of feminine behavior. She's too boringly conventional, and her coyness hides a will no less strong than that of her more honest, if sharp-tongued, sister. More important, she uses her feminine wiles to manipulate her various suitors. Thus Shakespeare implies that feminine "obedience" is a clever disguise women adopt to get what they want from men. So which sex is the victim?

Kate needs to temper her aggression with some of her sister's placidity, and Petruchio helps her to do this—it's just that his methods are extremely offensive to present-day women. If you can overlook this, you can see that their marriage promises to be far more interesting than that of Lucentio and Bianca. This doesn't mean that Shakespeare advocates feminine bitchiness or masculine aggression, but he *is* saying that a woman with a touch of wildness can make a man's life a lot more intriguing.

The play's misogyny, whether Shakespeare's or Petruchio's, has caused something of a problem in recent years. Some directors try to sidestep the issue by making Kate's submission a joke or by accepting the words at face value without irony or nuance, while others reinterpret Shakespeare to make him more acceptable to modern women. *Shrew* can be played any number of ways: as a Punch and Judy show, a war between the sexes, a bedroom farce, an ironic look at female power, a complicated exploration of sexual relations, or a savage indictment of patriarchal authority. Some productions, such as Franco Zeffirelli's movie, allow us temporarily to abandon contemporary biases and enter into the spirit of the play (and in doing so we are reminded that Shakespeare's robust comedies, particularly *Shrew,* are still incredibly sexy).

But no matter which interpretation a director chooses, he or she still has to confront that final stumbling block—Kate's speech of submission:

> Such duty as the subject owes the prince,
> Even such a woman oweth to her husband.
> And when she is froward, peevish, sullen, sour,
> And not obedient to his honest will,
> What is she but a foul contending rebel
> And graceless traitor to her loving lord?

(V.2.154–59)

We like to think of Shakespeare as modern, as someone who anticipated our concerns, and modern women want to identify with his heroines. This speech, once a favorite subject for girlhood samplers, makes such identification nearly impossible. Some actresses play the scene with a sly wink at the audience. The reviewer in *Newsweek* noted that in the 1990 New York Shakespeare Festival production starring Tracey Ullman and Morgan Freeman, Ullman ended the speech "by 'accidentally' sending [Petruchio] sprawling." The 1980 BBC production, with John Cleese as Petruchio, played it absolutely straight, reinforcing the idea of an orderly social system in which a man, no matter how loving, was still a woman's lord and master. In a celebrated production directed by Michael Bogdanov with the Royal Shakespeare Company, Kate delivers her final speech with smoldering resentment and hostility, while the men, uncomprehending, lie back and listen with smug satisfaction. The French theatre critic Caroline Alexander observed that without altering a word of the text, Bogdanov turned the play's perspective inside out by making Kate an intelligent girl who in spite of herself "falls in love with and compensates for Petruchio, the sort of rebel teenager whom a woman has to treat like a child."

An especially innovative interpretation is Charles Marowitz's adaptation *The Shrew,* in which he draws a chilling comparison between Petruchio's "taming" and the brainwashing techniques used on prisoners of war. Kate's speech at the end is uttered by rote in the expressionless tone of a Stepford wife. The play, says Marowitz, is "Shakespeare's revenge for his brutalization by Anne Hathaway."

SHAKESPEARE AND WOMEN

*W*omen are analyzed in terms of having to stay close to the sources of power, if they want to survive, which is why Gertrude in *Hamlet* has to marry another king, the stronger man. Bianca, as soon as she gets the ring on her finger in *The Taming of the Shrew,* says to Lucentio, "More fool you for betting on me!" That's what happens in the play. Men bet on women, as they bet on dogs; and so you find in Shakespeare the cyclical pattern of a society which, while apparently protecting women, actually batters them to pieces.

—MICHAEL BOGDANOV

Much Ado about Nothing

Best known for its brilliant lovers, the dazzling Beatrice and Benedick, *Much Ado about Nothing* resembles the screwball comedies of the thirties. Beatrice is one of Shakespeare's most loquacious—and engaging—heroines. As she puts it, "There was a star danced, and under that was I born." Throughout the play she and Benedick exchange insults when it's obvious to everyone but themselves that they are drawn to each other. As in *The Taming of the Shrew,* Shakespeare reveals that those who love deepest are usually those who are most guarded against it. Coolness and witty detachment are the best defense against the confusions of the heart. Tricked by friends into admitting their love, Beatrice and Benedick at last reluctantly do so, with Benedick's grudging offer to marry Beatrice "out of pity." There's also a serious (and less interesting) subplot involving the blandly decorous Hero and Claudio—who, unlike their livelier counterparts, conduct their courtship according to prescribed social rituals—and Don John, a pre-Iago villain whose motiveless evil threatens their union. Shakespeare reveals his zanier talents with Dogberry, his first great comic creation. An Elizabethan Keystone Kop, he's a constable on the watch who spouts malapropisms and unwittingly exposes the villain and brings him to justice.

The Merry Wives of Windsor

The only play set in Shakespeare's own middle-class suburbia, *The Merry Wives of Windsor* is an Elizabethan "I Love Lucy." And, indeed, according to legend, the play mocks Sir Thomas Lucy, who caught the young Shakespeare poaching deer on his territory and had him run out of town.

Some scholars maintain that the play was hastily written in two weeks to comply with the queen's request to see Falstaff in love. But Falstaff isn't in love; he simply wants to con the two merry wives, Mistresses Ford and Page (Lucy and Ethel), out of some cash. The pair manage to outwit Falstaff and, along the way, teach the jealous Mr. Page a lesson.

There are also several subplots, all amusing, which end with everyone going off to feast at the Page household.

*I*t's often said that the BBC does best with the minor Shakespeare plays. This is certainly true with *The Merry Wives of Windsor*. The cast of their 1982 production is superb. Ben Kingsley, as the frantic Mr. Page, departs from his usual intensity and reveals himself as a first-rate comedian. Judy Davis and Prunella Scales (a.k.a. Sybil Fawlty) play the Mistresses Ford and Page. Davis almost allows herself to succumb to Falstaff's advances, while the no-nonsense Scales shows us that in many ways Elizabethan housewives aren't all that remote from suburban homemakers today.

There's nothing heavy-handed about this play; it celebrates the solid domestic virtues of thrift, marital fidelity, and good humor. It's one of those plays that work better in performance than on the page, since it's filled with sight gags and spoken humor, including outrageous accents and bawdy malapropisms, that are hilarious on stage.

Love's Labour's Lost

Watching *Love's Labour's Lost* is like drinking champagne for the first time: unexpectedly wonderful. The play is elegant, its humor sparkling and sophisticated. And like rare wine, it was originally designed for an elite coterie. Scholars agree that it was written for a special occasion, and it was probably first performed at court or in a great house. The audience, which may have included the queen, dictated the play's style, so it's filled with allusions to fashionable life—its personalities, fads, and follies.

As usual in Shakespeare's comedies, *Love's Labour's Lost* is composed of symmetrical groupings of the sexes. Here, it's two quartets whose varied movements throughout the play are as patterned and stately as a minuet. The men are the King of Navarre and his three courtiers, Berowne, Longaville, and Dumaine. The play begins when the four form a scholarly academy and solemnly vow that for three years they will follow a strict re-

Love's Labour's Lost, a showpiece of linguistic bravura, contains between two hundred and two hundred forty puns and quibbles, most of them based on contemporary events and courtly in-jokes.

---

*F*rancis Meres, the sixteenth-century critic and avid Shakespeare fan, alludes mysteriously to a play entitled *Love's Labour's Found.* Whether or not this was a sequel we shall never know, but it's tempting to think that *Love's Labour's Lost,* like all of Shakespeare's other comedies, might have ended with happy marriages for all.

gime that will exclude women, delicacies, and excessive sleep. The young king arrogantly assumes that by pursuing knowledge and adopting the monastic life he will defeat "devouring time" and acquire eternal fame. But his oath is as meaningless as it is perverse: ironically, the men hope to gain time by throwing away three years of their youth.

No sooner have they sworn when, predictably, four women arrive on the scene: the French Princess and her three gentlewomen, Rosaline, Maria, and Katherine, who "invade" the academy on court business. It quickly becomes apparent that the four men will soon betray their oath. Part of the fun of the play comes from watching each hide his love from the others and their discovery of each other's secret.

Berowne and Rosaline are the central and most interesting couple. He's an intellectual cynic who mocks all pretensions, but he's also the hardest hit by love. She's just as sharp, but also sexy, and, unlike Berowne, she chooses her words with care. Their banter consists mainly of flirtatious puns and quibbles in which each tries to outdo the other, with Rosaline usually the winner.

BBC REVIEW

The 1984 BBC production of *Love's Labour's Lost* is absolutely luminous. By setting it in the eighteenth century, the director Elijah Moshinsky makes the most of the play's refined elegance. The backgrounds of the sets are a delicate wash of color, and the settings themselves are as beautifully romantic as a painting by Watteau or Fragonard. This production captures a gracious world of picnics on the grass, *billets-doux,* and nocturnal masques.

But at the same time, it's very funny. David Warner as Don Armado resembles Salvador Dalí at his most inane, but he also captures the "Fantastical Spaniard"'s melancholy romanticism. Best of all is the Princess's messenger, Boyet (Clifford Rose), who with one look manages to convey all the arch mannerisms of the French court.

The play is filled with obscure words and arcane allusions, but it also mocks pedantry, fashionable literary postures, amateur sonneteers, and linguistic pomposity. Each young man writes outrageously florid verse to his lady, which she quite rightly distrusts; and in the subplot, an unintelligible pedant named Holofernes drops a Latin phrase at every opportunity. (As one character says, "He's been at a great feast of language and stolen the scraps.")

Best of all is the melancholic lover-soldier, the funny yet sweet Don Adriano de Armado, whose love for the country wench Jaquenetta inspires him to such lines as "I do affect the very ground, which is base, where her shoe, which is baser, guided by her foot, which is basest, doth tread." Called a "Fantastical Spaniard" in the cast of characters, he's a quixotic hodgepodge of Shakespearean figures—a zany Hamlet, a sweet Malvolio, an idealistic Falstaff. At the end of the play, he ceremoniously enacts for the courtiers the "Pageant of the Nine Worthies," and as the butt of their mockery he makes *them* seem callow and brittle.

Love's Labour's Lost is ultimately more about language than about love. There is a profound disjunction between what the young men say and what they feel, and it's each lover's task to match his words to his feelings. Concerned with the tension between affection and affectation, the play asks if language can be a mouthpiece of the heart. The answer is finally voiced through Berowne, who, chastened by Rosaline, promises that from here on, he'll forswear

> Taffeta phrases, silken terms precise,
>   Three-piled hyperboles, spruce affection,
> Figures pedantical . . .
>
> (V.2.406–8)

and will speak nothing but "russet yeas and honest kersey noes" (russet was the color usually worn by peasants, kersey a plain spun fabric). But no sooner has he promised than he forgets himself and says,

> And, to begin: wench—so God help me, law!—
> My love to thee is sound, *sans* crack or flaw.
>
> (V.2.414–15)

To which Rosaline replies, "*Sans 'sans,'* I pray you."

But this is *Love's Labour's Lost,* not found. The play ends as it began, with a promise, not a deed. Each woman sends her lover away for a year with a task that will teach him how to balance his words with his affections. At the beginning of the play four men unthinkingly swear an oath and then are just as eager to dismiss it when it no longer suits them. In a year's time they must learn that words without action are hollow. *Love's Labour's Lost* begins with male vows that are found empty and ends with female promises that, one hopes, will be made good.

Tony Church as the "Fantastical Don Armado"

In a Shakespeare play, even minor characters relegated to a subplot are important; sometimes they are the most compelling characters in the play. A lesser playwright might have devoted all his powers to the courtly couples, but Shakespeare created the remarkably complex figure of Don Armado, who is not essential to the main action but underscores and highlights the play's major themes. The actor Tony Church played Armado twice for the Royal Shakespeare Company, in 1973 and in 1979. To dismiss this man as a buffoon, he says, is to miss a key element of the play.

NE: *What about Don Armado?*

TC: Oh, Don Armado! He's much more than just funny; he's partly a tragic figure. He's the most wonderful part of the play. Shakespeare takes the stock figure of the braggart soldier and gives him the soul of a poet.

NE: *But a bad poet.*

TC: No, no, no, no! Think of that last scene, when he's confronted with the hostility of all those courtiers mocking him about his pageant, and he then turns to them and says with such dignity: "The sweet war-man is dead and rotten. Sweet chucks, beat not the bones of the buried. When he breathed, he was a man."

The extraordinary thing is, we don't know if Shakespeare knew anything about Don Quixote. But Armado imagines himself tilting at various windmills, and he has his own Dulcinea in Jaquenetta. Of course, what's so touching is that though he has no valid reason for doing so, he takes the blame for breaking the Prince's oath—and it's not even an oath that's been administered to *him*. As he regards himself as an equal to the Prince, so he considers himself bound to the Prince's oath. He starts as a ridiculous figure and ends by being a semitragic one. Like all interesting comic roles, he has another side.

Armado is probably based in part on a bizarre dreamer named Pérez, who was a Spanish diplomat who got into trouble with the Inquisition and escaped the court of Philip II dressed as a princess. He hid out in the court of Navarre and became such an extraordinary figure that he was sent to the court of Essex. He wrote mad sonnets to ladies which he signed *"El Peregrino,"* the Wanderer. I don't know what happened to him.

The Merchant of Venice

*I keep saying Shakespeare, Shakespeare,
you are as obscure as life is.*

—*MATTHEW ARNOLD*

The *Merchant of Venice* is a troubling play. At the end, you may not know whether you've seen a tragedy or a comedy, a love story or a tale of hate. In its infinite ambiguity, it is quintessential Shakespeare. No sooner have you reached one conclusion about the play than it's immediately contradicted in the next scene—or line.

First, there's the question: Was Shakespeare an anti-Semite? The central drama of the play concerns the conflict between Shylock, a Hebrew usurer, and Antonio, a Christian merchant. Antonio's friend Bassanio has borrowed three thousand ducats—an enormous sum—from Shylock and offered Antonio as bond. Antonio agrees that if he can't meet the payment, the Jew is entitled to cut a pound of flesh from his side. Later, when the merchant can't pay him back, Shylock demands his due. By adhering to the letter of the law and demanding Antonio's death, Shylock refuses to extend to others the humanity he demands for himself. At the end, when Shylock is forced to convert to Christianity, the Christians offer mercy to a man who extended none to others. Thus *The Merchant of Venice* extols the Christian virtues of mercy and charity over the harsh legalism of Old Testament justice. Such was the standard interpretation of the play throughout the nineteenth century.

Today, we tend to view it differently. The Christians, Bassanio, Gratiano, and Salerio, fashionable men of the Venetian Rialto, are callow and spoiled, while Antonio is a rich merchant who keeps them all in pocket money in exchange for social cachet. Recent Shylocks have been portrayed as Jewish Lears, "more sinned against than sinning." How, then, should we view this play: through eyes that have witnessed a Holocaust or through the Elizabethan perspective, which renders the Jew as an agent of unimaginable cruelties? Then again, are these two views the only alternatives? Shakespeare is rarely that simplistic.

The play is not pro-Jewish, as some would have it, but it's not pro-Christian, either. It all depends on how you—or the director—choose to look at it. Admittedly, the character of Shylock is a Christian invention: dressed in greasy gabardine, he has the obligatory red hair (associated with the devil) and a big nose that quivers at the smell of pork. A crafty loan shark who preys upon the poor, he treats his daughter like a servant and his servant like a slave. He speaks in the Elizabethan equivalent of the singsong rhythm of the stereotyped ethnic Jew—quite unlike the patrician tones of the Gentiles. Most damning of all is his reaction to his daughter Jessica's elopement and theft. Shylock doesn't know what to lament first, his daughter or his ducats:

> My daughter! O my ducats! O my daughter!
> Fled with a Christian! O my Christian ducats!
> Justice! The law! My ducats and my daughter!
>
> (II.8.15–17)

Shakespeare gave his audience the cartoon Jew they loved to ridicule and to hate. In Elizabethan England, a Jewish character was a major draw, promising diabolical deeds and bizarre cruelties. Yet embedded within this caricature there's a real human being, and every so often Shakespeare lets him out. Shylock still mourns his dead wife, Leah, and respects and honors the traditions of his ethnic group. He's a lonely, pitiful old man imprisoned by greed. He's like a survivor of the Great Depression who grows up valuing money more than love. Although Shakespeare was a man of his time, he was capable of stepping outside of his age's prejudices and presenting the world from the alien's perspective. In one of the most quoted speeches in the play, Shylock says:

> He [Antonio] hath disgraced me and hindered me half a
> million, laughed at my losses, mocked at my gains, scorned

my nation, thwarted my bargains, cooled my friends, heated mine enemies, and what's his reasons? I am a Jew. Hath not a Jew eyes? Hath not a Jew hands, organs, dimensions, senses, affections, passions? . . . If you prick us, do we not bleed? If you tickle us, do we not laugh? If you poison us, do we not die?

(III.1.49–55, 58–60)

Just as we are laughing at this ludicrous man, Shakespeare turns around and gives him a speech that makes laughter impossible. Cited by those who don't want to see the play as anti-Semitic, this speech is frequently taken out of context; it's also here that Shylock commits himself to revenge. As the director John Barton points out, the speech is not simply an impassioned plea for racial tolerance but also Shylock's defense for murdering Antonio. In their zeal to make Shakespeare into a great humanitarian, people tend to forget the rest of the passage:

And if you wrong us, shall we not revenge? If we are like you in the rest, we will resemble you in that. If a Jew wrong a Christian, what is his humility? Revenge. If a Christian wrong a Jew, what should his sufferance be by Christian example? Why, revenge! The villainy you teach me I will execute, and it shall go hard but I will better the instruction.

(III.1.60–66)

Yet as many have pointed out, Shylock's desire for Antonio's blood isn't unprovoked. He wants revenge—the same desire that possesses the honorable Hamlet. In providing him with a motive, Shakespeare does something unprecedented on the Elizabethan stage: he makes the Jew comprehensible and human. Shylock's all-consuming hunger for his pound of flesh becomes an obsession only after his daughter has stolen his money and eloped with a Christian.

The character of Bassanio is equally troublesome. In Act I we learn that he's been borrowing money from his friend Antonio—and has already spent it. Now he needs more so that he can court the rich Portia in style, and then, after their marriage, use her money to pay his debts. Basically, he's asking his friend to invest in a new business venture called marriage. These Christians are too proud to walk with Shylock but not too proud to borrow his money. Is the genteel Gentile any

AUDIENCE BEWARE

There is more spit flying about in *The Merchant of Venice* than in just about any other play, Shakespearean or not. In the 1990 Peter Hall production with Dustin Hoffman, there was enough to fill several cuspidors. According to the editor Kenneth Myrick, spitting for the Elizabethans was as common as thumbing one's nose is to us today. The queen herself once "spat upon a courtier's cloak when he displeased her."

With *The Merchant of Venice,* dramatic history intertwines with politics. In 1943, the celebrated actor Werner Krauss was ordered by Joseph Goebbels, Hitler's minister of propaganda, to play Shylock in a manner that would incite hatred against the Jews.

Along with *Othello,* Shakespeare's other play concerning racism, *The Merchant of Venice* has sparked more controversy than any other Shakespearean drama. Jewish adults recall feeling ashamed when they had to read the play in high school. Since World War II, the play has been banned in more classrooms than any other Shakespearean work. When David Suchet planned to play the role of Shylock, he received letters from fellow Jews asking him to reconsider. Surprisingly, according to Sam Schoenbaum, *The Merchant of Venice* is the most popular play in Israel.

different from that shyster Shylock? The Christian likes money as much as the Jew; he just doesn't care to earn it, preferring instead to borrow or marry into it.

Shakespeare presents Bassanio as a Renaissance ideal. He's a handsome and dashing adventurer, careless with material possessions, disdainful of money, and always in need of it. In short, the paragon of the Renaissance courtier. His warm relationship with Antonio embodies the prototype of male friendship, which was almost a cult in Shakespeare's time. During the courtroom scene, Bassanio announces his willingness to give up Portia's life in exchange for Antonio's— a remark not exactly appreciated by his bride, who stands next to him disguised as his lawyer.

What about the enigmatic Antonio, the titular protagonist? Why is the play named after him? Why didn't Shakespeare call the play *The Jew of Venice* or *The Heiress of Belmont*? For a major character, he has very few lines. He is the silent, motionless mystery in a play composed almost entirely of speeches. The play's first words are his, and they contain the most personal information we'll ever get out of him: "In sooth I know not why I am so sad." We never learn the source of Antonio's melancholia or even why Shakespeare has him bring it up in the first place, since it's never mentioned again.

Since he's the only male Christian in the play who isn't interested in women, and because he is intensely involved with Bassanio, it's tempting to see Antonio as suffering from the futility of his homoerotic passion for his friend. Though editors define Antonio's love for Bassanio as friendship, the depth of his involvement goes far beyond this. Antonio's biggest rival in the play is not Shylock but Portia.

Seen one way, Antonio is a courteous gentleman, willing to do anything for a friend; seen in another, he's a Jew-hater and a social climber who publicly spits upon Shylock and curses him—gestures that are difficult to bring off with grace. One critic calls him an "ideal courtier," another a "homosexual pretty boy." Both are legitimate interpretations of Antonio's character.

Antonio's function in the play is essential to the plot, but as a character he's so passive that his personality is eclipsed by everyone else around him. Early audiences would have associated Antonio's willingness to be martyred— particularly at the hands of a Jew—with the Crucifixion. In our post-Freudian age, his apathy suggests a yearning for death.

Entwined with the realistic Shylock plot is a fairy tale of a subplot that raises questions concerning another powerless group—women. According to her dead father's edict, Portia can marry only the man who chooses the right casket from among three, made of gold, silver, and lead. Portia laments, yet she passively obeys this rigid patriarchal decree, which could cost her the only man she's ever loved. (Nevertheless, when Bassanio is about to make his choice, she gives him a nudge in the right direction by singing a song in which all the end rhymes suggest the word "lead": "Tell me where is fancy bred, / or in the heart, or in the head?")

Later, in the trial scene, we see a different Portia. Arguing Antonio's case, she's in complete control of the situation, and her common sense surpasses that of all the men in the courtroom. Is there an inconsistency in Shakespeare's portrait? Is Portia smart enough to argue legal fine points, but not intelligent enough to choose her own husband? Disguised as Balthasar, the male lawyer, she possesses strength, wit, and power, but as an unmarried woman she must wait demurely to be courted by a suitor not of her own choosing.

In addition to the two plots, the play shuttles back and forth between two settings. Venice, a bustling city, filled with a mélange of nationalities, races, and classes, is a practical world ruled by commerce. Belmont, where Portia lives, is a gilded fantasy by the sea—a "restricted" country club for the idle rich where no Jews are allowed. Belmont is the magic circle everyone wants to enter. Significantly, only two people remain outside its charmed interior: the "hero" and the "villain." Both end up as strangers and losers: Antonio loses Bassanio, and Shylock his daughter—and his ducats. And to some degree, everyone is betrayed: Portia and her confidante, Nerissa, realize that their husbands have given away their rings, their sacred pledges, to the young "lawyer" and his "page." The two wives have tested their husbands and found them wanting.

After the trial, as the Christians celebrate their victory and the Jew is humiliated and deprived of his wealth, Shakespeare has him murmur, "I am not well." Shakespeare could have had him rush out demanding revenge, yet these simple words humanize him in a way nothing else could. Precisely when we should be cheering the Christian victors, the so-called villain has become *their* victim. What should be joyous makes us feel strangely unhappy and uncomfortable. When Heinrich Heine saw the play, he cried out, "My God, the man has been wronged!" Yet at the same time, one must never forget that Shylock is both wronged *and* wrong.

The play doesn't end with Shylock's humiliation. Shakespeare gives the audience a final turn of the screw when the scene shifts swiftly from the austere courtroom to a moonlit night in Belmont, and Jessica and Lorenzo make us forget the nasty vision we have just seen by uttering the play's most sensuous poetry.

The Merchant of Venice is about power—being without it and wanting it. The ideal is to be wealthy, male, and Christian. Portia can successfully argue Antonio's case, but only when she's strengthened by male attire. Jessica begins the play poor, Jewish, and single and ends it rich, Christian, and married. In the interim, during her flight to Belmont, she inexplicably adopts masculine clothing. Through this gesture, Shakespeare seems to be saying that Jessica can acquire power, but only if she first "becomes" a man and a Christian.

Are all these contrary views ever resolved? Perhaps the answer lies in the riddle of the three caskets. Remember, it's the least ostentatious one that's the most valuable, and the choice is a test that reveals the character of the chooser and not just the contents of the casket. The play sets up a similar test with its audience. Throughout *The Merchant of Venice* Shakespeare insists that nothing is what it seems. The play, which seems so traditional, is actually quite subversive: villains possess secret virtues; heroes have a secret taint. Shakespeare offers at least two views of every character and situation, confronting us with a variety of possible interpretations. The play supports almost any reading you care to give it, and, like the caskets, the one you choose reveals more about you than about the play.

Shylock

*S*hylock overshadows everyone else in the play, but, in fact, he has a very small part, appearing in only five of the play's twenty scenes. Until the late nineteenth century, the character was played as a comic villain with a red fright wig, sidelocks, and a bulbous false nose. Edmund Kean was the first actor to explore the tragic dimension of Shylock's character, and until the late twentieth century it was considered *de rigueur* to play Shylock as the long-suffering Jew, as if the play were a Shakespearean *Fiddler on the Roof* with Shylock an Elizabethan Tevye. Today's actors are more concerned with

*T*here's a fascinating videotape of an actor's workshop, entitled "Playing a Character," led by John Barton of the Royal Shakespeare Company. Barton, who directed the actors David Suchet and Patrick Stewart as Shylock in two different productions of *Merchant*, comments on the various ways in which a role can be interpreted by two different actors. Stewart and Suchet alternate playing the same scene, after which they comment on their understanding of the character—his clothing, his accent, his demeanor, even his walk.

discovering the contradictions and ambiguities within a character, and they try to create a multifaceted human being who is shaped by the context of his time and place.

Patrick Stewart was reluctant to accept the part because of its recognizably Jewish trademarks: the sidelocks, the Semitic clothing, whether gorgeously Oriental or greasy, the skullcap, and, of course, the obligatory accent. These standard ethnic features, he felt, would lock him into a conventional interpretation. Stewart deemphasized Shylock's Jewishness, preferring instead to see him as an outsider who happens to be a Jew. In "Playing a Character," Stewart said, "If you see him as a Jew first and foremost, then he's in danger of becoming only a symbol."

Stewart's Shylock was an alien who tries to assimilate into Venetian society, and he spoke in the genteel tones of a foreigner who has mas-

© Donald Cooper/Photostage

*P*atrick Stewart as Shylock in John Barton's 1978 production.

tered the language better than the natives. In rejecting the orthodox approach, Stewart created a complicated man who artfully used irony and intelligence as a weapon against the more simplistic Christians, who couldn't possibly begin to understand his wit.

I find it impossible to think of Shylock as a really nice chap; he is just better-quality stuff than any of the Christians in the play. They are truly vile, heartless, money-grubbing monsters, and when Shylock makes his final exit, destroyed by defeat, one should sense that our Christian brothers are at last thoroughly ashamed of themselves. *The Merchant of Venice* is horrid, cruel, and one of the most popular plays in the whole collected volume of Shakespeare.

—LAURENCE OLIVIER

David Suchet

*D**avid Suchet, an associate artist of the Royal Shakespeare Company, played Shylock in the RSC production of* The Merchant of Venice *in 1981. He is probably best known to Americans as Hercule Poirot in the television series "Mystery!"*

NE: *How did you prepare for the role of Shylock?*

DS: I studied the history of how the Jew was portrayed in English drama. Up to that point he had always been represented as the devil with red hair. Until *The Merchant of Venice,* no Jew on stage had ever been given a reason for his diabolical actions. No one can say that Shylock is right to seek the life of anybody, even in revenge. But because you are dealing with a marvelous writer who knows about people, he gives Shy-

*D*avid Suchet as
Shylock in John
Barton's 1981
production.

lock a motive, and the motive is the loss of his daughter. The humor is that here is a man who at one moment doesn't know what's more important to him, his daughter or his ducats.

NE: *Doesn't that make us hate Shylock?*

DS: No, he's very sympathetic. He's an old man, a man who is confused, a man who doesn't know his values anymore. He's a man who ultimately learns his values. If you look at the scene where he is bewailing his daughter and his money, it might seem like an anti-Semitic, silly thing, but if you look at it again, if you see him as a human being, then Shakespeare is asking, What is more important in life? People, family, or money? It's a very subtle scene.

I disagree with every critic who says it is an anti-Semitic play. Shakespeare would never have done that—not with Marlowe's play *The Jew of Malta* playing down the road, which *is* very anti-Semitic. With *The Merchant,* Shakespeare gives two fingers to *The Jew of Malta.* And Shylock is redeemed at the end of the play.

NE: *Why? Because he is now a Christian? Many people find that scene very offensive.*

DS: We *must* not judge *The Merchant of Venice* in terms of the Holocaust! We must not! We must go back four hundred years and look at what Shakespeare was doing. By making Shylock convert at the end, Shakespeare is saving his soul, because the Elizabethans believed that the Jewish soul went to hell.

NE: *But he's a reluctant Christian.*

DS: That doesn't matter! We can't look at it in modern terms. It was quite a common punishment. We can only react to how the play was written and keep an open mind.

NE: *But don't the Christians in the play come off as rather bland and callow?*

DS: Yes, the Christians in the play come off terribly badly, and Shakespeare is very keen to make sure that the last scene is not just a happy reunion.

NE: *But what about Portia, the so-called heroine?*

DS: Portia is a totally confused, money-governed person, desperately wishing to find human values. The whole play has to do with money, not racism. Shylock comes on and his first line is "Three thousand ducats, well." Everybody wants to marry Portia because she is so wealthy. She has to find love in the play. That's what Shakespeare is saying throughout *Merchant*: the real value is in people, not money.

Tony Church

*T*ony Church, a founding member of the Royal Shakespeare Company in 1960, played Antonio in 1971 and 1972 in Terry Hands's production of The Merchant of Venice.

NE: *Antonio is the most ambiguous character in this maddening, frustrating play. I don't understand him.*

TC: Shakespeare didn't intend you to. He's creating a puzzle in the center of the play.

NE: *Does he have a secret? Is he gay?*

TC: You're not to know this entirely. Passionate male friendship is accepted in Shakespeare, and the men aren't necessarily gay. What you have is a title role—the center of the play—which by Shakespearean standards is purposely underwritten. Antonio's silences are some of the most powerful parts of the play. This had never been done in Elizabethan drama, which is the drama of the speaker.

The interesting thing is to look at Shakespeare's sources for a play and see where he departs from them. In two of the original sources, Antonio is either a godfather or stepfather [to Bassanio]. Shakespeare deliberately ignores these possibilities, thereby opening up the possibility of Antonio as Bassanio's lover.

NE: *Did you play him as a lover?*

TC: Partly. As a frustrated lover. I don't know whether their love is consummated or not. I don't think it matters. What matters is that Antonio is a rich man who is surrounded by a coterie of young men, one of whom, Bassanio, he's always lending money to. Bassanio is an aristocrat, a scholar, and a soldier. He isn't a nobody, but what he doesn't have is money.

Now, Antonio isn't an aristocrat at all. He is a self-made businessman—an Onassis, if you like, in modern terms. In fact, we very much thought of Onassis and Callas: she didn't need his money, but she was a star who entertained him and who, like Bassanio, was beautiful, witty, and clever. But the other side of Antonio is that he's predominantly a gambler. And his sadness is not that he loses but that he can't stop winning.

NE: *Why would that make him sad?*

TC: Have you ever met a gambler? Antonio offers his flesh as surety because Shylock challenges him to a gamble. Shylock suddenly challenges Antonio to a stupid dare that Shylock will definitely lose, but he does it to make Antonio the laughingstock of the Exchange. Shylock essentially says, Put your life on the line. That appeals to Antonio, since it's the only thing left he hasn't gambled. It has all the romantic appeal of the ultimate risk.

NE: *So what he is experiencing at the beginning is the ennui of someone who has nothing left to live for.*

TC: Yes, yes! And at the same time he knows he will potentially lose Bassanio. Shakespeare gives you a wonderful mixture of things to play. He never gives you a simple role.

NE: *The play drives me nuts.*

TC: That's why I love it so much. The only plays that really interest me are the ones that drive me nuts. I don't believe that Shakespeare is any more contradictory, confusing, or ambiguous than people are in life. He's only dramatizing what actually goes on. That's why he is the ultimate realistic writer.

A Midsummer Night's Dream

*Against May, Whitsunday, or other time
all the young men and maids . . . run
gadding over night to the woods, groves,
hills, and mountains where they spend all
the night in pleasant pastimes.*

—*PHILIP STUBBS,*
Puritan preacher

Like a dream itself, *A Midsummer Night's Dream* presents a startling mixture of disparate elements: homely and realistic characters are placed within a fantastic, almost surrealistic, plot; the lowest level of society mixes with the highest; prosaic speech is uttered along with sublime poetry; and the supernatural, the human, and the bestial worlds commingle. And, like a dream, this dramatic fairy tale initially appears to be a trivial diversion that bears little connection to our waking lives. Yet, upon closer examination, *A Midsummer Night's Dream* reveals, in disguised form, deep truths about our hidden emotional life.

In *A Midsummer Night's Dream* Shakespeare does something with his two central pairs of lovers that he had never done before and would do only once again (with Rosencrantz and Guildenstern in *Hamlet*): he creates characters who are interchangeable—a striking departure for a playwright who usually distinguishes every character, no matter how minor. Lysander loves Hermia, and Hermia, Lysander; Demetrius also loves Hermia; and Helena, odd woman out, is infatuated with

Demetrius. But any combination would serve the purposes of the plot. No matter how many times you read this play, you'll get Hermia and Helena confused. The only difference between them is that one is tall, the other short; they are the stock lovers found in any romantic comedy—except that, this being Shakespeare, they speak more beautifully. The same is true of the men: Lysander could suddenly become Demetrius and the audience would never be any the wiser. That's precisely Shakespeare's point; this play, which deals in magic, illusion, and enchantment, is about the mysterious power of love to transform an ordinary mortal into a rarity of perfection:

> Things base and vile, holding no quantity,
> Love can transpose to form and dignity.
> Love looks not with the eyes, but with the mind . . .
>
> (I.1.232–34)

But since we aren't under the lovers' spell, we see them with the cool eyes of reason, and they all look alike to us. And apparently to Puck as well. When Oberon orders him to sprinkle "love juice" in the eyes of an Athenian man, he mistakes Lysander for Demetrius, the intended recipient. Thus Lysander, once passionate about Hermia, is now deeply in love with Helena. Then, to rectify his error, Puck squeezes the juice onto Demetrius, and he, too, falls for the once-despised Helena. Love, long recognized as a form of enchantment, literally becomes a spell.

Modern audiences tend to resist the idea of magic, but many Elizabethans still believed in fairies, only their creatures were much darker and more sinister than the bland images manufactured by Walt Disney. Their traditional habitat, the dark forest where confused travelers lose their way, belongs more to the strange tales of the Brothers Grimm. Shakespeare's moon-drenched fairy world is a symbolic dreamscape where traditional distinctions blur and disappear. By entering the enchanted woods at nightfall, the lovers abandon the familiar daylight world, as represented by civilized Athens, and enter a mental landscape, a covert realm within the unconscious, a place of fearsome transformations and self-discovery. Just as insanity, poetry, and dreams possess their own fantastic logic, revealing an unsettling yet truthful vision of ordinary life, so the dark woodlands—as seen in countless myths and fairy tales—expose the flip side of civilization, revealing the tenuous boundary that distinguishes reason and madness, lust and love.

Although the characters have transferred their affections, the situation remains the same: Hermia is merely exchanged for Helena. If the play were translated into modern life, Lysander, Hermia, Demetrius, and Helena would be Bob and Carol and Ted and Alice.

Meanwhile, there are other visitors to the forest that night. The Athenian tradesmen have gathered there to rehearse the "tedious brief scene of young Pyramus and Thisbe," which they intend to perform for Duke Theseus in honor of his forthcoming nuptials. As he watches them rehearse, Puck snickers at their amateurish bungling, just as he mocks the inanity of the young lovers: "Shall we their fond pageants see? / Lord, what fools these mortals be!" ("Fond" meant foolish.) From Puck's superior perspective, the mortal world is a ridiculous farce, and he laughs at the confused lovers just as later the lovers will snicker at the artisans when they put on *their* show. If in *Lear* human beings are to the gods as flies are to wanton boys, in *Dream* they are sport for fairies.

But the fairy kingdom is not immune to disorder. In Oberon and Titania's bitter feud, the theme of love's delusion is carried to an even darker extreme. Enraged at Titania's refusal to give him her beloved Indian boy, Oberon sprinkles the love juice in Titania's eyes while hissing this malediction:

> What thou seest when thou dost wake,
> Do it for thy true love take;
> Love and languish for his sake.
> Be it ounce or cat or bear,
> Pard, or boar with bristled hair
> In thy eye that shall appear
> When thou wakest, it is thy dear.
> Wake when some vile thing is near!
>
> (II.2.33–40)

Unfortunately, it's the newly "translated" Bottom who, thanks to Puck's mischief, is now crowned with the head of an ass. Titania, that most ethereal queen, is immediately enamored of the animal that was regarded as the most lascivious—and sexually potent—in the Elizabethan bestiary. Only in this century have critics paid much attention to the grotesquely erotic implications of Titania and Bottom's love scene:

Come, sit thee down upon this flowery bed
While I thy amiable cheeks do coy,*
And stick muskroses in thy sleek, smooth head,
And kiss thy fair large ears, my gentle joy.

(IV.1.1–4)

*Coy means "caress."

Mendelssohn's "Wedding March," which usually picks up at about this point, suggests that this is a wedding night in the fullest sense. Although the language is undeniably erotic, and the implications of bestiality are certainly present, remember it's only Bottom's *head* that's been transformed: the rest of him remains a man. In *A Midsummer Night's Dream* the ordinary question, "What does she (or he) see in him (or her)?" is taken to an extreme: Who among us, Shakespeare seems to ask, hasn't fallen for an ass and believed him (or her) a god?

And who, upon awakening from the enchantment of love, has not been embarrassed to discover the mistake?

Released from her spell, Titania shudders, half remembering, not quite certain of what she has done, or if what has happened is real or an illusion. Similarly, the lovers, their confusion dispelled by Puck and Oberon, fall into a deep sleep and wake never knowing if their experiences have been a vision or reality. Perhaps a little of both. As Hermia says: "Methinks I see these things with parted eye, / When everything seems double." Exhausted by their ordeal, they all "to Athens back again repair / And think no more of this night's accidents / But as the fierce vexation of a dream." Demetrius still retains the effects of the love potion, leaving us to wonder if his love for Helena is "real"; but as Shakespeare has already shown us, all love—even "true" love—is a form of sorcery. And, after all, this is a comedy, and everyone must get married.

All the different plots and social strata come together in the final scene, when the artisans assemble before lovers and nobles to put on their play in honor of the weddings. Scholars believe that *A Midsummer Night's Dream* was written to grace the marriage of a noble couple, so in essence, Shakespeare's original audience watched a play that contained a play that was watched by courtiers. The levels of deception and mirror images in this play are astonishing, and it's easy to get trapped amid all the shimmering reflections. Ironically, it's the oafish Bottom who has the wisest comment on the night's experiences, and students and scholars of Shakespeare would do well to pay attention:

> I have had a most rare vision. I have had a dream past the wit of man to say what dream it was. Man is but an ass if he go about to expound this dream.
>
> (IV.1.203–5)

On Fairies and Spectacles

*M*odern directors generally try to translate Shakespearean sprites, ghosts, and fairies into images and concepts more meaningful to a skeptical audience, though why they feel they must do so in an age of science fiction and "Star Trek" is not quite clear.

*I*n . . . *A Midsummer Night's Dream*, the unavoidable question, "How do we stage fairies and spirits?" cannot be solved by aesthetic devices, because on an immediate level "fairy" suggests nothing to the modern mind. . . . A fairy is the capacity to transcend natural laws and enter into the dance of particles of energy moving with incredible speed. What theatre imagery could enable human bodies to suggest bodilessness? Certainly not gossamer schoolgirls. . . . Seeing Chinese acrobats, we found the key: a human being who, by pure skill, demonstrates joyfully that he can transcend his natural constraints, become a reflection of pure energy. This said "fairy" to us.

—PETER BROOK

*I*n Peter Brook's celebrated production of *A Midsummer Night's Dream* at Stratford in 1970, Titania and Puck swung on trapezes while observing the follies of earthbound mortals. According to the theatre critic Robert Brustein, "lovers were wooed on swings" and the play's "all-white environment became a freestyle gymnasium." The entire play was enacted within a stark white box.

*T*he Shakespearean biographer Peter Levi writes, "Most uneducated Elizabethans believed in fairies," and he notes that most literary fairies of the period were more obscene than those found in Shakespeare.

BFI Stills, Posters and Designs

*M*ax Reinhardt's 1935 Hollywood extravaganza, *A Midsummer Night's Dream* (co-directed with William Dieterle).

Levi cites a play called *The Maid's Metamorphosis* (1600), in which there are three fairies named Penny, Cricket, and "little, little Prick":

> *When I feel a girl asleep*
> *Underneath her frock I peep*
> *There to sport, there I play,*
> *Then I bite her like a flea*
> *And about I skip.*

A Midsummer Night's Dream has often inspired lavish stagecraft. A contemporary's description of Purcell's musical version, *The Fairy Queen* (1692), in itself sounds like pure poetry:

In the second act, Purcell introduced a whole new cast of supernatural and allegorical creatures such as "Secresie, Sleep, and their Attendants, Singers and Dancers." The fourth act included "Spring, Summer, Autumn, Winter, and their Attendants. Phoebus: A Dance of the Four Seasons." And the triumphant finale pulled out all the stops with "Juno. Chinese Men and Women. A Chorus of Chineses. A Dance of 6 Monkeys. An entry of a Chinese Man and a Woman. A Grand dance of 24 Chineses."

*E*very single person goes into a forest at night and encounters fairies. The question depends upon what you think of as a fairy. What sinks most productions of *A Midsummer Night's Dream* is the notion of a fairy as a nineteenth-century silly thing. Anytime you walk in the woods alone, they're there. Or when you dream. If a voice comes to you and says something you don't really understand . . . that's what Shakespeare means by fairy.

—PETER SELLARS

*I*n some respects, the comedy of musical beds and drugs and knockabout buffoonery seems almost made for MTV. The scene of two young men playing mixed doubles with their interchangeable girlfriends would not seem strange to the kids in Bret Easton Ellis novels, who fall into bed with anyone at all, scarcely stopping to ascertain identity, or even sex.

—PICO IYER

No-Holds Bard: A Glossary of Sexual Slang

Those who praise Shakespeare and condemn, say, Robert Mapplethorpe certainly don't know Shakespeare.

—*DAVID NIELDS,*
former residential directorial
assistant, Shakespeare Theatre
at the Folger Library

There's no denying it: Shakespeare was not merely bawdy—the usual term used to convey full-blooded Elizabethan lustiness—he was stunningly vulgar. And his audience loved it. Bodily functions, secretions, smells, references that we would consider tasteless or private, were to them the pinnacle of wit. Privacy, particularly concerning personal hygiene, is a relatively modern idea, and the Elizabethans were far less squeamish than we are today.

Shakespeare, as might be expected, used bawdy language with more verve than his contemporaries, the most neutral words often doing overtime as double, and sometimes triple and even quadruple, entendres (for instance, Shakespeare was fond of the word "will," which variously meant sexual desire, penis, vagina, and was, of course, his own name). Once you know the Elizabethan meaning of one or two words, a whole passage suddenly takes on a startling alternative meaning. Slang hunting in Shakespeare is amusing, and the underlying crudity doesn't necessarily detract from the beauty of the lines—it only adds another dimension. What makes Shakespeare unique is that he is capable of being tender, sexy, funny, and sad, all at the same time.

Since most Elizabethan sexual slang is no longer current, students today can study *Romeo and Juliet* without any idea of what they're reading. Editors tend to evade explicit annotation, resorting to the bland "This is a bawdy quibble," the editorial equivalent of a squirm. This is unfortunate, since understanding Shakespeare's earthiness might enhance his reputation among high school students. Guardians of morality who complain of obscene lyrics in rock music are unaware that teenagers hear a lot worse in their English class, albeit uncomprehendingly. Given the explicit nature of Shakespeare's works, one wonders if he could have received an NEA grant had he applied today.

If you're curious—or just prurient—look at Frankie Rubinstein's *A Dictionary of Shakespeare's Sexual Puns and Their Significance* or Eric Partridge's classic *Shakespeare's Bawdy*.

Anatomical Humor: The Bard was not above the locker-room school of humor, as in this exchange from *The Comedy of Errors*:

> DROMIO. She is spherical, like a globe. I could find out countries in her.
> ANTIPHOLUS. In what part of her body stands Ireland?
> DROMIO. Marry, sir, in her buttocks. I found it out by the bogs.
> . . . .
> ANTIPHOLUS. Where stood Belgia, the Netherlands?
> DROMIO. O, sir, I did not look so low.
>
> (III.2.120–25, 145–47)

("Bogs" was slang for the buttocks; Eric Partridge writes that "Belgia" is a pun on belly.)

Arise (or stand): To have an erection. Shakespeare belabors this word and its meaning in Sonnet 151: ". . . flesh stays [waits for] no farther reason / But, rising at thy name, doth point out thee / As his triumphant prize." ("Point" is another bawdy quibble, since it means, like "prick," to mark or point out and to rise.) In fact, the entire sonnet is an extended metaphor about the rise and fall of the flesh. When Titania tells Bottom "Arise, arise," she is not only telling him to wake up.

Banter (sexual): Perhaps the most famous sexual banter occurs in *The Taming of the Shrew*:

> PETRUCHIO. Who knows not where a wasp does wear his
>   sting?
>   In his tail.
> KATHERINA. In his tongue.
> PETRUCHIO. Whose tongue?
> KATHERINA. Yours, if you talk of tails, and so farewell.
> PETRUCHIO. What, with my tongue in your tail?
>
> (II.1.213–17)

Bottom: In *A Midsummer Night's Dream,* the word has a triple meaning: it is the name of a character; it means the buttocks, or ass, which is also a pun on the beast that Bottom is turned into; and the ass was regarded as the most well-endowed animal in the Elizabethan bestiary.

Cod: A common pun referring to the male organ. But anything to do with fish—of any species—was automatically suggestive and could start the audience laughing merely by association. (Mercutio upon seeing Romeo: "Here's Romeo without the roe.") The editor of the Folger Library edition of the comedies decorously defines "cod" as "strictly the husks containing the peas."

Codpiece: A fashionable item of clothing, resembling a jockstrap worn over a man's hose instead of beneath it.

Count: Often used for its similarity to the English vernacular for the female genitalia. When Hamlet, with his head on Ophelia's lap, tells her he is thinking of "country matters," he pointedly stresses the first syllable.

Die: Sexual intercourse or orgasm. The most common sexual pun in Elizabethan literature. According to Elizabethan physiology, each act of sexual intercourse shortened the lover's life by about a minute or so, owing to the discharge of "animal fluids." Thus, every orgasm was a miniature death. From *Antony and Cleopatra*:

> ENOBARBUS. Under a compelling occasion, let women die.
> It were a pity to cast them away for nothing,
> though between them and a great cause they
> should be esteemed nothing.

> (I.2.138–41)

Note how shrewdly Shakespeare slips in the double entendres. Women experience orgasm "under" something that compels them. "Nothing" was slang for sexual intercourse and the female genitalia. Between them and a "great cause" (a penis) lies nothing.

Double Entendres: Shakespeare's erotic poem "Venus and Adonis" proves that gorgeous lyrics are often the most suggestive:

> "I'll be a park, and thou shalt be my deer:
> Feed where thou wilt, on mountain or in dale;
> Graze on my lips; and if those hills be dry,
> Stray lower, where the pleasant fountains lie.

> "Within this limit is relief enough,
> Sweet bottom-grass and high delightful plain,
> Round rising hillocks, brakes obscure and rough . . ."

Eric Partridge notes that "bottom-grass" referred to the "hair growing in and about the crotch," "brakes" was pubic hair; "groves" referred to the pubic area. According to Frankie Rubinstein, "graze" meant to roam freely, but it also suggested promiscuity. "Park" connoted a woman's genitals. It was commonplace to apply topographical terms to the female anatomy.

Green: Connoted virility and potency. See the scene in *Henry V* in which Falstaff's former mistress, the Hostess, relates her discovery of his death. You'll never read this scene in quite the same way again:

> . . . for after I saw him fumble with the sheets, and play
> with flowers, and smile upon his fingers' ends, I knew

there was but one way; for his nose was as sharp as a pen, and 'a babbled of green fields. . . . I put my hand into the bed, and felt them [his feet], and they were as cold as any stone; then I felt to his knees, and so up'ard, and up'ard, and all was as cold as any stone.

(II.3.13–25)

Rubinstein annotates "flowers" and "nose" as penis; "green fields" suggested virility; "stone" was a common word for testicle. The Hostess mourns her old lover's death—both his literal end and his last erection. This speech, which unites a genuine elegiac tone with masturbatory imagery, is something few poets could get away with. Given Falstaff's earthiness and his role in the play as a symbol of the flesh, it's fitting that the Hostess can tell he's dead only by feeling his penis. The two sensibilities, the bawdy and the sentimental, don't cancel each other out; in fact, surprisingly, each enhances the other.

Hell: Slang often used in passages of sexual nausea to indicate a woman's genitals. See Sonnet 144, in which the poet suspects the friend of being inside the Dark Lady's hell.

Leaping House: A brothel.

Naught: Wickedness, with implications of sexual intercourse—usually adulterous. From *Richard III*:

> BRAKENBURY. With this, my lord, myself have naught to do.
> RICHARD. Naught to do with Mistress Shore? I tell thee,
>   fellow,
> He that doth naught with her, excepting one,
> Were best he do it secretly, alone.

(I.1.97–100)

Pricks and Bowls: Pricks referred to a game of archery, bowls to bowling, but both words are frequently used to suggest other games. According to Rubinstein, games were often metaphors for sex. From *Love's Labour's Lost*:

COSTARD. She is too hard for you at pricks, sir. Challenge
    her to bowl.
BOYET, I fear too much rubbing.

(IV.1.139–40)

"Rubbing" was a bowling term, when one ball grazed another. When Hamlet says, "Ay, there's the rub," he is using a bowling term.

Quaint, Queynt, or Coynt: Female genitalia. When a man said he "made" a woman's "acqueyntaince," he meant he knew her very well indeed. The word refers to the vernacular "cunt" and has undergone an interesting etymological evolution. At first, in addition to its anatomical meaning, it referred to something dark, secretive, and curiously wrought. It's a linguist's—or a psychiatrist's—task to figure out why, but through the ages the word has slowly been purged of its covert meanings, until now it refers to the opposite of its original definition: "quaint" now means something dainty, sweetly picturesque, and old-fashioned.

*H*ere's one brave editor who annotated with a vengeance. In 1723, the Shakespearean scholar and editor George Steevens published a volume of Shakespeare complete with graphic explications of all sexual puns and allusions. But Steevens didn't take credit for the edition, attributing it instead to two respectable clergymen with whom he had a score to settle.

Seduction: Falstaff to Mrs. Ford in *The Merry Wives of Windsor*: "Let the sky rain potatoes. Let it thunder to the tune of 'Greensleeves,' hail kissing-comfits and snow eringoes. Let there come a tempest of provocation, I will shelter me here." (V.5.18–21) (One wonders where Falstaff is pointing.) Potatoes, kissing-comfits (perfumed sweetmeats), and snow eringoes (sea holly) were believed to have aphrodisiacal properties; "provocation" meant sexual stimulation; the popular song "Greensleeves" was probably the Elizabethan equivalent to "Bolero" or Johnny Mathis, standard seduction fare.

Thing: A penis. Rosalind and Orlando's seemingly innocent banter in *As You Like It* is filled with double entendres:

> ROSALIND. Are you not good?
> ORLANDO. I hope so.
> ROSALIND. Why then, can one desire too much of a good
>   thing?
>
> (IV.1.110–12)

Whore: Elizabethan English had dozens of words to describe a prostitute, and Shakespeare seems to have used them all: beef, wench, jade, baggage, punk, slut, Winchester goose, taffeta punk, guinea-hen, bawd, quean, laced mutton, fish, stale, and doxy. (Prostitutes often dressed in taffeta; the bishop of Winchester owned the land where most of the brothels were located, and prostitutes had to pay him revenue out of their earnings; hence they were like geese, kept and fattened by the church.)

Will: Not only a pun on Shakespeare's name, but also a reference to sexual desire, as well as the male and female genitals. Shakespeare exploits the word to the maximum, particularly in Sonnet 135, where it occurs twelve times in fourteen lines:

> Wilt thou, whose will is
> large and spacious,
> Not once vouchsafe to
> hide my will in thine?

According to the novelist Anthony Burgess, this sonnet is a "hymn to the male thrust." When the poet learns that the lady has been sleeping with three men named Will, he cynically observes in Sonnet 136 that all these Wills have fulfilled—and filled—the lady's will: "Ay, fill it full with wills."

*A*fter a performance of *The Merry Wives of Windsor* at the Shakespeare Theatre at the Folger Library, an aide from Senator Jesse Helms's office called the theatre. After praising the performance, she said she had a question. Did she hear the word "erection" in Act III, scene 5 ("She does so take on with her men; they mistook their erection"), and, if so, was that in Shakespeare's text or was it the director's innovation? The theatre assured her that it was genuine Shakespeare.

The Sanitized
Shakespeare

As children, Harriet and Thomas Bowdler spent many delightful evenings gathered at the family hearth listening to their father read Shakespeare aloud, with Thomas Senior carefully improvising around any indelicate words. These evenings became the inspiration for *The Family Shakespeare,* a volume that promised to contain not one word to "raise a blush to the cheek of modesty."

Since it was considered unseemly for a woman's name to appear in print, Harriet published the first edition in 1818 anonymously, and then in all subsequent editions attributed the work to her brother, who for years has received the credit. (Harriet, however, was no stranger to literature: her earlier effort was the popular *Fragments in Prose and Verse, by a Young Lady Lately Deceased,* an edifying anthology popular in religious circles.) The edition included sanitized versions of *King Lear, Othello, Romeo and Juliet,* and *Hamlet.* Later, Thomas tried his hand at editing and added a few more plays to the volume.

For eleven years, *The Family Shakespeare* went unnoticed; after all, it was published during the age of the great Romantic writers, and sensuous poetry was in vogue. But it found a devoted following among the sober-minded Victorians. During Victoria's reign it went through thirty printings and was a staple in every genteel library. In fact, until the turn of the century, many middle-class women never read the real Shakespeare, and certainly no child ever did. The title page of *The Family Shakespeare* read:

THE FAMILY SHAKESPEARE

In Ten Volumes

IN WHICH NOTHING IS
ADDED TO THE ORIGINAL TEXT;
BUT THOSE WORDS AND
EXPRESSIONS ARE OMITTED
WHICH CANNOT
WITH PROPRIETY
BE READ ALOUD
IN A FAMILY.

Here are some of Harriet's "improvements":

❖ Juliet miraculously ages four years, thus becoming a more respectable seventeen. Her unmaidenly haste to lose her virginity is curtly excised.

❖ Macbeth's taunt:

> The devil damn thee black, thou cream-faced loon!
> Where got'st thou that goose look?
>
> (V.3.11–12)

has become softened to

> Now friend, what means thy change of countenance?

❖ Iago's malignant

> I hate the Moor,
> And it is thought abroad that 'twixt my sheets
> He's done my office.
>
> (I.3.380–82)

is duly altered to the anticlimactic:

> And it is thought abroad that with my wife
> He has done me wrong.

❖ Lear's raging challenge to the storm, "Rumble thy bellyful!" (III.2.14) is purged of its unpleasant digestive associations: "Rumble thy fill!"

❖ And finally, Hamlet's sexual disgust with his mother's haste "to post . . . to incestuous sheets" (I.2.156–57) is completely excised, thereby eliminating most of the motives for his erratic behavior.

Harriet at least was no hypocrite. Her life was as pure as *The Family Shakespeare* itself. The Earl of Minot, who met her when she was a young girl, described her as "a bluestocking; but what the colour is of that part of her dress must be mere conjecture; for she said that at the opera she always kept her eyes shut the whole time dancers were performing; it was so indelicate, she could not bear to look."

Although *The Family Shakespeare* is as quaint as a quilting bee, the Bowdlers live on through their name: to "bowdlerize" has come to mean to purge a work of any unmentionables, usually choice bits having to do with sex or violence.

As You Like It

*I cannot remember enjoying a
production so much. Even when
I was depressed, after a few
scenes the depression would lift.*

> —*JOHN BOWES*
> *(Orlando in the 1980
> RSC production of
> As You Like It)*

Along with *Twelfth Night* and *A Midsummer Night's Dream*, *As You Like It* is one of Shakespeare's greatest comedies. The first is manic, the second magical, and the third sublimely serene. Although it has dances, weddings, a masque, and a wrestling match, its activity is stylized and ritualistic. The play seems more like a tableau than a drama—very different from the anarchic goings-on in *Twelfth Night*. After the first act the play seems to consist almost entirely of talk.

In structure and character, *As You Like It* is composed of balanced contrasts. Almost every scene, setting, and character has a counterpart, and for every action there's a reaction. In fact, the play would be almost too symmetrical had Shakespeare not thrown in a few odd touches to keep it slightly off-center.

Life at Court

*T*he story begins at court, where foppish courtiers dwell on the latest gossip and enmity prevails: brother fights brother and a daughter is

FROM "AN OPEN LETTER TO WILLIAM SHAKESPEARE, OR, AS I DON'T LIKE IT . . ."

Now I must confess it. I don't like your *As You Like It*. I'm sorry, but I find it too hearty, a sort of advertisement for beer, unpoetic and, frankly, not very funny. When you have one villain repenting because he's nearly been eaten by a lion and another villain at the head of his army "converted from the world" because he happens to meet an "old religious man" and has "some question" with him, I really lose all patience.

—PETER BROOK

separated from her father. Duke Frederick has usurped the throne of his elder brother, "Duke Senior," who has been exiled to the Forest of Arden, where he lives "like the old Robin Hood" with his merry men. But the Dukes' daughters, the cousins Rosalind and Celia, live harmoniously in the castle, spending their days discussing men, love, and marriage. In this intricately patterned play, there's also a pair of young men—in this case, the siblings Orlando and Oliver—whose enmity is contrasted with Celia and Rosalind's devotion. In the first three scenes, Oliver arranges to have Orlando killed in a wrestling match, Orlando and Rosalind fall desperately in love, and Rosalind is banished. She disguises herself as a boy named Ganymede, and along with Celia (disguised as Ganymede's sister, Aliena) and their fool, Touchstone, they make their way to the Forest of Arden. Of course, Orlando, with his old servant, Adam, also flees the court, and ends up in the forest.

The Forest of Arden

*T*he Forest of Arden is a sylvan sanatorium for the politically exiled, the lovelorn, and assorted undesirables. It's not like any geographical place, its topography being a fantastical mixture of flora and fauna, including snakes, lions, and palm trees. Anything can happen in what the actress Janet Suzman calls "this improbable forest where a lot of crazy people are having an engagement party." *Billets-doux* "grow" on trees, one woman falls in love with another, an evil duke undergoes a miraculous conversion, and feuding brothers are suddenly reconciled. Anyone or anything can suddenly turn up at any moment: Celia finds a husband, Touchstone finds a wife, and Rosalind is reunited with the banished father and the lover she thought she'd never see again.

Shakespeare creates an extended analogy between the forest and the theatrical stage. At various times characters step back from the main action and observe the others, as if life were a comedy of manners composed of people watching their neighbors making fools of themselves. Rosalind observes Silvius and Phebe, Jaques watches the antics of Audrey and Touchstone, Rosalind and Celia eavesdrop on Jaques and Orlando, and Rosalind sees herself as a busy "actor" who meddles in the Sylvius-and-Phebe love plot. Thus we, the real spectators, are watching an onstage audience watch other actors.

The Love Plots

*R*osalind and Celia are like enthusiastic upper-class private-school girls. Celia pretends to be world-weary, Rosalind is keen on just about everything—but both girls have an acute sense of irony. They also have their own jargon, the private language of young women. Celia, bursting to tell Rosalind that she's just bumped into Orlando, can barely contain herself: "O wonderful, wonderful, and most wonderful wonderful, and yet again wonderful, and after that out of all whooping!"

Rosalind reminds us of the young Katharine Hepburn (who did, indeed, play the part on stage). She's usually regarded as Shakespeare's most adorable heroine, particularly when she is dressed as Ganymede, a male disguise that paradoxically only heightens her femininity. And lest we forget she's a woman, Rosalind frequently draws attention to her femininity: "Do you not know I am a woman? When I think, I must speak." Her first thought upon learning that Orlando is also in the forest is: "Alas the day, what shall I do with my doublet and hose?" (in other words, "Oh, my God, I look a fright").

Despite her sense of irony and apparent casualness, Rosalind is no less intense in her ardor than Juliet: "O coz, coz, coz, my pretty little coz, that thou didst know how many fathom deep I am in love!" Like many of Shakespeare's heroines, she's both a romantic and a realist. Her awareness that love is wonderful doesn't make her any the less pragmatic about it. Love is a marketplace, she tells the conventional and overly sentimental Phebe: "Sell when you can, you are not for all markets."

Rosalind meets up with Orlando, and the two play a game in which "Ganymede" will pretend to be Rosalind and, by pointing out typical feminine flaws, will cure him of his lovesickness. In these scenes, Rosalind shows herself capable not only of making fun of herself and her sex but of examining love with a critical eye. At the same time, she never lets her ironic self-awareness diminish her passion. Unlike Jaques, who mocks and negates life, Rosalind mocks life but gives herself to it with abandon.

Erotic role-playing also gives Rosalind a chance to observe Orlando secretly as she flirts and tests him. Orlando seems rather overly involved in the game. Can he be falling in love with this young boy/girl? The implication is not that he's a latent homosexual but that he's fallen for the deception that Ganymede actually *is* Rosalind, which is the whole point of game playing—and theatrical disguise. Remember, Shakespeare's original audience saw a boy playing a girl disguised as a boy.

Meanwhile, a typically complicated Shakespearean situation has emerged: Rosalind, disguised as Ganymede, who is pretending to be Rosalind, meets up with Phebe, a shepherdess, who falls passionately in love with him/her.

Jaques

*T*he play needs a focus aside from love; otherwise, it would be too cloying. Enter "the melancholy Jaques" (pronounced "Jayqueeze"—a dig at French affectation). The one solitary voice in this play of pairings and marriages, he emits a steady stream of mocking commentary that undercuts almost every idealistic thought or act, thus preventing the play from becoming too precious. It's Jaques, for instance, who, while everyone else munches on venison and praises the rustic life, points out that "pastoral life" is rather hard on the deer.

Jaques's encounter with Orlando is equally acerbic. Like characters played by the young James Stewart, Orlando is a nice, earnest guy who's not excessively bright. He writes excruciatingly bad love poems, which he insists upon carving into the bark of trees, an act that strikes Jaques as a crime, the equivalent of graffiti or vandalism. He further insults Orlando by comparing the lover's sentiments to a clichéd motto inscribed in a bourgeois wedding ring: "You are full of pretty answers," he sneers. "Have you not been acquainted with goldsmiths' wives, and conned them out of rings?" Today this remark would be like telling someone he sounds like the corny banality of a greeting card.

> Shakespeare found that the only thing that paid in the theatre was romantic nonsense, and that when he was forced by this to produce one of the most effective samples of romantic nonsense in existence—a feat which he performed easily and well— he publicly disclaimed any responsibility for its pleasant and cheap falsehood by borrowing the story and throwing it in the face of the public with the phrase *As You Like It*.
>
> —GEORGE BERNARD SHAW

Time

*E*ven in the forest, where time moves slowly, Jaques and Touchstone are *memento mori,* a continual reminder of death and decay. Jaques asserts that, far from being the capstone of existence, love is a passing whim, and every part of life is a brief scene in a larger drama. In the "Seven Ages of Man" speech, life, from birth to death, is defined in terms of bodily functions and physical disintegration. Infants are described as "mewling and puking," while the aged are deprived of all sensation. Each part of life is a predictable scene in which nothing endures, because nothing has value. Yet Shakespeare won't let Jaques have the final word on the matter. The very next moment, Orlando enters with his old servant Adam in his arms, a visual reminder that human existence can't be reduced to such cynical terms. Here, at least, two ages of man are linked by mutual love and support.

Touchstone

A touchstone is an object used to test the genuineness of another object, and whenever the aptly named Touchstone comes up against another character, he subjects him or her to his blistering comments, as if to test the person's mettle. Striking a pose of exaggerated sentimentality, he mocks Rosalind's love by reminiscing about his own great *amour fou*—one Jane Smile, whose charms inspired him to kiss "the cow's dugs that her pretty chopt [chapped] hands had milked." Once, in her absence, he wooed a "peascod" (codpiece) in her stead, and through his tears begged, "Wear these for my sake." Taking the lover's absurdity to its utmost and deftly undercutting its pretensions, he follows up his banter with a typically Touchstonian remark: "We that are true lovers run into strange capers; but as all is mortal in nature, so is all nature in love mortal in folly." Perhaps the strangest "caper" is that at the end of the play, the sophisticated fool joins the rest of the "country copulatives" and marries the illiterate goatherd Audrey (on whom his sarcasm is lost when he calls her "an ill-favoured thing . . . but mine own").

Marriage

*E*verything works out in the end with marriages for all, and the play closes with a fertility dance that imitates the rhythmic cycles of life. The four couples each embody a different type of love: Touchstone and Audrey are sexual and earthbound; Celia and Oliver's instantaneous love is self-consciously theatrical; Sylvius and Phebe represent sentimental and conventional romance. Only Orlando and Rosalind unite all these types—their union is romantic and realistic, physical and idealistic.

The two Dukes are reconciled, as are Oliver and Orlando, who just happens to save his brother from a lion. The reconciliation between

© Zoë Dominic

*R*onald Pickup (Rosalind) and Jeremy Brett (Orlando) in an all-male *As You Like It* at the National Theatre in 1967.

❧

*O*ne of the strangest productions of *As You Like It* must have been Clifford Williams's all-male version, performed in 1967 at the National Theatre. Despite its self-consciousness, it probably came close to depicting the sexual playfulness and ambiguity that Shakespeare explored in his romantic comedies. The production was inspired by Jan Kott's interpretation of the play in *Shakespeare: Our Contemporary,* particularly where he writes: "In the love scenes in Arden Forest . . . an actor disguised as a girl plays a girl disguised as a boy. Everything is real and unreal, false and genuine at the same time."

Orlando and Oliver parallels the reunion between the two Dukes, which in turn is further strengthened by their daughters' marriages. Human beings not only, as Jaques has it, "ripe" and "rot," but part and reunite like partners in a dance. *As You Like It* fittingly concludes with images of harmony: two atonements, four marriages, dancing, and a masque that is also a solemn betrothal ritual. Hymen, the god of marriage, magically descends and blesses all the couples: "Then is there mirth in heaven, / When earthly things, made even, Atone together."

In *As You Like It,* marriage is both a sacrament and a biological necessity, uniting the cosmic realm to the natural world. The play ends with joy in heaven and on earth—or, at least, almost. Jaques, the one figure left out of the general merriment and dancing, abruptly departs, leaving the others to their joy and vowing that he is "for other than for dancing measures."

The Epilogue

*T*he story ends, but the theatrical illusion has yet to be shattered. Shakespeare may be done with his characters, but he hasn't finished with his audience. The boy who played Rosalind who disguises herself as the boy Ganymede who pretends to be Rosalind and has just revealed herself as the *real* Rosalind now steps forth and addresses the audience directly as an actor. But just when we think we are faced with "reality," we remember that this "real" actor is still speaking lines written by a dramatist, and he's simply playing another part, an ambiguous and androgynous figure. Shakespeare thus left his original audience with the unsettling notion that perhaps we are all playing parts—and being laughed at by the gods themselves.

Jaques's "Seven Ages of Man" speech suggests that the play was first performed in 1599 to inaugurate the opening of the Globe playhouse, which bore a sign depicting Hercules holding a globe with the motto *Totus Mundus agit histrionem*—"All the world's a stage."

Twelfth Night, or, "What You Will"

Where there is no illusion,
there is no Illyria.

—OSCAR WILDE

With a lavish estate, plenty of amorous intrigues, upstairs-downstairs plotting, and two cases of mistaken identity, *Twelfth Night* is like an Edwardian house party where no one goes home. Yet there is something sweetly sad, unsettling, even bitter about this play. *Twelfth Night* is about love and grief, their pains and their pleasures, and how the two emotions are often indistinguishable.

Written just after the high-spirited *As You Like It* and just before the somber *Hamlet, Twelfth Night* contains elements of each. It is, oddly enough, both elegiac and manic. Named for a holiday, *Twelfth Night* is festive, but it also skirts madness, despair, sexual ambiguity, and cruelty.

Illyria

*T*he story begins with Viola shipwrecked on Illyria, a mythical kingdom by the sea whose inhabitants are on eternal vacation—all they seem to do is listen to sad songs, fall hopelessly in love, play practical jokes, and get drunk. Even grief has a pleasing melancholy in Illyria, where no one works, not even the servants.

The Upstairs Lovers

*L*ike Beatrice, Rosalind, and Portia, Viola is one of Shakespeare's plucky young heroines. Having endured shipwreck and believing her twin brother, Sebastian, to be drowned, she nevertheless sets briskly about trying to make her way in the world. For protection, she disguises herself as a young boy called Cesario and is hired by the handsome Duke Orsino as a page to carry love messages to the beauteous Olivia. Like Viola, Olivia has lost a brother, and she refuses to return the Duke's affections, having vowed to mourn her dead brother for seven years.

Orsino and Olivia isolate themselves by indulging in extremes of emotion: he is fixated on love; she, on sorrow. Olivia closets herself with an image of her dead brother, while Orsino languishes in his castle wooing Olivia by proxy and preferring an idealized image to the woman herself. He's in love not with Olivia but with the idea of himself as lover. For Orsino, love is grief; for Olivia, grief is love. Viola, however, despite her overwhelming love for Orsino and her grief over Sebastian, responds to life's vicissitudes with resiliency and courage.

*D*espite Eric Partridge's pronouncement that *Twelfth Night,* along with *A Midsummer Night's Dream,* is the "cleanest of all the comedies," the play, given the right production, must be one of the most erotic and sensual in all Shakespeare.

The Uses of Disguise

*O*livia's sorrow doesn't stop her from becoming quickly infatuated with Cesario, nor can Viola's disguise prevent her from loving the Duke. It's fitting that Olivia should initially fall for a woman—albeit a disguised one—since she is capable only of loving an image of herself.

"Poor Lady," says Viola, "she were better love a dream." And with the exception of Viola, each of the main characters loves a phantom—a dream of his own making rather than a flesh-and-blood person.

Olivia's futile passion for Cesario teaches the shallow girl what it means to suffer in love, and by chasing after Cesario, she's forced to leave her self-imposed prison. Similarly, by talking with "Cesario," Orsino comes to know Viola before he loves her, and in a way he could never know Olivia. He proves this by proposing marriage *before* he sees what she looks like as a woman. For once, this narcissistic man is able to transcend appearances and love a real woman, not an idealized image. When Orsino realizes he loves Viola, it's not for her beauty, her grace, her rank, or even her gender, but simply for herself. Ironically, Orsino learns to love a woman through a "man," while Olivia learns to love a man through a "woman." Confusing? Improbable? Wait. This Elizabethan *Some Like It Hot* gets even more complicated.

*M*alvolio's final cry of "I'll be revenged on the whole pack of you!" casts an even longer shadow over the play as it is going to have its answer forty years down the line when the Puritans come to power in England and every theatre in London is shut down.

—DAVID JONES

*W*e are not likely ever to know with any degree of certainty what it was, in Shakespeare's experience and awareness of life, that caused him to turn away from the pleasant world of his comedies to the topsy-turvy universe of *Hamlet* and *Troilus and Cressida,* [but] we can at least attempt to discover whether there is any factor of continuity in this frightful and apparently sudden unpredictable development. At first sight *Twelfth Night* seems hardly the place to look for such premonitory signs and portents. No one in his senses would dream of denying that the last of Shakespeare's comedies is also the purest gem of Shakespearean comedy....

But it is Shakespeare's farewell to comedy, and as such, it might carry some secret intimation that Shakespeare was beginning to outgrow the pure mirth of the comic vision.

—ALBERT GUERARD

Downstairs Plotting

*M*eanwhile, there are plots afoot downstairs, where "cakes and ale" reign supreme: the drunken inmates of Olivia's house—the servant Fabian, the clown Feste, the maid Maria, and hangers-on Sir Andrew Aguecheek and Sir Toby Belch (the houseguests who never go home)—convince Olivia's steward, the narcissistic Malvolio, that his mistress pines with love for him. With unabashed glee, they bait him with a forged love letter from his mistress.

Malvolio is a potentially tragic figure trapped in a comic world. He has the uncompromising nature of a Hamlet, yet he's as ridiculous in his world as Hamlet is heroic in his. Hamlet's integrity lies in his refusal to be integrated into society. But in comedy, the nonconformist is a poor sport and a party pooper.

The practical joke gets out of hand and is carried to outrageous, even sadistic, lengths. We almost feel sorry for Malvolio—and if he could laugh at himself, we would—but in comedy, misrule and revelry must prevail over the individual's humorless authority. By Act IV, scene 2, Malvolio has been cast in a dungeon, and thus the playwright creates an appropriate symbol for his character's suffocating egotism.

Time

*B*eneath all the revelry in *Twelfth Night* there's the haunting sense of fugitive time: "Youth's a stuff will not endure," sings Feste, who, with the possible exception of Lear's Fool, is the sanest clown in Shakespeare. The world of *Twelfth Night,* like a holiday itself, is ephemeral. But if time is a thief, it is also a healer. With time, the path to true love is made plain, difficulties smoothed, identities restored. This is the world of comedy, where such coincidences as the sudden appearance of a lost twin make perfect sense. The arrival of Sebastian works out perfectly for Olivia, who snatches him up with alacrity.

Marriage

*T*he only characters left alone at the end are Malvolio and Antonio, Sebastian's shipboard companion. Antonio is in love with Sebastian, and Malvolio is in love with himself. Malvolio rushes out like a character in a revenge tragedy, casting a slight pall on the merriment. This play about the nature of desire and love is confined by mirror images: twins, homosexuality, narcissism. Mature love, the play insists, of the sort Viola bears for Orsino occurs when the lover looks beyond the mirrored ideal and steps out of the prison of the self.

What to Look for in <u>Twelfth Night</u>

> If music be the food of love, play on,
> Give me excess of it, that, surfeiting,
> The appetite may sicken, and so die.
> That strain again! It had a dying fall.
>
> (I.1.1–4)

*T*he relationship between love and music is a major theme in *Twelfth Night*. The infatuated Duke Orsino is like a moody adolescent who listens to the same sentimental ballad again and again. These first lines of the play set its tone of melancholy yearning.

*I*n Act II, scene 4, the Duke is having a "man-to-man" talk with Cesario; this scene is both extremely erotic and excruciatingly painful for Viola. He tells Cesario that no woman could "bide the beating of so strong a passion" as he feels. The remark adds a splendid touch of dramatic irony (and shows how little Orsino knows about the opposite sex), for Shakespeare's audience would be aware that sitting next to him is the frustrated Viola, whose own heart is probably beating faster and faster. Shakespeare's audience would have appreciated a joke now lost to us today: Cesario was played by a male actor playing a woman who is disguised as a man.

Through Cesario, Viola hastily informs the Duke that women can and do feel such things—only they don't talk about it as much:

> We men may say more, swear more, but indeed
> Our shows are more than will; for still we prove
> Much in our vows, but little in our love.
>
> (II.4.115–17)

*P*eter Webster as Orsino and Kelly McGillis as Viola in Michael Kahn's 1989 production of *Twelfth Night* at the Shakespeare Theatre at the Folger. Of her performance, Frank Rich, drama critic of *The New York Times,* wrote, "Disguised as the page Cesario, Ms. McGillis pines for the unobtainable Orsino with such rapt, consuming desire that the duke need only idly graze her with his arm to fill the house with the hot currents of frustrated sexual passion."

The Gulling of Malvolio

*I*f you read enough Shakespeare, you'll eventually come across the word "gull." As a verb it means "to dupe or cheat"; as a noun it refers to a person who, through his own vanity or stupidity, is easily deceived. Malvolio, for instance, is Sir Toby's gull. Today we would call him "gullible."

Volio

*N*ote that several of the major characters' names contain or are near anagrams of the word "volio," which in Italian means "will." (Malvolio, for instance, means "bad will.") For the Elizabethans, "will" meant desire, specifically sexual desire. The play's subtitle, "What You Will," suggests the clichés of the 1960s: "Whatever turns you on" and "Do your own thing." Characters love whom they will in this comedy: male, female, upper-class, lower-class—it makes no difference. It's spring-time, the mating season, and everyone must fall in love.

Comedy in Drag

Shakespeare never heard the now-fashionable terms "sex role" or "gender reversal," yet he nevertheless delights in exploring what it means to be feminine or masculine—but in a manner more pleasing than that of today's humorless sociologists.

Why do so many of Shakespeare's comic heroines go about in drag? At some point, Julia (*The Two Gentlemen of Verona*), Portia, Rosalind, Viola, and Imogen (*Cymbeline*) all put on masculine attire. Disguise, of course, fulfills the demands of the story, allowing an adventurous woman to move about in a dangerous world and secretly test her man's fidelity. But further, a woman's disguise gives the lovers their sole opportunity to talk openly to each other without having to adhere to the rigid rules of courtship. Paradoxically, disguise reveals rather than hides the true self.

Cross-dressing implies that Shakespeare is advising us not to take sex, or life, so seriously. In the comedies, gender is a role one can adopt and remove at will; and for Shakespeare's original audience, comic transvestism had a special meaning: it was a witty visual pun that transcended plot and revealed something about the nature of theatrical illusion. Since women were not allowed to appear on stage, all female roles were played by prepubescent and adolescent boys. Shakespeare's audience entered into the illusion that a young man was a desirable woman, while the actor's gender and the playwright's hints coyly reminded them that "she" was really a "he." Shakespearean disguise invited the audience into a confusing world where the line between actor and role, illusion and reality, became blurred. Paradoxically, while he asked the audience to participate in the mass delusion of theatre, Shakespeare never let them forget that they were watching a play.

When women were finally permitted on stage, in 1660, the relationship between audience and actor irrevocably changed. Theatricality—

the idea that the actors were aware of their parts and enjoying a subtle joke with their audience—was diminished. Since a woman now *was* playing a woman, theatre became more realistic. After 1660, plays didn't call as much attention to their own artificiality (what critics call "metatheatre") and were more concerned with simply telling a tale.

Of course, when women began acting, a whole new dimension was added to theatregoing. When an actress disguised herself as a boy, the men in the audience got to see a tantalizing bit of a real female's leg—which is why these roles were called "breech parts."

Anachronisms

*D*on't be surprised when a character in *Julius Caesar,* set in 45 B.C., mentions clocks, or when the ancient Roman conqueror Titus Andronicus casually drops a "Bonjour" or "Merci." Even the prehistoric Lear, who should be swathed in animal hides, mentions tailors, and Gloucester says he needs his spectacles to read Edmund's letter. Though Shakespeare set his plays in the past, he wasn't particularly fussy about historical accuracy. Costumes were a hodgepodge of the contemporary and the ancient. As Anthony Burgess pointed out, "Our heads swim at the ease with which the Elizabethans fuse, or confuse, disparate times and cultures." An eyewitness sketch of a performance of *Titus Andronicus* reveals an incongruous assemblage of classical Roman togas and contemporary Elizabethan garb. Today, directors do the same thing: in the 1990 production at the National Theatre in London, Lear arrived on stage tooting happily on a party horn while zipping along in a wheelchair through a distinctly medieval dwelling.

*A*ll of Shakespeare's plays are so topical and he used anachronisms with such precision. It's not that he didn't know that there weren't any clocks in ancient Rome. He did. That's the point. The plays are topical. Shakespeare was interested in anachronisms. In watching the play we are both in the Roman period *and* in the Elizabethan age. And frankly, we live in an age very like Shakespeare's. We still take so much from previous societies.

—PETER SELLARS

Playing Havoc with the Bard

*A*lthough Shakespeare's plays are variously set in Denmark, Cyprus, Verona, Padua, Egypt, Athens, and Rome, the places named are so vaguely distinguished that, except for a few geographical details (which Shakespeare probably lifted from contemporary accounts, guidebooks, and maps), they could take place just about anywhere. Italy was popular, since it embodied everything sexy and foreign to the more sedate English. Associated with ancient tales of the gods, the pope, and Machiavelli, Italy also added a suggestive dash of sinfulness to a play. Shakespeare could easily have changed his source material and made Romeo and Juliet young lovers from his own Warwickshire, but the Veronese backdrop heightened the play's sensuous romanticism. Similarly, there's nothing intrinsically Danish about any of the characters in *Hamlet.* Hamlet himself is actually the ideal of the English gentleman: handsome, well-bred, and a good sport. Shakespeare used Denmark simply because it's where the source legend of Amleth took place.

The reverential attitude adopted by many people toward Shakespearean masterpieces leads them to treat his works as Holy Writ, sacred words that must be staged in the manner they assume Shakespeare intended. Yet this worshipful attitude is far removed from Shakespeare's casual sense of his "works" (an epithet the Elizabethans would have found pretentious when applied to drama). Shakespeare did not fight for the right to have his plays performed as he wrote them, nor did he much care about their historical accuracy. If directors are not willing to experiment, then Shakespeare becomes the embalmed icon of a vanished age. Better to be outraged than bored.

❖ Caesar's Rome in *Julius Caesar* has variously appeared, among other places, in Mussolini's Italy and De Gaulle's France.

❖ In the movie *Joe Macbeth,* the wild heath has been transformed into gangland Chicago.

❖ Mariana in a John Barton 1970 Royal Shakespeare Company production of *Measure for Measure* sat in a nightclub chain-smoking and nervously downing cocktails while waiting for Angelo to show. And in another RSC production (1986), her lonely moated grange was, according to critic Nicholas Shrimpton, a "Jazz Age Villa" on the French Riviera.

❖ The medieval poet Gower, who narrates many of the events in the romance *Pericles,* appeared as a jazz singer in a 1986 production of the play at the Shakespeare Festival in Stratford, Ontario.

❖ In a celebrated 1986 Royal Shakespeare Company production, dubbed by the critic Michael Billington "Alfa Romeo and Juliet," Tybalt enters for the duel scene in a red sports car. This flashy production, as described by Shrimpton in *Shakespeare Survey,* contained "roller-skates, rock-music (with Mercutio on lead guitar), a swimming pool, telephones, Alka-Seltzer and [a] romantic suicide by shooting-up with a hypodermic."

❖ Derek Jarman's controversial punk/gay movie version of *The Tempest* (1980), regarded by critics as one of the most unnerving Shakespeare productions on stage or screen, included the popular singer Elisabeth Welch singing "Stormy Weather."

❖ One of the most original interpretations of a Shakespeare play must be Orson Welles's 1936 "Voodoo *Macbeth,*" in which the Scottish heath became the wilds of eighteenth-century Haiti, a country that epitomizes the dark forces that permeate the play. The production, funded by the Negro Division of the Federal Theater Project, headed by John Houseman, was hailed as one of the most original dramatic events of the century. It featured ritual chanting, a twelve-foot-high mask of Banquo, a Hecate waving an enormous bullwhip, and a genuine witch doctor imported from Haiti. The play, while controversial, was a huge success. The voodoo motif was entirely in keeping with the play's atmosphere of superstition and dread, and the setting suggested was that of a place where truth and lies are conveniently confused according to the whims of a dictator. The only problem was that Abdul, the witch doctor, had the unfortunate tendency to lapse into deep trances, from which it was impossible to wake him.

Updating
Shakespeare

ou will never see a faithful production of *King Lear* as Shake-speare wrote it. All Shakespearean productions are modernized, in the sense that they are necessarily interpreted by a twentieth-century director, who must impose his own values and perspectives on a play. But certain productions are deliberately modernized or set in an era other than the one Shakespeare intended. It's hard to imagine a Chekhov play set anywhere but in nineteenth-century Russia. Masha and her two sisters and Uncle Vanya are rooted in their geographical and cultural landscape. Transcending time and culture, Shakespeare's plays can absorb radical transformations while remaining true to their original spirit. Without changing a line of dialogue, a clown in *Twelfth Night* can send out for a pizza. It all depends on your capacity to suspend disbelief and on the power of theatrical illusion. If you can accept fairies in *A Midsummer Night's Dream,* you should have no problem with a twentieth-century American Verona or an African Scotland.

The director's challenge lies in changing the setting and period without violating the meaning of the play. In one memorable production (1985), for instance, the director Terry Hands, of the Royal Shakespeare Company, set *The Merry Wives of Windsor* in the suburbia of 1959, complete with Formica, beehive hairdos, lacquered nails, and poodle skirts. Hands wasn't simply trying to jazz up an old play. His interpretation, as critics pointed out, is closer to Shakespeare's intention than the traditional doublet-and-hose-and-farthingale route. The original *Merry Wives* was set in middle-class Elizabethan England, and when it was transplanted to 1950s suburbia, a modern audience could immediately comprehend Shakespeare's jibes at middle-class snobbery and the characters' provincialism, and experience what an Elizabethan viewer might have felt when he saw the play. In this case Hands didn't modernize the play in order to shock, humor, or patronize the audience, but to make it comprehensible—and funny.

Such productions reveal that locations and time periods which seem remote from each other are often quite close in sensibility, spirit, and custom. The leisurely and jokey upper-class atmosphere of *Twelfth Night,* set in far-off Illyria, seems perfectly in keeping with the idyllic Edwardian age, a time of long country-house weekends filled with idle guests and practical jokes. Noël Coward would have been right at home in Illyria. Life at Elsinore seems remote; who, after all, still spies from behind an arras? (And what's an arras, anyway?) But set *Hamlet* dur-

© Joe Cocks

*T*erry Hands's 1985 Stratford production of *The Merry Wives of Windsor,* set in 1959 suburbia, captures the play's sitcom zaniness. While enjoying a good gossip at the beauty salon, the two merry wives compare notes and discover that Falstaff has sent them both the same love letter. They now join forces and scheme à la Lucy and Ethel.

ing the Watergate era and make that arras a wiretap, and an audience immediately understands the play's themes of clandestine evil, espionage, and betrayal. Claudius's "rotten" secret that festers in Denmark is akin to the cancer in the Nixon presidency. Also, we've seen Hamlet as a melancholy, black-clad Dane so many times that a modernized production can, in fact, force us to see him as if for the first time.

Perhaps the most ambitious modern-dress version of a Shakespeare play was Orson Welles's Mercury Theatre staging of *Julius Caesar* in 1937. Welles's production, subtitled "!!Death of a Dictator!!," drew parallels between Caesar's ancient Rome and the contemporary rise of Fascism. According to John Houseman, the production emphasized the "similarity between the last days of the Roman republic and the political climate of Europe in the mid-thirties. Our Roman aristocrats wore military uniforms with black belts that suggested but did not exactly reproduce the current fashion of the fascist ruling class; our crowd wore the dark, nondescript street clothes of the big-city proletariat." Restaging Shakespeare can be more than just an amusing venture. Topical parallels force viewers not only to understand Shakespeare but, more important, to re-examine the assumptions and beliefs of their own age.

The excessive reliance on Shakespeare in the standard repertory puts directors under pressure continually to come up with something novel. This is a challenge that can end in disaster. At worst, innovations can turn a play into a series of clever gimmicks or trivialize it by making it "relevant" to a modern audience (for example, *Lear* as an examination of the plight of the elderly and their problems with homelessness and retirement). Modernizing a play is generally more successful with comedy than with tragedy. Electronic special

> When we claim we suddenly understand Shakespeare because some director . . . has delivered an updating to it, we are kidding ourselves. At best we understand something about our post-human era that Shakespeare also perceived. . . . A "modern" Shakespeare will move us closer to the mystery of *the* Shakespeare primarily by chasing us back to the text, to rediscover the complexity and suggestiveness which modernizing tends to insult and flatten.
>
> —H. R. COURSEN

effects may enhance the magical spirit of *A Midsummer Night's Dream,* but a Shakespearean tragedy is timeless, and updating tends to violate its soul, turning depth into shallow trickery, leaving the audience cheated out of what should be a profound experience.

A common complaint is that directors arbitrarily insert innovations and adopt alternate settings without considering how they operate within the play's larger meaning. A nineteenth-century *Hamlet* may be amusing or interesting, but does it deepen our understanding of the play? Or, failing that, does it tell us anything about the audience's country during that time? Does the presence of a Walkman enhance or collide with the text? Can a character who says "prithee" and "forsooth" drive a Jaguar without the audience's becoming painfully aware of a strain between text and setting?

The Folger Shakespeare Library

"*T*he Plus Fours *Hamlet*": Colin Keith-Johnston in the first modern-dress *Hamlet* (1925), in which courtiers sported monocles, sipped cocktails, and played jazz tunes. Hamlet, most daringly, appeared in plus fours.

ॐ

Take Peter Sellars's controversial 1980 production of *Lear* (which he directed at Harvard's Loeb Theatre when he was only twenty-two), in which the King enters in a stretch limo—a bit of stagecraft that infuriated purists, who claimed that it was done merely for shock—or schlock—value. Sellars was trying to express a major theme of the play: that the rich are indifferent to the poor. The limo with its tinted windows suggests a powerful man who blinds himself to the suffering around him, a man who is as insulated from the weather as he is from the human condition. Lear's emotional turning point occurs when he is forced to spend a stormy night sleeping beneath his car because he is locked out of his house. In Sellars's production we glimpse Shakespeare's tragedy, but it is a diluted version, without mystery or depth. Sellars's *Lear* is topical, not timeless. It is arrogance to try to fit Shakespeare into our age without realizing that we belong to *his* wider vision. As Peggy Ashcroft said, "We don't need to justify Shakespeare."

Peter Sellars

*T**he director Peter Sellars is like a child prodigy who's been given a chemistry set for Christmas; by noon he's either blown up the house or discovered a cure for cancer. As director of the Boston Shakespeare Company, and later at the American National Theatre at the Kennedy Center, he managed to infuriate—and stimulate—everyone in the Shakespeare establishment, which is precisely what he had set out to do. Sellars refuses to create boringly sedate evenings with the Bard, and he wants to shake up an audience that's spent too many hours dozing instead of watching the plays. To Shakespearean purists, his interpretations are a form of shock treatment, but by staging a revered play such as* King Lear *in a flashy modern setting, he forces a jaded audience to re-examine what has become a familiar artifact.*

NE: *I'm afraid to ask, but what's your next Shakespearean project?*

PS: I like to take the plays that everybody says are the problem plays. But of course they're not! They're just great! They just don't fit into the traditional categories, and that's what makes them so interesting. So [*dramatic pause*] I want to direct . . . *King John!* [*Roars with laughter.*]

NE: King John? [John *is the most unfamiliar and disliked play in the canon.*]

PS: In *John* and other history plays, Shakespeare *really* diagrams mental illness and a sick society. And those elements of the play have been shortchanged. They're not weird! We know these things all too well from experience. I always test these plays against experience rather than against literary criticism or a perceived notion about what they are about.

NE: *What is your conception of Shakespeare?*

PS: For me, Shakespeare belongs to America and Americans.

NE: *What do you mean?*

PS: Because he wrote for England, a country that was the most power-ful country in the world, that dominated world trade, had the most impressive armada, and on and on. But Shakespeare didn't write for what Britain is today: an empire that's been out of it for years. He wrote for a country that was a promising adolescent. And America is the all-time adolescent country. I think *all* of Shakespeare is American. I don't think Shakespeare ever intended to sound like the Royal Shakespeare Company.

NE: *You don't like the RSC very much, do you?*

PS: I deplore it. It's this British thing, and it's all about words, words, words, words, words. They think words are the most important part about Shakespeare. But every Shakespeare play goes out of its way to insist that words aren't to be trusted! [*Laughs uproariously.*]

One of the things I do—I've done this with *A Midsummer Night's Dream* and *Macbeth*—is cut the plays and perform their skeletons. I think plot is the least interesting part of Shakespeare.

NE: *If neither words nor plot is important, what is?*

PS: Ideas. Character. The most extreme readings are the most interest-ing. The middle of the road doesn't wake you up. Every time we see Shakespeare we should see this free-spirited *WOW* thing where any-thing is possible.

NE: *Is that why people get angry with your work?*

PS: Yes, because they want Shakespeare to just lie there and not move! Most Americans have this notion that classical culture has to be good for you. They go to a museum and spend more time looking at the label next to the painting than the painting itself, because they want to say the right thing about it. I have directed some of these plays several times, and I still don't understand them. But you're not meant to *under-stand* Shakespeare! Everyone thinks that at the end of an art experi-ence they have to answer twenty questions and get nineteen right. No! What matters is your own personal interaction with the play. It doesn't yield itself to an easy reading. It's like life. There's enough there for everyone to find something for themselves.

NE: *What is the best way to understand Shakespeare?*

PS: What Shakespeare says again and again is that you have to mistrust everything. Most great Shakespeare plays ask, "Is that *really* true?" and "Do you buy this?" But so often in Shakespeare scholarship you have the Canon and the Text, and most people don't ask questions about them. Rarely is the point of the play what it seems to be. And *rarely* is the official version of the play adequate. And *rarely* do scholarly notes have anything to do with what's going on in a play. There's always something a scholar doesn't want to touch with a ten-foot pole; for instance, he'll give you this incredibly abstruse footnote for a simple bawdy word, like [a penis] is a "type of grain."

NE: *Can you sum up what you see as Shakespeare's greatness?*

PS: The guy did have a knack for words. He can put his finger on it when most of us are talking around in circles. My grandfather grew up on a farm in Ohio where there were no books except Shakespeare and the Bible. He had a brother named Floyd who was a postman, and Floyd knew most of Shakespeare by heart. So here's Floyd, a postman in Pittsburgh who could quote Shakespeare for every occasion. Of course, Floyd always had the perfect thing to say—no matter what was going on!

THE

First, a Word of Reassurance

*D*uring the intermission of a particularly good performance of *Richard III* at the National Theatre in London, with Ian McKellen as the deformed despot, I overheard a well-dressed, intelligent-looking woman say: "Now, who is Anne? Who's she related to? Could she be mar-

*H*ISTORIES

ried to her father-in-law? And is he Henry or Edward?" Don't be alarmed if *you're* completely lost. The history plays are notoriously confusing, and even veteran Shakespeareans have trouble keeping all the names and characters straight. You shouldn't expect to walk into a performance cold and understand everything that's going on.

One problem is that everyone seems to have the same name. The stage is filled with Edwards, Henrys, Annes, Margarets, and Richards, all related in one way or another. To complicate matters further, some characters have several names: their surname, the place of their inherited seat, their title, and their Christian name. Bolingbroke, Lancaster, Hereford, King Henry IV, and Henry all refer to the same person. The plots hinge on intricate genealogies, and you have to remember which side a character is on. And, to make that even more difficult, everyone continually changes loyalties, so that one character in his time may play many parts. The action tends to be chaotic, shifting rapidly from one setting to another, where something else monumental is happening. At times you may have trouble keeping up with a play's rapid pace; at other times the action may seem tediously slow.

So it's best to prepare a little before seeing a history play. You needn't read the play, but it wouldn't hurt to look at a history book with a genealogical table. Even the entry under "Wars of the Roses" in a good encyclopedia would help. The worst thing you can do is bring the play with you to the theatre and try to follow along. Most acting companies cut scenes and lines from the histories, and you'd find yourself frantically thumbing the pages rather than enjoying the action on stage.

Allow yourself to get carried away by the force and energy of what's going on. Richard III claimed that the world is an arena for him to "bustle" in, and the historical stage *is* a bustling world, filled with noise, intrigue, and action. Enjoy it.

The History Play Defined

*T*he terms "history" and "chronicle" plays refer to the two tetralogies, or the eight plays covering the reigns of English monarchs from that of Richard II to that of Richard III, roughly from the late 1390s through the establishment of the Tudor dynasty in 1485. The cycle begins with the abdication of Richard II and ends with the death of Richard III. Shakespeare also wrote two other history plays that don't fall within this time span, *King John* and *Henry VIII,* but they won't immediately concern us, since *John* isn't all that interesting and *Henry VIII* was written with a collaborator. Shakespeare probably invented this genre, and there is nothing like it today, although the old historical movie epics come close. The plays are a wonderful mix of battlefield heroics, familial relationships, feisty characters, power politics, and covert scheming.

Shakespeare's histories have been compared with "Dallas" and "Dynasty," but they also are a Tudor version of "Lifestyles of the Rich and Famous." Like these television shows, the history plays are about royalty and other moneyed people in high places, and their struggle for power. The Wars of the Roses, between the Houses of Lancaster and York, are nothing more than an elaborate family feud over the crown. By substituting a major corporation for England, the plot of, say, *Richard III* could easily be a miniseries about two warring scions fighting for corporate control. Thematically, however, the history plays perhaps most closely resemble the movie *The Godfather;* both are concerned with the father-son relationship, family honor, and the acquisition of power. More important, they both examine the question of dynastic succession—a particularly weighty issue for the Elizabethans, who had an aging virgin queen on the throne and no heir in sight.

Although the history plays can be—and often are—enjoyed as separate dramas, they are more fully understood when seen as a whole, since each play forms part of an ongoing saga. In each tetralogy, characters appear, rise to power, and are killed, only to be replaced by their descendants, who in turn emerge, rise to power, and are killed.

Outline of Events

*H*ere is a chronology of the history plays—not in the order Shakespeare wrote them, but according to the events they describe:

Richard II: Richard II renounces his throne and is later murdered, an act that divides the succession into two dynastic strains, Lancaster and York, primary contenders for the crown in the Wars of the Roses. Henry IV, formerly called Bolingbroke, is crowned.

Henry IV, Part 1:   Henry's old supporters, the Percys, raise forces against him. Relations between Henry and his heir, Hal, are strained; Hal comes of age when he valiantly fights in his father's cause.

Henry IV, Part 2:   Civil disruptions continue as Henry struggles to maintain his throne; he dies and is succeeded by his son, Hal, who becomes Henry V.

Henry V: Henry V conquers France and woos the French princess Katherine. The first tetralogy concludes with civil peace, triumph, and a royal marriage.

Henry VI, Part 1:   Henry V dies while Henry VI is still an infant; uncles vie for power; civil war is imminent; France is lost.

Henry VI, Part 2:   Henry VI grows up to become a weak and ineffectual ruler; the Wars of the Roses begin. (Henry is a Lancastrian.)

Henry VI, Part 3:   Henry is defeated; the House of York triumphs. Edward III, brother of Richard of Gloucester (soon Richard III), is crowned.

Richard III: Edward III dies; Richard, fourth in line for the throne, removes all obstacles and is crowned. At the Battle of Bosworth, he is slain by Henry Richmond, later Henry VII, the first Tudor king and Elizabeth's grandfather.

There is supposedly a moment in a grade B historical epic when a character yells, "Come on, men! Let's go fight the Hundred Years' War!" This ironic, retrospective view of history must have been similar to what the Elizabethans felt as they watched their own past being enacted on stage. The Wars of the Roses were still vivid in the minds of Shakespeare's audience; they knew the outcome of the plot and the fates of all the major characters. Lancaster and York were household names, with all the familiarity and appeal of the name Kennedy today. The members of the audience could smile at the irony of Richard III's boast of power, since they knew that in Act V he would be defeated at the hands of Henry Richmond. This double perspective allowed them to observe the past while knowing its outcome—both in history and on stage. Thus the characters' words were given an extra level of meaning that is lost to us today.

The Elizabethans loved watching their past come alive, and the histories were among Shakespeare's most popular plays. The *Henry VI* trilogy was a box-office smash that turned an unremarkable actor named William Shakespeare into the most successful playwright of the day.

Shakespeare's Epics

You don't read or see these plays for a lesson in English history. They're a little like those Classics Illustrated comic books: the educational content is hardly noticeable. Is history a good story, or is the story good history? It scarcely matters, because these sensational plays are filled with murders and duels, chivalry and betrayal, feasting and funerals. They also help to make the remote past comprehensible in our own terms. Politicians haven't changed that much: suddenly you glimpse Richard Nixon in Richard of Gloucester or Jimmy Carter in Henry VI (which is why modern directors often set the history plays in contemporary times). Facts, names, and dates, history's flotsam and jetsam, suddenly come together, so that in watching these plays you think, So *that's* how it happened.

Shakespeare domesticates history. Kings and queens are mothers and fathers. When not conducting state business, rulers eat, drink, make love, sleep, and gossip. We are privy to the dreams and secret yearnings of monarchs, the loneliness of queens, and the private rebellion of young princes. Minor characters, allowed to strut and fret their hour upon the stage, are given quirks and humors, making them instantly memorable.

The Elizabethans believed in the "Doctrine of the Two Bodies," which asserted that the king possessed two bodies, one immortal, the other mortal ("The king is dead, long live the king"). Shakespeare exploits this belief, so that audiences never forget the man beneath the ermine. Henry IV is always magisterial, but, like any father, he worries about a rebellious son who refuses to follow in the family business.

Richard II is a powerful tyrant, but he loves to play at bowls and dally with his courtiers. In odd moments, Henry VI yearns for the contemplative life of a shepherd.

But what's ultimately fascinating about the histories is their tremendous sweep and scope, the charisma of royalty, and the mad lust for power that lives on from one generation to the next.

Shakespeare's Sources

 S hakespeare based his history plays on various sources, drawing upon everything from medieval chronicles and Tudor propaganda to romances and rumors. He took a little bit here, a little bit there, to create a historical stew—a mixture of legend and fact that he blended with genius. His primary source of information was Raphael Holinshed, whose *Chronicles,* published in 1586–87, comprised a complete history of the English-speaking world.

While Shakespeare rarely altered basic historical facts, he didn't feel slavishly bound to them. Facts are subservient to the story. For instance, he would condense time, so that historical events spanning more than ten years would be telescoped into a day or a week. Hotspur in *Henry IV* was actually old enough to be Hal's father, but Shakespeare makes the two the same age to stress the theme of sibling rivalry. He creates characters, embroiders details, and invents new information to suit his dramatic needs. According to history, old Queen Margaret, the crazy wife of Henry VI, fled to France after the wars, but Shakespeare thought she might add a nice dramatic touch in the sequel, so he brought her back to England for *Richard III.*

In some cases, Shakespeare's fictional account of people and events have become more real than actual history. More people know Richard III as the humpback villain of Shakespeare's play than the real Richard, who by all other accounts was rather a nice man.

Elizabethan History 101

To understand the history plays, it's best to look at what history meant to an Elizabethan audience. For Shakespeare and his contemporaries, history was a morality play, written, staged, and directed by God. It had a pattern and a plot, and there was a reason for everything. A bad king, such as Richard II, was a form of divine retribution against the English people. By examining history, the Elizabethans traced their destiny as it worked itself out through the movements of kings, queens, tyrants, rebels, and pretenders.

Moreover, in the historical contest between the forces of Good and Evil, the good side (i.e., English, Tudor, Protestant) triumphs, while the bad (i.e., French, Italian, Roman Catholic) are defeated—if not in this generation, then in the next. (Hadn't the recent defeat of the Spanish Armada proved that God is an Englishman?) The cyclical pattern of the history plays bears this out: both tetralogies begin in discord and end in peace.

Excessively proud characters like Henry IV and Richard III boast that they *make* history when actually they are trapped by it and are the unwitting instruments of a divine scheme that must run its own inevitable course. Thus, when Henry Bolingbroke usurps the crown of Richard II, he unknowingly takes part in a historical process that triggers a chain reaction that ends with the butchery of the Wars of the Roses and the terror-filled reign of Richard III.

Yet Shakespeare's historical plots are not at all formulaic. The role of Providence in many of the plays is at times ambiguous and troubling, and the playwright's view of power and kingship can be cynical. A legitimate ruler can be just as bad as an illegitimate one. Henry IV is more capable than the rightful king he deposed, and the saintly Henry VI causes just as much damage to his country as the evil Richard III.

During the Renaissance, the Elizabethans began to develop a sense of their own past, and Shakespeare exploited this in his plays. The history plays helped the Elizabethans to see themselves as a nation—where they came from and where they were heading. They looked upon the past as a mirror of their own age that, if studied carefully, could teach them how to avoid the mistakes of their ancestors. History was a warning and a prophecy. In watching the *Henry VI* plays, audiences could look back to the Wars of the Roses and then at their present barren queen and draw terrifying conclusions for the future. The events enacted on the stage—the coronations, the abdications, the battles, and the truces—were not only entertainment but lessons that touched the Elizabethans' deepest anxieties and concerns.

History as Propaganda

*T*oday's playwrights fear only bad reviews; Shakespeare, if he displeased the queen, could have been hanged, drawn, and quartered. He lived in an age of censorship, when all literature was subject to review by the Master of the Revels, an ironically jolly title for a censor. It was the Master's job to examine all plays for political slander and to excise any line that seemed even remotely treasonous. Queen Elizabeth and all she stood for had to be presented in the best possible light, and Shakespeare's history plays bolster the Tudor myth. For instance, Richard III was probably not as bad as he's portrayed in the play, but he was viewed as an enemy to the Tudor line. Thus Shakespeare had to present Richard's conqueror, Queen Elizabeth's grandfather, as England's savior. As the playwright Rosemary Anne Sisson wrote, "If he had made Richard the hero and Henry VII the villain, it would have been just like writing a play about John F. Kennedy and Richard Nixon [and writing it] at the time of Watergate and making Nixon the hero."

One final point about the histories. Before the reign of Elizabeth, the English looked to the Continent for their literary models, their fashions and fads. All official documents, and most important works of literature, were written in Latin. English was a language used only for vernacular literature and ordinary affairs. Now, for the first time, the English had confidence in themselves as a nation, and they began to celebrate their language and all it could do. The outpouring of puns, sonnets, word-play, banter, and quibbles during this time reflects a reckless infatuation with language. Often Shakespeare will take a common word and in the course of a work use it in so many different ways that it takes on extraordinary significance and explodes into multiple meanings. Through a happy coincidence, historical moment and individual genius came together at the right time.

England at the end of the sixteenth century was just beginning to test its powers as a nation; this was an age of expansion and of newly won confidence, and it was a time of discovery both at home and on foreign shores. Above all, it was a time when this tiny island, subject for centuries to invasion and foreign influences, began to see itself as an autonomous nation. The history plays, with their jingoistic yet lilting allusions to "this sceptered isle . . . this England," and their celebration of the past, helped to fashion a national identity. Moreover, the attributes commonly ascribed to the English—reserve, bluntness, stoutheartedness, and a wry distrust of faddishness—were in part created by Shakespeare. One way he did this was by mocking anything foreign—one reason that so many of the plays sneer at the French as a nation addicted to its tailors, and why syphilis was "the French disease."

The Politics of
the Plays

*B*ut the histories go beyond pomp and circumstance and are more than propaganda. They pose serious philosophical questions that go straight to the heart of Elizabethan political life: What is the best way to educate a prince? The two parts of *Henry IV* deal specifically with the grooming of Prince Hal, and *Henry V* describes the fruits of his training. What is the proper way to rule? This question is taken up in *Henry V.* Is the king divinely appointed? And, most important, is it ever morally right to kill a bad king? *Richard II* examines these questions from various perspectives.

The divine right of kings was an ancient doctrine that was challenged during the Renaissance by such controversial ideas as the rational skepticism of Montaigne and the political pragmatism of Machiavelli. Machiavelli's treatise on statecraft, *The Prince,* written in 1513, was translated into English in 1602. It was not an abstract study by a scholar removed from the sources of power but an introduction to realpolitik by a statesman who knew the world all too well. "Politics," he wrote, "have no relation to morals." Machiavelli's cold appraisal of government and power had the same widespread cataclysmic effect on the Elizabethans that Darwin's *On the Origin of Species* would have on the Victorians two hundred fifty years later.

Machiavelli asserted that the achievement of political power necessitated unscrupulous methods and that the ethical man was an ineffectual ruler. It didn't matter what a prince did behind the scenes; he only had to make sure that he *appeared* honorable. Thus, in politics, at least, honor was a sham and morality was irrelevant. Machiavellian principles, which emphasized "policy," the prudent and underhanded management of affairs, subverted everything the Elizabethans believed about the divinity of kings and *noblesse oblige*. To them, "policy" and "political" were tainted words, and whenever they're used in Elizabethan literature, they signal that something is rotten in the state. During the Renaissance the medieval image of the devil was replaced by the Machiavel, a smooth-tongued villain with a genius for intrigue. According to one count, the Machiavel appeared more than four hundred times on the Elizabethan stage, and the figure inspired Shakespeare's greatest villains, Richard III and Iago. The French may have exported venereal disease, but the Italians presented a more dangerous contagion: Machiavelli.

Machiavelli's ideas influence almost every ruler Shakespeare created: Richard III sums up Machiavelli's moral isolationism when he says, "I am myself alone." And Henry Bolingbroke is referred to as "this vile politician"; yet despite his craft—or perhaps because of it—he's a far more competent ruler than the legitimate king he replaced. Even the exemplary folk hero King Henry has a touch of the Machiavel about him. To use the critic A. P. Rossiter's phrase, the histories are about "the survival of the slickest."

THE MEN WHO WOULD BE KING

*I*t seems that everyone in the history plays wants either to be king or to get close to one. It's the symbol rather than the actual job that they covet. As Richard of Gloucester says in *Henry VI, Part 3*:

> How sweet a thing it is to wear
>   a crown;
> Within whose circuit is Elysium
> And all that poets feign of
>   bliss and joy.
> (I.2.29–31)

The crown promises unlimited Faustian power and glory—until it's actually achieved. No sooner are Shakespeare's monarchs crowned than they start complaining about the burdens of kingship. Richard II protests that no one understands him; Henry IV regrets the crime that enabled him to achieve his greatest desire; Henry V laments his isolation; Henry VI longs for the simple life of a peasant; and even Richard III has a few contemplative moments. As Henry IV said, "Uneasy lies the head that wears a crown."

Shakespeare's Politics

Shakespeare is generally considered a conservative, but one with irony and compassion. His plays, seen as either subversive or elitist, depending on the viewer, are never dogmatic or ideological, and he never blindly accepts any single perspective at face value. He confirms and doubts, both at once, which is what makes the plays multifaceted and challenging. His views on kingship and power are at times reverent, at other times cynical. For instance, in the *Henry* plays the ruling class often behaves as foolishly as the buffoons of the subplots. Despite Shakespeare's understanding of the dangers of power and his fascination with Machiavelli's pragmatic view of kingship, in his plays and tragedies, the king is God's vicar on earth. Regicide leads to anarchy, the annihilation of cosmic and domestic order. Whether this was his private belief or a necessity in the age of censorship remains unknown.

Note: The Histories are discussed here not in the order Shakespeare wrote them but as they occur in the eight-part dramatic sequence.

Richard II

In Richard II *Shakespeare
deposed not only the king, but
the idea of kingly power.*

—JAN KOTT

This is the first play in the tetralogies, and it describes the crime
that will unleash a bloody civil war two generations later. *Richard II*
looks longingly back on a medieval past, when England was a "green
and pleasant land," and anticipates the social and political disorder of
the future.

The plot itself is straightforward: it's a chronicle of the abdication
and murder of Richard II which tells the story of his ambitious yet
reluctant usurper, Henry Bolingbroke (later Henry IV). Shakespeare
enhances historical fact with a psychological study of two very different
temperaments. The characters of Richard and Bolingbroke are Shakespeare's creations, not history's. As the conflict between the two men
develops, Shakespeare heightens dramatic interest by constantly
uncovering new and unanticipated sides to their personalities. Suspense comes from the surprising revelations of character, not from the
unfolding of the plot, which Shakespeare's audience would have
known, anyway.

When we first see Richard he is a capricious king who regards his
realm not as a responsibility but as an amusement. His court is composed of favorites and flatterers (the memorably named Bushy, Green,
and Bagot) rather than wise advisers. A spendthrift who loves the ceremonies and trappings of kingship, its privileges and prerogatives,

Richard has little taste or talent for the practical business of ruling. Worse than his neglect of duty is his abuse of power: he auctions to his courtiers the right to collect unlimited taxes from the common people, and shortly after the play begins he capriciously banishes Henry Bolingbroke, Duke of Hereford, seizing his lands, title, and inheritance.

Richard II is the embodiment of a bad king, but he *is* the king, God's anointed. The play reveals a generational conflict among the Elizabethans. To the old guard, like John of Gaunt, Bolingbroke's father, the monarch is to be obeyed no matter how badly he rules. To his son, the divine right of kings is a doctrine to be challenged.

Temperamentally, Henry Bolingbroke is everything Richard is not. He is down-to-earth, efficient, and practical. For the first third of the play, Richard is detestable and Bolingbroke admirable. Then something amazing happens: as Bolingbroke gains power and Richard loses it, the audience's affections gradually shift. (This has nothing to do with the adage "power corrupts," but rather with the way Shakespeare manipulates the audience's perception of the two men.) In the last section of the play Richard takes on the roles of poet and martyr, instantly winning us over with his exquisite language. In losing everything, Richard at last finds the part he was destined to play: the Martyred King:

> Of comfort no man speak.
> Let's talk of graves, of worms, and epitaphs,
> Make dust our paper, and with rainy eyes
> Write sorrow on the bosom of the earth.
> Let's choose executors and talk of wills—
> And yet not so; for what can we bequeath
> Save our deposed bodies to the ground?
>
> (III.2.144–50)

Richard is an extremely complex character. On the one hand, he is arrogant, self-dramatizing, and infatuated with his image; on the other, he is genuinely moving and tragic. If you simply *read* Richard's post-deposition speeches, his grief seems straightforward and simple. But when you *hear* them spoken by a skilled actor, a whole new level of meaning emerges. A good actor will convey Richard's ironic self-awareness that he's playing a role—the Exiled Ruler, or the Misunderstood Hero—but at the same time, he should express the character's very real grief.

Richard's abdication is his finest hour, and he plays it for all it's worth. Shakespeare gives him exquisite lines that have many levels of meaning: they are melodramatic, ironic, self-mocking, tragic, and moving—all at once.

> For God's sake let us sit upon the ground
> And tell sad stories of the death of kings—
> How some have been deposed, some slain in war,
> Some haunted by the ghosts they have deposed,
> Some poisoned by their wives, some sleeping killed,
> All murdered. For within the hollow crown
> That rounds the mortal temples of a king
> Keeps death his court. . . .
>
> (III.2.155–62)

Always one for the grand gesture, Richard demands a mirror so he can examine his face, to determine who he is, now that he's no longer king. Bolingbroke's reply after Richard smashes the mirror is right on the mark: "The shadow of your sorrow hath destroyed / The shadow of your face." Like us, Bolingbroke distrusts Richard's sorrow—and also like us, he grieves for him.

We never know if Richard gives up his crown voluntarily or under duress. Bolingbroke *says* he merely wants his lands, inheritance, and title restored, but Richard refuses to compromise. He insists upon renouncing the throne as well. He's like a child who won't play the game if he can't have it all his own way:

> What must the King do now? Must he submit?
> The King shall do it. Must he be deposed?
> The King shall be contented. Must he lose
> The name of king? A God's name, let it go.
>
> (III.3.143–46)

But at the end, imprisoned in Pomfret Castle, isolated, without audience, flatterers, applause, or crown, Richard no longer needs a mirror, and at last he looks within himself and sees the reality and not the shadow of his grief: "I wasted time, and now doth time waste me. . . ."

Has Bolingbroke planned all this? We never know. His role in Richard's downfall and murder is teasingly ambiguous. Later, after his coronation, Bolingbroke, now Henry IV, muses in front of his courtiers that he would like Richard out of the way. But when someone actually kills him, Henry is morally outraged: that's not what he meant at all. Henry, like any shrewd politician, has learned to preserve what in the Watergate era came to be called "deniability." He wants the nasty job done; he just doesn't want to know about it.

Richard II does more than simply capture a historical moment. It's the first play Shakespeare wrote that has a genuine tragic dimension. But the tragedy is neither Richard's nor Bolingbroke's: they are merely pawns who carry out the historical process. The tragedy is England's.

What to Look for in
<u>Richard II</u>

*J*ohn of Gaunt's deathbed speech ("This royal throne of kings, this sceptred isle . . . This blessèd plot, this earth, this realm, this England. . . .") is one of the most quoted passages in all Shakespeare. Bolingbroke's father, John of Gaunt, who reveres the divinely granted and immortal title of king, hates the man who fills it. Gaunt's deathbed speech is a parting shot at Richard. It's also a nostalgic lament for the old England and a terrible prophecy.

*I*n Act III, scene 4, Shakespeare provides a temporary respite from the turbulent world of politics by depicting a conversation among three gardeners. The men discuss Richard's private garden, which they insist must be well governed ("All must be even in our government"), pruned, and weeded. But then they discuss Richard's other "garden," England, which, owing to poor management, is overrun with "caterpillars" and "weeds" (i.e., court flatterers and traitors).

This type of scene is known as a mirror scene, because it doesn't advance the plot but reflects its deeper themes and concerns.

*R*ichard's soliloquies (III.2.144–77; III.3.72–100, 143–75; IV.1.162–76) are self-pity raised to high art, and they are perfect for reciting aloud. Not solitary meditations, they are designed for an audience, which the narcissistic Richard needs in order to inspire him.

Richard II and Essex's Rebellion

*H*istory plays weren't simply diversions for the masses. They could sometimes be a form of treason. A play could subtly plant subversive ideas in the minds of a populace that could neither read nor write, but that could, and did, go to the theatre. Drama, which tends to incite emotions, and government, which tends to suppress them, can be a highly explosive combination.

In 1601, six years after *Richard II* was first performed, a group of noblemen made a strange request: they asked Shakespeare's company, the Lord Chamberlain's Men, to revive the play for a special one-night-only performance. They gave the company only a day to rehearse. Later, a spokesman for the actors would tell the Privy Council that the players would have preferred some other play, but the fee offered was unusually high, and they were strictly told that no other play would do.

It turned out that the noblemen were the notorious followers of the Earl of Essex, a political outlaw and an enemy of the queen. And they weren't theatre fans, either. The command performance was scheduled for the eve of what would become known as Essex's Rebellion, which aimed at a complete governmental overthrow. His followers chose *Richard II* because of its deposition scene, which portrayed what they hoped would take place the following day.

The play was performed without mishap. But the next morning, Essex kidnapped the Lord Chancellor and other court officials, and then tried to raise a mob and storm the palace at Whitehall. By evening the rebellion had failed, and all the conspirators had been seized and were imprisoned in the Tower. Three weeks later, Essex was executed.

Richard's downfall remained a touchy point with Queen Elizabeth, whose own claim to the throne was tenuous. Once, upon examining court documents relating to Richard's abdication, she looked up at her secretary and said, "I am Richard the Second, know ye not that?"

When the play was published in 1597, the abdication scene was omitted.

RICHARD II: AN UNBALANCED KING

Richard II was only a boy at his accession: one day, however, suspecting that he was now twenty-one, he asked his uncle and, on learning that he was, mounted the throne himself and tried first being a Good King and then being a Bad King, without enjoying either very much: then, being told that he was unbalanced, he got off the throne again in despair, exclaiming gloomily: "For God's sake let me sit on the ground and tell bad stories about cabbages and things." Whereupon his cousin Lancaster (spelt Bolingbroke) quickly mounted the throne and said he was Henry IV Part I.

—W. C. SELLAR AND
R. J. YEATMAN,
1066 AND ALL THAT

Henry IV, Part 1 and Part 2

The title *Henry IV* is somewhat misleading. Henry is rarely on stage, and at times he seems to exist solely as a peg upon which to hang the more interesting tale of Prince Hal and Falstaff. *Henry IV* is ostensibly about Henry's struggle to maintain the throne against the Percys, the clan that helped him to attain it in *Richard II*. But the play centers on Prince Hal and his development from jokester into king. Two plots, one comic and one serious, are represented, respectively, by Falstaff and the Boar's Head Tavern in Eastcheap and by King Henry and the court at Westminster. Hal is the hinge upon which the two swing back and forth.

Hal and Falstaff

While the king presides over the court at Westminster, Hal, his wayward heir, presides over the taverns and brothels, where he spends his time wenching and plotting escapades with low companions, chief among whom is Sir John Falstaff. Even those who have never read or seen a Shakespeare play have heard of Falstaff, Shakespeare's greatest comic figure. He *is* funny, but his character transcends comedy. Painfully touching and sad, he's like an aging music-hall comedian. Buffoon, braggart, coward, parasite, and wit, he eclipses everyone else when he's on stage. Why is this fat old man so enchanting? "Banish plump Jack, and banish all the world," he tells Hal. And Falstaff *does* represent earthly pleasures; he's the epitome of Merrie Old England, all roast beef, wenches, wassail, and ale. A Freudian would say he represents the pleasure principle; to a moralist, he's the seven deadly sins in human form. But he can't be confined to any categories, psychological or moral. He touches us with all the sad eagerness of an old man grasping at endless youth. Significantly, the first words Falstaff addresses to Hal in the play are, ". . . what time of day is it, lad?" To which Hal replies:

> Thou art so fat-witted with drinking of old sack, and unbuttoning thee after supper, and sleeping upon benches after noon, that thou hast forgotten to demand that truly which thou wouldst truly know. What a devil hast thou to do with the time of the day?
>
> (I.2.2–5)

Hal basically belongs to two worlds, each a mirror of the other: the tipsy Falstaffian circus, where time is irrelevant, and the magisterial world of his father, where he must take his place in history.

In the upside-down world of the comic subplot, Falstaff is a surrogate father to Hal. Shakespeare develops this side of their relationship in a hilarious scene in Act II in which Falstaff does a sendup of the king reprimanding Hal for keeping such boorish companions—excluding Falstaff, of course—so that later, when the king *does* reprimand Hal, his words ring ironic and hollow. With his gift for parody and his need to subvert all authority, Falstaff undermines the order upon which government depends. He is thus a dangerous companion for the future king of England.

Hal stands between these two fathers, one real, the other a surrogate, and though he seems tempted to follow Falstaff, we never doubt which one he'll choose. In their first scene together Hal and Falstaff trade mock insults, and we are instantly charmed—and deceived—by their engaging camaraderie. We assume that despite his jests at Falstaff's expense, the fun-loving Hal is fond of the old man. But as soon as Falstaff leaves, Hal swiftly turns to the audience and confides his secret strategy: he's just using Falstaff until he's ready to assume his princely duties. By associating with the aging libertine and his unsavory companions, Hal will look all the more virtuous when he "reforms" and abandons them. This comes as an unpleasant shock: the delightful Hal, who seemed so full of boyish vitality, is cultivating his public image as carefully as any shrewd politician.

Falstaff, Hal, and Hotspur

*L*ed by the young Harry Hotspur, the Percys, Henry's old allies, are gaining strength. Henry compares Hotspur to his own dissolute son, and feels that he's being paid back for all his sins. As his name suggests, Hotspur is everything Falstaff is not. Whereas the old man symbolizes the flesh, Hotspur is pure volatile spirit. Hotspur and Falstaff embody two extremes of behavior, with the prudent Hal standing midway between them. Neither as impetuous as Hotspur nor as hedonistic as Falstaff, Hal adopts the expedient course of action. But extremes are always more intriguing than the safe middle ground, and Hal lacks Falstaff's and Hotspur's charisma. He *is* the hero, but by this point the audience is beginning to find Falstaff and Hotspur more attractive.

The End of Merrie Old England

*I*n *Henry IV, Part 1,* Hal grows up when he kills Hotspur in his father's cause, and in *Part 2* he truly becomes a king when he banishes Falstaff (an act that breaks the old man's heart and thus kills him). *Part 2* is both more wistful and more raucous than *Part 1.* The main leaders of the Welsh conspiracy are now dead; Falstaff has developed gout from too much sack, and syphilis from Mistress Quickly, the hostess at the Boar's Head. The tavern scenes are frantically madcap, as if everyone were trying to have one last debauched fling to forget the passage of time and its inevitable losses. The "chimes at midnight" are about to strike.

Most of the scenes at the Boar's Head now take place without Hal, as Shakespeare gradually prepares for his eventual rejection of Falstaff. Falstaff appears less lovable and more unscrupulous. He shamelessly exploits his connection with Hal, and during the war that breaks out against the Welsh rebels he abuses his military position by padding the payroll with fictitious men, using the king's cause to fatten his own purse—and stomach. (He also does this in *Part 1,* but since the scene was only talked about and not actually dramatized, it seems remote and innocuous, rather like a schoolboy prank.) Perhaps we are already

THE REAL BOAR'S HEAD TAVERN

*T*he site of the Boar's Head tavern in Eastcheap is now as deep sunk in the ooze of human forgetfulness as that of the palace of Haroun. But it was once a real hostelry, and must have meant much to Londoners of the reigns of Elizabeth and James. Records are scanty, but the very fact that Shakespeare makes it Falstaff's headquarters suggests that it was the best tavern in the city. And the further fact that he avoids mentioning it directly, though quibbling upon the name more than once, suggests, on the one hand, that he kept the name off the stage in order to escape complications with the proprietors of the day, and on the other that he could trust his audience to jump to so obvious an identification without prompting.

—J. DOVER WILSON

beginning to view Falstaff through Hal's eyes.

At the end of *Part 2,* just after Hal, now Henry V, has been crowned, Falstaff, proud as any father, rushes to London to present himself to his "sweet boy." But Hal no longer exists. He has been transformed into Henry V. There is no trace of the lovable young man in this austere ruler. When Falstaff cries out to his friend, now his king, he is immediately cut with a cold dismissal: "I know thee not, old man." What makes this so devastating is that the young monarch proceeds to deliver a smug sermon on the proper conduct for an old man, acting as if he never knew Falstaff, as if they had never shared a laugh or a drink.

The Falstaff Question

*S*hakespeareans are divided into two camps, the Falstaffians and the anti-Falstaffians. Falstaffians see Falstaff as the real hero of the play. They praise his gusto and view Hal as a hypocritical prig. The anti-Falstaffians see Falstaff as a corrupter of youth and believe that Hal's rejection is as necessary as it is honorable. Is Hal right to dismiss his old friend? Or is he simply a cold-blooded politician? Neither view is wholly right or wrong, and critics will probably go on arguing forever. Nonetheless, this is a history, not a comedy; it has a moral scheme in which law must win over lawlessness, order over disorder. Falstaff never has a chance. He would have turned the entire government of England upside down. As he tells Hal:

> . . . but I prithee sweet wag, shall there be gallows standing in England when thou art King? . . . Do not thou when thou art King, hang a thief.
>
> (I.2.57–61)

As prince, Hal can play around in taverns and brothels, but as king he cannot. This seems to be the only moral in a play where nothing is clear: a king must rule, and in doing so he must sacrifice everything Falstaff represents—vitality, spontaneity, and the freedom of youth.

The banishment of Falstaff and the coronation of Henry V mark the end of the Middle Ages and the beginning of the modern age. The play thus ends on a dual note of nostalgia and optimism.

What to Look for in <u>Henry IV</u>

*T*he king is a master of political rhetoric. We never know whether to believe him or not, and we can never tell what he's thinking. Is he sincere in repenting of Richard's death? In Henry's Opening Speech in *Part 1* he speaks piously about one day making a pilgrimage to Jerusalem, and he *sounds* genuine, but then abruptly we realize he had never intended to go at all. Then again, disconcertingly, he abruptly abandons his reverent tones as he reverts to state business (I.1.1–33). Such shifts reveal Henry's dexterity in manipulating any occasion to his advantage.

*T*he rebel Prince Hal of *Part 1* turns out to be just as shrewd as his father. Henry's pious cant is merely for show, just as Hal's rebellious behavior is merely a ploy to boost his public image. Like Richard III and Iago, he reveals his strategy to the audience:

> So when this loose behaviour I throw off,
> And pay the debt I never promisèd,
> By how much better than my word I am,
> By so much shall I falsify men's hopes.
> And like bright metal on a sullen ground,
> My reformation, glittering o'er my fault,
> Shall show more goodly, and attract more eyes
> Than that which hath no foil to set it off.
>
> (I.2.206–13)

Orson Welles said that Hotspur's death was the death of medieval chivalry and that Falstaff's was the end of Merrie Old England. Shakespeare also contrasts the two men in regard to their belief in a code of honor, a crucial Elizabethan concept. In a wonderfully impassioned speech in *Part 1,* Hotspur cries:

> By heaven, methinks it were an easy leap
> To pluck bright honour from the pale-faced moon,
> Or dive into the bottom of the deep,
> Where fathom-line could never touch the ground,
> And pluck up drownèd honour by the locks.
>
> (I.3.199–203)

Hotspur rushes into battle to preserve his precious honor and is killed. For all his idealism, he still ends up as "food for worms." In contrast, Falstaff would rather be dishonorable and alive. To him, self-preservation is all:

> Can honour set to a leg? No. Or an arm? No. Or take away the grief of a wound? No. Honour hath no skill in surgery then? No. What is honour? A word. What is in that word honour? Air.
>
> (V.1.131–35)

*I*n one of the funniest scenes in *Part 1,* the Gad's Hill robbery, Shakespeare condenses all of Hal's riotous past into one episode. The young prince appears as an Elizabethan version of one of Ken Kesey's Merry Pranksters. The game begins with Hal's invitation to Falstaff: "Where shall we take a purse tomorrow, Jack?" Falstaff, always eager for action, instantaneously replies: "Zounds, where thou wilt, lad. . . ." Falstaff, Hal, and the rest of the gang take part in a highway robbery at Gad's Hill. Later, Poins and Hal disguise themselves as robbers, steal the booty, and attack Falstaff and the rest, who flee, roaring in terror. But Falstaff makes a better storyteller than a fighter, and when he recounts the tale the next day, his own exploits grow ever more heroic and grandiose—just as Hal predicted they would. When Hal confronts him with his lies, Falstaff, thinking quickly on his feet, replies, "By the Lord, I knew ye as well as he that made ye. . . . was it for me to kill the heir apparent?" (In other words, "I knew it was you all along"). But what's funny during one moonlit night on Gad's Hill isn't amusing on the battlefield. The robbery scene finds its counterpart in Act V of *Part 1,* when Falstaff conducts himself less than admirably on the battlefield, and in his boastful lies about his military prowess in *Part 2.* Once again, Shakespeare shows how an action can have many interpretations, depending on the circumstance, and critics have spilled much ink arguing about whether Falstaff is a scheming coward or a fun-loving rogue.

Shakespeare, like Sylvester Stallone, knew the drawing power of a sequel. In an epilogue to *Henry IV, Part 2,* he promises the return of Falstaff (in *Henry V*): "One word more, I beseech you. If you be not too much cloyed with fat meat, our humble author will continue the story, with Sir John in it, and make you merry with fair Katherine of France. . . ."

The Language of
<u>Henry IV</u>

A Shakespearean character's speech is a verbal thumbprint: each one's is unique. In keeping with his dual nature, Hal speaks prose in the tavern, verse at court. Doll Tearsheet's tongue is as loose verbally as she is sexually. Her speeches are a linguistic orgy:

> Away, you cutpurse rascal, you filthy bung, away! By this wine, I'll thrust my knife in your mouldy chaps an [if] you play the saucy cuttle with me. Away, you bottle-ale rascal! . . .
>
> (II.4.124–27)

The Hostess is known for her malapropisms (though the term hadn't been invented yet): "I'faith, sweetheart, methinks now you are in an excellent good temperality. Your pulsidge beats as extraordinarily as heart would desire. . . ." Falstaff's language is as orotund as he is rotund. His need to talk is like an animal appetite. And he especially enjoys the sound of his own name: ". . . but for sweet Jack Falstaff, kind Jack Falstaff, true Jack Falstaff, valiant Jack Falstaff—and therefore more valiant, being as he is old Jack Falstaff. . ." He's continually talking and never seems to say anything of substance, but when you look closer, you'll find that his buffoonery can hide great wisdom.

Henry has the well-oiled voice of a politician. He's urbane and prudent, the consummate public speaker. What he says is true enough, but it sounds pat and rehearsed. He also makes repeated use of the royal "we," as if he can never grow too tired of hearing it. The fiery Hotspur speaks mainly in verse; his language, like his soul, is pure poetry.

Note, too, the sexual wordplay on "Doll Tearsheet" and "Mistress Quickly," women of dubious virtue. Often the names of minor figures are clues to their character, or the "humor" they are supposed to represent.

Henry V

Henry V is the only history play that doesn't revolve around the seizure of the crown. Hal, the young rebel of *Henry IV,* has become the glamorous hero of Agincourt, where the English, against all odds, roundly defeat the French (France's casualties, ten thousand; England's, twenty-five).

Just before leading his troops into what he believes to be certain defeat, Henry gives the stirring Saint Crispin's Day speech ("We few, we happy few, we band of brothers . . ." [IV.3.60]), one of the most thrilling speeches in drama. Then there's that wonderful moment when Henry utters his famous charge, "Cry, 'God for Harry, England, and Saint George!'" It's easy to see why Churchill, also an inspiring wartime orator, asked Laurence Olivier to make a movie of the play as a morale booster during World War II.

Henry may be an ideal ruler, but he is not a perfect man. The tension between the flawed man and the model king is what makes Shakespeare's portrait of Henry so intriguingly ambiguous. There's the democratic Harry who relaxes with his men and the majestical one who abandons his old companions. He both atones for his father's sins and perpetuates them. Pious and humble, he's also a ruthless war machine, a leader who orders his men to cut their prisoners' throats in violation of the medieval war code. He tries to be just, but he'll stop at nothing to get what he wants. Most important, behind his magnificent triumph at Agincourt there lurks the unsettling idea that his claim to England is just as spurious as his claim to France. Henry comes across as a medieval John F. Kennedy: he's virile, sexy, and patriotic, but he also has an unexplored darker side, which somehow adds to his charismatic charm.

What to Look for in
<u>Henry V</u>

*H*enry V is a masculine play. It has only four women, and they all have small parts. But in Act III, scene 4, the devastation and brutality of war are suddenly swept aside, and we are permitted a glimpse of a young princess's boudoir. In this delightfully feminine scene, Princess Katherine receives an English lesson from her attendant, Alice. Because it relies on verbal humor and puns, it's more funny on stage than in print.

Katherine is no shy maiden; she's giggly, and like any teenage girl, she enjoys a good joke, particularly one relating to anatomy. Squeamish editors become vague when annotating this scene, which luckily for them is in French. Katherine asks Alice for the English words for "*pied*" and "*robe*" ("foot" and "gown"), which Alice mispronounces as "fout" and "count." This to Katherine sounds suspiciously like "*foutre*" and "*con*," which when translated into the English vernacular, mean "fuck" and "cunt." She is both shocked and delighted.

*T*he comic subplot of *Henry V* is acted out by the same ribald Boar's Head gang of *Henry IV*, along with some new characters, such as Captain Fluellen, whose

*T*he expert on Shakespearean bawdy Eric Partridge considers *Henry V* the most obscene of all the history plays. Perhaps this is because it is the archetypal play about male bonding.

———◆———

*A*ntony Sher notes an intriguing historical fact that emerged from rehearsals for *Henry V* when Kenneth Branagh played the title role in Stratford: "The two-fingered sod-off sign comes from Agincourt. The French, certain of victory, had threatened to cut off the bow-fingers of all the English archers. When the English were victorious, the archers held up their hands in defiance."

Jerry Ohlinger's Movie Material Store, New York

The cinematic and historical version of *Henry V.* Note how Olivier directly modeled his appearance on the portrait in the National Portrait Gallery.

ᐒ

National Portrait Gallery

Welsh pride, thick accent, and scrupulous concern for military codes are a running gag throughout the play. (In Kenneth Branagh's movie of *Henry V,* Ian Holm gives the character just the right balance of humor and integrity.) Nym, Pistol, and Bardolph return, cowardly and craven as ever. Although the two worlds of heroic plot and comic subplot seem antithetical, there are ironically pointed similarities between them. Henry can be just as bombastic as the ignoble Pistol, and his order to slit his prisoners' throats recalls the dastardly behavior of Bardolph and the others.

Henry VI, Part 1, Part 2, and Part 3

Even many Shakespeare enthusiasts don't bother to read *Henry VI,* and it's rarely performed in its entirety. The plot is a sweeping panorama; there's no hero, just a succession of characters who temporarily hold center stage and then quickly depart. (Even Henry seems almost incidental at times.) Much of the play is made up of brief, episodic scenes, rather like a Cecil B. De Mille epic (e.g., Lancastrians rush from stage left; Yorkists from the right).

Henry VI is memorable for four reasons: (1) For its startling portrayal of Joan of Arc as a a crafty whore who tries to get out of being burned at the stake by proclaiming herself to be pregnant with the Dauphin's child. As a French Catholic, Joan was regarded as the enemy, so Shakespeare's portrayal was good English, Protestant, Tudor propaganda. To modern audiences, however, it's as shocking as blaspheming Mother Teresa. (2) For the line, nowadays emblazoned on T-shirts and coffee mugs, "The first thing we do, let's kill all the lawyers" (*Part 2,*

> *Henry VI* is one of those plays that are more fun to see than to read. The 1983 BBC version is excellent. The battle scenes are extremely well directed, and, as one newcomer to Shakespeare put it, "It's like watching a high-class soap opera."

IV.2.72), uttered by one of the followers of Jack Cade, the popular rebel who tried to overthrow the government. (3) The Temple garden scene of *Part 1* (II.4), in which the followers of Richard Plantagenet and the Earl of Somerset pluck, respectively, white and red roses, a symbolic event that prophesies the Wars of the Roses: ". . . this brawl today, / Grown to this faction in the Temple garden, / Shall send between the red rose and the white / A thousand souls to death and deadly night." And (4), most important, in *Part 3* a unique voice begins to take shape, which speaks out loud and bold:

> Why, I can smile, and murder whiles I smile,
> And cry "Content!" to that which grieves my heart,
> And wet my cheeks with artificial tears,
> And frame my face to all occasions.

(III, 2.182–85)

It is the voice of Richard of Gloucester, who will become one of Shakespeare's most famous creations.

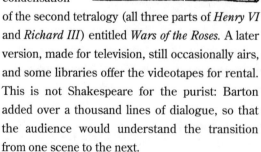

*I*n 1964, Peter Hall and John Barton directed the Royal Shakespeare Company in an ambitious ten-hour condensation of the second tetralogy (all three parts of *Henry VI* and *Richard III*) entitled *Wars of the Roses*. A later version, made for television, still occasionally airs, and some libraries offer the videotapes for rental. This is not Shakespeare for the purist: Barton added over a thousand lines of dialogue, so that the audience would understand the transition from one scene to the next.

Falstaff

. . . Falstaff *inimitated, unimitable*
Falstaff, *how shall I describe thee?*
Thou compound of sense and vice, of
sense which may be admired but not
esteemed, of vice which may be despised,
but hardly detested.

—*SAMUEL JOHNSON*

Falstaff is not just a character; he's a phenomenon. As he himself boasted, he's witty not only in himself but is the cause of wit in others. He's been the inspiration for songs, paintings, operas, and beer. Actors have made their careers playing him, and he's the only character to appear in four Shakespeare plays—once by royal request. Falstaff is so inimitable that his name has become an adjective, "Falstaffian," defined by the *Oxford English Dictionary* as "characteristic of or resembling Falstaff, a fat, jovial humourous knight." And the entry in the *Shakspere Allusion Book* pays him the supreme compliment: "For the purpose of this Index Falstaff is treated as a work."

An opportunistic schemer, a sad old clown, a corrupter of youth, and a philosopher, Falstaff has seduced the greatest actors: it was Orson Welles's life's ambition to play it, and the role capped Ralph Richardson's career. Like Hamlet, Falstaff transcends gender. The actress Pat Carroll earned accolades for her performance as the old knight in *The Merry Wives of Windsor.* Perhaps her part was made easier by the fact

Courtesy of The Shakespeare Theatre at the Folger. © Joan Marcus

*P*at Carroll transformed herself into the obese knight in Michael Kahn's 1990 production at the Shakespeare Theatre at the Folger. Carroll, however, is not the only female to play the role. During the nineteenth century it was more common for women to play nonromantic male parts such as Shylock and Falstaff.

ು

that although Falstaff boasts of his sexual prowess, he's usually too drunk to consummate his lust.

In the original version of *Henry IV,* Falstaff was called Sir John Old-castle. Oldcastle, later Lord Cobham, played a very slight role in Hol-inshed's *Chronicles,* and his character was nothing like Falstaff's. But through the years, the Oldcastle name somehow became entangled with the legendary high jinks of the Prince Hal crowd, and Shake-speare, always eager for a lively detail, used Oldcastle as the Falstaffian character.

One of Oldcastle's descendants, also Lord Cobham, was not amused. As the Lord Chamberlain, he wasn't pleased to see his illustrious ances-tor cast in such an unsavory light, and, through his position as censor, he rejected *Henry IV,* and the case was considered closed. (Ironically, the only reason Oldcastle is known today is through his coupling with his fictional nemesis.)

The name "Oldcastle" was changed to "Falstaff," Lord Cobham died a few months later, and the play went on—though a few "old castle" jokes were retained as a sly elbow in the ribs of the new Lord Chamber-lain. (At one point, Hal jovially addresses Falstaff as "My old man of the castle.")

Writing plays was often a battle of wits between censor and drama-tist, and here Shakespeare managed to get in the last word. Lord Cob-ham's successor, Henry Brook (also Lord Cobham), was to be installed into the Knights of the Garter in a ceremony at Windsor Castle. Since this was a great day for the Cobham clan, a play was commanded for the occasion. Just when he thought he was finished with the whole affair, poor Lord Cobham was once more reminded of the Falstaff-Oldcastle controversy. According to legend, Queen Elizabeth had been so taken by the character that she specifically requested a play in which Falstaff is in love.

In the new play, called *The Merry Wives of Windsor,* Shakespeare couldn't resist smuggling in a few "Brook" jokes at the expense of the honoree. "Brook" is the alias assumed by the ludicrous Mr. Page when, terrified of being cuckolded, he spies on his wife in a frenzy of jealous rage.

The Oldcastles obviously lacked a sense of humor, and "Brook" was changed to "Broom" in all subsequent productions.

Orson Welles on Falstaff

*F*alstaff is a man defending a force—the old England—which is going down. What is difficult for Falstaff, I believe, is that he is the greatest conception of a good man, the most complete good man, in all drama.

I have played the part three times in the theatre and now in the film, and I'm not convinced that I have realized it properly yet. It's the most difficult part I ever played in my life. . . . I feel he is a wit rather than clown, and I don't think much of the few moments in the film where I am simply funny, because I don't think that he is.

*O*rson Welles as Falstaff in *Chimes at Midnight.*

The Museum of Modern Art/Film Stills Archive

"Sweet Beef" Falstaff

*T*he epithets hurled at Falstaff—about his girth, his cowardice, his sloth, his lechery, and his wit—are some of the most inventive Shakespeare ever wrote. Most of them relate to brawn, roasts, and other meats.

❖ All-hallown summer [Late autumn; i.e., Falstaff is old.] (*Henry IV, Part 1*, I.2.156–57)

❖ fat-kidneyed rascal (*Henry IV, Part 1*, II.2.5–6)

❖ fat-guts (*Henry IV, Part 1*, II.2.30)

❖ sweet beef (*Henry IV, Part 1*, III.3.175)

❖ woolsack (*Henry IV, Part 1*, II.4.130)

❖ this bed-presser [lazy] (*Henry IV, Part 1*, II.4.238)

❖ this horse-back-breaker [fat] (*Henry IV, Part 1*, II.4.238–39)

❖ clay-brained guts (*Henry IV, Part 1*, II.4.223)

❖ knotty-pated fool [thick-headed] (*Henry IV, Part 1*, II.4.223)

❖ obscene greasy tallow-catch [tub for catching candle wax— Falstaff has a tendency to sweat] (*Henry IV, Part 1*, II.4.224)

❖ Sir John Sack—and Sugar [Sack, Falstaff's beverage of choice, has become synonymous with the character.] (*Henry IV, Part 1*, I.2.112)

❖ this huge hill of flesh (*Henry IV, Part 1*, II.4.239)

❖ my sweet creature of bombast [Bombast, a cloth padding, came to refer to anyone who was inflated in his speech.] (*Henry IV, Part 1*, II.4.320)

❖ whoreson candle-mine [Falstaff is so greasy you can make candles out of him.] (*Henry IV, Part II*, II.4.295)

❖ tidy Bartholomew boar-pig [Tidy means succulent and fat. Bartholomew pig was a special ham sold at Bartholomew's Fair.] (*Henry IV, Part II*, II.4.226)

Richard III

The curtain rises on a solitary misshapen figure. Humpbacked, limping, a withered arm dangling by his side, he slowly drags himself toward his audience and utters that astonishing soliloquy:

> Now is the winter of our discontent
> Made glorious summer by this sun of York,
> And all the clouds that loured upon our house
> In the deep bosom of the ocean buried.
> Now are our brows bound with victorious wreaths,
> Our bruisèd arms hung up for monuments,
> Our stern alarums changed to merry meetings,
> Our dreadful marches to delightful measures.
>
> (I.1.1–8)

War, winter, and death are over; it's now time for celebration, peace, and amorous play. You can almost see the speaker's lip curl. In his opening speech, Richard unfolds his strategy to us, revealing the man behind the smiling mask. He pledges himself to villainy, treachery, and conspiracy. By confiding in us, he pays us what for him is the supreme compliment: he makes us his accomplices. At once we are mesmerized by that droll, mocking voice, by the sheer charisma of the man. This is the tone of a highly refined villain:

> Plots have I laid, inductions dangerous,
> By drunken prophecies, libels, and dreams,
> To set my brother Clarence and the King
> In deadly hate the one against the other....
>
> (I.1.32–35)

We are hooked by this actor—not the one *playing* Richard, but by Richard himself, who is, after all, a consummate player who can slip into any role with ease.

Richard's world is a vast chessboard, and he's now plotting his moves: four jumps and the throne will be his. All he must do is remove the obstacles—his brother, King Edward (who conveniently dies); the Duke of Clarence (also, confusingly, called by his Christian name, George); then his nephews, the two young princes, Edward and York. And in the course of the play he also manages to dispose of his first wife, as well as several other persons who stand in his way.

Richard admits he isn't much to look at, but what he lacks in appearance he more than makes up in wit and charm. He doesn't need to admire his face; he's in love with his own ingenuity—the clever way his mind works, its plots and twists and turns. No matter that there's no one to appreciate his brilliance—except us, of course. Richard can't simply plot Clarence's death; he also has to make a joke about it:

> Simple plain Clarence, I do love thee so
> That I will shortly send thy soul to heaven,
> If heaven will take the present at our hands.
>
> (I.1.118–20)

Then he goes on to woo Lady Anne—quite a challenge, considering that he's just killed her husband, father, and father-in-law. In typically daring fashion, he proposes as she weeps over her father-in-law's bier. Shakespeare heightens the dramatic suspense by having Richard court her at the worst possible moment. Can he do it? She curses his face; she spits at him; he glories in her spit; she accuses him of murder; he says he did it for her beauty; she hates him; he wins her—all within six minutes.

Shakespeare does something remarkable here. We *know* Richard is playacting; he's just finished telling us that he's deliberately pursuing Anne to solidify his claim to the throne. But while he is seducing her we forget that it's all an act and believe him, just as she does. That's how convincing an actor he is. So when Anne leaves and Richard turns to us again, crowing over his power, we are shocked back to reality. We, too, have been seduced. His triumph gives way to one of the greatest speeches of self-congratulation ever written:

Was ever woman in this humour wooed?
Was ever woman in this humour won?
I'll have her, but I will not keep her long.

(I.2.227–29)

Richard has outdone even his own expectations, and success quickly follows success, until at last he attains the crown. So here's Richard of Gloucester, soon to be Richard III: an ugly brute with sex appeal, disabled, yet a brave warrior. With Richard, Shakespeare transcended the stock figure of the stage villain and created a fascinating, contradictory figure.

Richard III begins as a black comedy and ends like a military parade. The second part of the play is taken up more with war strategy than with Richard's intrigues, and it's therefore less compelling. It's as if Shakespeare got carried away by his own creation and then, at the last minute, realized he was writing a history play with a moral. Enter the Tudor hero Henry Richmond, who begins to raise troops against Richard.

Shakespeare alters Richard's character, so that the audience will root for the right (that is, Tudor) side. As soon as he's crowned in Act IV, scene 2, all smiles and jokes quickly cease. With his ugly head made all the more grotesque by the crown that's perched upon it, he sits in satanic splendor on the throne. Having achieved his goal, he no longer needs to placate or to pretend, and the genial mask is suddenly removed. Richard even stops trying to please the audience. After having addressed us six times in the first half of the play, he now turns to us only once. We thus feel more alienated from him—particularly in regard to his next move: his first act as king is to order the murder of the two young princes. "Cousin, thou wast not wont to be so dull," he tells the uncomprehending Buckingham. "Shall I be plain? I wish the bastards dead. . . ." Although they appear only briefly on stage, the princes are fully rounded characters, unforgettably sweet, honest, and wise—and, more important, the legitimate heirs to the throne. It is at this point that Richard utterly loses the sympathy of both the audience and his subjects. His enviable sangfroid is now simply chilling.

Shakespeare enjoys showing his public figures in isolation—those moments when events start closing in on them and they are forced to confront themselves. On the eve of Richard's death on Bosworth field, the ghosts of his victims visit his dreams and one by one, with haunting formality, cry out, "Despair, and die!" Momentarily stripped of his defenses, Richard replies: "I shall despair. There is no creature loves me. . . ." How different from the oily schemer of *Henry VI, Part 3,* when he declared:

> And this word "love," which greybeards call divine,
> Be resident in men like one another
> And not in me; I am myself alone.

(V.6.81–83)

To Richard, deathbed confessions are despicable, and he will have none of it. His final scene is his finest hour. His horse killed, ambushed on all sides, he nevertheless continues to fight, uttering the desperate cry of a man who will not be vanquished: "A horse! A horse! My kingdom for a horse!" Kingdom, crown, and power are gone. At the end, Richard *is* himself alone.

What to Look for in Richard III

*A*ct I, scene 2, reveals a perverse sexual chemistry between Anne and Richard. It's a reversal of the scene in which Romeo and Juliet first meet. The young lovers engage in repartee, but theirs are the balanced clauses of a love duet; Anne and Richard's verbal thrust and counterthrust suggest a sexual duel:

> ANNE. And thou unfit for any place, but hell.
> RICHARD. Yes, one place else, if you will hear me name it.
> ANNE. Some dungeon.
> RICHARD.   Your bedchamber.
> ANNE. Ill rest betide the chamber where thou liest!
> RICHARD. So will it, madam, till I lie with you.

(109–14)

Act IV, scene 4, has been described by the critic A. P. Rossiter as a "dismal catalogue of *Who Was Who* and *Who Has Lost Whom.*" One by one, each of Richard's female victims describes what he has done to her and her family. The repetitious, ritualistic quality of the verse can be monotonous, but it creates an atmosphere of incantatory power, rather like that evoked by the witches in *Macbeth.* There is unintentional humor in the way in which each victim tries to outdo the other in her complaints.

> I had an Edward, till a Richard killed him;
> I had a Harry, till a Richard killed him;
> Thou hadst an Edward, till a Richard killed him;
> Thou hadst a Richard, till a Richard kill'd him.

(40–43)

All those Richards and Edwards again! (The last two refer to the princes in the tower.)

*I*n Act I, scene 3, old Queen Margaret, crazed with grief and rage, blasts Richard and prophesies retribution on the house of York. There's nothing like it for sheer vitriol:

> No sleep close up that deadly eye of thine,
> Unless it be while some tormenting dream
> Affrights thee with a hell of ugly devils!
> Thou elvish-marked, abortive, rooting hog!

(224–27)

*J*ust after Richard is crowned, Buckingham requests the dukedom that's been promised him. But he has just committed a fatal error: he briefly hesitated when Richard asked him to murder the princes, and Richard demands nothing less than complete obedience. The icy hauteur of the king's reply sounds as if he were cutting off Buckingham's head as he cuts off his request: "I am not in the giving vein today" (IV.2.117). This line was uttered to perfection by Olivier in the movie.

Facts about
<u>Richard III</u>

✤ The Polish critic Jan Kott observes that after one hundred years of slaughter and intrigue, all aimed at achieving the crown, the final words spoken by a king in the entire history cycle are "My kingdom for a horse."

✤ One of the most celebrated lines in *Richard III* was written not by Shakespeare but by a third-rate actor and playwright named Colley Cibber. It is to him that we owe the line "Off with his head! So much for Buckingham." Although faux Shakespeare, it is recognized as quintessentially Shakespearean, and rather then disappoint the audience, some performances still retain the line, most notably Olivier's movie version.

✤ Richard III is a man of a thousand faces and has been played as everything from a lonely freak and a standup comedian to a Nazi and a gangster.

✤ Perhaps the most unusual bit of casting occurred in 1820, when the tyrant was played by Miss Clara Fisher, age eleven.

*O*ne of the first anecdotes recorded by a contemporary about Shakespeare attests to Richard's enormous sex appeal and reveals that stagedoor Johnnys are not a modern phenomenon. It's from the diary of John Manningham, a lawyer who might have known the playwright through mutual friends:

Once upon a time when Burbage played Richard III there was a citizen grew so far in liking him that before she went from the play she appointed him to come that night into her by the name of Richard III. Shakespeare, overhearing their conclusion, went before, was entertained and at his game ere Burbage came. The message was brought that Richard III was at the door. Shake-speare caused return to be made that William the Conqueror was before Richard III.

Manningham goes on to explain, "Shakespeare's name was William."

Ricardian Abuse

*I*n the course of the play, Richard gets plenty of abuse. Among other names, he is called:

- ❖ a cacodemon [hellish spirit] (I.3.143)

- ❖ that bottled spider [swollen] (I.3.241)

- ❖ thou lump of foul deformity (I.2.57)

- ❖ a hellhound (IV.4.48)

- ❖ a hedgehog (I.2.103)

- ❖ the bloody dog (V.5.2)

- ❖ a cockatrice [a monster who turns men into stone] (IV.1.54)

- ❖ this poisonous bunch-backed toad (I.3.245)

- ❖ hell's black intelligencer [secret agent] (IV.4.71)

- ❖ thou elvish-marked, abortive, rooting hog (I.3.227)

RICARDVS · III · ANG · REX ·

National Portrait Gallery, London

*A*ccording to members of
the Richard III Society,
Richard was good-looking.

&

The Richard III Society

*B*eing a member of the Richard III Society must be a little like belonging to the Al Capone fan club. Members are continually forced to defend their hero. Ricardians insist that Richard was neither crippled nor humpbacked, and they are passionately dedicated to proving that Shakespeare's portrait of the inhuman monster is based on Tudor propaganda used to bolster Henry's VII's weak claim to the throne. They believe that Richard was framed for the murder of the princes and that his alleged crimes are part of a six-hundred-year smear campaign. In 1933, the supposed bones of the princes were privately exhumed, and though they were proved to be the remains of young children, it could not be established whether they were male or female or in what century they had been killed.

The group was founded in England in 1924 as the Society of the White Boar (Richard's emblem). In 1960, the American branch was started, and today there are members in every state. Ricardians can be found picketing productions of the play and writing letters to cast members. (Antony Sher received one that began, "I read in the paper that you are yet another actor to ignore truth and integrity in order to launch yourself on an ego-trip by the monstrous lie perpetuated by Shakespeare about a most valiant knight.") They place memorial notices in the newspapers on the anniversary of Richard's death, make pilgrimages to Ricardian shrines, and, more seriously, maintain libraries devoted to their hero, sponsor scholarships and research, and publish several periodicals.

In 1973, the Ladies of the American Branch of the Richard III Society presented needlepoint covers for the kneeling hassocks of the Sutton Cheney Church, where there is a memorial tablet commemorating Richard III along with others who fell at Bosworth field. The "real" Richard would have sneered.

Edmund Kean's Richard

*E*dmund Kean (1789–1833) was one of the most famous Richard the Thirds of all time. The other famous Richard, Olivier, recounts this legendary anecdote in his book *On Acting*:

> When a friend asked Kean to help him out by appearing in his benefit performance in Liverpool, Edmund agreed with alacrity. He was to play Richard III to his friend's Duke of Buckingham. They repaired, naturally, to the local hostelry and talked about

good times, bad times and old times. By the time they got to the theatre, they were warm inside and in the head. After Edmund's first speech the audience began to scream, "Mr. Kean, you're drunk!" After a long pause, he stared with those penetrating eyes at the hostile house and replied, "If you think I'm drunk, wait till you see Buckingham."

*E*dmund Kean (1789–1833), one of the most famous—and frenzied—Shakespearean actors of his day. Coleridge wrote that "to see him act is like reading Shakespeare by flashes of lightning."

The Folger Shakespeare Library

On Playing Richard III

*M*ajor Shakespearean roles require the physical dexterity of an athlete, the intellect of a scholar, the sex appeal of a Don Juan, and the imagination of a poet. Richard III in particular is physically and emotionally demanding. He's on stage longer than any other character in any other Shakespeare play—and *Richard III* is one of the longest. (Tyrone Guthrie observed that during the course of one night's performance, an actor in a major Shakespearean role might walk several miles.) For three hours the actor playing Richard must limp, hunched over, while wearing a heavy cloak or armor, beneath which is the dead weight of a hump (sometimes made of heavy plaster)—all the while baking under hot lights. Then, in the last scene, just when he's utterly exhausted, he must summon up the energy for a violent and

A sketch from Antony Sher's notebook in preparation for the role of Richard III.

&

© Anthony Sher from Anthony Sher, *Year of the King*, Chatto & Windus, 1987, p. 114

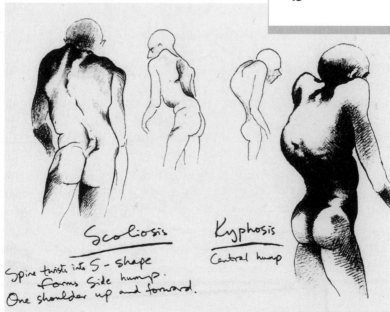

Scoliosis

Spine twists into S-shape forms side hump. One shoulder up and forward.

Kyphosis

Central hump

Antony Sher
as Richard III,
"the nightmare
creature."

© Reg Wilson

lengthy duel. The director Ron Daniels said, "Richard is notorious for crippling actors. They spend years afterwards on osteopaths' couches."

Should Richard be funny, cruel, or seductive? Should he be a standup comic or a thug? Should he alienate the audience or seduce it? And just how deformed is Richard, anyway? There are innumerable choices to be made by actor and director. Antony Sher, one of the finest Richards in recent memory, obsessively researched the role, visiting rehabilitation clinics, reading medical texts, and studying scoliosis and other diseases of the spine, as well as the effects of deformity on the psyche. Finally, after much doubt and wavering, he ended up playing the part—brilliantly—on crutches.

In addition to carrying that hump, the actor playing Richard must bear the symbolic weight of performances past. In *Year of the King,* Sher recounts the doubts, hesitations, and exhilarations that come with playing one of Shakespeare's superstars.

> Wake inextricably depressed about Richard III. Why bother playing the part? Olivier's interpretation *is* definitive and so famous that all round the world people can get up and do impersonations of it. At parties in New York, in bars in Naples, on remote Australian farms and forgotten South Sea Islands, people get to their feet, hoist one shoulder up, shrivel an arm, and limp across the room declaring, "Now is the winter" or its relevant linguistic equivalent.

Then Sher sees his hump for the first time:

> With my heart in my mouth, I hurry over to see my back. It's much softer than I imagined, lying on the floor like a big pink blancmange, a slice of blubber, a side of Elephant Man. I can hardly get my clothes off fast enough to hoist it onto my back.

Olivier's Richard III

*L*aurence Olivier's Richard III, with his hooded eyes, thin voice, and black pageboy haircut, remains the definitive portrait. His conception of the humpbacked psychopath came to him with visionary intensity. First there was the voice:

> It came to me: the thin reed of a sanctimonious scholar. I started putting it on at once. It arrived and set the vision going: thin and rapier-like, but all powerful. Somewhere between the bridge of the nose and the sinuses at first.

The New York Public Library/The Billy Rose Theatre Collection

Bettmann/Hulton

*J*ed Harris, the much-despised American director.

❧

*O*livier getting made up for *Richard III*.

❧

This voice, described by Olivier as "a mixture of honey and razor blades," was to haunt Antony Sher when he prepared for the role of Richard more than thirty years later. Freakish yet alluring, Olivier's Richard, with his languid slouch, twisted leg, one fixed and deadened eye, and shriveled claw of a hand, was inspired by a particularly loathsome American theatre director named Jed Harris.

The completed image: Olivier's Richard III.

❧

"The Big
Bad Wolf."

Nose on, wig on, make-up complete. There, staring back at me from my mirror was my Richard. . . . My revenge on Jed Harris was complete.

Years later, Olivier learned that a man who worked at Disney studios also had a vendetta against Harris, and that in addition to inspiring an image of history's monster, the director was also the model for the cartoon villain the Big Bad Wolf.

John Waller: Swordplay and Dueling

*I*t's not enough that a Shakespearean actor speak the lines and act; he must also appear to be an accomplished duelist. As a choreographer of combat, a fight director must make terrified actors look like fierce adversaries. John Waller has been directing fights, battles, and duels for over twenty-five years, and his numerous credits include Ian McKellen's 1989 Richard III *at the National Theatre in London and the films* Anne of the Thousand Days *and* The French Lieutenant's Woman.

NE: *What is a fight director's goal?*

JW: To have an actor do ten blows and have the audience believe that the characters are trying to kill each other. Too much stylistic choreography isn't convincing. It must be a matter of life and death.

NE: *How do you get an actor to want to kill someone and at the same time hold back?*

JW: The actor shouldn't feel like killing; the character he plays should. Actors are not all that physical, so someone who's really aggressive and strong can be truly frightening. Though one opponent may be baring his teeth and flashing his eyes, his partner should be able to see that he's in control. But all the audience should see is the aggression—that's the hard bit.

NE: *How do you go about staging a fight?*

JW: What you first do is assess an actor's physical presence, and then you try to persuade him that the character would have been good at fighting. If he's big and heavy, then you choreograph in character. You combine the actual fight with the actor's physique and choreograph around that.

NE: *How about staging big battle scenes?*

JW: You just have to get everybody moving to fill all the spaces. If you get three people fighting, two against one, and they're the main focus, then you get them to hold center stage. When it's time for them to move, their space is immediately filled by another couple. The other characters fight, but they put slightly less intensity into their movements; otherwise, the audience's eyes would stray from the central actors. If you have two young spear carriers swashbuckling away on stage and you find yourself looking at them instead of the main actors, well, that's wrong. That's not where the emphasis should be.

NE: *What sort of fights do you think Shakespeare staged?*

JW: They must have been phenomenal, and he always put them at the end of the play as a climax. The actors would have been laughed off the stage if they weren't any good. He wrote at a time when nearly all men fought with swords, from the aristocrats who knew all the newfangled Italian fencing styles and terms, to the apprentice boys who fought with sword and buckler in the English manner. Shakespeare even has Mercutio poking fun of Tybalt's Italian techniques in *Romeo and Juliet*. What Shakespeare seems to be saying is, It's all a bit fancy for us English.

NE: *How can Richard be a great warrior if he's handicapped?*

JW: That's always a problem with *Richard III*. All actors want to play him with a deformity. But the play is set in about 1480, when the essence of being a knight was to ride horses—the knight on horseback was the equivalent of a tank. When a person is as deformed as Richard is portrayed as being, with a withered arm and a gamey leg, then he logically wouldn't be able to ride a medieval war-horse, which you ride with your left hand because your right hand is the one you fight with.

NE: *So how did the real Richard III fight?*

JW: It's Olivier's portrayal that everyone copies. Richard had been fighting hand to hand for years and was still fighting when he was

*T*he final duel sequence in Olivier's *Hamlet* lasted ten minutes and took fourteen days to shoot.

🦢

killed. Though an actor can play him with some deformity, it shouldn't hinder him from proving what a great warrior he was. If he is too deformed he wouldn't be able to ride a medieval war-horse, so there would be little point in him saying, "A horse! A horse! My kingdom for a horse!"

NE: *What's your opinion of the famous duel in Olivier's* Hamlet*?*

JW: It's exciting. But if you ask me if I believe in it, well, not completely. It doesn't tell the story of *Hamlet* as much as it should. Hamlet's duel is a very difficult thing to direct. Hamlet sets out to patch up the argument with Laertes, and he thinks the duel is just an ordinary fencing match. But Laertes intends to cheat him with a poisoned sword. So they begin to fence, and Hamlet keeps scoring the points, and Laertes can't get him with the sharp sword. So when Hamlet finally is hit and sees his blood, he becomes upset, because he's trying to be a nice guy and his opponent is going for him with a sharp sword. But he still doesn't realize he's dying. So he tries to get the sword away from Laertes, and then he goes for *him* with it. Now he thinks Laertes is frightened because he has a sharp sword, but he doesn't know that Laertes is frightened because he's got a *poisoned* sharp sword! Do you see what I mean? It's quite complicated to dramatize. And then, of course, the match turns into a brawl. So you've got an ordinary fencing match and then an aggressive fencing match with Laertes actually fighting for his life. All the while Hamlet never knows that he's *also* fighting for his life. Although Olivier's duel is exciting, it didn't show all of this.

NE: *Wouldn't this be lost on an audience?*

JW: If it's done properly and they know the story, no. The movement and the choreography should tell the story of the play. Most of all, the audience has to believe that the characters are fulfilling the demands of the plot. At no time must the audience believe that the actor is in danger. That's the hard part.

Prose and Verse

When I read Shakespeare I am struck
with wonder
That such trivial people should muse
and thunder
In such lovely language.

—D. H. LAWRENCE

hakespeare basically uses two kinds of language, prose and
verse. As a general rule, prose is reserved for ordinary conversation
and common folk, while verse is usually spoken by kings and other serious talkers. As he matured, Shakespeare came to use more prose;
Hamlet's magnificent speech, "What a piece of work is a man," which
sounds like verse, is, surprisingly, written in conversational prose.

One character may use both verse and prose, depending upon
the situation, his social status, and whom he's addressing. In *Henry IV,
Part 1,* Act I, scene 2, for instance, Prince Hal uses prose because he's
with his cronies in the tavern, but as soon as they leave, he addresses
the audience in blank verse. The abruptness of the change frames his
speech, setting it apart from what went before. Our attention is more
focused, and we instinctively recognize that what he's saying is crucial.
Verse catches the ear in a way prose cannot.

Some people are alienated by Shakespearean dialogue because no
one really talks like that. To them verse sounds stilted and artificial,
particularly when it takes the form of rhymed couplets, which have the

capacity to make the most elevated thought sound like a jingle for laundry detergent. The humorist Robert Benchley wrote, "It is hard to ask an actor to make an exit on a line like:

> I am glad on't. I desire no more delight
> Than to be under sail and gone tonight."

(The Merchant of Venice, II.6.67–68)

It was his opinion that Shakespearean actors felt compelled to exit in gales of laughter to disguise the artifice of what they had just said. But rhyme only sounds strange when the actor mindlessly follows the stresses of the syllables, giving the lines a tedious, singsong quality. The trick to reading verse is to emphasize two or three important words. You might try this with Benchley's example, emphasizing "glad" and "gone." The line now sounds like ordinary speech, only with emphasis and weight.

Part of the problem is that many American actors aren't trained to speak in verse. A true Shakespearean actor, like a musician, has to know when to breathe, when to pause, when to rush forward, and when to stress or unstress a syllable. More important, he or she must understand what the words mean. Part of the problem also lies with *our* training as readers and spectators. We've grown accustomed to movies and plays in which characters speak in flat, nasal cadences, as in this exchange from the movie *Marty*:

> ANGE. What do you feel like doing tonight?
> MARTY. I don't know, Ange, what do you feel like doing?

(Screenplay by Paddy Chayefsky)

Speaking in rhyme is not natural to us, but it was to the Elizabethans, so we have to understand what language meant to them, and what language does *not* mean to us today. If I were an Elizabethan and I wanted to impress you as a lover, I wouldn't send you flowers. I would come and woo you at your feet and recite to you a sonnet I had written just for you—no matter how bad it was. Elizabethan England was a world where people sang, talked, and breathed language.

—DAVID SUCHET

This would not be art to an Elizabethan audience. To them, art *heightened* reality; nature was enhanced, not slavishly imitated.

Shakespeare should be made intelligible to the average listener. If an actor sings the words without feeling them or understanding why his character says them, then they will sound unnatural or rhetorical, or what we sometimes, wrongly, call "Shakespearean." If the verse *sounds* beautiful but you don't have a clue as to what's being said, blame the actor, not Shakespeare.

Shakespeare Is Not "Shakespearean"

When people parody Shakespeare they tend to go in for those lengthy death scenes in which the victim keeps rallying to cram in a few last words. But Shakespeare could also be remarkably restrained. The loquacious Hotspur in *Henry IV, Part 1,* for instance, could have had a protracted death scene, but instead Shakespeare wisely has him die in mid-sentence. The abrupt silence and the disturbing sense of incompleteness it evokes expresses the untimely end to this garrulous young warrior. Hotspur's anguished cry, "O Harry, thou hast robbed me of my youth!" finds an auditory parallel in his last, unfinished sentence.

Shakespeare was an actor. He probably said the words aloud as he wrote them. He knew what worked—what sounded natural and right. It's hard to hear, "O, what a rogue and peasant slave am I!" without instinctively knowing what Hamlet means. Though he was not averse to writing ornate, Latinate lines like "the multitudinous seas incarnadine," Shakespeare was also a master of the simple phrase, such as Lear's "Pray you undo this button." He knew the force of wry understatement: "Well, this is the Forest of Arden," says Rosalind as she glances at her new home. And when Romeo learns about Juliet's supposed death, he doesn't feel much like speechifying: "Then I defy you, stars!" is all Shakespeare has him say on the subject. The best example of all is the scene in which Lear begs his daughter's forgiveness. Cordelia is so moved, so pained by her father's humility, that she's barely able to speak: "No cause, no cause," she murmurs. A lesser playwright would have indulged in a long setpiece on forgiveness, but these two words say it all.

Shakespearean "Bombast"

I hear a great deal, too,
of Shakespeare, but I
cannot read him, he is
such a bombast fellow.

—*GEORGE III*

*T*here's no getting around it: Shakespeare's language *can* be dense—
but it's never bloated. Look at this obscure passage from *The Winter's
Tale,* when Leontes begins to suspect his wife of infidelity. The language is thick, and as he grows increasingly more suspicious it
becomes more parenthetical, tortured, and rambling. Notice how the
passage turns back on itself, as if he can barely complete a thought. It's
precisely this kind of utterance that turns people away from Shakespeare:

> Affection, thy intention stabs the centre.
> Thou dost make possible things not so held,
> Communicat'st with dreams—how can this be?—
> With what's unreal thou coactive art,
> And fellow'st nothing. Then 'tis very credent
> Thou mayst co-join with something; and thou dost,
> And that beyond commission, and I find it. . . .
>
> (I.2.138–44)

Reading this passage, one appreciates Ben Jonson's wish that Shakespeare had blotted out a thousand words. But there's a reason for its
labyrinthine density. Leontes is struggling both to deny and to convince
himself that his wife is unfaithful, and thus his language pulls in two
directions at once. As the director Peter Sellars said, "Shakespeare is
perfectly capable of writing the clearest and most lucid English sentence. If he decides to get tangled and obscure, then there's a reason
for it."

Hints on Reading Shakespeare Aloud

❖ First, and most important, figure out what the words mean, and you'll almost instinctively know how to say them. At the same time, allow yourself to be swept along by the sound, the music of a line, and you'll find you understand more than you think. Shakespeare used rhythm to help his actors and audience. Rhythm—whether a line is fast or slow, irregular or smooth—will help you know what a character is saying. For instance, Juliet's impassioned "Gallop apace, you fiery-footed steeds" recreates the swift regularity of hoofbeats and thus expresses the urgency of her passion. Macbeth's weary "Tomorrow and tomorrow and tomorrow" is slow and repetitious, suggestive of the speaker's deadened state and his sense of life's monotony. Shakespeare usually places the punch, the word that should be emphasized, at the end of a line.

> *T*he Elizabethans were an audience of listeners. They would say, I'm going to *hear* a play, not I'm going to see a play. The Elizabethan audience would pick up on words and their various meanings that we wouldn't.
>
> —MARJORIE GARBER

❖ The director John Barton of the Royal Shakespeare Company advises his actors to pause slightly at the end of each verse line; Shakespeare, he notes, gives his actors an evocative image at the end of the line, which is continued much more strongly in the first three words of the next line.

❖ For the novice, it's usually best to begin by using punctuation as a guide. If the line ends with a period, give it a full stop; a comma takes a half stop, and if the line runs on, keep reading. You'll be surprised at the difference it makes.

✤ One final note: an accent mark over the suffix "ed," as in "per-fumèd," indicates that it should be pronounced as an extra syl-lable. Perfumèd in Elizabethan English has three, not two, syllables.

✤ Those rich sounds we hear on stage in that plummy British accent are nothing like the sounds the playwright's audience would have heard. Scholars who have reconstructed Elizabethan diction say that the closest approximation today would be the English spoken by hillbillies in Appalachia.

SHAKESPEARE'S IMAGERY

Speaking on Shakespeare's poetry, the actor Ian McKellen pointed out that poetic imagery reflects more than just a pretti-fied expression, or "poetic charm"; Shakespeare's imagery is a concrete picture grounded in the reality of the moment. Cit-ing the line from *Romeo and Juliet,* "It was the nightingale, and not the lark, / That pierced the fearful hollow of thine ear," McKellen asked, "How near the hollow of an ear do you have to be to see that it is hollow and not that it is pink, beautiful or ugly? In other words, when the two lovers heard the bird, . . . they were very close to each other, they were in bed, they were making love. Juliet doesn't speak it poetically. . . . In other words, this line is not 'nice,' but sensual, real, passion-ate and youthful."

Shakespeare's Vocabulary

*I*f there were an "Elizabethan Guinness Book of Records," Shakespeare would be the unchallenged record breaker in his use of language. Nobody ever used so many words so well.

❖ It's estimated that Shakespeare used between 25,000 and 29,000 *different* words in his plays and poems. To give you a sense of just how extraordinary this is, consider that the King James Bible is made up of only six thousand different words.

❖ One out of every dozen or so words was a new one that Shakespeare would never repeat in any play or poem.

❖ The longest word in all Shakespeare is "honorificabilitudinitatibus," and it's found in *Love's Labour's Lost*—Shakespeare uses the Latin ablative plural to stretch it out even further. It means, quite simply, "honorableness."

❖ *The Harvard Concordance to Shakespeare,* which lists every word Shakespeare ever wrote, is 14 inches long, 10½ inches wide, and 2½ inches thick.

❖ Although it's been attributed to him often enough in numerous parodies and burlesques and in countless Renaissance faires, Shakespeare never used the word "gadzooks."

Shakespeare's Characters

Shakespeare created about 1,280 characters—and this doesn't include spear carriers or Third Lord from the Left.

When people praise Shakespeare it's often for his ability to create "realistic personalities with psychological depth." This phrase, or variations of it, has been cited so often that it's easy to dismiss as just another example of Shakespearean hyperbole. The realism of Shakespeare's portraits isn't immediately obvious, since his characters speak Elizabethan English and they usually find themselves in extreme or improbable situations.

For me, "psychological depth" means that you could, if so inclined, hold an imaginary conversation with Hamlet and envision him outside his particular setting. Hamlet isn't defined by Denmark or even by his need for revenge. The best characters seem to transcend the confines of their immediate dramatic situation.

Seem. For of course, they don't. As works of fiction, they exist only in our minds. But Shakespeare's ability to create multidimensional characters has seduced generations of bardolators into treating his creations as if they were intimate friends or, as Hartley Coleridge put it, "deceased acquaintances." Much Victorian and early-twentieth-century criticism consisted of investigations into the early lives of characters, such as a study of Horatio's and Hamlet's schooldays or the girlhoods of Shakespeare's heroines, a form of scholarship that prompted one of the first modern pieces of Shakespearean criticism, G. Wilson Knight's landmark essay, "How Many Children Had Lady Macbeth?"

It's easy to see why many people have felt closer to Lear than to their own fathers. Unlike his contemporaries, Shakespeare took pains to create complex figures capable of eliciting our sympathetic identification.

Hamlet's sorrow is specific to him but readily understood by anyone who has ever lost and missed a parent. Also, since they are composed of contradictory elements, Shakespeare's characters, like people in real life, are subject to change and can seem different every time you encounter them. There are few choices an actor confronts when playing a Jonsonian character, but with Shakespeare, the possibilities are endless. Just look at Falstaff: he has been portrayed as devoted friend, callous exploiter, and sad spendthrift. Ophelia has been a sexual tease, political spy, and virginal martyr; Othello, a dignified idealist and virile warrior.

And yet, although the personality may change, the characters possess an enduring identity from which their actions spring. Macbeth must kill Duncan; Lear must exile Cordelia; Juliet must die, just as Rosalind must marry. The best Shakespearean figures are dear and familiar, strange and new.

Even minor characters, the anonymous stream of murderers, messengers, and servants, are distinguished in some way that sets them apart from one another. Some are obsequious, some terrified or breathless. Clarence's assassins in *Richard III*, known simply as First and Second Murderer, could have been faceless assassins, but for Shakespeare, sin is never abstract. Just as they are about to commit the deed that will send them to hell, Second Murderer suddenly hesitates. Not only does this moment heighten dramatic tension, but for an instant this emissary of evil, this killer without a name, is transformed into one of us, an ordinary man caught in extraordinary circumstances, poised between damnation and grace.

On Quoting Shakespeare

Shakespeare was a dramatist of note;
He lived by writing things to quote.

—*H. C. BRUNNER*

Will a dab of Shakespeare daintily
perfume my wit or just sound like the
literary belching of a compulsive nerd?

—*GARY TAYLOR*

Many of us are like the person in the famous joke who admired *Hamlet* because it was so full of quotes. The impact of Shakespeare on our language is so great that we often quote him without realizing it, his expressions having become "household words" (*Henry V*).

It doesn't hurt to have a line or two of the Bard readily available. Quoting Shakespeare at the appropriate moment can make you appear instantly knowledgeable about any subject. As Prince Philip purportedly said, "A man can be forgiven a lot if he can quote Shakespeare in an economic crisis."

Some Popular Shakespearean Lines

* Something is rotten in the state of Denmark (*Hamlet*, I.4.90)

* Good night, sweet Prince (*Hamlet*, V.2.353)

- ❖ To be, or not to be—that is the question (*Hamlet*, III.1.56)

- ❖ Once more unto the breach (*Henry V*, III.1.1)

- ❖ Now is the winter of our discontent (*Richard III*, I.1.1)

- ❖ Lay on, Macduff (*Macbeth*, V.6.72)

- ❖ A horse! a horse! my kingdom for a horse! (*Richard III*, V.4.13)

- ❖ Friends, Romans, countrymen, lend me your ears (*Julius Caesar*, III.2.74)

- ❖ Alas, poor Yorick! (*Hamlet*, V.1.172)

- ❖ Out, damned spot! (*Macbeth*, V.1.33)

- ❖ All the world's a stage (*As You Like It*, II.7.140)

- ❖ What's in a name? (*Romeo and Juliet*, II.2.43)

- ❖ Oh Romeo, Romeo! wherefore art thou Romeo? [Incidentally, "wherefore" means "why," not "where."] (*Romeo and Juliet*, II.2.33)

- ❖ Beware the Ides of March! (*Julius Caesar*, I.2.18)

- ❖ The lady doth protest too much, methinks (*Hamlet*, III.2.240)

- ❖ Parting is such sweet sorrow (*Romeo and Juliet*, II.2.185)

*H*ere are some of the most common phrases, words, and everyday expressions that were first used, and in most cases invented, by Shakespeare. I omit those that are commonly attributed to Shakespeare but have been found to be proverbial expressions popular when Shakespeare was writing (e.g., "All that glitters is not gold," "It's Greek to me," and *"Et tu, Brute?"*). Some of the following expressions might already have been part of contemporary idiom, but Shakespeare was the first to use them in writing. For a fuller list, see Michael Macrone's *Brush Up Your Shakespeare.*

Household words (*Henry V*, IV.3.52)

Bated breath (*The Merchant of Venice*, I.3.121)

More in sorrow than in anger (*Hamlet*, I.2.232)

Brevity is the soul of wit (*Hamlet*, II.2.90)

Neither rhyme nor reason (*The Comedy of Errors*, II.2.48)

The primrose path (*Hamlet*, I.3.50)

Laughing-stock (*The Merry Wives of Windsor*, III.1.77–78)

Devil incarnate (*Henry V*, II.3.30)

We have seen better days (*As You Like It*, II.7.121)

What's done is done (*Macbeth*, III.2.12)

Eaten me out of house and home (*Henry IV, Part 2*, II.1.72)

Till the crack of doom (*Macbeth*, IV.1.116)

Out, out, brief candle! (*Macbeth*, V.5.23)

Full of sound and fury (*Macbeth*, V.5.27)

What the dickens ["Dickens" was slang for "devil."] (*The Merry Wives of Windsor*, III.2.17)

Dead as a doornail (*Henry VI, Part 2*, IV.10.38)

An eye-sore (*The Taming of the Shrew*, III.2.100)

Foregone conclusion (*Othello*, III.3.426)

One fell swoop (*Macbeth*, IV.3.217)

Bag and baggage (*As You Like It*, III.2.157)

Hoist with his own petard [A petard was a mine filled with gunpowder; to be hoisted by one's own petard means to be destroyed by one's own machinations.] (*Hamlet*, III.4.208)

Let's kill all the lawyers (*Henry VI, Part 2*, IV.2.72)

A lean and hungry look (*Julius Caesar*, I.2.193)

Such stuff as dreams are made on (*The Tempest*, IV.1.156–157)

Wear my heart on my sleeve (*Othello*, I.1.65)

Laid on with a trowel (*As You Like It*, I.2.99)

More fool you (*The Taming of the Shrew*, V.2.128)

The green-eyed monster (*Othello*, III.3.164)

Uneasy lies the head that wears a crown (*Henry IV, Part 2*, III.1.31)

This was the noblest Roman of them all (*Julius Caesar*, V.5.68)

Hoodwinked (*All's Well That Ends Well*, IV.1.80)

Fortune's fool (*Romeo and Juliet*, III.1.134)

The apple of her eye [The apple was the pupil.] (*Love's Labour's Lost*, V.2.475)

Pomp and circumstance (*Othello*, III.3.351)

One that loved not wisely but too well (*Othello*, V.2.340)

Frailty, thy name is woman! (*Hamlet*, I.2.146)

Sweets to the sweet (*Hamlet*, V.1.239)

As white as driven snow (*The Winter's Tale*, IV.4.220)

Stony-hearted villains (*Henry IV, Part 1*, II.2.25)

Budge an inch (*The Taming of the Shrew*, Induction 12)

Too much of a good thing (*As You Like It*, IV.1.112–13)

Neither a borrower nor a lender be (*Hamlet*, I.3.75)

To thine own self be true (*Hamlet*, I.3.78)

Paint [*not* "Gild"] the lily (*King John*, IV.2.11)

Into thin air (*The Tempest*, IV.1.150)

Not a mouse stirring (*Hamlet*, I.1.10)

Speak the speech I pray thee trippingly on the tongue (*Hamlet*, III.2.1)

The play's the thing (*Hamlet*, II.2.604)

Benedick: the married man (*Much Ado about Nothing*, I.1.247)

The game is afoot [Made popular by Sherlock Holmes.] (*Henry IV, Part I*, I.3.272)

The game is up (*Cymbeline*, III.3.107)

Strange bedfellows (*The Tempest*, II.2.39)

I will tell you my drift (*Much Ado about Nothing*, II.1.358)

The naked truth (*Love's Labour's Lost*, V.2.706)

Breathe one's last (*Henry VI, Part 3*, V.2.40)

The course of true love never did run smooth (*A Midsummer Night's Dream*, I.1.132)

The better part of valour is discretion (*Henry IV, Part 1*, V.4.118–19)

Fair is foul, and foul is fair (*Macbeth*, I.1.9)

It smells to heaven (*Hamlet*, III.3.36)

Remembrance of things past (Sonnet 30, line 2)

To make a virtue of necessity (*The Two Gentlemen of Verona*, IV.1.62)

Trueborn Englishman (*Richard II*, I.3.309)

Of comfort no man speak! (*Richard II*, III.2.144)

Salad days (*Antony and Cleopatra*, I.1.73)

I have immortal longings in me (*Antony and Cleopatra*, V.2.279–80)

There's a divinity that shapes our ends (*Hamlet*, V.2.10)

To the manner born [*not* "manor"] (*Hamlet*, I.4.15)

Caviar[y] to the general (*Hamlet*, II.2.435)

Suit the action to the word (*Hamlet*, III.2.17)

Get thee to a nunnery (*Hamlet*, III.1.121)

O, my prophetic soul! (*Hamlet*, I.5.40)

O, brave new world (*The Tempest*, V.1.183)

Short shrift (*Richard III*, III.4.95)

A tower of strength (*Richard III*, V.3.12)

Murder most foul (*Hamlet*, I.5.27)

The time is out of joint (*Hamlet*, I.5.188)

Ay, there's the rub (*Hamlet*, III.1.65)

Knock, knock! Who's there? (*Macbeth*, II.3.3)

In my heart of hearts (*Hamlet*, III.2.73)

For goodness' sake (*Henry VIII*, III.1.159)

Thus conscience does make cowards of us all (*Hamlet*, III.1.83)

What a piece of work is a man (*Hamlet*, II.2.303)

Ripeness is all (*King Lear*, V.2.11)

The readiness is all (*Hamlet*, V.2.216)

As flies to wanton boys are we to the gods (*King Lear*, IV.1.36)

Sharper than a serpent's tooth (*King Lear*, I.4.285)

More sinned against than sinning (*King Lear*, III.2.59)

What fools these mortals be! (*A Midsummer Night's Dream*, III.2.115)

Now gods stand up for bastards! (*King Lear*, I.2.22)

When shall we three meet again? (*Macbeth*, I.1.1)

Double, double, toil and trouble (*Macbeth*, IV.1.20)

Unsex me here (*Macbeth*, I.5.39)

Star-crossed lovers (*Romeo and Juliet*, Prologue, 6)

*S*hakespearean quotations run to eighty-eight pages in Bartlett's *Familiar Quotations.*

The quality of mercy (*The Merchant of Venice*, IV.1.181)

Milk of human-kindness (*Macbeth*, I.5.16)

Stood on ceremonies (*Julius Caesar*, II.2.13)

What's past is prologue (*The Tempest*, II.1.245)

The be-all and the end-all (*Macbeth*, I.7.5)

Good riddance (*Troilus and Cressida*, II.1.119)

Good night, ladies (*Hamlet*, IV.5.72)

The rest is silence (*Hamlet*, V.2.352)

Shakespeare Abused: "Full of Wise Saws and Modern Instances"

 S hakespeare uses many adages and proverbs in his plays—and usually they're said by the wrong people, thus undermining the efforts of those who would adapt the Bard for edifying purposes. Much of the advice gleaned for books of quotations and calendars is uttered by such disconcerting mentors as the wily Iago, the evil Lady Macbeth, and the dull Polonius.

The critic Malcolm Evans notes that on March 15 of the Reverend A. E. Sims's *A Shakespeare Birthday Book,* a calendar containing 365 improving sentiments sifted from the plays, the Reverend approvingly cites Lady Macbeth's exhortation to regicide:

> Wouldst thou have that
> Which thou esteem'st the ornament of life,
> And live a coward in thine own esteem,
> Letting "I dare not" wait upon "I would,"
> Like the poor cat i'the adage?
>
> (I.7.41–45)

(The cat in the adage is a cat who wanted fish but didn't want to get his feet wet.)

Similarly, taken out of context, the irony of Polonius's much-quoted advice to Laertes—"This above all: to thine own self be true"—is lost. It *sounds* like solid paternal advice, but the words take on a totally different meaning when we look at the speaker: as the court toady, Polonius is true *only* to himself. Similarly, the much-quoted precept "Neither a borrower nor a lender be" suggests Polonius's wary view of the world, in which everyone, including himself, is on the make. Here's some advice on making sense of Shakespearean advice: trust the speaker, not the speech.

According to Stanley Wells, associate editor of the New Penguin Shakespeare, "What Shakespeare says over and over again is that you've got to keep your mind open. His villains, such as Edmund and Iago, are rationalists who think they know all the answers; his heroes know they don't know. Viola in *Twelfth Night* gives herself over to fortune. She has an open mind to experience and she's continually learning. Shakespeare would have approved of this."

THE PROBLEM

The term "problem plays" refers specifically to three works, *All's Well That Ends Well*, *Troilus and Cressida*, and *Measure for Measure*. Often attributed to Shakespearean angst, the plays probably were, more prosaically, the result of the playwright's desire to capitalize on the interest in satire current during the early years of the seventeenth century.

Although grouped with the comedies in the First Folio, they are pungent satires on human vice, sexuality, folly, and greed. Today we would call them "black comedies," because they make us laugh at what we would normally find distasteful. Neither purely comic nor purely tragic, they fall into a disturbingly ambivalent limbo—which is

PLAYS

why they are considered problematical. Shakespeare offers no clear-cut answers to the social problems he presents in these plays. In fact, many of them finish without any resolution. By the end of *Troilus and Cressida,* the world hasn't changed and no one has reformed: the Trojan War continues its tedious course. And even the plays with "happy endings," *All's Well That Ends Well* and *Measure for Measure,* fail to provide the unqualified joy of a comic resolution. Their equivocal conclusions seem too glib, as if the play's complex issues and problems were now conveniently ignored—indeed, hadn't even existed. Moreover, the speedy repentances that conclude the comedies can be accepted with goodwill because their evil seems as fanciful as that of a fairy tale. But the realism of the problem plays, their explicit portrayal of infidelity, sexual dishonesty, and civic corruption, make such last-minute conversions unsatisfying and disturbing.

With clinical detachment, the problem plays reveal the more unsavory side of human nature. In the comedies we laugh at human folly with the joyous laughter of self-recognition; laughter in the problem plays is more reluctant, representing a less ready self-awareness.

The atmosphere in these plays is naturalistic, lacking the transcendent good humor of comedy and the cosmic redemption of tragedy. In the problem plays life is worldly and profane without a suggestion of any existence beyond the one portrayed. Their locations are starkly realistic: there's no magical Illyria or Forest of Arden here. The Vienna of *Measure for Measure* is a portrait of urban blight, a place where officials are no different from the underworld of pimps, whores, and thieves.

Finally, though they depict an amoral world, the plays themselves aren't lacking in moral standards. By exposing the worst of human existence, they hold a corrective mirror up to our vices. Like all satires, they are tacitly based upon a moral ideal, which though it exists in theory is consistently ignored in practice.

Troilus and Cressida

"**L**echery, lechery, still wars and lechery" pretty much sums up what must be one of the most disturbing plays ever written. First performed in about 1603, *Troilus and Cressida* is set in the Greek and Trojan camps during the Trojan War. According to most accounts, the war began when a young Trojan named Paris abducted the beautiful Helen from her husband, King Menelaus. But this glorious war, set off by the face that launched a thousand ships, and the inspiration for Homer's epic, is reduced in *Troilus and Cressida* to a locker-room joke. Shakespeare's version is about a whore named Helen and her cuckold husband. When the play opens, the war has been going on for seven years, without any end in sight. The soldiers are bored, their cause banal, yet they continue to fight and to die for a piece of soiled goods. Some of the Trojans want to return Helen, since her cause no longer means anything to them. But honor, by now a pointless ideal, bids them continue their tedious fight. Although classed with the tragedies in the First Folio, the play is not tragic. Tragedy deals with a hero's fall in a world of absolute good and evil; the world depicted in *Troilus and Cressida* is morally ambiguous and deals with the entire pageant of human vice and folly. The play's comedy derives from its mordant wit, not its dramatic situation.

Considered one of Shakespeare's least attractive plays, *Troilus and Cressida* was performed only sporadically after 1602, and then only in revised and refined versions. There is no record of any performance between 1734 and 1898, but after World War I its popularity increased, reaching a peak during the Vietnam era, when teachers and directors seemed obsessed by "relevance." Ignored for centuries, *Troilus and Cressida* took on new life in the twentieth century—an age all too familiar with the spiritual emptiness the play describes. Its despair, disillusionment, and disgust reassuringly confirm our own view of the world.

Most of the play's humor arises out of the bitter contrast between a superficial idealism and sordid reality. For example, all the great warriors of legend are here, but they're not the heroes we remember from history books: Achilles is a petulant homosexual who spends his days sulking in his tent and mimicking his superiors with his "masculine whore"; Ajax is a brainless jock; the wise Nestor is a long-winded bore, much given to talking about the good old days; and Hector, the most heroic character in this most unheroic of plays, is stabbed while unarmed by Achilles' thugs. So much for honor. The Greeks are political double-talkers, and the Trojans are filled with fruitless idealism.

The Trojan lovers, a grotesque parody of Romeo and Juliet, are the teenaged Troilus and Cressida, children of a country at war. Troilus is wildly infatuated with Cressida, so he coaxes her uncle Pandarus to procure her (hence our word "pander"). The two sleep together and then pledge undying love and fidelity. Like Shakespeare's star-crossed lovers, Troilus and Cressida have but one night of tenderness before they are forever parted. In less than twenty-four hours, Cressida, now a hostage to the Greeks, is already making her way to the enemy camp—and the bed of Diomedes. Cressida is no Juliet, willing to die for her beloved, but a shrewd woman who quickly assesses her chances for survival. As soon as she enters the Greek camp, it's clear she has no intention of honoring her pledge to Troilus. She will soon become just another camp whore, as experienced as Helen. The scene in which the romantic Troilus and the cynic Thersites watch Cressida succumb to another man (Act V, scene 2) is one of the most repellent—and fascinating—in all drama. The young man's disillusionment is counterpointed by Thersites' cackling as he, too, watches his nasty vision of life confirmed. Because this isn't a tragedy, Troilus, unlike Romeo, doesn't die, but survives in a world where survival is all.

Shakespeare's tragic heroes learn from their suffering: Lear achieves self-knowledge and humility; Othello acquires tragic grandeur. But Troilus is only diminished by his knowledge that love and war are simply other names for lust and power. As T. S. Eliot said in another context, "I should have been glad of another death."

What to Look for in
<u>Troilus and Cressida</u>

Thersites

A cynical observer, or "railer," who comments on all the action, Thersites sees through everything, reducing all human activity to war and lechery—and the characters in *Troilus and Cressida* vindicate his debased assessment of humanity. His ironic perspective, seen also in Jaques in *As You Like It,* is that of the detached outsider. He alone sees the discrepancy between the ideal and the real, and the conflict between what characters say and what they do. Out of all the characters, only Thersites sees and states the truth. His diatribes and curses, spat out with venomous rage, reflect his disillusionment and disgust with humanity. He acknowledges courage, honesty, and loyalty, but only as abstract ideals, for he knows that human beings will always act out of their own greed and lust. Inspired by his disgust with the world, Thersites is stunningly vulgar. The imagery of disease—plagues, ulcers, "guts-griping ruptures," venereal disorders, skin ailments, sores, and itches—permeates his speech, suggesting that humanity itself is festering.

Thersites has been compared to a war correspondent, and the analogy is apt, since he merely notes events without committing himself to either the Greeks or the Trojans. He also fulfills the traditional role of a fool; but unlike Feste, Touchstone, or Lear's Fool, he has no loyalty to anyone. Shakespearean fools defend their master's virtue, taking his side against a sinful or foolish world. In *Troilus,* however, both sides are unscrupulous, thus fidelity is pointless.

But as always in Shakespeare, a character has more than one dimension. At the end, we realize that the scurrilous Thersites is the most idealistic of the lot. His pessimism is born out of disenchanted idealism. Cressida, who seemed so romantic, turns out to be a worldly whore. And by Act V, Troilus, the amorous dreamer, has become as soured as Thersites.

*U*lysses' speech in Act I, scene 3, is one of the most famous passages in Shakespeare, and one that's traditionally used to illustrate the Elizabethan world picture. Modern critics say that the speech must be looked at in context; it is, after all, spoken by a shrewd politician and is a superb piece of rhetoric. The speech is about authority, order, hierarchy, the rhythms of the universe, the revolutions of the stars, the ebb and flow of the seas. Ulysses describes the universe as a stringed instrument: "untune" one string and all harmony collapses and chaos reigns. War on earth provokes disturbances in the heavens as well as anarchy within the heart of man: see page 61.

*S*hakespeare continually reminds us that we, too, are implicated in his sick vision of society. He won't let us leave the theatre thinking, Well, that's all right for the stage, but I'm different. In an epilogue, the leering Pandarus steps out and addresses the audience directly: we are his brothers, fellow "traders in the flesh," and he ends his speech by bequeathing us his diseases.

Troilus and Cressida is definitely not a crowd pleaser; at times the language is tortured and hard to follow. But it reveals that poetry doesn't need to be about love and beauty, and can, in fact, spring from the most sordid circumstances. While the play disturbs, it also makes us think, question, probe. If the romantic comedies depict a life better than our own, the problem plays reveal humanity at its worst. *Troilus and Cressida* challenges our assumptions about the "glory" of war, heroism, and love. We may laugh at its wit—but with the laughter of the damned.

A Glossary of Shakespearean Invective

Shakespeare loved insults, invectives, and curses, whether a full-blooded volley of words or a short, pointed barb. Some, like those in the comedies, are deft jabs of wit. But others, like Lear's curse on Gonerill's fertility and Timon's execration on the Athenian senators, are almost too appalling to say aloud, the language is so potent.

The All-Purpose Insult

❖ Whoreson: Similar to our SOB; used to connect a string of epithets, e.g., "thou clay-brained guts, thou knotty-pated fool, thou whoreson obscene greasy tallow-catch." [A tallow-catch was a large tub used to collect the waxy drippings from candle making.] (*Henry IV, Part 1*, II.4.222–24.)

❖ Thou slander of thy heavy mother's womb! (*Richard III*, I.3.230–31)

❖ Thou loathèd issue of thy father's loins! (*Richard III*, I.3.231)

❖ Were I like thee I'd throw away myself. (*Timon of Athens*, III.4.100)

❖ You are as a candle, the better part burnt out. (*Henry IV, Part 2*, I.2.158–59)

❖ If he were opened and you find so much blood in his liver as will clog the foot of a flea, I'll eat the rest of the anatomy. (*Twelfth Night*, III.2.58–60)

❖ Thou are a boil, / A plague-sore, or embossed carbuncle, / In my corrupted blood. (*King Lear*, II.4.218–20)

❖ Go suck the subtle blood o' th' grape / Till the high fever seethe your blood to froth. (*Timon of Athens*, IV.3.425–26)

❖ Fouler than heart can think thee, thou canst make / No excuse current but to hang thyself. (*Richard III*, I.2.83–84)

Bores

❖ Well said, that was laid on with a trowel. (*As You Like It*, I.2.99)

❖ Harp not on that string. . . . (*Richard III*, IV.4.364)

❖ You cram these words into mine ears against / The stomach of my sense. (*The Tempest*, II.1.108–9)

❖ More of your conversation would infect my brain. . . . (*Coriolanus*, II.1.88–89)

Curses

❖ Now the rotten diseases of the south, guts-griping ruptures, catarrhs, loads o'gravel i'th'back, lethargies, cold palsies, and the like . . . take and take again such preposterous discoveries! (*Troilus and Cressida*, V.1.17–20)

❖ To general filths / Convert o' th' instant, green virginity! / Do it in your parents eyes! (*Timon of Athens*, IV.1.6–8)

❖ Son of sixteen, / Pluck the lined crutch from thy old limping sire; / With it beat out his brains! (*Timon of Athens*, IV.1.13–15)

❖ The devil damn thee black, thou cream-faced loon! (*Macbeth*, V.3.11)

Get Lost!

❖ Out, you green-sickness carrion! Out, you baggage! / You tallow face! (*Romeo and Juliet*, III.5.157–58)

❖ I thank you for your company, but, good faith, I had as lief have been myself alone. (*As You Like It*, III.2.246–47)

❖ Direct thy feet / Where thou and I henceforth may never meet. (*Twelfth Night*, V.1.166–67)

❖ Go thou, and fill another room in hell. (*Richard II*, V.5.107)

❖ Go, shake your ears. [An allusion to an ass's gesture.] (*Twelfth Night*, II.3.121)

❖ Away, you scullion! You rampallian! You fustilarian! I'll tickle your catastrophe! [A rampallion is a ruffian; "fustilarian" is a made-up word, suggestive of "fusty" or "fustian," a poor homespun fabric; "I'll tickle your catastrophe" was a popular phrase of the time.] (*Henry IV, Part 2*, II.1.57–58)

Hypocrisy

❖ Live loathed and long, / Most smiling, smooth, and detested parasites, / Courteous destroyers, affable wolves, meek bears, / You fools of fortune, trencher-friends, time's flies, / Cap-and-knee slaves, vapors, and minute-jacks! / Of man and beast the infinite malady / Crust you quite o'er! [Minute-jacks are the mechanical jacks that strike bells in clocks; "cap-and-knee" means obsequious, i.e., with one's cap held to the knee; "trencher-friends" refers to those who eat table scraps, the remains left on a trencher, or the flat wooden board used to serve meat.] (*Timon of Athens*, III.6.90–96.)

Insults Impugning Masculinity

❖ Zounds, an I were now by this rascal I could brain him with his lady's fan. (*Henry IV, Part I*, II.3.23–24)

❖ . . . such a dish of skim milk . . . (*Henry IV, Part 1*, II.3.34)

Obesity

❖ She is spherical, like a globe. I could find out countries in her. (*The Comedy of Errors*, III.2.120–21)

❖ [He] sweats to death, / And lards the lean earth as he walks along. (*Henry IV, Part 1*, II.2.106–7)

❖ [She's so fat] I warrant her rags and the tallow in them will burn a Poland winter. ["Tallow" means grease and sweat.] (*The Comedy of Errors*, III.2.101–2)

❖ . . . that trunk of humours, that bolting-hutch of beastliness, that swollen parcel of dropsies, that huge bombard of sack, that stuffed cloak-bag of guts, that roasted Manningtree ox with the pudding in his belly . . . ["Humours" are secretions; "Manningtree ox" refers to an ox that was often roasted whole at fairs; "pudding" means "stuffing."] (*Henry IV, Part 1*, II.4.437–41)

Personal Hygiene

❖ . . . I do smell all horse-piss, at which my nose is in great indignation. (*The Tempest*, IV.1.199–200)

❖ You are the musty chaff, and you are smelt / Above the moon. (*Coriolanus*, V.1.32–33)

❖ Would thou wert clean enough to spit upon! (*Timon of Athens*, IV.3.356)

❖ She sweats a man may go overshoes in the grime of it. (*The Comedy of Errors*, III.2.107–8)

Repartee

❖ PETRUCHIO. Nay, come, Kate, come, you must not look so sour.
KATHERINA. It is my fashion when I see a crab. (*The Taming of the Shrew*, II.1.226–27)

❖ LUCIO. . . . I know what I know.
DUKE. I can hardly believe that, since you know not what you speak. (*Measure for Measure*, III.2.144–45)

❖ APEMANTUS. When I know not what else to do, I'll see thee again.
TIMON. When there is nothing living but thee, thou shalt be welcome. (*Timon of Athens*, IV.3.351–52)

❖ OSWALD. What dost thou know me for?
KENT. A knave, a rascal, an eater of broken meats, a base, proud, shallow, beggarly, three-suited, hundred-pound, filthy-worsted-stocking knave; a lily-livered, action-taking, whoreson glass-gazing super-serviceable finical rogue, one-trunk-inheriting slave; one that wouldst be a bawd in way of good service, and art nothing but the composition of a knave, beggar, coward, pander, and the son and heir of a mongrel bitch; one whom I will beat into clamorous whining if thou deniest the least syllable of thy addition. ["Broken meats" are table scraps; "three-suited" refers to the amount of clothing allotted to servants; "action-taking" is one who sues rather than fights, thus "unmanly"; "glass-gazing" means narcissistic; "super-serviceable" means meddlesome and servile; "finical" means foppish; "one-trunk-inheriting" is one who owns enough to fill only one trunk; "bawd" and "pander" mean "pimp"; "addition" means name.] (*King Lear*, II.2.12–22)

Stupidity

❖ AJAX. I shall cut out your tongue.
THERSITES. 'Tis no matter; I shall speak as much as thou afterwards. (*Troilus and Cressida*, II.1.109–11)

❖ . . . he has not so much brain as ear-wax. (*Troilus and Cressida*, V.1.49–50)

❖ Thou has pared thy wit o' both sides and left nothing i'the middle. (*King Lear*, I.4.183)

Threats

❧ Guard thy head; for I intend to have it ere long. (*Henry VI, Part 1,* I.2.127)

❧ Let me go grind their bones to powder small / And with this hateful liquor temper it; / And in that paste let their vile heads be baked. (*Titus Andronicus,* V.2.198–200)

❧ I'll unhair thy head! / Thou shalt be whipped with wire and stew'd in brine, / Smarting in lingering pickle! (*Antony and Cleopatra,* II.5.66–68)

Ugliness

❧ The tartness of his face sours ripe grapes. (*Coriolanus,* V.4.17)

❧ ...his face is the worst thing about him. (*Measure for Measure,* II.1.148–49)

❧ I never can see him but I am heart-burned an hour after. (*Much Ado About Nothing,* II.1.5)

❧ Thou elvish-marked, abortive, rooting hog! ["Elvish-marked" means disfigured by elves; "abortive" means monstrous.] (*Richard III,* I.3.227)

Womankind

❧ Paint till a horse may mire upon your face. / A pox of wrinkles! (*Timon of Athens,* IV.3.148–49)

❧ Dear goddess, hear! / Suspend thy purpose if thou didst intend / To make this creature fruitful. / Into her womb convey sterility, / Dry up in her organs of increase, / And from her derogate body never spring / A babe to honour her. If she must teem, / Create her child of spleen, that it may live / And be a thwart disnatured torment to her. (*King Lear,* I.4.273–81)

❖ Her beauty and her brain go not together. (*Cymbeline*, 1.2.24–25)

❖ Could I come near your beauty with my nails, / I could set my ten commandments on your face. (*Henry VI, Part 2*, I.3.139–40)

❖ God has given you one face and you make yourselves another. (*Hamlet*, III.1.144–45)

❖ Triple-turned whore! (*Antony and Cleopatra*, IV.12.13)

The Unfriendly Shakespeare

*N*ot everyone likes Shakespeare—and some are quite eloquent in their disgust.

I remember, the Players have often mentioned it as an honour to Shakespeare that in his writing, (whatsoever he penned) he never blotted out a line. My answer hath been, would he had blotted a thousand.

—BEN JONSON

*S*hakespeare never has six lines together without a fault.

—SAMUEL JOHNSON

*W*hen you pick him up later in life you find it almost impossible to overcome the prejudice established against him by the school-masters, by their way of presenting him. Shakespeare was just the pompous, flatulent sort of giant whom the English *would* convert into a sacred bull. Lacking depth, they gave him girth and a girth that ill conceals the stuffed pillows.

—HENRY MILLER

*T*olstoy diligently tried to like Shakespeare, but without much success:

My perplexity was increased by the fact that I have always keenly felt the beauties of poetry in all its forms; why then did Shakespeare's works, recognized by the whole world as works of artistic genius, not only fail to please me, but even seem detestable?

He paid Chekhov the supreme compliment, telling him that his plays were "even worse than Shakespeare's."

*S*hakespeare should not be put into the hands of the young without the warning that the foolish things in his plays were written to please the foolish, the filthy for the filthy, and the brutal for the brutal; and that if out of veneration for his genius we were led to admire or even tolerate such things, we may be thereby not conforming ourselves to him, but only degrading ourselves to the level of his audience. . . .

—ROBERT BRIDGES

*S*hakespear, (whom you and ev'ry Play-house bill
Style the divine, the matchless, what you will)
For gain, not glory, wing'd his roving flight,
And grew immortal in his own despight.

—ALEXANDER POPE

*S*hakespeare's name, you may depend on it, stands absurdly too high and will go down. He has no invention as to stories, none whatever. He took all his plots from old novels and threw their stories into a dramatic shape, at as little expense of thought as you or I could turn his plays back again into prose tales. . . . Suppose anyone to have had the dramatic handling for the first time of such ready-made stories as *Lear, Macbeth,* & c. and he would be a sad fellow indeed if he did not make something very grand of them.

—LORD BYRON

I do not believe that any writer has ever exposed this *bovaryisme,* the human will to see things as they are not, more clearly than Shakespeare.

—T. S. ELIOT

*S*hakespeare is a drunken savage with some imagination whose plays can please only in London and Canada.

—VOLTAIRE

*T*he most insipid ridiculous play that I ever saw in my life.

—SAMUEL PEPYS (On *A Midsummer Night's Dream*)

Shaks versus Shav

*W*ith his usual astuteness at pointing out the mindless follies of the common herd, George Bernard Shaw deplored the unthinking worship of Shakespeare and invented a word for it: bardolatry. Only Shaw, or so he believed, truly saw through Shakespeare's bloated reputation—everyone else was a participant in a mass delusion. Shakespeare's reputation rankled Shaw, who hated sharing top billing with anyone. To Shaw, whose plays are social commentary, Shakespeare's ideas were "platitudinous fudge," a remnant of the tired old order:

The fact is we are growing out of Shakespeare . . . he is nothing but a household pet. His characters still live; his word pictures of woodland and wayside still give us a Bank-holiday breath of country air; his verse still charms us; his sublimities still stir us; the commonplaces and trumperies of the wisdom which age and experience bring to all the rest of us are still expressed by him better than by anybody else; but we have nothing to hope from him,

---

TWO RIVALS OF SHAKESPEARE COMMENT

He was not of an age, but for all time!

—BEN JONSON

He was of an afternoon, but not for all time.

—GEORGE BERNARD SHAW

and nothing to learn from him—not even how to write plays, though he does that so much better than most modern dramatists.

According to the critic Edwin Wilson, Shaw blamed Shakespeare for failing to anticipate the contemporary problems that Shaw considered important. Yet despite his disgust with Shakespeare, Shaw continued to write obsessively about him, like a son who wants to be free of his father but continually returns home to berate him. Whenever Shaw mentions Shakespeare, he seems to be mentally tallying up their respective merits and liabilities, and he can't think about Shakespeare without considering himself: "With the single exception of Homer, there is no eminent writer, not even Sir Walter Scott, whom I can despise so entirely as I despise Shakespear [sic] when I measure my mind against his." Shaw even rewrote the final scene of *Cymbeline,* which he called "stagey melodramatic trash of the lowest order," and in 1949 he wrote a puppet drama called "Shaks versus Shav."

Jan Kott

*I*t's no exaggeration to say that Polish critic Jan Kott's Shakespeare
Our Contemporary *is this century's most influential work on Shake-*
speare. His disciples are legion, most notably Sir Peter Hall and Peter
Brook; their debt to Kott is seen in Hall's erotic A Midsummer Night's
Dream *and Brook's nihilistic* King Lear.

Translated into English in 1964, Shakespeare Our Contemporary
revealed a new Shakespeare, one who was part of modern experience and
spoke directly to contemporary anxieties and concerns. Looking beyond the
clichés of the doublet-and-hose tradition, Kott saw Hamlet not as a rarefied
prince who speaks in operatic blank verse, but a rebel who doubts his
cause, a young man who questions the validity of existence. Kott's Lear
peers into the abyss and sees that life is a purposeless journey from cradle
to grave. This is not predigested Shakespeare, but a new and darker one
who speaks to us today.

NE: *What do you mean when you call Shakespeare "our contemporary"?*

JK: The answer is quite easy. Of course Shakespeare is universal—
because he is alive after over four hundred years, and in so many countries and for so many times. At times, and especially in the second half
of our century, he is very, very topical.

NE: *Why is he more topical now?*

JK: Shakespeare was topical when I wrote my book twenty-five years
ago in Poland, because it presented a new interpretation of history, of
the terror of history, of that kind of terrorism. The politics of Shakespeare were relevant, especially his depiction of a cruel king, which
could be a reflection of Hitler or Stalin.

Shakespeare is topical today because he's connected by the screen and television—the machine—to different cultures and through different cultures and traditions. Shakespeare is again and again interpreted. For example, there's Kurosawa's *Throne of Blood,* his Japanese version of *Macbeth,* and *Ran,* his Samurai *King Lear.* Of course, any great interpretation of Shakespeare on screen must be topical and new. An example of this would be Branagh's *Henry V.* The play was understood for a long time as Olivier's wartime patriotic movie. Now it's a bloody antiwar film.

Shakespeare is also topical because of our interest in sex and sexism. Sexuality and its ambiguity in Shakespeare is very strong. It relates to our own sexual revolution and to the idea of homosexuality. This generation can find in Shakespeare a different kind of sexual relationship, such as homosexuality, which in other ages was hidden.

NE: *Is there one play that's more topical than most?*

JK: *Troilus and Cressida.* I was always very touched by Cressida. Of all Shakespeare's women, she is our vision of a modern girl. I would choose Cressida over Portia any day.

Many, many years ago, when I was teaching, I would ask my students, "Out of all Shakespearean characters, who would you most like to have as a lover?" And I had a nun in my class. Later, I thought my question was not very tactful, to ask a nun who she would like to sleep with! But she was very wise and very blunt. And she told me, "Hamlet, of course, because Hamlet would say, 'Let's go to the nunnery'!"

*F*elicia Londré, professor of theatre at the University of Missouri, notes that after the fall of the Berlin Wall, the critic Thomas Engel said that all contemporary German plays suddenly became obsolete; the only contemporary dramatist was Shakespeare.

Is Shakespeare
Still Our
Contemporary?

*I*n 1989, a public seminar organized by the British division of the International Association of Theatre Critics met at the Old Vic Theatre in London in honor of the twenty-fifth anniversary of the publication of *Shakespeare Our Contemporary.* The panel was composed of scholars, critics, poets, and directors, and its purpose was to address the question, "Is Shakespeare Still Our Contemporary?" John Elsom, who edited the conference's proceedings, wrote:

> The fact that Shakespeare's plays are performed more widely around the world, and more often, than those of any other dramatist, living or dead, is itself a phenomenon as startling as the proposition that he could be our contemporary. If it could be somehow proved that one man's plays really had overcome the barriers of language, race, creed, and custom, as well as time, if it could be demonstrated that the proclaimed "universality" of Shakespeare was something more than poetic license on the part of his enthusiasts, than we might not have added much to the libraries of Shakespearean criticism, but we would have gained a valuable insight into the cultural software which drives our mental computers.

Participants vociferously disagreed with one another on such questions as Shakespeare's suitability for television, his sexism, and his Englishness. But for the most part they agreed that different plays are topical at different times, while others, like *Love's Labour's Lost,* are more embedded in the Elizabethan experience and thus are less likely to bridge the gap that separates today's audience from Shakespeare's. Specifically political plays, such as *Julius Caesar* and *Coriolanus,* are especially topical at certain historical moments; other plays indirectly address contemporary social issues, such as anti-Semitism in *The Merchant of Venice* and racism in *Othello.* A play becomes "contemporary" when it transcends its particular setting and speaks to the audience about their own experience, whether personal, political, or social. Of course, that one generation can applaud a "tamed" Kate, and another rejoice to see her give Petruchio a sly kick, says more about the two ages than about Shakespeare or the play. Here are some examples of plays that have been topical in our own century:

❖ With its emphasis on trust, eavesdropping, and spying, *Hamlet* is regarded as ideal for the Watergate era, the only difference being that Polonius spies from behind an arras, while Nixon's "courtiers" used electronic means. The analogy between the Nixon presidency's hidden "cancer," which permeated the entire government from the highest official on down, was likened to Claudius's festering Denmark.

❖ Prospero's usurpation of Caliban's island in *The Tempest*, and his enslavement of the native, upon whom he imposes his own, "civilized" values and language, is now regarded as a critique of imperialism.

❖ Hamlet's incredulity that thousands would willingly die for a tiny plot of ground—all for the sake of honor—has been used as a comment on the Falklands war.

❖ *Romeo and Juliet* took on new meaning during the 1960s, when the two teenagers were perceived as flower children ("Make love, not war") rebelling against the older generation.

❖ In light of the women's movement, *The Taming of the Shrew* has been interpreted as a scathing examination of sexual politics: marriage, a product of capitalism, is nothing more than an auction in which a woman is sold to the highest bidder. Once bought, she is her husband's possession, to do with as he likes.

❖ In its depiction of the futility of war and its indictment of honor without conviction, *Troilus and Cressida,* never before a popular play, flourished during the Vietnam War.

❖ *A Midsummer Night's Dream* contains all the elements to make it a perfect play about the sixties: parents who don't understand, partner swapping, and drug-induced madness.

❖ *Coriolanus* and *Julius Caesar* have been used to indict totalitarian regimes, with Caesar variously appearing as De Gaulle, Mussolini, and Hitler figures.

Sonnet Boom

*With this key, Shakespeare opened
his heart.*

      —*WILLIAM WORDSWORTH*

*Did he?
If so, the less Shakespeare he!*

      —*ROBERT BROWNING*

*With this key, Shakespeare let
down his pants.*

      —*ALDOUS HUXLEY*

"Sonneteering" was the major literary fad when Shakespeare began writing his own sequence in the early 1590s. Imported from Italy, the sonnet form was regarded as continental and elegant, and practically every fashionable courtier tried his hand at writing at least one. When a gentleman wanted to seduce a lady, he didn't send her chocolates; he sent her a "sugared sonnet" of his own invention. Most of these were clichéd confections about anonymous mistresses with lips like cherries and hair like golden wires. A favorite bit of flattery was to compare a lady's breath to perfume, and since the Elizabethans hadn't yet discovered dental hygiene, this was a genuine compliment. After reading hundreds of sonnets populated by blond angels with milk-white skin, it's easy to see why Shakespeare's Dark Lady, with her swarthy complexion and raven hair, makes such a stunning entrance—precisely because she is nothing like the sun and her breath "reeks."

C. S. Lewis conveniently divided late medieval and Elizabethan verse into the Drab and the Golden, categories that beautifully express the difference between Shakespeare's verse and that of his predecessors and less gifted contemporaries. Inheriting a lusterless tradition, Shakespeare, a poetic Midas, gilds it with his touch to dazzling effect. After plowing though line after line of Drab verse, with its wooden if earnest compliments and lumbering eight-syllabic lines, you not only see but *feel* the impact and power of Shakespeare's sonnets—how direct they are, infused with irony and passion. Compare this Drab beginning by an anonymous poet: "A sweet attractive kind of grace / A full assurance given by lookes, / Continual comfort in a face / The lineament of Gospel books," or "When dreadful death with dint of piercing dart . . ." to Shakespeare's sardonic opening to Sonnet 138: "When my love swears that she is made of truth / I do believe her, though I know she lies, / That she might think me some untutored youth, / Unlearnèd in the world's false subtleties." There is a unique voice behind the words—not a generic courtier mouthing flattery, but a speaker of originality and depth.

Unlike drama, verse was regarded as a personal and aristocratic art form. It wasn't aimed at the general populace—in fact, it was considered *infra dig* actually to publish sonnets. Before their unauthorized publication, Shakespeare's sonnets were privately circulated in manuscript form. His early poems, "The Rape of Lucrece" and "Venus and Adonis"—and, some say, the Sonnets—were dedicated to the Earl of Southampton, Henry Wriothesley (pronounced, in the usual improbable English manner, as "Risley"). For a relative unknown it was a coup to get the Southampton name on the title page. No one knows how Shakespeare met Southampton, but the Earl was a well-known patron of the arts, and certainly Shakespeare was not averse to a little social climbing.

Scholars generally agree that Shakespeare took more care with his verse than with his dramas. Popular drama was his livelihood, what he did to survive; but verse was his art, what he did to ensure immortality.

The Sonnet

A sonnet is a highly structured poem with fourteen lines and a specific rhyme scheme. Each line must have ten syllables with a steady unstressed, stressed beat: "Shall I compare thee to a summer's day?" rhythmically translates into da DA daDA da DA da DAda DA. The challenge of fitting a thought or an idea into a strict rhythmic structure forces a poet to be more creative. As if entering a labyrinth in which all traditional avenues are cut off, the poet must explore new and more circuitous routes to reach his goal. The difficulty lies in trying to compress all that passion into such a tight, formal structure.

The Sequence

*A*mbitious poets wrote sonnet sequences, or cycles, that detailed the ups and downs of an extended love affair, with each sonnet describing a different mood or stage in the process. Contemporary poets often divulge intimate details of their private lives, so we modern readers might automatically assume that Shakespeare did the same. While it's tempting to read these intensely introspective sonnets as the key that unlocked Shakespeare's heart, we can't identify the speaker of the poems with the historical Shakespeare. Like most great artists, Shakespeare probably created a persona, or mask, through which he expressed his intimate thoughts. We'll never know if the Sonnets were inspired by actual relationships or were impersonal literary exercises. To be cautious, let's just say that Shakespeare used his life experiences as he used the sources for his plays: as inspiration, not slavish transcription. The Sonnets aren't true confessions, but works of art.

Cast of Characters

The Poet: Serious, triumphant, self-loathing, witty, wistful, flirtatious, avuncular, and bitter by turns, he is unmatched in English poetry for the complex variety of his voice. Although his mood changes from one sonnet to the next, his prevailing tone is one of middle-aged weariness, and he is obsessed by the passage of time.

The Fair Young Man: Variously referred to by critics as "the friend," "the fair friend," and "the sweet boy," he is a young, callow, and beautiful aristocrat who is not as good as he should be. As Sonnet 94 suggests, he is a man "who, moving others, [is himself] as stone." Sonnet 136 punningly indicates that his name could also be Will.

The Dark Lady: A vamp, "mad, bad, and dangerous to know." She appears at Sonnet 127. It's likely she is married (Sonnet 152), and if critics are right in their interpretation of Sonnets 135 and 136, then her husband is also named Will.

The Rival Poet: Another poet, also writing poems to the fair young man. He is learned, worldly, and prosperous, and the speaker is jealous of his success in worldly ventures. He appears in Sonnets 78 to 86.

Shakespeare's Ménage à Trois

*T*he 154 Sonnets make up a poetic sequence—a melodramatic tale of love, lust, and betrayal. More important, they are serious meditations on the quintessential Shakespearean themes of love, death, art, and time. While individual sonnets are magnificent (some are mediocre) and can be appreciated independently, when read as a whole they have a cumulative power. Since they unfold sequentially, the reader can trace the vicissitudes of the poet's love life, its torments and pleasures. Moreover, groups of sonnets work together, as if the poet were conducting a debate in which one poem raises a problem or question that is then explored and answered in others.

Most of the sonnets are addressed to a young nobleman, a man blessed with beauty, birth, and charm. In the first section, composed of Sonnets 1 to 17, the poet—an older, less attractive man of inferior birth—urges his dashing friend to get married and procreate so that he can multiply his loveliness and immortalize his rare beauty. But the young man bristles at this paternal advice, preferring more casual attachments. His obstinacy, however, becomes our good fortune: in Sonnet 18 the poet says that he'll immortalize his friend "in eternal lines." Throughout the sequence, he dwells obsessively on the ravages of "devouring time" and the transcendent power of verse to preserve beauty and youth "to the edge of doom."

But more than homages to beauty, the Sonnets are also about the difficulty of writing sincere verse. In several, particularly Sonnet 18, the poet struggles to find the exact simile that would convey the boy's astonishing beauty: "Shall I," he tentatively begins, "compare thee to a summer's day?" But all the usual tropes won't do: "Thou art more lovely and more temperate." To the Elizabethans, the short lyric was like a snapshot—a desperate attempt to capture an elusive moment.

In Sonnets 78 to 86, the speaker complains of a rival for the young man's affections, a more successful poet to whom the speaker compares himself unfavorably. And as if all this weren't enough, he occasionally hears disquieting rumors about his friend's unruly behavior and hopes that they aren't true. In Sonnet 42, we learn that the boy has stolen the poet's mistress; but, ever ready to excuse his friend, the poet eagerly and wittily turns disaster into good fortune: "If I lose thee, my loss is my love's gain, / And, losing her, my friend hath found that loss. . . ." Torn by his love for the boy and his horror at his conduct, the poet both accuses and absolves. In some sonnets, notably 41, 93, and 94, he offers advice: "Lilies that fester smell far worse than weeds" (i.e., the moral fall of a virtuous man is worse than that of an ordinary mortal).

Abruptly, in Sonnet 127, the notorious Dark Lady makes her entrance, and immediately she holds the poet in thrall. This lady of darkness evokes all the mystery of Shakespeare's powerful women, and, as her epithet suggests, she's the antithesis of the fair young man. Neither blond, nor male, nor virtuous, she is nothing like the sun or a summer's day: the Dark Lady is pure midnight witchery, a dangerous female who has seduced centuries of readers since her first appearance in 1609.

With the Lady's arrival, the Sonnets become more explicitly sexual, with bawdy puns (particularly in Sonnet 151) flying fast and loose. The poet's tone is sardonic and knowing. What's so compelling about this relationship is his cold-eyed appraisal of his mistress's character. Acknowledging that she is neither good nor true, not even conventionally pretty, he is caught in a curious state, seeing what she is but remaining nonetheless enslaved. He knows he is lying to himself, and yet he continues to believe his self-deception: "Thou blind fool, Love, what dost thou to mine eyes / That they behold and see not what they see?" And although he is "frantic-mad" with love that threatens at times to undermine his self-control, he preserves an icy self-possession that never lets him forget that this lady is a whore. Man and mistress are locked in a mutual web of falsehood and deceit in which each pretends to believe the other's lies. Their love is thus a cynical contract in which each agrees to wink at the other's frailties.

> When my love swears that she is made of truth
> I do believe her, though I know she lies,
> That she might think me some untutored youth,
> Unlearnèd in the world's false subtleties.

(Sonnet 138)

The Dark Lady sonnets are filled with images of syphilis and sin, damnation and despair. Sex is a bait; the lover is haunted, maddened with desire and self-disgust, by turns yearning and remorseful. His desire—along with his language—is harsh and violent and tormented, yet Shakespeare the poet is always in perfect control. "My love is as a fever, longing still / For that which longer nurseth the disease. . . ." ("Still" means "continually.") Lust, he asserts, is "perjured, murd'rous, bloody, full of blame, / Savage, extreme, rude, cruel, not to trust. . . ." He can barely spit out the words. He is locked in a perpetual cycle of frustration and satiation; his appetite is always "had, having, and in quest to have . . ." The lines end with "in quest to have," because his desire is never sated. In the early sonnets, married sexuality produces an abundance of beauty; but the poet's perverted desire for the Dark Lady is "a waste of shame." And "waste" refers not only to the poet's sense of degradation but to a literal waste as well: the squandering of the life force on a relationship that will bear no fruit.

Finally, in the concluding sonnets, the poet discovers that his fair friend has also been bedding the Dark Lady, and the sequence concludes with all three entangled in a sordid *ménage à trois.* The poet is damned, the woman lost, the friend forgotten, and the Sonnets end on a note of cynicism and disgust, with nothing resolved. But because they are ultimately about art, which captures and transfixes pain and passion, the poems transcend the immediate and the ephemeral and, triumphantly, defeat time.

The Mystery of the Sonnets

With the exception of *Hamlet,* the Sonnets have generated more speculation and controversy than any other Shakespearean work. The intrigue begins with the curious title page, with its cryptic epigraph, and ends with the question of the poet's sexuality. The printer's address on the Sonnets' title page reads, "To the onlie begetter of these ensuing sonnets Mr W.H." This is where the hunt begins, taking the dogged literary sleuth into both the sexual habits and the printing practices of the Elizabethan age.

Commentators have variously speculated about the term "begetter," a word that suggests a plethora of meanings. Since the Sonnets were first published in an unauthorized, "pirated," edition, "begetter" could refer to the person who procured the Sonnets for Thomas Thorpe, their printer. It could refer to the young man whose beauty is the subject of so many of the poems; or it could even signify the author himself. Some say that "Mr W.H.," by a reversal of initials, is a cryptic allusion to the poet's patron, Henry Wriothesley, who *was* beautiful, younger than the poet, and of dubious sexuality. But a nobleman wouldn't be called "Master," an honorific reserved for an untitled gentleman. Most likely, "Mr W.H." was the recipient of the printer's dedication and not Shakespeare's patron or lover. More amusing is the hypothesis of the scholars Katharine Wilson and D. Bernstorff that "W.H." stands for "William Himself" and is a joking reference to the poet. The critic Donald W. Foster convincingly argues that the analogy between writing poems and childbirth was an Elizabethan commonplace often used in dedications, and thus the Sonnets' "begetter" is, of course, the author. According to Foster, "Mr W.H." is a printer's error for "Mr W SH," which, if true, would make it the most celebrated typo in literary history.

Who is the fair friend? Several candidates have been named, but

Henry Wriothesley remains the top contender. William Herbert, the Earl of Pembroke, is another choice, since the First Folio is dedicated to him, although there's no evidence Shakespeare ever knew him. Imaginative speculation has provided more possibilities. The hero of Oscar Wilde's short story "The Portrait of Mr W.H." is convinced that "Mr W.H." is a boy actor by the name of Willie Hughes. His main evidence is line four of Sonnet 20, where the poet praises the young man as "A man in hues all hues in his controlling. . . ." Since Willie played women's parts, he could easily have been the "master-mistress" of the poet's passion. Typically, Wilde became enamored of his own fiction: "You must believe in Willie Hughes, I almost do myself," he reportedly said.

Who is the Dark Lady? At one time the primary candidate was Mary Fitton, a lady-in-waiting to the queen, until her portrait was discovered and dashed all hopes: Mary was decidedly blond. Then the Elizabethan historian A. L. Rowse discovered the private journals of the astrologer Simon Forman (1552–1611), who, consulted by ladies on matters sexual and personal, was the Elizabethan equivalent of a gynecologist-astrologer-psychiatrist. His daily records allow us a glimpse of Elizabethan women, their anxieties and desires. Through the pages of Forman's records, Rowse discovered Emilia Lanier, née Bassano, who he believes was Shakespeare's mysterious lover. Emilia was the mistress of Lord Hunsdon (the patron of Shakespeare's first company), and after her noble lover had made her pregnant, he married her off in 1592 to Captain Alfonso Lanier, a musician of the court. Rowse notes that Mrs. Mountjoy, Shakespeare's landlady, also was a frequent visitor to Forman's establishment, and thus Shakespeare may have met Emilia through the Mountjoy/Hunsdon/Forman connection.

The Diary of Simon Forman, by A. L. Rowse, yields fascinating insights into the sex lives of ordinary and upper-class Elizabethans. Among other idiosyncrasies, Forman couldn't bring himself to write "sexual intercourse," preferring the inexplicable code word "halek," as in "I did halek with her."

Was Shakespeare Gay?

*I*f Shakespeare were to apply for an NEA grant on the basis of the Sonnets, he would probably be denied one. There is profound resistance to accepting Shakespeare, the icon of Western civilization, as gay. High school teachers introduce Shakespeare's Sonnets as passionate love lyrics, neglecting to mention that they were written to a man, while many scholars read the poems as expressions of male friendship, ignoring their frank homoeroticism. But there's no getting around it: the Sonnets are clearly addressed to a young man, and even allowing for what professors call the "Renaissance cult of male friendship," many of the poems are quite ardent. It could be that editors have overemphasized the importance of this cult as a way of explaining away what would otherwise be undeniably homoerotic. Nonetheless, no other straight poet has ever written such ardent poems to another man. This doesn't mean that the poems can be understood or appreciated only as homosexual poems; they are universal lyrics about love—which happen to be addressed to a man. We'll never know whether the eroticism went beyond poetic imaginings or if the relationship was ever consummated. There has, however, been a conspiracy of silence concerning Shakespeare's sexuality.

*J*oseph Pequigney, the first critic to treat the Sonnets convincingly as a homosexual love sequence, describes in his book *Such Is My Love* a lecture by W. H. Auden on the Sonnets, which would later become the introduction to the Signet edition of the poems (1964). In it, Auden "chides" the homosexual reader who ignores the fact that Shakespeare was a husband and father. But Robert Craft in his diaries reveals that at a dinner party at Igor Stravinsky's house shortly afterward, Auden said, "It won't do just yet to admit that the top Bard was in the homintern."

In the ambiguous Sonnet 20, the poet suggests his sexual attraction to the young man, the "master-mistress of my passion," but he ends the sonnet by wittily pointing out that Nature has thwarted his amorous intentions:

> And for a woman wert thou first created,
> Till Nature as she wrought thee fell a-doting,
> And by addition me of thee defeated,
> By adding one thing to my purpose nothing.
> > But since she pricked thee out for women's pleasure,
> > Mine be thy love, and thy love's use their treasure.

("Thing" refers to penis, while "treasure" refers to the female genitalia.)

For some, this sonnet is the frank expression of the poet's sexual desire for the young man, and the addition of the "one thing" defeats the poet's procreative, but not his sexual, desire. Others see the sonnet as proof that the poet's lust for the young man is never consummated; women "use" the friend for sex, but the poet's love transcends physical gratification. He says, in effect, Give women your body; I'll take your mind. Incidentally, the pun on "pricked" has been blandly annotated "to mark" (which it does) but the word also refers to the "addition" that defeats the poet's intentions.

We'll probably never know Shakespeare's sexual preferences, though it's likely he was bisexual. He was fascinated by sexual ambiguity and the way in which one sex could behave like the other, and some of the most passionate relationships in the plays and poems are between men—Valentine and Proteus in *Two Gentlemen of Verona,* Antonio and Sebastian in *Twelfth Night,* Bassanio and Antonio in *The Merchant of Venice,* Iago and Othello in *Othello,* and Coriolanus and Aufidius in *Coriolanus.*

The Western ideal of romantic love, which traditionally refers to heterosexual desire, doesn't go very far in illuminating what Shakespeare means in the Sonnets. The poet uses a deceptively simple word, "love," to convey a complex range of emotions and objects. Viewed as a whole, the entire sequence is a full expression of the diverse ways human beings can love—homosexual, heterosexual, intellectual, companionable, paternal, the purely idealistic as well as the purely carnal. In some poems, the lover's agony is so closely aligned with his pleasure that the two are indistinguishable. To classify the Sonnets as either heterosexual or homosexual would be to oversimplify them, ignoring Shakespeare's great achievement.

Critics' Comments
on the Sonnets

*H*ad Southampton seen all these Sonnets, he might well have been amazed at the immensity of the feelings he had inspired. Probably Shakespeare put many of them in his private drawer.

—G. P. V. AKRIGG

*S*hakespeare, a husband, a father, a moral man, addressed a hundred and twenty, nay a hundred and twenty six *Amorous* sonnets to a *male* object! (Chalmers resolved his dilemma with the happy conclusion that the one hundred twenty-six Sonnets addressed to the fair young man must really have been written for Queen Elizabeth, since she was often "considered a man.")

—GEORGE CHALMERS

*A*bout all that one can get out of the Sonnets, considered as transcripts of experience, is the reflection that pederastic infatuations with beautiful and stupid boys are probably very bad for practicing dramatists.

—NORTHROP FRYE

*H*omosexuality? No, I know nothing about the joys of homosexuality. My friend Oscar [Wilde] no doubt can tell you all about that. But I must say that if *Shakespeare* asked me, I would have to submit.

—FRANK HARRIS

"Come Kiss Me, Sweet and Twenty, Youth's a Stuff Will Not Endure"

*A*lthough Proust is associated with the phrase, it was Shakespeare who coined the expression "remembrance of things past." Shakespeare's best love poems are also meditations on death, as he is constantly aware of the fugitive nature of time and its ravenous effect on love and beauty:

> Three winters cold
> Have from the forests shook three summers' pride,
> Three beauteous springs to yellow autumn turned
> In process of the seasons have I seen,
> Three April perfumes in three hot Junes burned,
> Since first I saw you fresh, which yet are green.
>
> (Sonnet 104)

In the Sonnets, Shakespeare repeatedly emphasizes springtime, beauty, and youth—things that can't survive—and the seasons, the tides, and the moon—things subject to change. According to Elizabethan cosmography, everything beneath the moon, "the sublunary sphere," was influenced by the rhythms of the tides and thus was subject to flux and decay.

The Elizabethans were obsessed with death, and the skull was a fashionable household *objet*, a *memento mori*, that, kept on writing desks and in bedrooms, was a tangible reminder of the vanity of human endeavor. It's not surprising that the object most closely identified with Hamlet, that quintessential Elizabethan, is a skull.

Although no one dies in a comedy, death is never far away, haunting even the loveliest moments, making them all the more precious for their fragility. Right in the middle of the radiant *As You Like It,* Jaques studies the antics of the lovers and sourly comments, "And so from hour to hour we ripe, and ripe, / And then from hour to hour we rot, and rot. . . ." This, at least from one perspective, is what love comes down to: procreation ultimately means putrefaction.

Death for the Elizabethans was common, a biological truth rather than a poetic convention. Surrounded by reminders of their own extinction, they witnessed the dead being carted out into the streets, family members died at home, and no parents could assume that their children would survive past puberty. In the sixteenth century a woman lived to about forty, if she was lucky. She was married by fourteen, and after years of childbirth and hard work she was considered old by thirty. That brief flush of early beauty must have been all the more poignant, and Elizabethan poets couldn't see a pretty face without imagining the skull behind those cherry-red lips:

> Golden lads and girls all must,
> As chimney-sweepers, come to dust.

The startling pun on the last word reminds us that all "quick bright things" return to earth.

The metaphor of comparing the brevity of youth to the short-lived summer is more than a poetic trope; it is a geographical reality. "And summer's lease hath all too short a date," writes the poet in Sonnet 18. The notoriously brief English summer, associated with the green world of the comedies, is followed by autumn and winter, common metaphors for absence, negation, old age, and death:

> That time of year thou mayst in me behold
> When yellow leaves, or none, or few, do hang
> Upon those boughs which shake against the cold . . .

(Sonnet 73)

Although Shakespeare was a Christian and presumably believed in an afterlife, his attitude toward mortality is strangely close to our own secular age: "What is love? 'Tis not hereafter," sings the clown Feste in *Twelfth Night.* "Present mirth has present laughter . . . / Youth's a stuff will not endure." In *The Tempest,* the magician Prospero says, "We are such stuff / As dreams are made on; and our little life / Is rounded with a sleep"; Hamlet's overactive imagination traces the dust of Alexander the Great until it eventually ends up as a plug for a beer barrel; and the valiant Hotspur ends up as "food for worms." Through Lear, Hamlet, Timon, and the speaker of the Sonnets, Shakespeare continually asks, Is life meaningless because it ends with death?

In the late plays and in the Sonnets, Shakespeare states that there are two ways of defeating time: one is through procreation—and Shakespeare lost his sole male descendant in 1596; the other is through fame—and this, of course, he has had in abundance.

The Authorship Question

*It is impossible to rob Shakespeare
of his mystery.*

—*PETER LEVY*

*It is the greatest detective story there
ever was. . . . It's the greatest story
in literature.*

—*CHARLTON OGBURN*

Shakespeare is the only writer whose authorship has been called into question. Although most people don't care whether or not a man named Homer wrote *The Iliad,* Shakespeare's identity has been the subject of furious, and often vindictive, attacks and counterblasts. Those who doubt Shakespeare's authorship are called "anti-Stratfordians," and although many are quite rational, they earned a reputation for being cranks and lunatics during the nineteenth century, when a few obsessive types were found haunting the graves of minor Renaissance figures, digging for manuscripts in moldy castles, or decoding cryptograms that translate to read "I AM SHAKESPEARE." Today, as conspiracy theories of all kinds proliferate, anti-Stratfordians claim more adherents than ever.

Anti-Stratfordians never deny that there was a man from Stratford named William Shakespeare; they just don't believe that an uneducated yokel from a backwater could have written the poetic masterpieces attributed to him. Some theorize that the Stratford man was a front for an anonymous aristocrat. Others believe that "William Shakespeare" was the pseudonym of the real author and that his identity and that of the man from Stratford became somehow confused.

The "Grassy Knoll" of Shakespeareana, the anti-Stratfordian argument, often involves complex conspiracies involving everyone from Queen Elizabeth to a country bumpkin named Shaxpere. Their arguments, which *sound* plausible, tend to impenetrable excursions into the minutia of the Elizabethan legal and political systems and are filled with references to minor personalities, all of whom are somehow intimately linked in a plot to use "Shaxpere" as a front for an anonymous nobleman or spy who may or may not be pretending to be dead.

Anti-Stratfordians tend to regard Shakespeare with contempt, as if he were a shifty relation who conned the rightful heir out of his birthright. Refusing to call him "Shakespeare," they prefer the less eloquent-sounding, derisive Shaxper, Shagsber, or, more disdainfully, the "Stratford Man." Their passion—some might call it an obsession— is born out of an intense desire to restore the man they believe to be the legitimate heir to his literary throne and to right the injustice they see as being perpetuated against some unknown, unhailed author.

Anti-Stratfordians are as divided among themselves as they are from their enemies the Stratfordians. Within the "anti" camp are many sects and splinter groups, the major ones being the Oxfordians, proponents of Edward de Vere, the Earl of Oxford (a major contender, with the most convincing case), the Baconians (the first to claim authorship, but growing steadily less popular), the Marlovians (a romantic theory, since Marlowe died in 1593), and the group theorists (those who believe that the plays were the product of a committee, an idea that is steadily gaining more converts). Then there are the "agnostics," who remain uncommitted, waiting for more evidence to emerge. Finally, a few brave souls maintain that Queen Elizabeth wrote the plays, poems, and sonnets in her spare time. (During my recent trip to England, a London cab driver, insisting that the plays must have been the work of royalty, confidently asserted, "They didn't have as much to do in those days.")

The Shakespearean faithful—academics, editors, scholars, and all those who work in what anti-Stratfordians call the "Shakespeare establishment"—dismiss these claims as rot. Most professors refuse to discuss the issue, preferring instead to concentrate on the works themselves; and if the question of authorship is mentioned in academic circles—which it rarely is—it's usually with a tone of complacent derision that dismisses the anti-Stratfordians as literary paranoiacs searching for mystery where none exists.

Anti-Stratfordians, for their part, mutter darkly about the Shakespeare establishment's vested interest in covering up their research. If, for instance, they *were* to prove that de Vere was Shakespeare, all lecture notes would have to be rewritten, millions of books would become instantaneously obsolete, and Stratford-upon-Avon would be as dead as Miami Beach in the summer.

The History of the Authorship Question

*T*he first mention that Shakespeare might not have written the works attributed to him was made in 1785 by the Reverend James Wilmot, who suspected that Bacon was the real author. But Wilmot was so afraid of offending people that he never published his radical theory, and it died with him, unnoticed. It became known only when a guest at a dinner party happened to mention Wilmot's idea to a man named James Corton Cowell, who then presented a  paper on the subject to his local philosophical society—a talk that must have disarmed his hearers with its opening admission, "I am a Pervert."

The next mention of Bacon as Shakespeare occurred in a book with the improbable title *The Romance of Yachting,* written by a New York lawyer named Colonel Joseph C. Hart in 1848. The book is presumably about the nautical life, but interspersed between talk of longitude and latitude, Hart manages to smuggle in his views on the Bacon/Shakespeare controversy.

After this, the gospel began to spread, with Sir Francis Bacon taking his place as the leading contender to the throne. Bacon found his foremost crusader in Delia Bacon (no relation, though later in her madness she claimed kinship), a fervent woman who needed a cause and who in an earlier age might have become a saint. There's something touching about her humorless persistence, which led her to devote her entire adult life to a man who had been dead more than two hundred years. To use Ivor Brown's evocative expression, Delia suffered from "tomb-lust," the intense need to haunt graveyards in search of any relic or scrap of information. Poor Nathaniel Hawthorne somehow got embroiled in Delia's madness and tried to help her publish her book, *The Philosophy of the Plays of Shakespeare Unfolded* (1857), which, when published, turned out to be 672 pages of prose so turgid it verges on the hysterical. Here's an example, chosen at random by Charles Hamilton:

> That sanguinary passion which the heat of conflict proves is but the incident: it is the natural principle of absorption, it is the instinct that nature is full of, that nature is alive with; but the one that she is at war with, too—at war with in the parts—one that she is for ever opposed to and conquering in the members, with her mathematical axioms—with her law of the whole, of the "worthier whole," of "the great congregation"; it is that principle of acquisition which it is the business of the state to set bounds to in the human constitution—which gets branded with *other* names, very vulgar ones, too, when the faculty of grasp and absorption is smaller.

Bacon, the ostensible subject, has disappeared behind a hopeless muddle of words. One can only sympathize with Hawthorne, who after his ordeal with Delia wrote, "This shall be the last of my benevolent follies and I never will be kind to anybody again as long as [I] live."

Then, in 1920, a shy English schoolmaster named J. Thomas Looney (pronounced *Lawney*) put a sealed envelope into the hands of the librarian at the British Museum. It contained the name de Vere, the candidate Looney had selected as the only one who could possibly have written the plays and poems attributed to Shakespeare. Looney arrived at his decision by compiling an arduous list of all the attributes he thought that "Shakespeare" should possess. After searching for a suitable candidate who matched these qualities, he came up with his man,

Edward de Vere, the seventeenth earl of Oxford. In 1922, Looney published *Shakespeare Identified,* which has become the bible of the Oxfordian movement.

Since then, the anti-Stratfordian movement has steadily grown, splitting off into various divisions, each with its own candidate. Through the years, at least fifty-eight persons at one time or another have been proposed as possible contenders for the Shakespearean throne, ranging from the traditional Bacon and de Vere to the outrageous Queen Elizabeth, King James, and an Arab sheik named El Spar. Surprisingly, he's not the only sheik on the list. In 1989, Radio Tehran announced that Muammar Qaddafi had declared that Shakespeare was a sixteenth-century Arab sheik named Zubayr bin William. Through some strange linguistic alchemy, "sheik" had become translated to "Shake," hence Shake Zubayr William.

Finally, in 1987, after a mock trial held in Washington, D.C., three U.S. Supreme Court justices pronounced that Shakespeare was the true author of Shakespeare's works. The following year a similar trial was held and presided over by three lords of appeal at the Inns of Court in London, with similar results.

Researchers at the Shakespeare Clinic at Claremont Colleges use computer analysis to compare commonly used words, punctuation, and spelling of the leading contenders, but so far, having already eliminated most of them, they are no closer to establishing Shakespeare's identity. Those the computer selected as possible contenders are Queen Elizabeth, Sir Walter Raleigh, a minor poet named Fulke-Greville—and Shakespeare himself. The Oxfordians are not amused.

The Basis for the Claim

Why do some people believe that the works of Shakespeare were written by someone else? What is the basis for their claim? The major reasons for the claim are extremely persuasive.

❖ A glove maker's son lacks the breeding, education, and background necessary to write the most sophisticated lyrics and plays the world has ever seen.

❖ Very little is known about Shakespeare. If you visit Stratford, you'll be taken on a delightful tour of his cottage and the Stratford Grammar School, but there's no proof of his birth date, that he was born at the famed Birthplace, or that he attended school.

❖ Shakespeare's plays exhibit an extraordinary depth and range of learning in such specialized and courtly disciplines as classical philosophy, literature, music, law, military strategy, art history, ancient and foreign languages, ancient history, natural history, foreign lands, falconry, government, politics, rhetoric, and medicine—precisely the sort of knowledge only a university-educated man of high birth could have possessed.

❖ The Stratford Man's parents, and his daughters as well, were probably illiterate.

❖ The plays demonstrate a sophisticated awareness of the inner workings of courtly intrigue and political life—knowledge that would have been unavailable to an Elizabethan bumpkin from Warwickshire but second nature to an aristocrat. As the former British cabinet minister Enoch Powell said in 1989, the plays "are written by somebody who has . . . been part of a life of politics and power. . . . It's not something on which an author can be briefed. . . . It comes straight out of experience."

❖ Although there are portraits of Shakespeare, none is drawn from life. If Shakespeare was so famous, why didn't he have his portrait painted, as his more renowned contemporaries did?

❖ The name on Shakespeare's birth certificate is spelled "Shaksper," and the six undisputed signatures are of varied spellings. The name on the quartos, however, is either "Shakespeare" or "Shake-speare," thus suggesting that the playwright and the man from Stratford were two different persons. Moreover, the hyphenated form suggests that the name might have been a pseudonym—a common practice at the time for authors who wished to remain anonymous.

❖ Only six examples of Shakespeare's signature survive, and his script appears to be the laborious scrawl of an illiterate—hardly someone who penned some of the most glorious lyrics the world has ever known.

To face the last page of Shakespear's Will

These laborious scribbles, the only undisputed examples of Shakespeare's hand-writing, are cited by anti-Stratfordians as evidence that he was illiterate. Note that each one is different.

❖ Shakespeare never exhibited any commercial interest in printing his plays, and although pirated editions were published in his lifetime, he never took any legal action against them. Nonetheless, in other, less important matters he was never reluctant to prosecute, and throughout his life he was excessively concerned about protecting his property.

❖ Legal documents reveal "Shaxpere" as a tight-fisted, hard-headed, litigation-happy, middle-class toady—certainly not the subtle genius who created *Hamlet* and *Lear.* Anti-Stratfordians happily note that Shakespeare was sued for hoarding grain during famine, that he sued people for paltry sums, and that he angled in a most undignified manner for a coat of arms.

❖ Except for the title pages of nine quartos, there's nothing to connect the man from Stratford with the dramatist known as William Shakespeare.

❖ Stratfordians point out that in his will, Shakespeare left his fellow actors money to buy mourning rings, thus proving his theatrical associations, but since the bequest is interlineated, it could very well have been forged when the will was found in 1747, a time when the Shakespeare industry was beginning to take off. Aside from this, the will is an entirely businesslike document with nothing in it to suggest that its writer was in any way connected to the stage other than as an actor.

❖ Inexplicably, Shakespeare retired to Stratford in about 1613, at the peak of his career.

❖ Shakespeare's death entry in the parish registry lists him as "Gent." There's no mention of him as either a dramatist or an actor. On the original monument on his grave, Shakespeare was represented as holding a sack of grain. When the monument was refurbished in 1747, at a time when Shakespeare was beginning to rise to prominence, the sack had been replaced with the quill pen tourists now see.

♣ Although Shakespeare was regarded as the leading dramatist of the day, not one person wrote an elegy or offered any written homage when he died. His death passed virtually unacknowledged until the publication of the First Folio seven years later.

♣ Not one person living in Stratford thought enough of Shakespeare to remember an anecdote or save a letter he had written. All that remains are rumors and legends, which were "suddenly" recalled years after his death, just when he started to become famous.

In short, there is no solid evidence for attributing the works to the man whose name they now bear.

FAMOUS DOUBTERS

Mark Twain

Sigmund Freud

John Galsworthy

Ralph Waldo Emerson

Henry James (though he was more of an agnostic)

Charlie Chaplin

Walt Whitman

Leslie Howard

*T*he Stratfordians would argue that it's like spontaneous generation. They're like the Christian fundamentalists who believe that life was created, bang, like that, overnight, all complete as it is, just the way the plays of Shakespeare were completed, bang, in his brain, without any background at all. How could anybody have thought that a man who could barely sign his name was the greatest writer in the English language? Who nobody while he was alive ever—to the best of our knowledge—ever identified as a dramatist?

—CHARLTON OGBURN

*I*n the ... debates I argued for the theory that King James himself was the real poet who used the *nom de plume* Shakespeare. King James was brilliant. He was the greatest king who ever sat on the British throne. Who else among royalty, in his time, would have the giant talent to write Shakespeare's works?

—MALCOLM LITTLE
(later known as Malcolm X),
speaking at a debate at Norfolk Prison Colony

*T*hose who believe in de Vere must believe in a giant conspiracy. Those who believe in Shakespeare of Stratford must believe in miracles.
—AL AUSTIN,
producer of "The Shakespeare Mystery"

I don't know if Bacon wrote the works of Shakespeare, but if he did not, he missed the opportunity of his life.

—JAMES BARRIE

*T*he Oxfordian case rests in part on the common-sense theory that a glove maker's son of apparently limited education could no more have written *Hamlet, Macbeth,* and *King Lear* than a Russian serf could have penned *War and Peace.*

—NOEL HOLSON

I am "sort of haunted" by the conviction that the divine William is the biggest and most successful fraud ever practised on a patient world. The more I turn him round and round the more he so affects me. . . . I find it *almost* as impossible to conceive that Bacon wrote the plays as to conceive that the man from Stratford, as we know the man from Stratford, did.

—HENRY JAMES

*I*f you get Shakespeare wrong you get the Elizabethan Age wrong.

—CHARLES VERE, EARL of BURFORD, a descendant of Edward de Vere

*I*n typically salty language, Mark Twain dubbed all Stratfordians "troglodytes, thugs, Stratfordolators, Shakespearoids, bangalores, herumfradites, bandoleers, blatherskites, buccaneers, and muscovites."

"*W*illiam Shakespeare. His Method of Work." Max Beerbohm on the Authorship Question.

WILLIAM SHAKESPEARE, HIS METHOD OF WORK.

The Stratfordian Rebuttal

"**A**nti-Stratfordians argue that there's little to connect Shakespeare with the 'Stratford Man,' and there's some truth in that. If pressed in a court of law, you couldn't say for certain that the two men are the same person. But that's not surprising." What is surprising is that the speaker is Stanley Wells, the eminent Shakespeare critic and an editor of *Shakespeare Survey* and the new Penguin edition of the plays. "But," he continues, "there are a few suggestions that the two men are linked. One piece of evidence is the bust in the Stratford parish church, whose epitaph makes it quite clear that Shakespeare was a commanding figure. And in the First Folio, Ben Jonson calls Shakespeare the 'Sweet Swan of Avon.'"

Here are some of the major arguments in Shakespeare's favor:

❖ John Shakespeare, the dramatist's father, was not of the lower class, as anti-Stratfordians claim, but a solid and prominent citizen of Stratford who, until he lost most of his fortune, was a prosperous tradesman. For a while he was the high bailiff of Stratford, the equivalent of being mayor of a small city today.

❖ The anti-Stratfordian theory that the writer of the plays and poems had to have been of noble birth is based more on snobbery than on fact. "You don't need to be a nobleman to be learned," says Wells. "That's a crock. Look at British noblemen today."

❖ Roger Pringle, the director of the Birthplace Trust, says of Shakespeare's dubious schooling and knowledge: "Twentieth-century research of the Tudor educational system reveals that grammar schools were open to the sons of all but the poorest ranks of society. It makes perfect sense that a man of John Shakespeare's standing would have been anxious that his heir take advantage of the local schooling opportunities."

❖ The anti-Stratfordian charge that a grammar school education is insufficient to account for the depth of classical learning revealed in the plays is countered by the argument that the Stratford Grammar School was regarded as one of the finest in England, and that its students received as much Latin training as graduates of a modern British university. Finally, most poets are definitely not intellectuals or scholars.

❖ According to Pringle, "There's no question that Shakespeare's plays were written by an author who was thoroughly familiar with the curriculum taught in an Elizabethan grammar school. The cumulative work of several scholars for the past eighty years or so has demonstrated Shakespeare's indebtedness for ideas for plots and characters to textbooks that were an essential part of the syllabus prescribed in the schools of the time."

> *A*sking if Shakespeare wrote Shakespeare's works is about as real as asking "Is Elvis dead?"
> —GARY TAYLOR

> *T*here are so many unbalanced people in the anti-Stratfordian camp who are excessive in their view that their candidate has never been acclaimed. I think there are a lot of absolute nutters in that field.
> —ROGER PRINGLE

❖ Stratford was not a sleepy backwater, as most anti-Stratfordians like to believe, but an important stopping point for traveling players. Shakespeare probably saw enough plays to quicken his young imagination. He did not arrive in London an uncultured bumpkin.

❖ Little is known about Shakespeare because Elizabethans didn't keep records as we do today. Newspapers, directories, census reports, report cards, doctor's records, and résumés were nonexistent. And since manuscripts and personal ephemera tend to get lost or destroyed after four hundred fifty years, it's not surprising that Shakespeare's manuscripts and personal papers no longer exist. (It's likely that they were burned during the Globe fire in 1613.)

❖ It's impossible and futile to infer anything about anyone's character on the basis of a few legal documents and business records. If, four hundred fifty years from now, all that survived about you were a few unpaid traffic tickets and some receipts, what image would you convey to posterity? The frequency of Shakespeare's name in lawsuits should be regarded in the context of an age that, like our own, was highly litigious.

❖ On the apparent contradiction between Shakespeare's alleged covetousness and the sensitivity of the works, Wells points out: "I can't accept the view that you're debased if you're concerned with money. There's nothing to suggest that Shakespeare exploited people. He was reasonably acquisitive, concerned with his family and their well-being. Modern playwrights are interested in their investments, and we don't see anything wrong with that."

❖ None of the fifty-eight candidates, including de Vere, Marlowe, and Bacon, writes in a style remotely like Shakespeare's. As Wells points out, "Bacon was a learned man; Shakespeare's works are imaginative. His voice is unique."

❖ To those who argue that the plays were a group effort, or part of an elaborate conspiracy beginning with the queen and ending with a dupe named Shaxpere, the Stratfordians argue that it's highly unlikely that so many could have kept a secret so long. Odd, too, that not one of Shakespeare's contemporaries claimed authorship.

❖ Shakespeare's allusions to various pursuits and careers aren't as profound as anti-Stratfordians would have us think, but are smatterings of lore that all artists pick up and use to give the illusion of knowledge. Shakespeare probably kept his ears and eyes open to all sorts of information about seamanship, foreign countries, the military, law, and politics. The novelist Robertson Davies dismisses the claim for Shakespeare's expertise in every field as "all hooey. Shakespeare had a few telling details which he injected into his plays that made them seem realistic, and I have done the same in my novels."

❖ Shakespeare's name was not generally printed on the quartos because his plays belonged to the company, not the author. A byline wasn't crucial to the Elizabethans, since plays were not considered to be great literary masterpieces. The Shakespearean Louis Marder counters: "Do you know who writes your favorite TV show? Their plays were like TV to us. They were popular theatre for the people. We know the actors in a TV show, but not the writers. It was the same with the Elizabethans." Shakespeare did, however, take unusual care with his two narrative poems, "Venus and Adonis" and "The Rape of Lucrece," and apparently supervised their printing.

> *I*f Bacon wrote Shakespeare, who wrote Bacon?
>
> —WILLIAM KITTREDGE
>
> ———————
>
> *T*he thing about the anti-Stratfordians is that they really would prefer any crackpot theory rather than the simple idea that Shakespeare really was Shakespeare.
>
> —LEONORA EYRE

❖ As for Shakespeare's will, just because he didn't cite books in it specifically doesn't mean he didn't own any. Few Elizabethans mentioned personal belongings in their wills, and books were usually given by oral bequest. Shakespeare didn't mention his jewelry or clothing, but we assume he owned some.

❖ According to Charles Hamilton in *The Search for Shakespeare,* Shakespeare's signatures are excellent examples of the secretary hand taught in all grammar schools of the period.

❖ "Gent." is engraved over Shakespeare's tomb because being a gentleman meant more to him than being a playwright, which was considered an inferior status.

❖ Shakespeare *was* mentioned several times by his contemporaries, most particularly by Ben Jonson in the First Folio's dedicatory poem and by the critic Francis Meres, who lists Shakespeare's plays and compares him with the Latin dramatists Plautus and Seneca.

❖ In short, the anti-Stratfordian argument is based on circumstantial evidence, snobbery, and the scarcity of details con-cerning Shakespeare's daily existence. But a paucity of facts doesn't necessarily lead to the conclusion that Shakespeare was someone else. Up to now there's been no evidence that disproves that Shakespeare was Shakespeare, and it would seem, as Wells notes, that "the burden of proof falls on the anti-Stratfordians—and they have yet to meet it."

Edward de Vere, Seventeenth Earl of Oxford

*E*dward de Vere (1550–1605) is now regarded as the leading contender to Shakespeare's crown. Oxfordians claim that out of all the
claimants, only Oxford had the experience, the education, and the aristocratic and political background necessary to have written the plays we
know as Shakespeare's. They have built up an enormous case, which mostly consists of parallels between the Earl's private life (which is fairly well
documented) and incidents described in Shakespeare's plays. Oxfordians
read the plays as romans à clef about various Elizabethan personalities
who would have been among Oxford's intimate circle.

Here are some of the more compelling arguments in de Vere's favor
(this selected argument is based entirely on the research and work of
the noted Oxfordian Ruth Loyd Miller):

♣ One of de Vere's coats of arms depicts a lion shaking a broken
  spear.

♣ A contemporary of de Vere hailed him as a "Man whose countenance shakes speares."

♣ The plays reveal minute details about Italy, where de Vere spent
  a good deal of time.

♣ De Vere was extremely interested in drama and was a patron of
  the private Blackfriars theatre. As a young man he wrote poetry, but then abruptly ceased all literary efforts, an indication
  that his alter ego, Shakespeare, had already taken over.

❖ Oxford inherited the title Lord Great Chamberlain of England, (which he kept for more than forty years), which is frequently abbreviated to Lord Chamberlain, the name of Shakespeare's acting company, thus suggesting that de Vere named the company after himself.

❖ De Vere's father died when he was twelve and his mother quickly remarried, a situation that parallels the plot of *Hamlet*.

❖ Polonius's advice to Laertes in *Hamlet* is similar to precepts offered in a private letter written by Lord Cecil, de Vere's father-in-law, to his son. (Even orthodox scholars allow that Cecil was lampooned as Polonius in *Hamlet*.) Only someone like de Vere would have had access to this letter. For instance, Polonius says:

> Neither a borrower nor a lender be,
> For loan oft loses both itself and friend,
> And borrowing dulleth edge of husbandry.
>
> (I.3.75–77)

Lord Cecil offered this precept: "He that payeth another man's debt seeketh his own decay."

❖ The speaker in the Sonnets was a middle-aged man obsessed with his own mortality, yet Shakespeare was in his thirties when he supposedly wrote them. The Oxfordians date the Sonnets later than orthodox scholars, asserting that they were written between 1593 and 1603. Since De Vere died in 1605, he was closer to the sensibility described in the Sonnets.

Charlton Ogburn

*N*ovelist, social critic, gadfly (and former State Department official), Charlton Ogburn is the most vociferous of all the Oxfordians. He can outargue any Stratfordian with the opponent's own ammunition. On William Buckley's "Firing Line" he debated the prominent Shakespearean professor Maurice Charney and came off the more convincing advocate.

His book The Mysterious William Shakespeare: The Myth and the Reality *is a nine-hundred-page argument for de Vere, and even traditional academics acknowledge grudging admiration for the work. Like many anti-Stratfordians, Ogburn knows the period intimately; his evidence takes the reader through the intricate alleyways and detours of Elizabethan life—its laws, politics, and personalities. It is not just his command of facts that makes Ogburn an eloquent spokesman for de Vere, but also his zealous dedication to the cause. In an episode of PBS's "Frontline" titled "The Shakespeare Mystery," he charmed, convinced, and moved audiences when, seated on the front porch of his Beaufort, North Carolina, home, he wept while reciting Hamlet's last words to Horatio.*

NE: *Do you agree with anti-Stratfordians who believe that Shakespeare was used as a front for de Vere?*

CO: I think he was. In 1598, de Vere's father-in-law, Lord Cecil, was about to die, and he wanted to get this mess cleaned up. By that time, fourteen of Shakespeare's plays had been produced, and no author was named. I think that Elizabeth and Cecil decided that a name was going to have to be attached to these plays. They were just too darned good: the public would insist on knowing who wrote them. So they decided to use "William Shakespeare," the name with which de Vere had signed the dedications of "Venus and Adonis" and "The Rape of Lucrece."

NE: *So the queen and Cecil were in on the conspiracy?*

CO: Yes. In fact, they created it.

NE: *So they didn't know that there was already a real William Shakespeare in existence?*

CO: There *wasn't* a real William Shakespeare! There was a William Shaxper, an obscure fellow. I think what happened was that his name was enough like the pseudonym William Shakespeare that if a real man *had* to be attached to the name—as one obviously did—he was a good one to pick. Nicholas Rowe in 1709 said that the Earl of Southampton gave William Shakespeare one thousand pounds to make a purchase. I think they gave him an enormous sum to get the hell out of London so that his obvious disqualifications for the job wouldn't queer the whole game. He then had to lie low in Stratford. That's when the man we call Shakespeare retired. And when he died, nobody in London heard that the person who was supposed to be Shakespeare had died, and nobody in Stratford realized that Shaxper was Shakespeare.

NE: *Why would de Vere use a front?*

CO: I don't think de Vere wanted to use a front at all! The pressure on him was simply too great. Queen Elizabeth said, You've got to be concealed!

NE: *Why?*

CO: Well, it was utterly unimaginable for the leading earl in England to write for the common theatre. The queen and Cecil were determined not to have the true name of the author come out because to do so would reveal too much about what was happening at court. Elizabeth didn't want to be identified with Gertrude in *Hamlet.* Certainly Cecil didn't want to be identified with Polonius, though even Stratfordians admit that Cecil was the model for Polonius.

NE: *Why can't we find a manuscript of the plays in Oxford's handwriting?*

CO: That's a good question. How do we explain the total disappearance of Shakespeare's manuscripts? The only explanation I can think of is that someone deliberately destroyed them—to the last page. The other alternative is that they were hidden. I think they are hidden somewhere, with conspicuous clues as to their location.

NE: *Where would those clues be?*

CO: Well, one clue is in the inscription on the Stratford monument. Listen to the beginning of this inscription: "Stay, passenger, why goest thou by so fast?" Well, here we're led to wonder immediately why it is assumed that a visitor would go by the monument to the greatest writer in the English language without knowing what it was. It goes on: "Read if thou can'st. . . ." Well, if he passed to visit, and he can't read, what's the use of appealing to him about reading and writing? "Whom envious death hath placed within this monument Shakespeare." You know that "envious death" didn't put Shakespeare in that monument. There isn't any room for a body in there. What the inscription says is "Look you, the body of Shakespeare couldn't be in this monument; I'm talking about the body of Shakespeare's *works* as being in the monument. The only way you can find out is to take the monument apart."

NE: *Why has no one done that?*

CO: The authorities won't let them do it.

NE: *Why would he bury his manuscripts in a monument?*

CO: It's a very clever dodge; it's very amusing and very Elizabethan. You bury them in a monument that you don't think anyone is going to connect with William Shakespeare for a long time. When they finally did, the great disadvantages of having the plays identified with Oxford would have passed. The device assumes that posterity wouldn't be composed completely of idiots.

Claimant or Pretender?

*Did you ever notice that you never
see a picture of Bacon, Queen
Elizabeth, and Shakespeare in the
same room together?*

—*JOHN C. THOMAS*

George Elliott Sweet, a geophysicist and author of numerous articles and books on the authorship question, believes that Queen Elizabeth was responsible for Shakespeare's works. According to Sweet, Elizabeth was the only one intelligent enough to have written the plays and poems, which he believes reveal a decidedly feminine sensibility: "Thirty-six plays and not a single hero. The great characters in Shakespeare's plays are all women," he says. "All the men have various failings, and that's exactly what an educated, feminist woman would have put in her plays."

Sweet believes that Elizabeth chose the actor Shakespeare as her front because "he had the proper name. In one of her speeches to Parliament the queen spoke of 'swaying the scepter.' The name 'Shakespeare,' of course, is a slight variation on that phrase." Elizabeth paid Shakespeare a salary to "keep his mouth shut," and in 1597 he was given one thousand pounds, with which he immediately bought the largest house in Stratford.

Sweet supports his claim by matching episodes in the plays with parallel events that occurred during Elizabeth's reign and in her private life. As evidence, he cites the Epilogue to *Henry VIII:* "'Tis ten to one this play can never please," which he interprets to mean, "There are ten kings in Europe and I am the one queen."

Codes, Ciphers, and Cryptograms

*T*he Shakespeare authorship controversy has become less exciting of late. In the early days of the controversy the Baconians were the Indiana Joneses of scholarship, and their adventures led them to graveyards, mausoleums, castles, and remote excavation sites, all in the hope of finding a long-lost manuscript. The years from 1888 to 1957 were the palmy days of Baconian ciphers, cryptograms, and codes. Since Bacon had invented ciphers, it seems logical that he would confess his authorship to posterity by slipping a secret message into his plays and poems. This is the basic premise behind the cipher theory, though each Baconist developed his or her own decoding system.

Tormented by an obsession not unlike the late-1960s belief that led people to play Beatle albums backward in search of messages about Paul McCartney's death, Baconists would look at certain Shakespearean passages backward, upside down, and diagonally, inventing elaborate Latin acrostics, skipping every five letters or every third word—it didn't really matter, as the system was usually arbitrary. If you accept the Baconian premise in the first place, then all sorts of crazy ideas assume their own peculiar logic.

One of the most zealous adherents of the theory was a man named Ignatius Donnelly, who was dubbed "Prince of Crackpots" by one of his contemporaries. His *The Great Cryptogram* (1888) asserts that Bacon revealed his identity through certain key words, around which he then wrote the plays. Embedded within *Henry IV* is an entire narrative relating crucial events of the period, which Donnelly explains in excruciating detail in the 998 pages of his magnum opus. One can only echo Sam Schoenbaum's query in *Shakespeare's Lives*: "Why should a super-subtle mind have resorted to the juvenile device of incorporating hidden cipher messages in his plays?" Donnelly (who was also a great believer in the lost island of Atlantis), held that Bacon, in addition to writing Shakespeare's plays, was also responsible for most of the literary output of the Renaissance, including Spenser's *The Faerie Queene* and Sir Philip Sidney's *Arcadia.*

Sometimes decoders would look to Shakespeare's epitaph instead of the plays for clues. A Hugh Black of Canada deciphered the first four lines of Shakespeare's tombstone as "FRA BA WRT EAR AY," which he interpreted as reading: "Francis Bacon wrote Shakespeare's plays." But Edward Gordon Clark went further: through a curious method of backward spelling and phonetics, he turned the last line of Shakespeare's epitaph, "curst be he ty [that] moves my bones" into "S E No Y'M S. E VOMYTE He B'T. S, R, U, CD, N A!," which he said means: "Shakespeare—he is no Bacon; I'm Shakespeare. He vomits out the claim that HE be it. Shakespeare, Ah, You Seed, Nay!"

Then there is the great "Honorificabilitudinitatibus Anagram." The longest word in Shakespeare, from *Love's Labour's Lost* (V.1.41.), it has become the basis for numerous Baconian theories. Isaac Hull Platt announced that the word was the Latin anagram for "Hi ludi, tuiti sibi Fr. Bacono nati": "These F. Bacon's offspring are preserved for the world." Another theorist spelled the word backward and came up with the intriguing statement: "Suddenly into a useful nest steals Francis Bacon."

Especially endearing is Dr. Orville Owen's "Cipher Machine," an ingenious Wheel that he designed about 1895 upon the secret advice of Lord Bacon himself. In a key passage discovered by Dr. Owen, Bacon told Owen to

> *Take your knife and cut all our books asunder*
> *And set the leaves on a great firm wheel*
> *which rolls and rolls. . . .*

According to Sam Schoenbaum, "The machine consisted of two huge reels mounted on horizontal axles. Seated on a stool on a raised platform, an operator rotated the drums by means of a crank. Stretched onto them was a canvas, a thousand feet long and over two feet wide, on which Owen had mounted four neat rolls of the printed pages of Bacon's works, his acknowledged writings, plus the plays of Shakespeare, Marlowe, Greene and Peele, *The Faerie Queene,* and Spenser's other poems." With the help of two assistants, Dr. Owen turned the wheels on their axles, locating key words, which he would decipher and then dictate to a secretary, who was seated nearby. The resulting narrative filled one thousand pages with nearly impenetrable prose. It soon became apparent to Owen that the spirit of Bacon was trying to communicate to him the whereabouts of the manuscripts. Through a new cipher system, devised especially for the purpose of locating them, he learned that the manuscripts were buried in a box where the River Wye meets the Severn. Financed by a Boston physician, Owen, along with patrons and friends, traveled to England in 1909, expecting to stay six weeks. His visit lasted six years.

When he failed to find any manuscripts, the diligent doctor reworked the code and discovered the reason: Bacon was afraid that the weathering of the river rocks would damage his manuscripts. The new code now led Owen to the riverbanks, where he continued his efforts. And so it went: always a new code to explain the failure, always a new location. Like a man pursued, Owen went from one spot to another. In 1915, he finally gave up and returned to the United States, exhausted and ill. Just before his death, Owen passed on some advice to a young friend: "Never go into the Bacon controversy for you will only reap disappointment."

Oxfordians have their codes as well. For instance, it is known that de Vere signed his name as "de ver" or "Ver." Thus Oxfordians translate Sonnet 76 to read:

> *Why write I still all one, E. Ver the same*
> *And keep invention in a noted weed,*
> *That E. Very word doth almost tell my name,*
> *Showing their birth and where they did proceed?*

Nor are Stratfordians impervious to the lure of cryptograms. In an article in the London *Times* of April 24, 1976, Bishop Mark Hodson writes about a little-known cipher:

If you look up Psalm 46 in the Authorized version of the Bible and count 46 words from the beginning of the psalm, you will find that you have arrived at the word "Shake." Now, discounting the word "Selah," count 46 words from the end of the psalm and the word

FAINT

He lends thee vertue, and he ftole that word,
From thy behauiour, beautie doth he giue
And found it in thy cheekes: he can affoord
No praife to thee, but what in thee doth liue.
Then thanke him not for that, which he doth fay,
Since what he owes thee, thou thy felfe dooft pay,

K

80

O How I faint when I of you do write,
Knowing a better fpirit doth vfe your name,
And in the praife thereof fpends all his might,
To make me toung-tide fpeaking of your fame.
But fince your worth(wide as the Ocean is)
The humble as the proudeft faile doth beare,
My fawfie barke (inferior farre to his)
On your broad maine doth wilfully appeare.
Your fhalloweft helpe will hold me vp a floate,
Whilft he vpon your foundleffe deepe doth ride,
Or (being wrackt) I am a worthleffe bote,
He of tall building, and of goodly pride.
Then If he thriue and I be caft away,
The worft was this, my loue was my decay.

THOU

E

&1

OR I fhall liue your Epitaph to make,
Or you furuiue when I in earth am rotten,
From hence your memory death cannot take,
Although in me each part will be forgotten.
Your name from hence immortall life fhall haue,
Though I (once gone) to all the world muft dye,
The earth can yeild me but a common graue,
When you intombed in mens eyes fhall lye,
Your monument fhall be my gentle verfe,
Which eyes not yet created fhall ore-read,
And toungs to be, your being fhall rehearfe,
When all the breathers of this world are dead,
You ftill fhall liue (fuch vertue hath my Pen)
Where breath moft breaths, euen in the mouths of men.

FATE

S

I grant

FANT is the only example where the signal is in one Sonnet and the link is in the next one (faint).

FAYT in Sonnet 81 was apparently spelled this way to distinguish from the several instances of FAT and yet to avoid too frequent use of four letter signals in straight-forward spelling.

A case of inspired lunacy from
Wasn't Shakespeare Someone Else?
by Ralph L. Tweedale.

then revealed is "Spear." This astonishing cryptogram is virtually unknown. Psalm 46, 46th word from the beginning, 46th word from the end: "Shakespeare."

What makes the good bishop find this cryptogram so remarkable is "the date when the translated version of the psalm was so arranged as to admit it." Work on the Authorized King James Version of the Bible began in 1607, and by 1610 it was being polished and readied for the printer. In 1610, Shakespeare was forty-six years old. "To honor Shakespeare on his birthday, the translator . . . placed this cypher in Psalm 46, 46th word from the beginning, 46th word from the end."

The King James Version of the Bible, one of the major achievements of the Renaissance, contains the most magnificent cadences and rhythms in the English language. The project to translate the Bible, sponsored by James I, Shakespeare's dramatic patron, began at the peak of the dramatist's powers, and it wouldn't be surprising to find out that Shakespeare might have played some part in writing its magnificent poetry.

Author Martin Gardner, writing in the January 19, 1992, "Book World" section of *The Washington Post,* points out two more Shakespearean mysteries, discovered by Leigh Mercer, the English wordplay genius to whom we owe the palindrome "A man, a plan, a canal—Panama!"

The first is from Titania's plea of love addressed to Bottom the Weaver in *A Midsummer Night's Dream* (III.1.137–43):

> Out of this wood do not desire to go.
> Thou shalt remain here, whether thou wilt or no.
> I am a spirit of no common rate,
> The summer still doth tend upon my state;
> ANd I do love thee. Therefore go with me.
> I'll give thee fairies to attend on thee,
> And they shall fetch thee jewels from the deep. . . .

If you read the capitalized letters beginning each line, in order, they spell "O Titania."

Gardner next cites a passage from Act I, scene 1, lines 141–50, in *The Comedy of Errors*:

To bear the extremity of dire mishap,
Now, trust me, were it not against our laws,
Against my crown, my oath, my dignity,
Which princes, would they, may not disannul,
My soul should sue as advocate for thee.
But though thou art adjudged to the death,
And passed sentence may not be recalled
But to our honour's great disparagement,
Yet will I favour thee in what I can.

If you read the capital letters up from the word "My" in line 5, then return to "My," and then read down from "My" to the end, you get "Want My Baby."

"Coincidence?" Gardner asks. "Or did Shakespeare, who enjoyed wordplay as much as Joyce and Nabokov, intend both these acrostics?" We'll never know.

SHAKESPEAREAN

*H*amlet, Othello, Lear, Macbeth. Shakespearean tragedy involves solitary men struggling with the most basic fact of all: human existence. Any literary handbook will include Aristotle's definition of tragedy and lofty rhetorical terms such as "denouement," "hamartia," and "catastrophe." But for now, simply allow yourself to be moved: tragedy is defined not by what it does but by what it does *to* us. We watch comedy, but we experience tragedy.

In comedy, the parade of human folly is presented through the wrong end of the binoculars, from a perspective of detached amusement. But

*T*RAGEDY

with tragedy, the binoculars are turned the other way: everything is up close, intense, and immediate. Shakespeare, like Hamlet, "considers" life "too curiously," exposing everything to minute scrutiny, and he takes his examination to the furthest, most terrible limit. Hamlet walks in a graveyard and imagines "the noble dust of Alexander" being used to "[stop] a bunghole," and he forces himself to consider the skull beneath the skin ("That skull had a tongue in it, and could sing once," a fact that most of us would rather ignore). In tragedy we are stripped of the defenses that keep us from looking at life's dark underside. In the process of watching a tragedy, we momentarily forget the details of everyday life, and a world of absolutes—mortality, time, death, decay, good and evil—is revealed.

Shakespearean tragedy exposes those dark impulses that lie below life's smooth surface: the well-regulated Danish court in *Hamlet* hides something rotten; the charming and loyal Iago is a psychopath; Antony's legendary passion for Cleopatra is sexual slavery. For some of the plays, the binocular metaphor is insufficient to convey the intensity of Shakespeare's tragic vision: in *Othello* and *Hamlet,* Shakespeare seems to take an X ray of the soul. Shakespeare, as E. M. Forster wrote in *Two Cheers for Democracy,* "was subconsciously aware of the subconscious," and this is nowhere more evident than in the great tragedies, in which he probes humanity's deepest impulses, desires, and fears.

The heroes of Shakespeare's greatest tragedies are pushed to the furthest limits of human endurance: a young prince is compelled to avenge the murder of his father; an exiled king wanders homeless on a stormy heath; a husband strangles his wife on their marriage bed; a loyal subject murders his king. Shakespearean tragic heroes, unlike the everyman of a play by Sam Shepard or Arthur Miller, are lofty figures, princes or other noblemen who live life to the fullest—and fall. To the Elizabethans, the death of a salesman would be not tragic but commonplace.

This doesn't mean that we can't identify with tragic heroes. In many instances their lives are our own, magnified. Most of us will never, like Macbeth, assassinate a king, but many of us are ambitious and tortured by conscience. Shakespeare keeps his heroes anchored to the earth by adding subtle touches, words or gestures, that make them recognizably human: Macbeth calls his imperious wife "dearest chuck" (the Elizabethan equivalent of "sweetie pie"). One moment Lear is a towering figure of fallen majesty, but then, turning to Kent, he asks, "Pray you undo this button," and at once the powerful king has become a tired old man.

The hero's tragic temperament is a compound of opposites. Macbeth has a conscience, yet he commits a horrible crime. An evil man who kills a king is sordid; a good man who does so is tragic. Hamlet's treatment of Ophelia is abusive and cruel, yet he's not a monster; he's sensitive and poetic. Antony is a world-famous soldier who ruled the world while behaving like a love-struck teenager. Othello is self-possessed yet succumbs to the most shallow trickery.

Aristotle said that the tragic hero is a noble man who possesses one fatal flaw. It is this one imperfection in an otherwise perfect nature that leads to his downfall. Shakespeare's greatest tragic figures are fierce absolutists who find compromise impossible. Once they have decided on a course of action, there's no turning back. As Gloucester says, "I am tied to the stake, and I must stand the course." After Macbeth assassinates Duncan, he understands, "I am in blood / Stepped in so far, that, should I wade no more, / Returning were as tedious as go o'er." Macbeth sees the creature he has become but cannot change. Lear divides his kingdom; Hamlet swears vengeance; Othello believes Iago's lies—their fates are sealed. In comedy, characters can always turn back. In tragedy, every move is irrevocable—a link in the chain of the hero's doom.

Catharsis

*T*he violence of tragedy must be transformed into the sublime, the most horrific suffering given a strange beauty. The images that remain with us are Lear staggering with Cordelia's corpse limp in his arms, the asp slowly coiling around Cleopatra's breast, Othello kissing Desdemona just before he strangles her. The nature of tragedy dictates that it do more than just depict agony and death; if adversity does not lead to redemption, the play becomes a pointless succession of cruelties, and we leave the theatre depressed rather than uplifted. So the hero's anguish must find release—or, at least, the relief of self-acceptance. At the end, when the hero has lost everything, he must find himself. Hamlet accepts his destiny and kills his father's murderer; Lear achieves self-knowledge; Macbeth sees the emptiness of ambition. All gain an insight that allows them to transcend their immediate situation. If they did not, Lear would remain a doddering old man, Macbeth a common assassin, and Hamlet a sullen adolescent. The tragic paradox is that the hero rises to emotional and spiritual heights only as his earthly fortunes plummet.

Shakespearean tragedy takes place on an epic scale. In modern life, where terrible events recur with numbing regularity on television news, Hamlet and King Lear and Othello shock us back into feeling, giving us a chance to participate in one of the most moving experiences imaginable. It's like staring into the sun.

Tragedy Can Be Funny

*E*ighteenth-century critics complained that Shakespeare's tragedies weren't consistently serious enough. According to classical rules, tragedy should be uniformly sober. But Shakespeare took some dramatic risks, sensing when his audience needed a break. Tragedy, according to Thomas Hardy, details the gradual closing in of a situation, that moment when the hero no longer has any options; it thus has a tendency to create a sense of suffocation in the audience. The Nurse's ribald humor in *Romeo and Juliet,* the antics of Lear's Fool, the Gravedigger's jests and Polonius's verbosity in *Hamlet,* give spectators a chance to catch their breath and mentally prepare themselves for what follows. For instance, immediately before Cleopatra's final scene in *Antony and Cleopatra,* a country bumpkin noisily enters and breaks the dramatic tension. The comic interlude prevents us from becoming satiated by Cleopatra's heightened language, so that when her magnificent poetry resumes ("Give me my robe; put on my crown; I have / Immortal longings in me" [V.2.279–80]), we are ready to hear it with fresh ears. The contrast between the Clown's prosy jocularity and Cleopatra's solemn grandeur throws her nobility into high relief.

The most famous example of "tragic mirth" occurs in Act II, scene 3,

> *Y*ou can't write tragedy without wit, irony, and a sense of comic timing. *Hamlet,* to me, has far funnier lines than *Private Lives* and the heath scenes in *King Lear* provide better jokes than twenty years of television comedy.
>
> —JOHN MORTIMER

of *Macbeth*. After Macbeth has killed his king, and the castle is an airless hell of blood and whispers, there's an abrupt knocking on the castle gates. We have become so engulfed by Macbeth's nightmare that the sharp noise comes as a shock, wrenching us back to reality. Like the Clown in *Antony and Cleopatra,* the Porter provides a frame of reference, a glimpse into ordinary life, revealing the extraordinary isolation of the tragic figure. The scene occurs just when we psychologically need it. The Porter's salty humor, his references to lechery and impotence, highlight the macabre scene, but at the same time they reassure us that there still exists a normal world beyond the castle walls:

> MACDUFF. What three things does drink especially provoke?
> PORTER. Marry, sir, nose-painting, sleep, and urine. Lechery, sir, it provokes and unprovokes: it provokes the desire but it takes away the performance.

The Revenge Play

What do *Hamlet, Robocop,* and Chuck Norris movies have in common? They all belong to the tradition of the revenge play—one of the few tastes we still wholeheartedly share with the Elizabethans. Blood, guts, and gore will never go out of fashion, and revenge tragedies were Elizabethan blockbusters. There must be something universally satisfying about seeing a villain get rough justice at the hands of his victim rather than an impersonal judicial system.

In the typical Elizabethan revenge play, the violence is evenly distributed throughout all five acts. In *Hamlet,* however, Shakespeare subverts the pattern by creating a complex hero who delays his revenge, thus building the dramatic suspense until the last bloody scene, when Hamlet completes his revenge.

Most revenge plays follow a specific formula: most of the play consists of the hero's plot to avenge an injustice or a crime committed against a family member. In their obsession with family honor and the violent means they'll take to preserve it, the characters of a revenge play resemble the tightly knit Corleone family in *The Godfather.* A rape, a dismemberment, or an act of incest might add sensationalism, and often a ghost incites the avenger to do his bloody business. By the last act, the stage is usually littered with carnage—much to everyone's delight.

The revenge hero takes the law into his own hands and works outside traditional avenues. Such individualism is exciting because it is morally ambiguous. According to Christian precepts, only God can exact revenge: "Vengeance is mine . . . saith the Lord." In our own secular age, justice belongs to the legal system. Thus the avenger, whether Hamlet or Charles Bronson, by taking the law into his own hands, becomes a romanticized outlaw and a champion of the individual over the "system."

Although seriously concerned with retribution, family honor, and justice, revenge plays can also be quite funny, and some may even be considered black comedies. Elizabethans didn't have the word "camp," but they had a sense of it. As the audience's appetite for poisoning grew jaded, a playwright was forced to invent new and more ingenious methods of torture, and the plays self-consciously flaunt their lavish brutality. It's hard to believe that Shakespeare didn't relish writing these lines for Aaron, the inventive villain in *Titus Andronicus*:

> Even now I curse the day, and yet I think
> Few come within the compass of my curse,
> Wherein I did not some notorious ill:
> As kill a man, or else devise his death;
> Ravish a maid, or plot the way to do it;
> Accuse some innocent, and forswear myself;
> Set deadly enmity between two friends;
> Make poor men's cattle break their necks;
> Set fire on barns and haystalks in the night
> And bid the owners quench them with their tears.
> Oft have I digged up dead men from their graves
> And set them upright at their dear friends' door,
> Even when their sorrows almost was forgot,
> And on their skins, as on the bark of trees,
> Have with my knife carvèd in Roman letters
> 'Let not your sorrow die, though I am dead.'
> But I have done a thousand dreadful things
> As willingly as one would kill a fly,
> And nothing grieves me heartily indeed
> But that I cannot do ten thousand more.

> (V.1.123–44)

Titus Andronicus

What can you say about a play that contains the stage direction "Enter the Empress' sons, with Lavinia, her hands cut off, and her tongue cut out, and ravished"? T. S. Eliot called *Titus Andronicus* "one of the stupidest and most uninspiring plays ever written." At various times it's been described as "a heap of rubbish" and "a horror comic"; others, with scholarly restraint, refer to it as a precursor of the modern "theatre of cruelty."

When it was new, *Titus Andronicus* was one of Shakespeare's most popular plays, and it was still being staged several years after its first performance—unusual at a time when the audience craved variety. But tastes eventually became more refined. Academic critics of the eighteenth century banished it to theatrical limbo, and the priggish Victorians disdained it. In fact, *Titus* wasn't seriously performed until Peter Brook's famous Stratford production with Laurence Olivier and Vivien Leigh in 1955.

The play is so offensive that people hesitate to attribute it to Shakespeare, maintaining that he reworked or collaborated on an existing play, also called *Titus Andronicus*. But, like it or not, most scholars concur that Shakespeare wrote at least most of it. It's probably his first play, or at least his first tragedy, so its baroque excesses can be excused as the understandable high spirits of a novice who wants a hit. Whether you view it as high camp or, as scholars would say, an "interesting example of the immature Shakespeare," the play is fascinating both *because* of its horror and for what it tells us about Elizabethan popular taste.

The Romans have been fighting the Goths, and Titus returns to Rome with his prisoners, including Tamora, Queen of the Goths, and her three sons. In keeping with the Roman custom, Titus sacrifices

Tamora's eldest son (by hewing his limbs and throwing him into the fire) despite his mother's pleas for mercy. This act sets off a chain of plot and counterplot that makes up the rest of the play. Shortly after this, Titus kills one of his own sons when he disobeys him. We are still in the first act.

Tamora, in league with her sons and her black paramour-slave, Aaron, are now busy plotting against Titus. The basic goal of the traditional revenge play is to cram as many ingenious methods of torture into five acts as possible. Lavinia, Titus's daughter, and her husband, Bassianus, are next on the hit list. After they murder Bassianus, Tamora's sons rape Lavinia, using her husband's decapitated head as a pillow for their deed. Lavinia's tongue and hands are then sliced off so she can't identify her rapists, and her brothers are framed for the murder. We can only be grateful that the rape occurs off stage, but Shakespeare is not so discreet with the rest of the play's ten murders (not to mention numerous other atrocities), which take place in full view of the by-now sickened—and enthralled—audience. This is still Act II.

Unlike Shakespeare's later villains (except Iago), Aaron is thoroughly evil, but his evil, like that of Richard III, is ingeniously droll. Adding a fillip to his cruelty, he reassures the father that if he will chop off his own hand, the emperor will spare his two sons. Titus chops off his hand, the sons are executed anyway, and their heads, along with the hand, are returned to him, thus inspiring the memorable stage direction: "Enter Messenger with two heads and a hand." In another nice touch, Lavinia carries her father's hand in her mouth. Between acts of mayhem, Titus, now understandably insane, repeats a litany of his wrongs, and the list keeps growing like one of those children's songs in which a new line is added to each new refrain.

It's hard to believe that Shakespeare could come up with still more, but the highlight comes in the last act, when Titus gets his ultimate revenge. In a macabre game of charades, Lavinia indicates the identity of her two rapists:

> [*Lavinia turns over with her stumps the books which Lucius has let
>   fall.*]
> TITUS. Why lifts she up her arms in sequence thus?
> MARCUS. I think she means there were more than one
>   Confederate in the fact.

(IV.1.37–38)

Then, guiding a staff in her mouth, Lavinia spells out her ravishers' names in the dirt (stage direction: *She takes the staff in her mouth and guides it with her stumps and writes*). Pretending to be insane, Titus kills Tamora's sons, grinds their bones to a powder, bakes their heads in a crust, and serves them up to their unsuspecting mother. After she's had her fill, he gives her the recipe, and the play ends with an orgy of stabbings.

*T*o parody *Titus Andronicus* would seem to be painting the lily. But the Reduced Shakespeare Company does a hilarious sendup of the play in which they turn the grotesque dinner scene into a cooking show in the flamboyant manner of Julia Child.

Is there anything aesthetically worthwhile about this play? As usual with matters Shakespearean, opinion is divided. Some see in the uncompromising Titus the future seeds of Lear and Othello. Jan Kott writes: "No doubt Titus's sufferings foretell the hell through which Lear will walk. As for Lucius [Titus's grandson], had he—instead of going to the camp of the Goths—gone to the university at Wittenberg, he would surely have returned as a Hamlet. Tamora, the queen of the Goths, would be akin to Lady Macbeth, had she wished to look inside her own soul." But none of the characters *do* look inside their souls—and this is the difference between a true tragedy like *Lear* and a superficial tragedy, in which characters wallow in suffering and death. The characters in *Titus* get their revenge or comeuppance without achieving salvation, redemption, or self-knowledge. Unlike the brutalities of *King Lear,* the horror of *Titus* is gratuitous.

Despite all the critical disapproval of *Titus,* there's something full-blooded and endearing about this apprentice work. It's much more lively than the later *Timon of Athens,* an ugly play that seems to have been written by a tired and angry old man. More than any other Shakespeare play, *Titus* shows the writer as a practical man of the theatre whose instincts tell him exactly what his audience craves—and who gives it to them in spades.

Peter Brook's
<u>Titus Andronicus</u>

*T*he headlines said it all: "Brook's production has them dropping in the aisles." Literally. Patrons, sickened by the spectacle on stage, had to be carried out gasping for air while an ambulance stood ready and waiting at curbside. The usually genteel Shakespearean crowd was unaccustomed to anything quite so shocking. There were generally at least two fainting spells per night, with an all-time record of twenty-two. The victims usually succumbed during the hand-cutting episode, which was accompanied by the realistic sound of crunching bone. Nonetheless, people flocked in droves to see the production, and *Titus* was the most popular play of the 1955 Stratford season, with every performance playing to a full house. "We are doing wonderful business. We are booked right up to the end of the run . . . and there are always long queues for standing room," one theatre official was quoted as saying at the time. Even the refreshment stand did a booming business. "Perhaps people need a tonic," he explained.

Such visceral reaction is one of the best responses a Shakespearean director can hope for; it is precisely the reaction Shakespeare himself probably intended. Because *Titus* is so crude, and thus less subject to cerebral analysis, it may be the only Shakespeare play in which people respond from their gut rather than their brain or heart. Watching the play, a modern audience experiences what it must have been like to be an Elizabethan playgoer in 1589.

How could Shakespeare's worst play inspire what many consider to be one of the best productions of any Shakespeare play, ever? Despite the audience's revulsion, Brook revealed that cruelty could be transmuted into a stylized beauty. He directed it seriously, cutting away Shakespeare's melodrama and crudities, which might have made an audience laugh inappropriately. Jan Kott notes that in Brook's production, "Shakespeare is taken literally. The King really sets out for a hunt; Tamora and Aaron really meet in a forest; Lavinia is really raped." This was not an *imitation* of an Elizabethan play—a quaint period piece done up with ruffs, doublets, and farthingales—but a violent, darkly glamorous tragedy.

*V*ivien Leigh in Peter Brook's *Titus* (1955) made an unearthly Lavinia. Her anguish was stylized and muted. Note that instead of blood, red ribbons trail from her stumps.

Harvard Theatre Collection

© Sarah Ainslie

*I*n contrast to Brook's production, the 1985 *Titus* at the Swan was starkly realistic. The expression on Lavinia's face (Sonia Ritter) is shocking—and, as this picture reveals, it is as if she had stubs instead of hands.

ᘒ

Romeo and Juliet

*There has been a recent fashion
in the theatre to define a certain
kind of play as a "black comedy."
I would define Romeo and Juliet
as a "golden tragedy."*

—*DAME PEGGY ASHCROFT*

"**F**or now, these hot days, is the mad blood stirring." It is summer in Verona, the air shimmers with heat. The tension is palpable, with street brawls, family feuds, and ancient animosities. Welcome to the hothouse atmosphere of *Romeo and Juliet,* where everything happens quickly: Romeo and Juliet meet, grow up, and die in less than five days.

Like adolescence itself, the play has many moods: it is delicate yet intense, occasionally obscene, sometimes funny, and always heart-breaking. If you can forget those tired parodies of the balcony scene with their "wherefore art thous," you're in for a delightful surprise. This play is terrific. Unfortunately, it's usually performed by actors who are far past their adolescence. Ellen Terry's remark is probably true: as soon as a woman is old enough to understand Juliet, she's too old to play her. Norma Shearer was thirty-five when she played the thirteen-year-old virgin in the 1936 movie version, with Leslie Howard as her middle-aged Romeo. The play is supposed to capture the exhilaration of first love. That's why Franco Zeffirelli's 1968 film version, with its seventeen- and fifteen-year-old stars, Leonard Whiting and Olivia Hussey, comes closest to Shakespeare's intention; not surprisingly, it's the most successful Shakespearean movie ever made.

Norma Shearer (age thirty-five) and Leslie Howard (age forty) in George Cukor's 1936 version of *Romeo and Juliet*.

Olivia Hussey (age fifteen) and Leonard Whiting (age seventeen) in Zeffirelli's 1968 film.

The play opens with a Chorus who speaks the Prologue, informing us that the "star-crossed" lovers will "take their life." This foreknowledge is important, because it gives the action a double perspective: rapture and love framed by the awareness of time and death. Too, the revelation of the play's tragic conclusion heightens rather than steals from the drama, suggesting that the lovers are fulfilling their rightful destiny and that their deaths are not an end but an erotic consummation.

Romeo and Juliet don't meet until the end of Act I. Shakespeare has us see them alone initially, so that we can observe how their love matures and deepens them. When we first see Romeo, his hormones are beginning to peak. However, he doesn't just want sex; he wants ideal romance. A conventional lover (a favorite Shakespearean caricature), he speaks in language that is stale and rhetorical. His poetry could be applied to any generic mistress. Yet in his desire for solitude and his sensitivity, he stands apart from his more boisterous friends. Juliet is playful and girlish, a sheltered child who unquestioningly obeys her parents, and yet she, too, exhibits moments of gravity and depth, flashes of the woman she will soon become. In the course of the play, suddenly wise in the ways of love and desire, she quickly outgrows her parents. Love awakens both Romeo and Juliet to their deeper natures, and their potential selves, briefly glimpsed in the preceding scenes, become more fully realized as the play unfolds. Once he has a real woman to inspire him, Romeo's clichés blossom into expressions of extraordinary vigor and individuality: "O, she doth teach the torches to burn bright! / It seems she hangs upon the cheek of night / As a rich jewel in an Ethiop's ear. . . ."

It is the night Romeo and his friends disguise themselves and crash the Capulets' banquet that the two legendary lovers first meet; they begin flirting in sonnet form, each picking up where the other leaves off. The raucous ball fades into the background, and we are immediately thrust into the timeless realm of poetry and love. Their exchange, while stylized, conveys a sense of suppressed excitement: they are spellbound, caught immediately by love, delighted with each other. Shakespeare stresses their ardor, so that their tragic end becomes all the more unbearable. They speak breathlessly, as if there isn't enough time to say everything they feel. And, of course, there isn't. In the midst of all this excitement, there are intimations of death, and both Romeo and Juliet mysteriously sense their imminent doom; the themes of love and death are entwined until the two are indistinguishable.

For the first three acts, however, we can almost forget that we are watching a tragedy. After all, the play's subject, thwarted young love, is typical comedic fare. But the comedy that began with a dance ends with a duel—an incident that sets off a chain of events that force the play to tragedy. In Act II, scene 6, Romeo and Juliet are married, but the next scene begins a whole new mood, and almost a new play. In Act III, scene 1, Juliet's cousin Tybalt kills Romeo's best friend, Mercutio; Romeo retaliates, killing Tybalt, and is banished by the Duke; Juliet's father orders her to marry Paris within three days; and Juliet, to escape her fate, downs the potion that will simulate her death. Upon hearing of Juliet's "death," Romeo rushes to her crypt and, thinking her dead, swiftly drinks poison. Shakespeare exploits the dramatic tension by making every event happen with split-second precision. Had Romeo waited a few moments, how differently the play would have ended! Seconds later, Juliet wakes up, finds her husband's corpse, and turns his sword against herself.

Is *Romeo and Juliet* a tragedy of fate or a tragedy of character? In Shakespeare's other tragedies, the fault lies within the hero's nature, and he dies with the knowledge of his fatal flaw. But Romeo and Juliet are victims of a universe not of their making. They are "star-crossed," born in a fateful hour; Shakespeare's only romantic tragedy is a drama of missed chances, poor timing, accidents, and mistakes. The teenaged lovers are also victims of the older generation who, failing to understand them, contribute to their deaths.

The Prince of Verona pronounces the play's final words. Romeo and Juliet are no longer breathing flesh-and-blood but a part of history, a lesson and a legend. Lying still in their silent vaults, frozen in time, they are as cold as the marble that entombs them. But while the play is going on, they are pure fire: young, doomed, and vibrant.

What to Look for in
<u>Romeo and Juliet</u>

THE POETRY

*F*irst performed in about 1594, *Romeo and Juliet* opens Shakespeare's mature period, and the poetry is richer and deeper than anything he had done before. Much of it relies upon paired opposites, or oxymorons: "brawling love," "loving hate," "heavy lightness"—fitting emblems of youth that ends in death. Shakespeare's poetry captures all the violence and the tenderness of illicit love.

QUEEN MAB SPEECH

*M*ercutio's setpiece in Act I, scene 4, about Mab, the Fairy Queen, soars with the speaker's exhilaration. It's a fantastic journey into an imaginary realm, and Mercutio gets there through language that he rides like a horse. But the Queen Mab speech is no whimsical flight through fairyland. She's the demon who rides through the night and lands in their dreams—dreams that aren't pleasant fantasies but sinful desires. The sleepers form a picture of the universal libido: grasping lawyers, women greedy for sweets and sex, covetous parsons, a soldier hungry for honor. This speech, which grows steadily nightmarish, concludes with an obscene allusion to Mab:

> This is the hag, when maids lie on their backs,
> That presses them and learns them first to bear,
> Making them women of good carriage.
>
> (92–94)

Beginning as a soaring fantasy, the speech descends into images of rape and pregnancy.

But while he's spouting this tour de force, Mercutio remains detached, aware that what he's spewing is the "vain fantasy" of an "idle brain." He's in love with the *sound* of his voice, but he's never taken in by what he says. Thus the speech is both impassioned and cynical. Mercutio in some ways anticipates Hamlet; he is intensely self-aware and a genius with language.

JULIET'S PASSION

*D*irectors and teachers do *Romeo and Juliet* a disservice by making the play too ethereal and refined. Mercutio is one of Shakespeare's most obscene characters, and Juliet one of his most passionate. Make sure your edition is fully annotated, with all the bawdy puns explained. Double entendres allowed Shakespeare to be sexual and romantic at once. In Act III, scene 2, when Juliet sighs, "Come night; come Romeo" (a speech that inspired the song "Tonight" from *West Side Story,* a modern adaptation of the play), she longs not only to see her lover but to feel him as well.

On her wedding night, poised between virgin and wife, girl and woman, Juliet speaks the language of paradox, which reflects her transitional state: ". . . learn me how to lose a winning match, / Played for a pair of stainless maidenhoods." (III.2.12–13) In losing her virginity, she will win Romeo; in surrendering, she will triumph.

[*Romeo and Juliet*] offered a completely novel experience, one disturbingly capable of challenging traditional authority. *Romeo and Juliet* was one of the hits of the decade [the 1590s], at least in part because it argued in favour of marrying for love against marriage by parental choice.

—ANDREW GURR

Comparing herself to a whore in a brothel who is bought yet unpossessed, she cries, "O, I have bought the mansion of a love, / But not possess'd it; and though I am sold, / Not yet enjoyed." (26–27)

Her speech is astonishing for the depth of its passion. Juliet is both shy and eager, inexperienced and womanly. Shakespeare emphasizes that love, not wantonness, makes her ready to embrace her first sexual experience: "Spread thy close curtain, love-performing night, / That runaways' eyes may wink, and Romeo / Leap to these arms untalked of and unseen." (5–7) Shakespeare wouldn't let Juliet lose her virginity while she was unmarried, but conjugal sex is another matter entirely. For his heroine's wedding night he gives her some of the most achingly ardent lines he ever wrote:

> Give me my Romeo, and when he shall die,
> Take him and cut him out in little stars,
> And he will make the face of heaven so fine
> That all the world will be in love with night
> And pay no worship to the garish sun.
>
> (21–25)

The speech begins with a plea to Night to hasten, so that she, Juliet, can lie in Romeo's arms. Night is associated with death and sex, which are united by the image of orgasm (to "die" in Elizabethan English). At the moment of sexual ecstasy ("and when he shall die"), Romeo will soar to the heavens and explode into starry fragments that will illuminate the night. In imploring night to hasten, Juliet invokes her own death, both sexual and literal. Thus their wedding night and its ecstasy anticipate their final consummation in the crypt. With one word, "die," Shakespeare combines three different meanings, all of which are thematically related: sex, death, and night.

In Act IV, scene 3, Juliet, alone in her bedroom, prepares herself to drain the potion that will lead to her presumed death and burial. She is afraid that the poison will do its work too well, yet she also dreads waking up alone in a cold, damp crypt. Just when an ordinary dramatist would play up the grand gesture, Shakespeare brings Juliet down to human level by having her cry out for her nurse one last time. Suddenly, we see an isolated girl inside the tragic heroine, and her agony becomes all the more real.

MISREADING SHAKESPEARE

⟶➤●◄⟵

One of the most quoted lines in the play is also the most misunderstood in all Shakespeare. "Wherefore art thou Romeo?" is often assumed to mean "Where are you, Romeo?" since Juliet usually utters these lines while leaning over the famous balcony, as if looking for her lover. Actually, what Juliet says is "Why are you Romeo?" that is, Why must you be Romeo, a Montague, the enemy of my family?

⟶➤●◄⟵

Shakespeare's primary source for *Romeo and Juliet* is a popular poem, *The Tragicall Historye of Romeus and Juliet*, by Arthur Brooke (1562). Among other sources, Brooke's poem is based on Luigi da Porta's tale of Romeo and Giulietta. Although the tale exists in previous adaptations—it probably originated as a folk tale—da Porta was the first to insist that the lovers were historical figures, a conviction that persists today. Visitors to Verona can stand on the "actual" balcony where the legendary lovers first confessed their love. Interestingly, Brooke's version was a cautionary tale, which alerted young people to the consequences of filial disobedience. Shakespeare subverts this moral of the original and turns his young lovers into the victims of parental control. In Shakespeare's version, it is the adults who must accept responsibility for the fate of their young.

On First Sitting Down to Read (or See) <u>Hamlet</u>

*What I'll have to do is, I'll have to
read that play.*

—*HOLDEN CAULFIELD*
in J. D. Salinger's
The Catcher in the Rye

O ver and over again, we're told that *Hamlet* is the greatest play by
the greatest playwright. If people are daunted by Shakespeare, then
Hamlet must be terrifying. Everything is in it: grieving and death,
fathers and sons, fathers and daughters, political deceit, revenge, and,
of course, the fundamental question of whether it's better to live or die.
While the play is unanimously hailed as "universal," it's also very particular—there's no character quite like Hamlet in dramatic literature.
He's a sensitive poet who is unable to act, yet he manages in one way or
another to kill almost everyone in the play.

Even if you've never seen or read the play before, you probably still
have a vague notion of what it's about. Nevertheless, try to approach it
fresh, without interpreting or analyzing it. Don't try to insist upon any
one meaning. Let the play contradict and frustrate you; follow it as it
unfolds and changes from one scene to the next.

At first, it's hard to see Hamlet as a person rather than a waxwork
dummy who utters a famous quote every few minutes. We tend to focus
on the operatic soliloquies and forget the man who says them. But the
heart of the play is in Hamlet himself. Although all the other characters
(even the minor Rosencrantz and Guildenstern, as Tom Stoppard's play

reveals) could be the heroes of their own plots, the play is Hamlet's and Hamlet's alone. The other characters revolve around him.

In *Hamlet,* the play, there's a play within a play; in Hamlet, the character, there's a character within a character. Like one of those Russian dolls that open to reveal sequentially smaller ones inside, Hamlet's psyche continually unfolds; there's always another level waiting to be explored. The only constant is his overwhelming sadness, which remains with us long after we've forgotten the plot.

John Gielgud is regarded as the quintessential Hamlet of the century. ". . . the voice of John Gielgud . . . introduced me to classical acting and now I can't read *Hamlet* without hearing it."
—JOHN MORTIMER

Raymond Mander and Joe Mitchenson Theatre Collection

Hamlet

Hamlet opens in the darkness of winter, when it is "bitter cold" and the night watchman guarding Elsinore castle is "sick at heart." The first words of the play set the tone at once: "Who's there?" In just two syllables, Shakespeare creates an atmosphere of tension and anxiety. The two sentries have just seen a strange and terrible creature stalking the castle walls—a ghost, a visitor from the underworld. In the literal and figurative darkness that envelops this scene, it is difficult to distinguish friend from foe, spirit from flesh. Shakespeare's first scene suggests an atmosphere of imminent danger and the need to be wary. What we eventually learn, of course, is that danger is lurking not outside the castle walls but inside the human soul.

Without pause or transition, the scene next shifts to a brightly lit room of state inside Elsinore. Courtiers and statesmen cheerfully toast the new king, Claudius. This is the world of enlightenment, politics, ritual—and false appearances. The scene is an official occasion—an inauguration and a wedding toast. Old King Hamlet has mysteriously and inexplicably died, and just six weeks after the funeral, Gertrude, Hamlet's mother, has married her dead husband's brother. The new king's voice sounds bland and rehearsed as he thanks everyone for making his transition a smooth one:

> Nor have we herein barred
> Your better wisdoms, which have freely gone
> With this affair along. For all, our thanks.
>
> (I.2.14–16)

What is the precise nature of this "affair"? Is it merely his transition to power? Or is the entire court, save Hamlet, involved in a massive conspiracy and coverup? Shakespeare subtly creates an aura of unreality, as if the court ceremony were not simply a state occasion but a staged event. Everything is too perfect, and later Claudius's words will take on a sinister aspect.

Shakespeare economically conveys what would take a lesser playwright several scenes to accomplish. Instead of *first* depicting the ceremony at court, he reveals the darkness threatening the castle, and thus makes us vaguely uneasy about what we would otherwise trust. We're uneasy because we've already heard those hushed whispers in the night, the talk of spirits. Like Hamlet, we suspect that something is wrong, though we can't articulate what it might be. Not yet understanding what the appearance of the Ghost portends, we sense that this smiling court hides a darker truth.

Only Hamlet, still in mourning, sits apart from the group, alienated by his clothing and his posture. He grieves for his father, whom everyone else seems to have forgotten, and he grieves knowing that the mother he loves (and who he believed loved his father) is just another woman, with appetites and needs. To Hamlet, it seems as if everyone else were acting a part, and he won't assume his expected role. His mother and stepfather chide him for his persistent mourning. "Thou knowest 'tis common. All that lives must die. /... Why seems it so particular with thee?" asks Gertrude. Hamlet, always ready to quibble, picks up on "seems"—a crucial word in a play obsessed by the conflict between being and seeming: " 'Seems,' madam? Nay, it is. I know not 'seems.' " He pronounces the word contemptuously, as if it were a foreign concept. His tone is at once adolescent, princely, haughty, sneering, and sad. He also stresses the word "I." Everyone else can pretend; Hamlet proudly sets himself apart from this sham court. He can only be himself—though he's not quite sure who that self is.

At the moment, Hamlet dwells upon the discrepancy between the courtly veneer and what he alone can't forget: his father has died and his mother has remarried. He longs to recapture the innocence of the time when his father was alive, when the world was as good as it seemed, and what seemed simply was. Not only Hamlet's dilemma, this is the crisis everyone faces when he grows up. Hamlet is the perennial adolescent, who in our own age is represented by J. D. Salinger's Holden Caulfield in *The Catcher in the Rye.* Like Holden, Hamlet has a precocious sense of what's "phony" and what's genuine.

Later, when the ghost of Hamlet's father imparts the truth about his murderer, Hamlet's instincts are confirmed ("O my prophetic soul!"). The Ghost's information both liberates and burdens him. It confirms his nameless suspicions—that life, which had seemed so promising, is in fact a sham; that you can't trust anybody; and that nothing matters. He becomes exhilarated by the revelation, uttering "wild and whirling words" reckless with discovery. But at the same time, the Ghost forces him to vengeance, an act Hamlet finds foreign and repugnant: "The time is out of joint. O, cursed spite, / That ever I was born to set it right!" Hamlet's task is to discover how he can honor his filial duty while remaining true to himself.

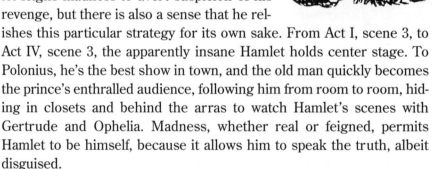

Oddly, Hamlet first responds to the Ghost's information in the same excited way in which he reacts to the news that an acting troupe has arrived at Elsinore. The two scenes are connected in that both allow Hamlet to indulge in his love of theatrics. Hamlet learns not only that his uncle has killed his father but that "one may smile, and smile, and be a villain." He, too, decides to don a mask, or, in his words, "put an antic disposition on" ("antic" here means "fantastical" and "insane," along with the theatrical implications of disguise). Hamlet feigns madness to avert suspicion of his revenge, but there is also a sense that he relishes this particular strategy for its own sake. From Act I, scene 3, to Act IV, scene 3, the apparently insane Hamlet holds center stage. To Polonius, he's the best show in town, and the old man quickly becomes the prince's enthralled audience, following him from room to room, hiding in closets and behind the arras to watch Hamlet's scenes with Gertrude and Ophelia. Madness, whether real or feigned, permits Hamlet to be himself, because it allows him to speak the truth, albeit disguised.

Hamlet thus works on two levels: on the surface, it's about its hero's revenge, but in the deeper realm of metaphor, *Hamlet* is a play about writing a play, Hamlet's inner drama, in which he struggles to become a new kind of hero. Titus Andronicus or any other stock figure might hack off limbs and cook them, but Hamlet is torn between being the furious medieval avenger, who "out-Herods Herod," and the thoughtful modern hero, who doesn't go around killing stepfathers upon the advice of a ghost, who may or may not be trusted. He simply doesn't know what to do. Should he believe the Ghost? Is his mother implicated in his father's murder? Is Ophelia guiltless? Whom can he trust? The Ghost has told him to take revenge, but not how to go about it; nor has he left him with a script or a prompt book that would cue him at the right moment. All the different moods and whims that critics find so puzzling and contradictory reflect Hamlet's need for direction, to find the one "acting" style that best suits him.

Despite the conventional wisdom about his inertia, Hamlet is not immobilized. Like Richard III, he bustles about, generating activity, moving from madness to lucidity and back again. One second he admits he never loved Ophelia; the next, he says he did. One minute he's languidly brooding on his inability to act and on the insubstantial nature of existence; the next, he's happily organizing the players for the evening's entertainment. He's cruel, angry, tender, depressed, clownish, manic, and filled with loathing for women, humanity, life, and himself.

He doesn't know *what* to do or feel. He's floundering; he's overwhelmed. Just when he's finally decided on a course of action—the staged re-enactment of the murder, which will betray Claudius into confessing his guilt and thus determine if the Ghost told the truth—he suddenly does an about-face. In the famed soliloquy, he admits that he's reached an impasse and questions whether he should go on with it at all—not just the plan, but the entire drama, life itself: "To be, or not to be—that is the question." He wants to know whether it's more honorable to suffer passively or to act; it's not simply a question of whether to live or to die, but what's the most *noble* thing to do. Hamlet *wants* to be a hero, but he needs to create his own brand of heroism and not just follow a predetermined course. By the end of the soliloquy, Hamlet decides not to die, but he doesn't exactly embrace life, either. He decides to live by default: "Thus conscience doth make cowards of us all." And in a sense, Hamlet's interior play, which never really took off, starts up all over again. In Act III, scene 2, Hamlet energetically resumes his plot to avenge his father's death.

The celebrated play-within-a-play, with its re-enactment of the murder, brings Shakespeare's play back to its beginning; it is followed by the prayer scene with Claudius and then immediately by the closet (bedroom) scene with Gertrude—*Hamlet* is structured around major dramatic scenes, with few transitions and little comic relief. Frantically,

Hamlet rushes from one room of Elsinore to another, and, in fact, almost every stage direction reads "In another part of the castle." Though Claudius reacts to the players exactly as planned, Hamlet still refrains from killing him. Hamlet's movements are unrestrained and unthinking, as if he were hastily improvising his interior drama as he went along, without seeing any one scene to completion.

Hamlet's first act of violence takes place in Gertrude's bedroom, where he recklessly stabs Polonius, an extreme gesture, seemingly  illogical and unnecessary, that leads to Ophelia's madness and Laertes's betrayal. Our reaction to this act depends upon how the actor chooses to portray Polonius. If he's portrayed as a well-meaning bumbler whose garrulousness is comic, then his murder is shockingly wanton; if as a sinister old man, we applaud his end and Hamlet's action. Hamlet *says* he mistook Polonius for Claudius, but this is impossible, since he left Claudius only a few seconds earlier. At this point, Hamlet comes dangerously close to violating the audience's trust in him as a hero. Then, after indulging in a long speech in which he imagines his mother's carnal pleasures, Hamlet forces her to promise to abstain from sex with that "bloat King."

All these major scenes don't add up to anything more than a series of false starts, and for a good part of the play Claudius and Hamlet play cat-and-mouse with each other. Each suspects that the other knows, but neither is convinced enough to act, until Polonius's death incites Claudius to action, and Hamlet, his drama pretty much played out, makes his exit. Packed off to England, along with Rosencrantz and Guildenstern, who bear instructions for his murder, Hamlet, the man and the play, seem to be over.

But, of course, heroes never die until the last act, and Hamlet pops up again, rejuvenated, in Act V. Having triumphed over death, he realizes that he *is* a hero, and that he's meant to stay on stage and see the play through to its finish. Having learned that "There's a divinity that shapes our ends, / Rough-hew them how we will," Hamlet finally allows Providence to direct his revenge. What seemed like delay and folly, Hamlet's attempts to maneuver and direct his fate, were, in fact, part of a larger plan: "Our indiscretion sometime serves us well / When our deep plots do pall." He no longer fears death, nor does he long for it: "There is special providence in the fall of a sparrow. If it be now, 'tis not to come. If it be not to come, it will be now. If it be not now, yet it will come. The readiness is all. . . . Let be."

Hamlet is an enigma, but the real surprise comes at the end, when all the seemingly pointless acts, hysterical scenes, and delays are revealed as part of a larger, coherent drama. Polonius's murder, for example, which initially seems gratuitous, is a link in a chain of events that fulfills Hamlet's destiny. Without knowing it, Hamlet had been waiting for the right "cue."

In the end, Providence and, of course, Shakespeare reward their leading man with a spectacular finale that is every actor's dream. Not only does Hamlet avenge his father's murder, but he also plays out a thrilling conclusion to his own inner drama. The self-consciously theatrical finale is filled with breathtaking dueling, dramatic suspense, murder, poisoned chalices, carnage, deceit, forgiveness—all ending with Hamlet's own magnificent death. In every other Shakespeare play, the climax comes in the middle. In *Hamlet,* Shakespeare saves the best for last. At last he has resolved the question of his soliloquy. He passively bore his troubles *and* took arms against them.

Hamlet's feigned madness allowed him to avoid taking responsibility for his actions. He could say what he liked to Ophelia and recklessly stab her father. Now, at the point of death, he realizes that to act means to be judged, sometimes unfairly. This is the essence of Hamlet's new maturity. In the end, without confusion, hesitation, or disguise, he acts. At that moment, he becomes most completely himself.

Ultimately, Hamlet depends upon Horatio, the sole survivor and witness to the truth, to relate his story; otherwise, future generations would see him as a mass murderer and not as a hero: "O God, Horatio, what a wounded name, / Things standing thus unknown, shall I leave behind me!" For Hamlet, Horatio becomes the poet who will relate the truth about his friend, granting him the immortality he craves.

Like so many of Shakespeare's dramas, *Hamlet* is about writing a drama, and Hamlet himself encourages us to consider the parallels between the Danish prince in a play called *Hamlet* and Hamlet the fictitious character who will achieve immortality through generations of future actors. As he tells Polonius, actors are "the abstract and brief chronicles of the time. After your death you were better have a bad epitaph than their ill report while you live."

Amleth

Shakespeare's source is known as the *ur-Hamlet,* a lost play that was popular in London during the 1580s. The tale and all its variations derive from a ninth-century saga about a pre-Viking prince called Amleth that was recorded by the Danish monk Saxo Grammaticus in his *Chronicles of the Danish Realm.* "Amleth" means "dim-witted," a reference to the prince's feigned madness, which he assumed to protect himself from his uncle, who killed his father. (According to Viking lore, killing a madman released his soul to fly into your own.) After avenging his father's death, Amleth went on to become a hero. He died in Jutland, and his grave still stands on a bleak heath known as Ammelhede.

Ophelia

It is Ophelia, not Hamlet, who most commands our sympathy. One of destiny's casualties, she's swept along by political events just as she is borne by the river at her death. Although Hamlet complains about being alone, he at least has Horatio. Ophelia, abandoned by brother, father, and lover, is completely isolated throughout most of the play. And while Hamlet's madness is feigned, Ophelia's is all too real: by committing suicide she actually does what he only contemplates. Shakespeare provides his hero with a triumphant finale, but, as usual, there's a catch. Just as in the comedies an outsider is left out of the communal marriages, so in this tragedy a solitary figure remains outside the collective deaths.

At her first appearance we see an innocent, trusting, and spirited young girl, but by her last scene she is contaminated, mad, and knowing. Whatever she might have become has been blighted. Insane, Ophelia at last speaks the truth, although no one understands her, and Shakespeare gives her one of the most cryptic lines in the play: "Lord, we know what we are, but know not what we may be." Ophelia goes mad because she discovers what others "may be." Tragically, she never learns what she might have become.

Just before he leaves for university, Laertes warns Ophelia that Hamlet is toying with her affections. Priggishly exhorting her to hold fast to her virginity (while he goes off to the whorehouses of France), he plants the idea in her mind that love is untrustworthy, that words of love mask physical desire. Virginity is something to be warily guarded in a world where all men are false. Then, to emphasize this sordid point, Ophelia's father enters and crudely forces her to confess the exact nature of her intimacies with Hamlet.

Polonius exhibits no tenderness toward his daughter. He's interested in her only as a source of information to pass along to Claudius, and thus make himself politically useful. His indelicate language and cruel insinuations poison her mind with the smut, spying, and sexual innuendo that infect the Danish court. Hamlet then abuses and deserts her,

In a landmark essay in feminist criticism, "Ophelia: The Responsibilities of Feminist Criticism," Elaine Showalter writes about Ophelia's negative status:

> HAMLET. That's a fair thought
>   to lie between maids' legs.
> OPHELIA. What is, my lord?
> HAMLET. Nothing.

In Elizabethan slang, "nothing" was a term for the female genitalia. . . . To Hamlet, then, nothing is what lies between maids' legs. . . . When Ophelia is mad, the Queen says, "her speech is nothing," mere "unshaped use." Ophelia's speech thus defines the horror of having nothing to say in the public terms defined by the court. Deprived of thought, sexuality, language, Ophelia's story becomes the Story of O—the zero, the empty circle or mystery of feminine difference, the cipher of female sexuality to be deciphered by feminist interpretation.

—ELAINE SHOWALTER

believing that she, along with his mother, has betrayed him. In a sense, Ophelia *is* a double agent. Dutiful daughter and loyal mistress, she is torn between her allegiances to her father and her lover.

After her lover has killed her father, Ophelia's mind snaps. The stage direction of the mad scene in the First Quarto has her entering with "her hair downe," an Elizabethan shorthand for dementia and grieving. During this time women wore their hair tightly bound, a coiffure that serves as a metaphor for their social and physical constraints. Thus, to "let your hair down" meant total liberation, and, to Shakespeare's audience, madness. Ophelia's mind, molded and shaped by her father, her brother, and the court, has at last burst free. The lewd ballads and ditties she sings have puzzled critics and inspired varied interpretations of her character: how could such a guileless maiden know of such "country matters"? They have been imprinted there precisely by those who sought to shield her from such knowledge. All the secret filth that lies rotting in the heart of the Danish court rises to the surface—within Ophelia's mind.

Hamletology

*H*amlet is the only play that has inspired its own cult, and there's even a name for it: Hamletology, the study of all things *Hamlet*. Like ardent sports fans, Hamletologists readily cite every record-breaking statistic about the play.

❖ It's been performed more than any other play in the world, and more has been written about it than any other literary work.

❖ It's been translated more than any other play and has inspired more spoofs, spinoffs, offshoots, sendups, burlesques, and adaptations, including a spaghetti western called *Johnny Hamlet* and a four-minute cartoon, *Enter Hamlet,* narrated by Maurice Evans. Believe it or not, there's even a Popeye version of the play.

✤ There are more than forty-five movie versions of the play, ranging from *Amleto* (Italy) and *Khoon ka Knoon* (India) to *Moi, Hamlet* (France), *Hamile: The Tongo Hamlet* (Ghana), and *Hamlet: The Trouble with Hamlet* (United States).

✤ The first book written on *Hamlet—Some Remarks on the Tragedy of Hamlet*—was published in 1736.

✤ The line "To be, or not to be" is the most quoted phrase in the English language.

✤ According to the British critic John Trewin, "There has been a debate on every minute" in the play.

✤ There have been hippie Hamlets and nude ones, too; the role has been played by dwarfs, fat men, tiny men, women (one with a wooden leg), and twins (to show his divided nature). It's been performed by the five-year-old prodigy hailed as "Master Betty, the Infant Phenomenon of the Regency Period," and by the octogenarian Sir Johnston Forbes-Robertson.

✤ It has inspired twenty-six ballets, six operas, and dozens of musical works from Tchaikovsky and Liszt to Shostakovich to the contemporary composer David Diamond.

✤ In 1964, Jan Kott wrote that the bibliography of works on Hamlet was longer than the Warsaw telephone directory. Today it's probably twice as large.

DISTRIBUTION OF LINES

Although the lines vary with each production, this is roughly the number of lines attributed to each character in the Folio version. Hamlet has more lines than any other Shakespearean character:

Hamlet, 1,530

Claudius, 524

Polonius, 338

Horatio, 265

Laertes, 185

(The list was compiled by Guy Boas, headmaster of the Sloane School, Chelsea, London.)

❖ The Hamletologist Ib Melchior notes, "There have been Hamlet cigars, bicycles, beer and laundry mats, Hamlet jewelry, games, paper dolls, and the maps of the world abound with towns, streets, and business establishments called Hamlet."

❖ Rarely performed in its entirety, Hamlet is the longest play Shakespeare wrote. The uncut version, dubbed the "eternity Hamlet" by the critic John Trewin, takes four and a half to five hours to perform.

❖ According to the novelist Laurens van der Post, the play's first performance outside England occurred in 1607, when a group of sailors enacted it off the Cape of Good Hope. The performance was entered in the ship's log as "this popular play now running in England."

Hamlets on Hamlet

*T*hen there's the lines. I know them. I've read them so many times. I go to sleep thinking about them, but the character is so confusing. It doesn't matter how many times you nail him or you think you've nailed him. It's the most [expletive] elusive thing. Every time you go back to it [the text] there's something else there which completely negates what you were thinking about before.

—MEL GIBSON (1991)

*A*s a crowning glory, I was allowed to study half a dozen scenes of *Hamlet*. When the day of the performance came, however, and my costume arrived, I was so delighted with the long black cloak I had to wear that I spent most of the first scene draping it over my arm and looking over my shoulder to see if it were trailing on the floor to my satisfaction.

—JOHN GIELGUD (see page 340)

*I*n every actor is a Hamlet struggling to get out.

—STEPHEN BERKOFF (1989)

*H*amlet is considered the most elusive character there is. And I can see what they mean. It can drive you mad.

—MICHAEL PENNINGTON (1980)

*H*amlet, Prince of Stretchmark, is a terrifying part to play.

—ROGER REES (on being too old for the part, 1984)

A heck of a part, tosh!

—RICHARD BURTON (1945, 1953, 1964)

Some Famous Hamlets

Ira Aldridge: The first great black American Shakespearean actor. In fact, during the nineteenth century he was considered one of the greatest American actors on the London stage. Shakespeare's plays may be without racial prejudice, but American audiences were not. Like Paul Robeson a century later, Aldridge found foreign audiences more tolerant than his own countrymen. When playing Hamlet, he had to paint his face and hands white.

John Barrymore: Regarded as a matinee idol, Barrymore stunned everyone with his 1922 Shakespearean debut. He was probably one of the most beautiful Hamlets to grace the stage, and as Orson Welles pointed out, he was a true prince, both virile and sensitive.

Jack Benny: In the 1942 movie *To Be or Not to Be,* he played a Polish actor whose specialty is Hamlet.

Sarah Bernhardt: At age fifty-five, with a wooden leg. Of her performance, Max Beerbohm wrote: "Her friends ought to have restrained her. The native critics ought not to have encouraged her. The custom house officials at Charing Cross ought to have confiscated her doublet and hose."

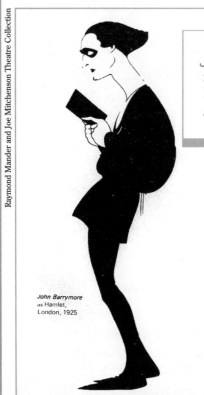

John Barrymore
as Hamlet,
London, 1925

A caricature of the famous profile by Nerman.

🙢

*B*efore Mel Gibson, Barrymore was the most famous Hamlet. When we imagine John Barrymore we think of that classically noble profile, the features perfectly still as though etched in marble. In contrast to his Hamletesque appearance, Barrymore's views on the role were wickedly irreverent. He particularly hated wearing the tights so closely identified with the part: "What an ass a grown man can become on occasion!" The first time he wore them, he drank until he didn't give "a damn how they looked."

🙢

Sarah Bernhardt as
the Danish Prince.

Mel Brooks: In a 1983 remake of the movie *To Be or Not to Be.*

Richard Burton: Directed by John Gielgud in 1964, this *Hamlet* became the longest-running Shakespeare play on Broadway. Clad in a black turtleneck, Burton made an intense yet fiery Hamlet. Hume Cronyn played Polonius and Alfred Drake, Claudius.

Richard Chamberlain: First at the Birmingham Repertory Theatre in England, in 1969. In his chronicle of Hamlet watching, *Five and Eighty Hamlets,* Trewin notes that Chamberlain, while not a major Shakespearean, did a respectable job.

Maurice Evans: In a 1935 production at the Old Vic and then in Margaret Webster's 1938 production, the first full-length performance of the play in America. During World War II he toured the Pacific in "GI *Hamlet,*" an abbreviated version of the play.

Sir Johnston Forbes-Robertson: Bridging the gap from the Victorians to the moderns, he acted in the grand manner and yet was one of the first Hamlets on film (1913); see page 494.

Mel Gibson: A visceral Hamlet; see page 514.

John Gielgud: His portrayal is considered definitive, the one with which all others are compared. Philosophical, gentle, a true poet, Gielgud has been associated with the play more than any other actor in the century: 1930 (in two separate productions), 1934 (also directed), 1935, 1936 (twice), 1937, 1939 (twice, and as director), 1944, 1945, 1964 (director).

Alec Guinness: In Tyrone Guthrie's modern-dress production of 1938.

William Hurt: Circle Repertory, 1979.

Derek Jacobi: In the 1980 BBC production, widely available on video.

Stacy Keach: 1971–72 season of the New York Shakespeare Festival.

Mel Gibson's *Hamlet:* The Publicity Still.
ૐ

Buster Keaton: A deadpan Hamlet in doublet and hose, more baleful than melancholy, in the movie *Day Dreams.*

Kevin Kline: In a Joseph Papp production in 1986, and then in 1990, when he directed and starred in Papp's production at the New York Shakespeare Festival Marathon (number thirteen), to mixed reviews.

Laurence Olivier: The actor who most closely resembles our collective image of Hamlet, he played the role in 1937 on stage, and in 1948 on screen (also directed).

Peter O'Toole: A hectic Hamlet (1963) whose "passion was barely more than external," according to John Trewin.

Christopher Plummer: In a 1964 television production filmed at Elsinore castle, with Michael Caine as Horatio and Donald Sutherland as Fortinbras.

Maximilian Schell: In *Hamlet Prinz von Danemark,* a 1960 West German television production that was later dubbed in English and aired in the United States.

Nicol Williamson: Hamlet as the frenzied academic, Hamlet, Prince of Neurotics; see page 507.

On <u>Hamlet</u>

*I*n the tragedy of *Hamlet,* the ghost of a king appears on the stage. Hamlet becomes crazy in the second act and his mistress becomes crazy in the third. The Prince slays the father of his mistress on the pretense of killing a rat, the heroine throws herself into the river. In the meanwhile another of the actors conquers Poland. Hamlet, his mother and his father all carouse on the stage. Songs are sung at table. There's quarreling, fighting, killing. It is a vulgar and barbarous drama which would not be tolerated by the vilest populace of France or Italy. One would imagine this piece to be the work of a drunken savage.

—VOLTAIRE

*T*he impractical length of *Hamlet,* together with the existence of varying authoritative versions, suggests a protracted period of composition. Shakespeare may have added to the tragedy over a period of time. Certainly *Hamlet* has always registered as a mysteriously personal play: the sort of work an author composes primarily to please himself.

—ANNE BARTON

*S*o far from being Shakespeare's masterpiece, the play is most certainly an artistic failure. In several ways the play is puzzling, and disquieting as is none of the others. Of all the plays it is the longest and is possibly the one on which Shakespeare spent most pains; and yet he has left in it superfluous and inconsistent scenes which even hasty revision should have noticed.

—T. S. ELIOT

I am trying to recall attention from the things an intellectual adult notices to the things a child or a peasant notices—night, ghosts, a castle lobby where a man can walk four hours together, a willow-fringed brook and a sad lady drowned, a graveyard and a terrible cliff above the sea, and amidst all these a pale man in black clothes with his stockings coming down, a dishevelled man whose words make us at once think of loneliness and doubt and dread, of waste and dust and emptiness and from whose hands to our own, we feel the richness of heaven and earth and the comfort of human affection slipping away.

—C. S. LEWIS

*T*his monstrous Gothic castle of a poem with its baffled half-lights and glooms.

—C. E. MONTAGUE

*O*ne of the reasons audiences admire the play so much is that everybody in their own lives almost every day faces the kind of crisis that Hamlet faces, that is, do you behave like a reactive savage or like a rational and sensitive human being?

—MICHAEL PENNINGTON

*I*t's nonsense to pretend that Hamlet is the story of Everyman. It isn't. It's Hamlet, *Prince* of Denmark. And that's the whole motive of the story; it's not just you or me growing up in a corrupt role, it's somebody who's obliged to take a public role.

—RICHARD EYRE, director, Royal Shakespeare Company

*W*hat's really getting him down is that his mother has gone and married the other guy straight off the bat, like within two months. He loves his mother, and she's like deserting him in his really grief-stricken time of need. He's only about fifteen years younger than her. He's pretty upset about the whole family thing. . . . He's in a pretty heavy mood.

—MEL GIBSON

Who Is Hamlet?

*H*amlet is loathsome and repugnant. The fact that he is eloquent has nothing do with him being obnoxious. He's an aging playboy. The only time he gets animated is when he bosses around the players, telling them how to do their own business. Imagine telling actors to insert some extra lines!

—CHARLES MAROWITZ

*A*n Anglo-Saxon bore who talked too much.

—HENRY MILLER

A rich kid from Denmark.

—DIANE SAWYER

A sad, screwed-up type of guy.

—HOLDEN CAULFIELD

A half a dozen characters rolled into one.

—GEORGE BERNARD SHAW

*H*amlet doesn't care if he bites the dust. He's dangerous. He's a human time bomb.

—MEL GIBSON

*W*e can visualize him in black sweater and blue jeans. The book he is holding is . . . by Sartre, Camus or Kafka. Occasionally he is tormented by thoughts of the fundamental absurdity of existence.

—JAN KOTT

*W*hat Hamlet is, before he is anything . . . is an authentic tragic hero who is himself a man of genius. And once Shakespeare had written him he never wrote [about] a man of any genius at all again. . . . Once he'd written [*Hamlet*] and discovered that there was no actor who could play him . . . he turned to something else.

—ORSON WELLES

How to Play Hamlet

[The actor Forbes-Robertson] . . .

does not utter half a line; then stop to act; then go on with another half line; and then stop to act again, with the clock running away with Shakespear's chances all the time. He plays as Shakespear should be played, on the line and to the line, with the utterance and acting simultaneous, inseparable, and in fact identical.

Not for a moment is he solemnly conscious of Shakespear's reputation or of Hamlet's momentousness in literary history; on the contrary, he delivers us from all these boredoms instead of heaping them on us.

—GEORGE BERNARD SHAW

*Y*ou can play it standing, sitting, lying down, or if you insist, kneeling. You can have a hang-over. You can be cold-sober. You can be hungry, overfed, or have just fought with your wife. It makes no difference as regards your stance or mood. . . . Why, one night in London, after I had been overserved with Scotch at the home of—never mind her name—I got halfway through my "To be" soliloquy when it became expedient to heave-ho, and quickly. I sidled off to the nearest folds of the stage draperies and played storm-at-sea. I then resumed the soliloquy. After the performance one of the fine gentlemen who had sponsored me for membership in the Garrick Club confided: "I say, Barrymore, that was the most daring and perhaps the most effective innovation ever offered. I refer to your deliberate pausing in the midst of the soliloquy to retire, almost, from the scene. May I congratulate you upon such an imaginative business? You seemed quite distraught. But it was effective!" To which I replied, "Yes, I felt slightly overcome myself."

—JOHN BARRYMORE

On "To Be, or Not to Be"

"To be, or not to be": I wish I'd said that.

—CLIVE JAMES

By now that speech has been translated into every major language on earth and some minor ones, and it's remarkable how the first line always seems to come out sounding the same. "Sein, oder nicht sein?" runs the German version, "das ist die Frage." Which perhaps lacks the fresh charm of the English subtitle in a recent Hindi film version: "Shall I live, or do myself in? I do not know."

—CLIVE JAMES

To illustrate how the glorious cadences of the English language have been reduced to flat, slangy dullness, Charles, Prince of Wales, translated the Prince of Denmark's famous speech into modern clichés:

"Well, frankly, the problem as I see it
At this moment in time is whether I
Should just lie down under all this hassle
And let them walk all over me,
Or, whether I should just say, 'OK,
I get the message,' and do myself in.
I mean, let's face it, I'm in a no-win
Situation, and quite honestly,
I'm so stuffed up to here with the whole
Stupid mess that, I can tell you, I've just
Got a good mind to take the quick way out.
That's the bottom line. The only problem is:
What happens if I find out that when I've bumped
Myself off, there's some kind of a, you know,
All that mystical stuff about when you die,
You might find you're still—know what I mean?"

Hamlet on Film

Well, can I see the script?

—ANONYMOUS HOLLYWOOD BACKER,
on being asked to contribute
financial support to Zeffirelli's *Hamlet*

❖ In Olivier's movie, Eileen Herlie was twenty-eight years old when she played Gertrude; her son, forty-one.

❖ Olivier opened his movie with this facile statement, uttered in weighty, oracular tones: "This is the story of a man who could not make up his mind."

❖ Christopher Plummer's *Hamlet* opens with the ponderous utterance:

"On a Promontory on the Sound Leading to the Baltic Sea Stands a Fortified Palace, symbolic of the Power of the King of Denmark."

✤ The true heroes of Christopher Plummer's *Hamlet,* filmed on location at Elsinore castle, must surely be the cameramen, who had to shoot their scenes during the twenty-four-second intervals between the foghorn's blasts.

Hamlet Controversies

The Delay

Does hesitation to murder need all the argle bargle that the professors have bestowed upon the psychology of Hamlet?

—*IVOR BROWN*

*T*he simplest reason for Hamlet's delay is, of course, that Shakespeare needs him to procrastinate; otherwise, the play would be four acts too short. Instead of turning those five acts into one violent binge, as in *Titus Andronicus,* Shakespeare created a psychological drama and set off an endless debate that has tantalized, puzzled, and annoyed people for over four hundred years.

Romantics read Hamlet as a sensitive poet, morbidly filled with thoughts of death. To the Victorians, Hamlet simply brooded too much: all he needed was a good tonic. In the age of Freud, Hamlet's failure to act was not so much explained as diagnosed: he was a neurotic, obsessed with his mother's sexuality. During the mid-twentieth century, Hamlet became an existential hero, clad in jeans and a black turtleneck, who peered into the abyss, saw the fundamental absurdity of existence, and concluded that all action, including revenge, was meaningless.

Gertrude Dearest

*T*hanks to Freud and his disciple Ernest Jones, the theory that Hamlet is in love with his mother has become commonplace, but when Olivier introduced it in his film in 1938, it was revolutionary. Since then, this idea has made its mark on almost every subsequent production—particularly in the famous closet scene. This doesn't mean that Hamlet and his mother are huddled together in a clothes closet. During the Elizabethan age, a closet was a chamber, though not necessarily a bedroom. As the Freudian interpretation became more orthodox, the closet slowly became "refurbished" as a bedroom, with an enormous bed occupying center stage. With each decade since Freud advanced his theory, Hamlet's goodnight kiss to Mother has grown progressively longer.

Hamlet Diagnosed

*T*he play is based on Hamlet's hesitation in accomplishing the task of revenge assigned to him; the text does not give the cause of or the motive of this hesitation, nor have the manifold attempts at interpretation succeeded in doing so. . . . The plot of the drama shows us that Hamlet is by no means intended to appear as a character wholly incapable of action. What is it then that inhibits him in accomplishing the task which his father's ghost has laid upon him? Hamlet is able to do anything but take vengeance upon the man who did away with his father and has taken his father's place with his moth-

ON HAMLET AND INCEST

Did Hamlet sleep with his mother?

Only in the Chicago company.

—JOHN BARRYMORE

er—the man who has shown him in realization the repressed desires of his own childhood. The loathing that should have driven him to revenge is thus replaced by self-reproach.

—SIGMUND FREUD

Is Hamlet Even Male?

*T*here's a famous nineteenth-century scholar and indeed there's a twentieth-century German film that argues that Hamlet was, in fact, a woman and that a lot of his problems stem from this misunderstanding.

—MARJORIE GARBER

Is Hamlet Fat?

*P*eople not only need a flattering image of Shakespeare; they also need one of Hamlet. In our collective imagination, Hamlet is blond and slender, with an aquiline nose usually seen in profile. But our imaginations are brought up short with that jarring comment in Act V, scene 2, when Gertrude, watching Hamlet duel with Laertes, says, "He's fat and scant of breath." For centuries, this remark has disturbed those who feel that obesity is incongruous with the inherited image of Hamlet as an ethereal, pale young man. The role, as the critic Martin Esslin points out, was created for the thirty-seven-year-old Richard Burbage, who weighed about 235 pounds, thus proving that our idealized conception of the melancholy prince is, in fact, a distortion of the truth. Nonetheless, "fat" has been variously glossed to mean out of breath or sweaty. The notion of Hamlet's physical fragility is cherished so highly that two journalists reportedly fought a duel over his weight. In 1989, the word "fat" was the subject of a heated debate conducted through the letters pages of the *Times Literary Supplement*.

Is Hamlet Insane?

I don't think any madman ever said, "Why, what an ass am I." I think that's a divinely sane remark.

—ORSON WELLES

Forrest Collection/Birmingham Public Library

*S*tephen Kemble, a Fat Hamlet in Scotland. (Kemble was one of the few actors who could play Falstaff without padding.)

*H*is father dies suddenly, cut off in his prime. His mother marries within two months. Now I challenge anybody who's very young and sensitive and imaginative not to feel the most chronic grief and the most chronic emotional disturbance as a consequence of those two things. And anybody who disputes that simply has never experienced grief or has never experienced any kind of jealousy or disturbance concerning the sexuality of their parents.

—RICHARD EYRE

*T*he Victorians needed to see Hamlet as mad. They worried about this. Because if he was sane, how could they justify the terrible way he acts through the play. Madness would explain his murder of Polonius and the terrible way he talks to his mother.

—RUSSELL JACKSON

*F*rom the burlesque *Rosencrantz and Guildenstern,* by W. S. Gilbert, first performed in public in 1891. Said by Ophelia:

> *. . . Opinion is divided some men hold*
> *That he's the sanest, far, of all sane men—*
> *Some that he's really sane, but shamming mad—*
> *Some that he's really mad, but shamming sane—*
> *Some that he will be mad, some that he was—*
> *Some that he couldn't be. But on the whole*
> *(As far as I can make out what they mean)*
> *The favourite theory's somewhat like this:*
> *Hamlet is idiotically sane*
> *With lucid intervals of lunacy.*

How Old Is Hamlet?

*W*hen the play begins, we assume that Hamlet is about eighteen: he has just interrupted his studies at the University at Wittenberg to attend his father's funeral. By Act V, scene 1, after he's just returned from England, we learn that Yorick died twenty-three years ago and that Hamlet remembers playing with the jester when he was a young boy. Then there's the Gravedigger's remark that he came to the job thirty years ago, "that very day that young Hamlet was born." Are there two Hamlets in the play, an adolescent and a man? Was Shakespeare simply being careless, or was Hamlet in England for over ten years? The play never gives a clue.

*T*he textual evidence from the grave-digger's scene indicates that Hamlet was thirty and in Elizabethan society, girls were married when they were twelve. And so you have a thirty-year-old son of a king messing around with a twelve-year-old girl. That was the social situation, but our inherited view of Hamlet is very different.

—MARTIN ESSLIN

Does Hamlet Believe in the Ghost?

*I*n the "To be, or not to be" speech, Hamlet says that death is a country from which "no traveller returns." This statement is startling, since the Ghost's appearance in Act I should have assured him that travelers *do* return from beyond the grave. This is one of the many contradictions that drove literal-minded Victorian scholars crazy.

Nunnery or Brothel?

*T*he line "Get thee to a nunnery" has long been a source of critical controversy. "Nunnery" means "convent," but it has been interpreted as Elizabethan slang for "brothel." Nonetheless, the duality of the word's meaning is in keeping with the play's ambiguity.

Is Hamlet in Our Blood?

*I*f you were to ask most people who haven't read or seen the play about it, they would probably tell you Hamlet dresses in black, has Scandinavian fair hair, says "To be or not to be" and holds up a skull of somebody named Yorick.

—DEREK JACOBI

HAMLET BANNED

———————

*U*nder Stalin's regime, *Hamlet* was banned, the official reason being that Hamlet's indecisiveness and depression were incompatible with the new Soviet spirit of optimism, fortitude, and clarity.

———————

*W*illiam Shakespeare's *Hamlet* has been banned from an Israeli detention camp for those arrested during the Palestinian uprisings, a human rights group said yesterday in Jerusalem. It has something to do with Hamlet's wondering at one point if it's better to take up arms or suffer in silence.

—*The Boston Globe*, OCTOBER 15, 1989

*T*o see *Hamlet* is one of our natural functions, one of our needs. How restful the play is, in its hold on us, how intimate and cosy! No-where, I protest, have I such a sense of home as in the Castle of Elsinore. Whenever the curtain rises on that "Room of State," I seem to recognize every brick in those arches ... [and] columns, every fold in those arrases of neutral-colored serge. I am too much at home in Elsinore. I seem to have stayed there so often, to have written so many letters on its notepaper.

—MAX BEERBOHM

*I*gnoring the fact that Hamlet is a fictitious character, people tend to regard him in the manner of Hartley Coleridge, the critic and son of the poet, who in 1828 wrote: "Let us for a moment, put Shakespeare out of the question, and consider Hamlet as a real person, a recently deceased acquaintance."

Jan Kott on <u>Hamlet</u>

NE: *When you wrote about Hamlet over thirty years ago, you referred to him as a young man who read Sartre, or as a James Dean figure. You also said he was like a sponge that absorbs the needs and feelings of each generation. Has Hamlet's image changed since you wrote your book?*

JK: There are many different Hamlets. The new Hamlet is a young Hamlet. He's not necessarily sympathetic; very often he is cruel and arrogant. In the past, Hamlet was a young boy walking through the corridors of Elsinore in love with Ophelia, always undecided. Hamlet is one of the Shakespearean characters, or the only Shakespearean character, who is a hero for every generation.

NE: *Why is Hamlet chosen as our cultural hero?*

JK: He is in some ways a very complex character. *Very* complex. He is like Swiss cheese, with all the holes.

Courtesy Deutsches Schauspielhaus, Hamburg, © Laurence Burns

The new and crueler *Hamlet* as seen in Michael Bogdanov's 1990 production at the Deutsches Schauspielhaus in Hamburg.

❧

NE: *You mean there are gaps to his character?*

JK: Much of the play is open to interpretation. According to the text, Hamlet could be a very young boy or a man of almost forty. Also, we can look at the relations between Hamlet and the mother in different ways—from a Freudian perspective, for instance. We never know what part Gertrude had in her husband's murder, and so on. And the relations between Hamlet and Ophelia are not completely transparent. You can say that she was his mistress or that she was absolutely virginal. Every director has a different vision. If the relationship between Hamlet and Gertrude is different, then the relationship between Hamlet and Ophelia must be changed, and then the character of Hamlet himself must also be different. Everything is connected.

NE: *Is this more true of* Hamlet *than of any other Shakespearean character?*

JK: It's more true of Hamlet than of any other character because Shakespeare's other characters are not as open to so many different interpretations. Look at Richard III: you can change him in one way or another, but he's always the same person; that's also true for Lear, and the same, but even more so, for Romeo. But not for Hamlet. He's always different.

Melchior Goes to Elsinore

In 1954, Life *magazine followed the dramatist, screenwriter, director, and novelist Ib Melchior to Elsinore castle in search of the original manuscript of* Hamlet. *Here is Melchior's story.*

I was in the American counterintelligence and the OSS, and in one of our textbooks we had a picture of Shakespeare's tombstone as an example of a concealed cipher. It's called a concealed cipher because the code is contained in something else—in this case, the tombstone inscription. Now, the inscription is a random compilation of upper-case and lower-case letters that really don't make much sense. There was no reason to spell "dig" as "diGG," or "EncloAsed" with a capital *A* in the middle. There's no reason—unless there's a cipher.

The original tombstone (the present one now has all capital letters) reads:

> Good Frend for Iesus SAKE forbeare
> To diGG ÆE Dust EncloAsed HE.Re.
> Blese be ÆE Man $\frac{T}{Y}$ spares ÆEs Stones
> And curst, be He $\frac{T}{Y}$ moves my Bones

For twenty years in my spare time I worked on solving the cipher. And I did, using a cipher invented by Francis Bacon. Putting it all together, I came up with a solution that said that the original *Hamlet* manuscript was buried in Elsinore *castle* in a place called "the Wedge." (The translated cipher read, "Elsinore [laid] in wedge first *Hamlet* edition.") It turned out that the Wedge is a cell in the lowest dungeon of the castle, where the prisoners were kept.

I then took my work to what they called the "Black Chamber" in Washington, where they have top cryptanalysts, and they looked it over and said it was okay. I then took it to the New York Cipher Society, where they sat around all night and tried to find out what was wrong with it. But finally even they had to agree with my interpretation.

Next, I had a helluva time getting permission from the Danish authorities to go and dig at Elsinore. I finally went to Denmark and found Kronborg castle, the real name of Shakespeare's Elsinore, and I rounded up as many members of the castle's council as I could, and everyone said, "Don't ask me." They were afraid of being ridiculed, you see. They then asked if I wanted to address the council, and of course I agreed. "Where would you like to meet?" "Elsinore," I said, "and what about in the Wedge itself?"

Two days later, the biggest caravan I'd ever seen arrived at the castle. The Wedge, by the way, is down two dungeons. So everybody trooped down, and it turned out that the electricity didn't work, and all we had was one little lantern. And we all followed that little lantern down the steps, into the dampness, past the torture chambers, down, down, down, and people's voices got lower and lower, until we were just whispering. We all trooped into the Wedge and I said only one sentence: "Gentlemen, you may be standing on Shakespeare's *Hamlet.*" No one said a word. Finally, somebody said, "Go ahead."

After hours of digging, we found a box-shaped affair which was lined inside with some compressed vegetable matter. The top had been broken open, so whatever had been contained in this protective covering had been removed. But something *had* been there.

We brought the vegetable matter back to the States, and we were sitting around the editorial office at *Life* magazine wondering what to do with it, when somebody said, "There's only one way we can find out what this stuff is: send it to the New York City forensic lab and ask them." So they sent it to the police department in New York, and the report came back. And this, I think, was the most interesting part of all. Without knowing anything about our expedition, they identified the material as eelgrass, a seaweed that only grows in Northern Europe. They also said that eelgrass was used as packing material in the Middle Ages. This particular eelgrass was old, at least two or three centuries, and it had been lying under pressure, and it had some sand in it, and in that sand were little pieces of something called "Danish flint." Now, Danish flint occurs only in the northeastern part of Denmark, so therefore they derived that this particular eelgrass had been lying under pressure for at least two or three centuries either in a cave or in a dungeon. And it was probably in the dungeon of Elsinore castle. Can you imagine that? Without knowing anything they came up with exactly the right answer, which is incredible! But it's also fascinating that eelgrass was used as packing material, like excelsior, thus proving that something had been there which was protected. Now, we'll never know what was in that empty box, but for all we know, perhaps the manuscript is still in the Wedge waiting to be discovered.

Parodies, Adaptations, and Versions of <u>Hamlet,</u> or, <u>Hamlet</u> for Hams

*P*arodies of *Hamlet* were especially popular in the nineteenth century, a period when practically everyone, even the illiterate, knew the play well. Charles Marowitz, who has written his own version of *Hamlet,* notes, "There's a lot of humor to be had out of *Hamlet* because so much of that stuff is familiar. You take 'To be or not to be' out of context and put it in a different setting and you've already got a gag line."

Here are some examples from nineteenth-century music-hall turns:

Hamlet the Ravin' Prince of Denmark!! or the Baltic Swell!!! And the Diving Belle!!!! A Burlesque Extravaganza in Three Acts

❖ Hamlet Revamped

❖ Hamlet à la Mode

❖ Hamlet the Hysterical: A Delirium in Five Spasms

❖ A Thin Slice of Ham-let

❖ A Black-Faced Minstrel Show *Hamlet*: Hamlet the Dainty: An Ethiopian Burlesque: A Performance by Griffin and the Christy Minstrels

❖ Hamlet: Not Such a Fool as He Looks [in which Ophelia calls Hamlet "Hammy dear" and Hamlet sings a burlesque tune]:

> *'Tis now the very witching hour of the night*
> *When Ghosts begin to toddle*
> *I'll keep my promise to the sprites*
> *And punch my uncle's noddle.*
> *Oh, what a row in Denmark! oh oh heigh ho!*
> *(Repeat)*

Finally, by 1905, the humorist P. G. Wodehouse had had enough. In "Too Much Hamlet" he writes:

> *I went into a music-hall but soon came out of it*
> *On seeing some comedians in a painful "Hamlet" skit;*
> *And a gentleman who gave some imitations, all alone,*
> *Of other people's Hamlets, plus a Hamlet of his own.*
> *It's "Hamlet" this and "Hamlet" that,*
> *And Hamlet day by day.*
> *Shakespeare and Bacon must regret they ever wrote the play.*

Then, more recently, there's Richard Curtis's "Skin Head *Hamlet*," a condensation that reduces the play's many scenes and incredibly rich language to four pages and a few words, one of which is the most common four-letter expletive in the English language.

Curtis's adaptation begins with the description:

Shakespeare's play translated into modern English. "Our hope was to achieve something like the effect of the New English Bible." Eds.

Here, translated into contemporary skinhead vernacular, is Claudius's response to the play-within-a-play:

> 1 PLAYER. *Full thirty times hath Phoebus' cart . . .*
> CLAUDIUS. I'll be fucked if I watch any more of this crap.

At the final act, Fortinbras enters to find Claudius, Gertrude, Hamlet, and Laertes dead:

> FORTINBRAS. What the fuck's going on here?
> HORATIO. A fucking mess, that's for sure.
> FORTINBRAS. No kidding. I see Hamlet's fucked.
> HORATIO. Yer.
> FORTINBRAS. Fucking shame: fucking good bloke.
> HORATIO. Too fucking right.
> FORTINBRAS. Fuck this for a lark then. Let's piss off.
> (*Exeunt with alarums.*)

Henry Miller's Hamlet

*H*enry Miller takes *Hamlet* and spins a Milleresque fantasia on the play, its themes, and its characters, which only vaguely resembles the original play. As Miller wrote, "Here I am in the land of Hamlets . . . such Hamlets . . . as Shakespeare never dreamed of."

ON THE ENGLISHNESS OF HAMLET

"*A*nd after each murder he scrupulously cleans his sword. . . . There is something about Hamlet's gestures which reminds one instinctively of the English gentleman. For me [the play] is England and nobody can convince me to the contrary. It's the very heart of England, too. I should say somewhere in the neighborhood of Sherwood Forest."

ON GERTRUDE

"Somehow I can't detach her from the image of the red queen in the *Alice* tale."

ON OPHELIA'S DEATH

"[Ophelia is] floating sweetly downstream, her ears stopped, but still smiling sweetly as is expected of the English upper classes, even in death. It is this sickly sweet smile of a waterlogged corpse which enrages Hamlet."

ON THE FINAL ACT

"Hamlet quaffs the poison goblet, but does not die immediately. He runs the King through like a piece of cold pork, with his sword. Then turning to the Queen Mother, he runs her through the stomach—gives her the high enema once and for all.

"Hamlet's now dying. . . . So he begins his last and best speech which, unfortunately, is never terminated. Rosencrantz and Guildenstern sneak out the back door. Hamlet is left alone at the banquet table, the floor strewn with corpses. He is talking a blue streak. The curtain slowly falls."

Charles Marowitz

heatre critic, director, and playwright, Charles Marowitz began his career as codirector with Peter Brook at the Royal Shakespeare Company during the mid-sixties, a collaboration that included such celebrated productions as the Paul Scofield King Lear *and* Marat/Sade. *Like Brook, Marowitz is experimental, but he does more than direct Shakespeare—he actually rewrites him. Ignoring the traditional linear plot, he "shatters" a well-known Shakespearean play—which he compares to a vase—and then, taking its fragments, reassembles them to form a new creation, a collage-like fantasia he calls recycled Shakespeare. In a way, Marowitz uses Shakespeare the way Shakespeare used his sources—as a way of telling a whole new story. There is more than one way to tell the tale of Macbeth—Shakespeare chose one way, Marowitz another, a point he emphasizes by calling his version* A Macbeth. *In his most famous creation,* The Marowitz Hamlet *(a title he finds pretentious—though it does take a certain amount of audacity to rewrite Shakespeare's masterpiece), Hamlet is an aging playboy and garrulous armchair liberal, all talk, little action. Marowitz also turns other familiar Shakespearean characters on their heads: his Othello is an Uncle Tom; Titania, a male homosexual; Prospero, an inmate in an insane asylum; and Shylock, a passionate Zionist.*

In a typically Marowitzian manner, he hopes to write and produce an extravagant multimillion-dollar musical version of Timon of Athens, *the sparsest, nastiest, most repellent play in the canon—one could scarcely imagine a less likely candidate for the musical theatre.*

NE: *How can we approach reading Shakespeare?*

CM: If you're sensitive and intelligent, you're going to get a reading of the play that's better than anything you'll see on stage; if you're a putz, you'll probably get a warped or scaled-down version. So the more sensitive and intelligent the reader, the better the play is going to be performed in their heads.

NE: *What's your view of Shakespeare?*

CM: What Shakespeare is all about, it seems to me, is that the plays can be revered as deeply traditional and yet at the same time they are about everything that goes on in most people's minds today.

Some of the plays have taken on mythic proportions. *Hamlet* has. *Romeo and Juliet, Macbeth, King Lear* to a certain extent. *Julius Caesar,* perhaps. By mythic, I mean we grow up knowing certain things about those characters but we don't know how we know them. Kids don't know how they know that Romeo and Juliet are ill-fated lovers, but they do. How do we know Hamlet can't get his act together, but we do. We don't know how we know that Macbeth is jinxed by witches. We know it because we have been immersed in this imagery for almost four hundred fifty years, and it has come down to us from generation to generation. There are lots of Shakespearean microchips lodged in our heads.

When people come to see a Shakespeare play they almost invariably come with an expectation—they've read it, they've heard about it, or they've probably seen other productions—and that anticipation is one of the most useful things for a director. Because once you know what an audience anticipates, you can frustrate those expectations and reangle them in interesting ways. What's interesting is not the beaten path, but how one creates highways and detours using the plays as starting points.

NE: *Is this what you try to do?*

CM: Yes, I create that difference exclusively.

NE: *How can you tell the difference between gimmicks for their own sake and ideas that are really in the play?*

CM: You *can* make a lot of points that are not in the original play. But some people are furious if they don't see what they expect to see in Shakespeare. They want that traditional experience. You will never please them unless you do Shakespeare boringly straight.

The first time we did our version of *Hamlet* it caused riots in Berlin. The major critic there wrote a negative review, but the students liked it and handed out leaflets in front of the theatre as a sort of counterblast.

It divided people very heavily, but it wasn't supposed to be Shakespeare's *Hamlet*: it was a ninety-minute free adaptation. If you came expecting the traditional *Hamlet*, then you would of course have been disappointed or outraged. But if you didn't go with those kinds of expectations, you could have appreciated it in a different way.

NE: *Why do you think they were outraged?*

CM: I blame the academics. Shakespeare's language comes down to us as embalmed and if people don't hear that language they feel as if something sacred has been violated. I'm looking forward to seeing this Branagh production of *Henry V*, but I have no real hope for it. Branagh is just a child of the establishment; he's been brought up on a love for Shakespearean language. I know what I'll see is some version of a straightforward conventional work. To me, the language is incidental. I'm much more concerned with the imagery that's evoked *by* language.

NE: *Is this the first generation to rewrite Shakespeare?*

CM: Innovation isn't new. In the past they rewrote *Romeo and Juliet* to give it a happy ending; there were a lot of burlesques of Shakespeare in the nineteenth century—probably because they were more familiar with him than we are. Today we want Shakespeare's plays to represent our values and our times, so we fragment them. We make them go off into all different directions. We take a negative, ironic, or cynical approach to the material. So we're not doing anything very different from any other age, which is to ask the material to speak to us in our own way.

Improbable
Shakespeareans

*I*n the nineteenth century, to be an actor meant to be a Shakespearean
*actor. Today, however, we tend to associate a certain type of actor and style
of acting with Shakespeare. Nonetheless, the least likely figures have
appeared at one time or another in a Shakespeare play. Type casting can
be dangerous, however: the terribly British Rex Harrison admitted he never wanted to do Shakespeare, while no one could have imagined that Mel
Gibson (or Richard Chamberlain) would make a credible Hamlet. Of
course, strictly speaking, not all of the following are straight Shakespeare,
but there is something touching about Hollywood's adaptations of the
Bard—how can one resist the idea of Tony Curtis in* Othello: Black Commando*?*

❖ **Abdul:** A real witch doctor in Orson Welles's "Voodoo *Macbeth.*"

❖ **Louis Armstrong:** Bottom in "Swingin' the Dream," a 1939
jazz adaptation of *A Midsummer Night's Dream;* see page 371.

❖ **Marlon Brando:** Marc Antony in the 1953 *Julius Caesar.*
Although Brando refused to take a screen test for the role, he
did agree to make an audiotape. John Houseman writes in his
autobiography that according to Hollywood rumor, "Brando
had persuaded Laurence Olivier to make the tape for him and
that we had fallen for the substitution." Houseman also recalled
that the inexperienced and nervous Brando was continually

Marlon Brando as Antony in the 1953 film *Julius Caesar.*
ã

Jerry Ohlinger's Movie Material Store, New York

coached on verse speaking by John Gielgud, who played Cassius. The funeral oration required a week of shooting, but Brando "never questioned the necessity for so much repetitious coverage."

✤ **Humphrey Bogart:** Henry IV in a radio adaptation of the play.

✤ **James Cagney:** Nick Bottom in Max Reinhardt's movie of *A Midsummer Night's Dream* (1935). According to Jack J. Jorgens in *Shakespeare on Film,* Cagney was a cross between a "union weaver, Chicago hood and the Ugly Duckling."

✤ **Richard Chamberlain:** Hamlet and Richard II. Chamberlain first performed Hamlet at the Birmingham Repertory Theatre in 1969. A television production of his performance was aired in the United States on "Hallmark Hall of Fame." Americans, accustomed to seeing Chamberlain wearing a white coat and with a stethoscope around his neck, disdained his performance, but the British, who had no such associations, rated it highly.

✤ **Quentin Crisp:** In an example of casting against type, the urbane and witty Crisp plays the cliché-spouting Polonius in Celestino Coronado's 1976 punk *Hamlet,* in which Helen Mirren plays both Ophelia and Gertrude.

✤ **Tony Curtis:** Iago in *Othello: Black Commando,* a 1982 movie in which the screen credits spell "Shakespeare" as "Sheakspeare."

✤ **Marianne Faithfull:** The popular singer and Mick Jagger's former girlfriend playing Hamlet's former girlfriend, Ophelia, in Tony Richardson's 1969 film *Hamlet.*

✤ **Morgan Freeman and Tracey Ullman:** Although Freeman and Ullman are gifted actors, the two together made an odd couple as Kate and Petruchio in Joseph Papp's 1990 *The Taming of the Shrew.* The innovative casting was enhanced by the play's Old West setting, in which Ullman played Kate as an Annie Oakley spitfire.

✤ **Lorne Greene:** In blackface as Othello in a 1953 Canadian television production.

❖ **Richie Havens:** In the rock opera inspired by *Othello* called *Catch My Soul;* see page 462.

❖ **Ted Lange:** Television viewers will remember Lange as the bartender on the inane TV show "The Love Boat." Lange, however, is a dedicated Shakespearean who directed and starred in a 1988 film version of *Othello* (with a black Iago) and staged a flashy *Richard III* (1975); see page 341.

❖ **Piper Laurie:** Lady Macbeth in a 1981 video *Macbeth* produced by the American-based Bard Production Series video. The production was described by a reviewer in the *Shakespeare on Film Newsletter* as "a deed without a name" and a fulfillment of the play's curse.

❖ **Norman Mailer:** Himself in Jean-Luc Godard's mafioso *Lear.*

❖ **Walter Matthau:** Iago in the 1953 "Philco Television Playhouse" production of *Othello.*

❖ **Nichelle Nichols** (Uhura) and **Walter Koenig** (Chekov) of "Star Trek" appear as Charmian and Lepidus in the Bard Production Series video of *Antony and Cleopatra*. **Tony Geary** of "General Hospital" fame played Octavius Caesar.

❖ **Michelle Pfeiffer:** Olivia in Joseph Papp's star-filled 1989 *Twelfth Night* in Central Park. According to Mimi Kramer, a drama critic at *The New Yorker,* "You've never seen a woman who would be more at home in a singles bar." With Gregory Hines as Feste, Jeff Goldblum as Malvolio, and Mary Elizabeth Mastrantonio as Viola.

❖ **Edward G. Robinson:** Hotspur in a radio adaptation of *Henry IV.*

❖ **Mickey Rooney:** At age fifteen, Puck in Reinhardt's *A Midsummer Night's Dream.* In his autobiography, Rooney admits, "I'd never read Shakespeare before or since"; see page 496.

❖ **Jimmy Smits:** Messenger in *Hamlet* in Joseph Papp's New York Shakespeare Festival, 1982.

Novelty Shakespeare

*A*ctors and directors feel free to take liberties with Shakespeare. After all, he's been dead for almost five hundred years and can't complain about copyright laws, colorization, bowdlerization, and other distortions of his plots, characters, and settings. Directors can assure themselves that Shakespeare would have approved of their efforts, since they are simply following Shakespeare's own dramatic strategy: borrow other artists' material and make it your own.

❖ **Ben Donenberg's Starship Shakespeare: A Sort of Elizabethan Star Trek** (1985): Al's Bar, and the Odyssey Theatre, in Los Angeles. The plot is Shakespeare for Trekkies: ten characters—Hamlet, Lady Macbeth, Juliet, Prospero, Richard III, Othello, Lear, Iago, Bottom, and God—scheme for control of the starship and try to subvert one another. The play ends with Hamlet and Richard III in an elaborate sword-and-pie fight, and when everyone is finally killed, Bottom, the ship's janitor, waltzes in and asserts, "I who was Bottom am now the top." "Star Trek" motifs and conventions are interspersed with Shakespearean turns of phrase (e.g., Hamlet declaims, "To eat, or not to eat").

❖ **The Reduced Shakespeare Company:** A Los Angeles–based theatrical company that presents *The Complete Works of William Shakespeare (Abridged)*. This company, the *other* RSC, is composed of three actors, who perform thirty-five plays in just under two hours—that is, the entire canon except *Othello,* because, as one member of the group explains in the program notes, "Let's face it, we're honkeys." According to one reviewer, the performance is a Reader's Digest Condensed Book version of the Bard as acted by Monty Python. The Wars of the Roses become a football match played by two teams, the Yorks and the Lancasters, which breaks up when King Lear sneaks onto the field from another play. The company's program notes warn that the show is harmful to those with English degrees or inner-ear disorders.

✤ **Lee Breuer's** *Lear*: In this 1990 New York production, partly underwritten by AT&T, Shakespeare's king undergoes a sex and geographical change and becomes a matriarch in the American South of the 1950s. The review in *The New Yorker* says it all: "We are accustomed to Shakespeare performances in un-Shakespearean settings and to actresses undertaking male roles, but Mr. Breuer not only reverses the sexes of all the characters, he sets much of the action on a pitch n' putt golf course, and mixes race and type so that the storm-racked heath is no longer populated by the dispossessed British king and his familiar remnant but by two elderly women (Kent and Lear), a drag queen (the Fool), and a young black woman disguised in the rags and dirty dreadlocks of a street person (Edgar)."

✤ **Kristin Linkletter's Company of Woman:** An all-female acting troupe that debuted in Boston in 1990 with *Henry V*—quite a challenge, considering that the play pretty much consists of one long battle scene and most of its characters are men. Not a jokey burlesque but genuine "straight" Shakespeare, this female *Henry V* asks us to take the Chorus's request in the Prologue to a new dimension. If we can momentarily suspend disbelief and imagine a "cockpit" as the "vasty fields of France," why can't a woman become Henry V?

✤ **Richard III:** Directed by actor Ted Lange and performed by the Oakland (California) Ensemble Theatre in 1977, this production began with all the flashy brilliance of a floor show. Lange described the opening: "We began with Neil Diamond's 'Hot August Night,' which starts off with a solo cello, then a guitar picks up, and then it goes into hard rock 'n' roll. The actor playing Richard steps into a pin spot of light where there are four ballerinas. The first one holds a glove, the second a jacket with a hump attached to it, the third a shoe of a different height, and the fourth a sword. They dance in a classical manner around him, one by one, and then the first slips the jacket on him, and his body changes; the second puts his foot in the shoe, and it's now deformed; the third slips the glove on his hand, which immediately withers; and the fourth kneels and hands him the sword. Richard takes the sword just as the guitar starts playing, and cuts them all down. Stabs them. He is now Richard III."

❖ **Swingin' the Dream:** Set in New Orleans at the turn of the century, this 1939 jazz adaptation of *A Midsummer Night's Dream* starred Louis Armstrong as a trumpet-playing Bottom, Butterfly McQueen (Prissy in *Gone With the Wind*) as Puck, Juan Hernandez (*Intruder in the Dust*) as Oberon, Jackie "Moms" Mabley as Quince, and the three Dandridge sisters, Dorothy, Vivien, and Etta, as fairies. The Benny Goodman Jazz Sextet, the Rhythmettes, and the Deep River Boys supplied the music to which this dream was swung.

*L*ouis Armstrong as Bottom in *Swingin' the Dream.*

New York Public Library/The Billy Rose Theatre Collection

Othello

*I had this fancy ... Shakespeare
and Burbage went out on a
binge one night, each trying to
outdrink the other. . . . Just before
one or the other slid under the
alehouse table, Burbage looked at
Shakespeare and said, "I can
play anything you write—anything at all." And Shakespeare
said, "Right. I'll fix you, boy,"
and wrote* Othello.

—LAURENCE OLIVIER

thello is both riveting and repellent. If you're like most people,
you won't be able to take your eyes off the stage, but at the same time,
that's all you'll want to do. The play's visceral hold on an audience is
unmatched in Shakespeare. People hate it, love it, or fear it. Its emotions are so highly pitched, its plot so improbable, its action so compressed, that without the right touch it can easily collapse into
melodrama or farce. *Othello* is the archetypal tale of the jealous husband, the butt of countless Elizabethan cuckoldry jests; but in the
hands of Shakespeare, what would normally be the subject of coarse
humor becomes one of the most moving spectacles of the stage.

Structured like a contrapuntal piece of music that harmoniously combines two opposing melodies, the play's plot *is* sensational—and, indeed, it seems more fitting for an opera, which it became. Othello's speeches are pure music, his diction ornate and formal, but the play is also about ordinary men and women, and its opposing voice, as represented by Iago, is colloquial, obscene, and knowing. Thus Shakespeare demands that viewers stretch their imagination, even as he presents them with a very familiar situation. An audience can't dismiss *Othello* as preposterous, because Shakespeare is writing about sexual jealousy, an emotion that touches a nerve in almost everyone. Most of us accept that jealousy makes people behave outrageously. From one perspective, Othello's murder of Desdemona is a romantic apotheosis; from another, it's extremely vulgar—crimes of passion can be found on the police blotter of any city. (Shaw despised the play for what he called its "police-court morality and commonplace thought.") Both aspects, represented by Othello and Iago, work together: without poetry, *Othello* would be squalid; without realism, it would be histrionic.

Several things set the play apart from Shakespeare's other great tragedies. First, it isn't about kings and queens; its tragedy is domestic and private. Usually, when an unnatural crime occurs in Shakespearean tragedy, the heavens open up and nature revolts, but Othello's crime is simply Othello's. A private act in the conjugal bedroom, it doesn't affect the universe or the state. And unlike Shakespeare's other plays, *Othello* concentrates on one emotion: sexual jealousy. It is relentless in its narrow focus. Neither a subplot nor an amusing character diverts us from the inevitable climax; there is not a fool nor a good joke in the whole play. (There is a character called "Clown," but he has only five lines, and his part is usually cut.) The only joker in Shakespeare's tragic pack of cards is Iago.

Everything in the play contributes to its claustrophobic atmosphere. Most of it takes place in one locale, which grows ever more claustrophobic as Othello's thoughts become increasingly narrow and monomaniacal. Contributing to this stifling quality is the fact that the play is an interior drama, with very little physical action. (As W. H. Auden pointed out, Iago is the only character who acts; all the others react.) Most of the drama consists of the struggle within Othello's psyche.

At first, Iago merely hints at Desdemona's infidelity with Cassio. Othello's imagination supplies the rest. Suspicion then becomes a vile odor from which he can't escape, polluting everything—his wife, his reputation, his occupation, even his language. Othello begins the play poised and confident, at the height of his powers and uttering the most sublime poetry. But by the time Iago has done his work, Othello's "music" has disintegrated into linguistic chaos:

> Lie with her? Lie on her? We say lie on her when they belie her. Lie with her! Zounds, that's fulsome! Handkerchief—confession—handkerchief!

(IV.1.35–37)

Othello's downfall is measured not so much by what happens to him as by what happens to his language.

From beginning to end, Iago's motives remain unfathomable. We never know what perverse spite drives him. Early in *Othello,* Iago, in one of his numerous asides, offers a possible reason:

> I hate the Moor,
> And it is thought abroad that 'twixt my sheets
> He's done my office. I know not if't be true
> But I, for mere suspicion in that kind,
> Will do as if for surety.

(I.3.380–84)

One excuse will do as well as another. He decides to destroy Othello and then finds reasons for it. Critics have come up with various motives for Iago's behavior: Iago is a racist and his superior is a black man; Othello has passed him by for promotion; perhaps Othello *did* have an affair with Emilia, Iago's wife; Iago is subconsciously attracted to Desdemona—or even to Othello. But ultimately, Iago destroys Othello because it's his nature to do so. When asked for his motives, the loquacious villain remains surprisingly silent:

> OTHELLO. Will you, I pray, demand that demi-devil
>   Why he hath thus ensnared my soul and body?
> IAGO. Demand me nothing; what you know, you know;
>   From this time forth I never will speak word.

(V.2.298–301)

We thus leave asking Othello's question: Who is Iago? Like Satan himself, Iago has the ability to transform himself into the shape of his enemy's secret fears and desires. Auden claimed he was a practical joker "of a peculiarly appalling kind." Maybe he's just bored, or a frustrated playwright who enjoys plotting real, instead of fictional, tragedies. Perhaps the answer is more simple: he is a psychopath, a type all too familiar to us today. Shakespeare is one of the first writers to create such a character—the charming man without a conscience. And Iago *must* be seductive; otherwise Othello's downfall wouldn't be convincing.

For the play to work as tragedy, however, the audience must sympathize with Othello, not Iago. Ultimately, Iago alienates the audience by the way in which he reduces everything to sex and money. To him, Othello is just "an old black ram . . . tupping your white ewe," and the faithful Desdemona, a "super-subtle Venetian" who will dismiss Othello "when she is sated with his body. . . . She must change for youth." To Iago's leering eyes, she is simply an upper-class debutante nymphomaniac enjoying a new sex game, with Othello as her boytoy.

Iago *is* loathsome, but at times Othello also seems despicable. How could he let this happen? One answer may lie in his inexperience with women: he's a middle-aged soldier whose dealings have been primarily with men, and his irreproachable past has made him idealize what he does not know. (A few critics and actors have speculated that he's sexually innocent, and John Gielgud confessed that he couldn't act the part unless he played him as a virgin.) As a romantic idealist with a trusting nature, he has little knowledge of sin. He places all his faith in Desdemona, and when she falls in his eyes, his entire world falls with her.

The climax of the play is terrible to watch. Desdemona pleads and bargains for her life: "Kill me tomorrow: let me live tonight!" He doesn't want to kill her; she doesn't want to die; but the scene relentlessly proceeds. When he finally strangles her, he's not insane—and this is what makes the scene so chilling. Coldly and in complete control, he murders her out of his uncompromising sense of justice—and his love. To Othello, Desdemona deserves to die.

Symbolically, it is particularly fitting that Desdemona should be smothered. As Othello falls deeper into madness, the play's atmosphere becomes increasingly airless and enclosed. Trapped within Othello's psychic nightmare, Desdemona, lovely and vibrant, can't possibly breathe—let alone thrive. Her last panicked gasp is not simply that of a dying woman, but a choking attempt to break free from the suffocating fantasy in which her husband has imprisoned her.

Desdemona isn't the play's only victim. Othello, too, is engulfed by Iago's snare of deceit, and once entrapped, he never considers any alternative to madness. His all-or-nothing integrity denies him the freedom of choice. Iago has done his work all too well. Only at the end does he, heartbreakingly, regain his sanity, and he dies knowing that he has destroyed what he loved best on earth.

Modern audiences want to know why Othello doesn't simply ask Desdemona if she's been unfaithful. But this is to put the play into the twentieth century, when couples seek marital counseling, and infidelity is the stuff of cocktail-party gossip. In *Othello,* we enter a rarefied world where logic seems irrelevant. The tragedy is that Othello wouldn't believe her denials; Iago's poison has already affected him too deeply. The tragedy is that this hero who is larger than life can't do the simple thing, and that this man with such a "free and open nature" is so vulnerable to Iago's covert machinations.

The one question that remains unanswerable is the one Shakespeare obsessively explores in all his major plays—the conflict between appearance and reality. Othello's black skin hides his innate aristocracy; "honest" Iago is treacherous; and the chaste Desdemona is branded a whore. In a world of false impressions, can we ever really know the truth? When truth masquerades as lies, and lies appear so true, can we ever know anything with certitude? If Othello, who by his own admission is not a jealous man, who seemed so self-possessed, could lose everything, who among us is safe?

❖ The bond between Iago and Othello is more powerful than that between any of the playwright's romantic lovers. It's not enough that each actor play his role well; there must be a potent chemistry between them. Here are some of the most famous pairings:

OTHELLO	IAGO	
Ralph Richardson	Laurence Olivier	(1938)
Paul Robeson	José Ferrer (New York)	(1943)
Orson Welles	Michael MacLiammòir	(1952)
Laurence Olivier	Frank Finlay	(1964)
James Earl Jones	Christopher Plummer	(1982)
Ben Kingsley	David Suchet	(1985, 1986)
Anthony Hopkins	Bob Hoskins	(1983)
Raul Julia	Christopher Walken, Richard Dreyfuss	(1990)

❖ If you can't see a live performance of the play, try to rent the 1983 BBC video from your local library. Bob Hoskins's Iago, a plainspoken cockney with a nervous giggle, makes an effective contrast to Anthony Hopkins's frantically earnest Othello. Penelope Wilton is a refreshingly commonsensical Desdemona. Breaking with tradition, Hopkins's Othello is a light-skinned Arab rather than a black Moor, since Jonathan Miller thought that the presence of a black Othello would obscure the play's fundamental theme of jealousy. (Director and actor Ted Lange scoffs at this interpretation: "British Equity wouldn't let the BBC hire American actors, so James Earl Jones, their first choice, was out. The British don't have any black stars, so Miller had to come up with a rationale to explain why they had a white actor in the role.")

❖ You might also want to look at Michael MacLiammòir's *Put Money in Thy Purse,* a day-to-day account of his experience playing Iago to Orson Welles's Othello.

What to Look for in <u>Othello</u>

*T*he first scene is extraordinary—and very confusing. At once we are plunged into an atmosphere where the differences between appearance and reality, truth and lies, are obscured. This is the world of *Othello*. It is night; two men are having a secret conversation, and though we don't know it yet, they are Iago and Roderigo talking of the unnamed Othello. Apparently, Iago has been taking money from Roderigo to advance the latter's suit with an unnamed woman. Roderigo has just learned that this woman has eloped with another man, and he now calls Iago to account for leading him on. Shrewdly, Iago deflects Roderigo's anger from himself onto the abductor, an unnamed man whom they both hate, Roderigo because he has eloped with the woman, and Iago, because he has neglected to promote him. Iago comes off as bluff, practical, and honest, a worthy soldier. We sympathize with his sense of injured merit, and we suspect this mysterious Moor, also called "thicklips" and "the devil," of treachery.

But one glance at Othello in the next scene reveals how false first impressions can be (and our willingness to trust appearances makes what happens to Othello all the more convincing). The difference between what "honest" Iago says about Othello and what Othello truly *is* emphasizes the conflict between appearance and reality.

*I*n Act IV, scene 3, haunted by premonitions of death, Desdemona sings an old ballad of betrayal while Emilia undresses her for what will be their last night on earth. The two women chat while they contemplate their own mortality. The scene achieves the impossible: it is homey and unearthly, ordinary and ominous. Paradoxically, it heightens the dramatic tension while at the same time serving as a relief from the play's relentless pace.

*A*long with Richard III, Iago is Shakespeare's greatest Machiavel. In the course of *Othello,* he is called "honest" fifteen times by everybody in the play, including himself. (The word is mentioned a total of forty-two times in the play.) His philosophy is summed up when he says, "I am not what I am," and in Act I, scene 3, he sneers, "Virtue? A fig!" His credo, adapted for all situations, is "Put money in thy purse."

Othello:
Shakespeare's Most
Intense Play

*F*ew people leave a performance of *Othello* untouched. Racial tension, sexual jealousy, and a lurid, melodramatic plot make for dramatic dynamite. Only recently have audiences of mainstream theatregoers been permitted to see an older, black man touching a young, white woman, and even when the black man is a white actor in blackface, the sight has stirred people's deepest anxieties about sex as well as about race.

The *Othello* editor Julie Hankey writes, "*Othello* has laid hold of people, primitively, in a way that no other Shakespearean tragedy could hope to do. Women have shrieked and fainted, old men have laid their heads down on their arms and sobbed, young men have lost their sleep and gone about for days in a trance. The story comes very near to ordinary people's lives." It's safe to say that there's been more audience participation with *Othello* than with any other Shakespearean play, and critical responses are rarely tepid.

❖ During one production in the Old West, a member of the audience took out his pistol and shot the actor who was playing Iago. On his tombstone were the words "Here lies the greatest actor."

*Exasperation is the word I should choose to express the state of feeling which the reading of *Othello* induces in me.*

—TOLSTOY

❖ In 1752 the *Virginia Gazette* reported that a Cherokee chief and his squaw visited Williamsburg to take part in a friendship treaty. As a peace offering, they were invited to attend a performance of *Othello* at the local playhouse. When, however, it came time for the sword-fight scene, the squaw became so distraught that she ordered one of her braves to ascend the stage and separate the two actors.

❖ During Paul Robeson's famed performance in 1943, the director Margaret Webster overheard a young girl in the audience murmur to herself, "Oh God, don't let him kill her . . . don't let him kill her, oh God."

❖ When Edmund Forrest played Iago to Edmund Kean's Othello, a member of the audience was heard to say, "You damn'd lying scoundrel, I would like to get hold of you after this show is over and wring your infernal neck."

❖ Ivor Brown, the theatre critic for the London *Observer,* dreaded having to review the play: "The spectacle of criminal lunacy and the epileptic screamings of an ignoble savage, who for a whisper of tattle would chop his wife into messes is revolting."

Actors and directors have an equally difficult time with the play:

❖ Michael Redgrave confessed to reservations about playing the title role: "I'm afraid of Othello. . . . I don't think I could do it."

❖ Worst of all is when the actor playing Othello (such as Paul Scofield in 1980) embarrassingly overacts, and the audience ends up laughing at a farce instead of weeping at the tragedy. According to one critic, Scofield "rather carefully lies on the floor and knocks his head against it [or] lowers himself onto the deathbed and moos three times like a cow."

❖ Desdemona's handkerchief, which Iago plants in Cassio's chamber, is the evidence used to convince Othello of his wife's guilt. It's this bit of flimsy stage business that drives the "anti-*Othello*ans" crazy.

One day during rehearsal, Margaret Webster, who played Emilia, walked onstage in Act III, scene 3, only to find that Desdemona's handkerchief was missing. Suddenly she realized something crucial about the play: "No handkerchief, no play. I couldn't give it to Iago, he couldn't plant it on Cassio, Othello couldn't see Cassio give it to Bianca, Iago couldn't use that to prove Desdemona's guilt—the whole play fell to pieces like a pack of cards."

Iago

*I*ago comes into *Othello* as a malignant and destructive plotter, and is there because the play could not do without him, and Desdemona's handkerchief would never have been stolen or the fatal flaw of jealousy in a noble mind exposed. It can be left to Victorian professors to search endlessly for explanations for Iago's behavior, as if he were a nineteenth-century politician scheming for power; it can be left to modern actors to invent such absurdities as Iago's frustrated homosexual passion for his Moorish master. . . . By behaving as he does, [Iago] makes the play work.

—JOHN MORTIMER

I think that few who have had experience in the armed forces can find Iago hard to understand. One only has to glance round a wardroom table and take note of the ageing, hard-bitten faces of those passed over. When I was a two-striper in the Royal Navy, one of my fellow officers was given a half-stripe more than I, and from this favourable position decided he would amuse himself by taking the mickey out of me. There was no way I could get back at him, and resentment began to fester. One evening I suddenly thought of a way: "Of course; he's married!" Flushing with horror, I realized—God, I've become Iago!

—LAURENCE OLIVIER

*A*ny consideration of *The Tragedy of Othello* must be primarily occupied not with its official hero but with its villain. I cannot think of any other play in which only one character performs the personal actions—all the *deeds* are Iago's—and all the others without exception only exhibit behaviour. . . . Nor can I think of another play in which the villain is so completely triumphant; everything Iago sets out to do, he accomplishes (among his goals, I include his self-destruction).

—W. H. AUDEN

*I*ago [Orson Welles] went on to say . . . was in his opinion impotent; this secret malady was, in fact, the keystone of the actor's approach. Realized, as the talk grew more serious, that I was more in agreement than ever, but felt no necessity to assume appropriate expression so just sat there looking pleasant. (Sudden hideous thought: maybe pleasant, slightly doped expression, habitual with me during meals, *is* the appropriate one for suggestion of impotence and this why O. who has watched me consume several meals, thinks me so made for the part? Must remember to sound him on this and prove him mistaken.)

"Impotent," he roared in (surely somewhat forced) rich bass baritone, "that's why he hates life so much—they always do."

—MICHAEL MACLIAMMÒIR

*O*thello is no dummy. He believed what Iago said. Iago was his trusted lieutenant. The two men fought side by side; they killed together;

they drank together; they womanized together; they dreamt together. Iago was wronged. Othello *should* have given him the lieutenancy. Not that what Iago did was justified, but remember, that promotion was given to *Cassio,* a guy who never fought in a war, never knew the anguish of battle, and who was wealthy and sheltered—basically a Dan Quayle. Why couldn't Iago be the man who is out of control instead of the man who is calculating? He has a right to be pissed.

—CHARLES "ROC" DUTTON

*A*t [Tyrone] Guthrie's request, Olivier accompanied him to [the psychoanalyst Ernest] Jones's office . . . for two long evenings of textual analysis, during which the Othello–Iago relationship was easily interpreted for them by the Freudian acolyte. Iago was not, they were told, jealous of the Moor; rather, he was subconsciously in love with him, and this homosexual attraction led to his destruction of Othello's marriage to Desdemona. . . .

But the odd idea of Iago's subconscious love became quite overt as rehearsals proceeded: Othello's third-act line "Now art thou my lieutenant" evoked an almost amusingly lascivious tone in Iago's reply, "I am your own forever." [Ralph] Richardson coped with all this by ignoring it—until the moment Olivier threw his arms around his neck and kissed him full on the mouth. "There, there, now, dear boy," Richardson said gently.

—DONALD SPOTO, OLIVIER'S BIOGRAPHER

A nasty bastard.

—BOB HOSKINS

David Suchet

*C*onvincing *portrayals of Shakespearean characters often depend upon the actor's understanding the character from the inside out—sometimes even inventing a background from which the character evolves. Before staging* Othello, *Stanislavsky devised a fictional biography for the hero that would account for his gestures, speech, and actions. Other actors, like Olivier, work from the outside in, creating idiosyncratic mannerisms that physically convey a character's psyche. Whatever route an actor chooses, he must convey a sense of depth behind a character; otherwise, his Othello or Lear would be an automaton reciting beautiful lines, rather than a flesh-and-blood creature.*

David Suchet, who played Iago to Ben Kingsley's Othello in Terry Hand's Royal Shakespeare Company's production at Stratford in 1985, imagines a past for Othello that Shakespeare probably never envisioned.

DS: I think it could be argued that Desdemona and Othello never make love.

NE: *Othello? The warrior who seduces Desdemona by merely* talking *to her?*

DS: Don't look at it from a 1960s point of view! He meets this young girl who falls in love with his . . . stories. He has this magnificent voice, *and* this charm, and incredible grace. . . . But he's an *old* soldier; we never see him fight. He's had it. If I were to play him, I'd play him with slightly gray hair and a potbelly.

Othello marries this young girl, but at the first sign of a fight on his wedding night he prefers to look after his friend Montano's wounds rather than go back to bed with his bride. Why? We *know* why—and so does Iago. Why does Desdemona decide to get out the wedding sheets just before she's killed by her husband? Do you think she's going to take out sheets if they're stained with blood? What's that going to do? But if she gets out the clean wedding sheets that have never been used, *then* when Othello enters the bedroom and sees *those* sheets and touches them, he goes bananas! *Then* he thinks she has had Cassio *in his bed*! And there she is, lying on *those* sheets—which *he's* never used with her. . . .

NE: *With this in mind, how would you play the strangulation scene?*

DS: Crying my eyes out as I murder what I love.

Bettmann/Hulton

*T*he climactic scene: Sarah Stephenson as Desdemona and Bruce Purchase as Othello in the 1971 production at the Swan Theatre in London. In this erotic production, Othello was hardly virginal.

Smother, Stifle, or Strangle?

In the original Italian tale of the Moor from Giraldi Cinthio's Hecatommithi (1565), the Othello's counterpart kills his wife by causing their bed to fall on her. Shakespeare wisely changed this when he wrote the play. Nevertheless, this scene, interpreted variously from one production to the next, must be one of the most unforgettable in drama. The original stage direction read "stifles her," but others say "smothers" or "strangles." Most actors take advantage of the scene's charged eroticism. Olivier strangled his Desdemona, and the sight of his excessively blackened hands gripping Maggie Smith's whitened neck heightened the scene's stark cruelty. In his movie version, Orson Welles stretches a scarf across Desdemona's mouth and then kisses her through it. In several productions, the murder takes place offstage to the accompaniment of snorting, grunting, and gurgling.

Early productions were especially violent: the actress Madge Kendall complained that her Othello, Ira Aldridge, made her wear toed stockings with sandals to suggest nudity: "He used to take me out of bed by my hair and drag me round the stage before he smothered me. So brutal did it seem that the audience hissed the business vociferously."

Less exciting, perhaps, but a more ingenious interpretation, is that in the Garson Kanin–Ruth Gordon film *A Double Life* (1948), in which a Shakespearean actor (played by Ronald Colman) wins critical raves by smothering Desdemona not with a pillow but with a kiss.

The Victorians were fascinated by the scene, and one nineteenth-century literalist wrote an article detailing the exact method Othello used, complete with diagrams of Desdemona's throat, larynx, and trachea.

Charles Marowitz's
An Othello

*I*n his version of Othello, *the avant-garde director and writer Charles Marowitz emphasizes the element of racism, a theme that is subtly explored in Shakespeare's play. Drawing upon Shakespeare's basic plot, Marowitz wrote* An Othello *in 1972, a time of race riots in London.*

NE: *What do you think of Othello as a character?*

CM: My attitude toward Othello is very un-Shakespearean. I don't see him as a great noble savage but as a toady and as someone who made a contemptible adjustment to his white masters. Because, as you know, in *Othello,* Othello is sent as a general of a white force to battle against brown-skinned men. What we tried to do was indict the kind of black man who lends himself to being exploited by a white establishment society.

NE: *What did you want* An Othello *to say?*

CM: We wanted to say something about black power, so we incorporated material from Malcolm X and Eldridge Cleaver, and we added some contemporary scenes. Iago is black, a black-power type, and Othello is an Uncle Tom. Iago tries to make Othello aware that he's a toady who sucks up and caves in to white men's views.

NE: *How else did you change the play?*

CM: Iago speaks a street argot filled with obscenity. Everyone always goes on about the Othello "music." I wanted to find a contrast to this beautiful music. The best contrast I could find was the sort of gutter obscenity that is very much a part of the black lingo [e.g., Iago says: "All that . . . about how you was hip enough to leave all those cotton-pickin' coons behind you, because you knew where all that gravy lay. . . . And it weren't with those . . . watermelon munchin' darkies"].

Iago notes that Othello, by killing himself night after night on stage, is a sacrifice to a white audience's pleasure. Just as Othello is about to commit suicide, Iago asks, "Are you going to be a tool of white audiences just to give them a catharsis?"

NE: *What would people get out of your production if they hadn't seen Shakespeare's* Othello*?*

CM: A very warped view of what the play is about.

Paul Robeson's Othello

*M*argaret Webster's 1943 production of *Othello* with Paul Robeson at the Schubert Theater in New York was a sensation, owing to the presence of Robeson, who drew a most un-Shakespearean crowd: taxi drivers, soldiers, union officials, all lined up for Shakespeare. One cab driver asked Uta Hagen, who played Desdemona, if someone had rewritten the play, he was so surprised he had understood it. It was one of those rare times when people went to see Shakespeare and were surprised by the outcome of the story. Julie Hankey comments, "People said to each other during the interval, 'Now for heaven's sake, don't tell me what happens.' "

But the most touching tribute came in a letter to Margaret Webster from a GI who saw the play while on leave:

Last Saturday night I saw *Othello.* It took a lot of coaxing to get four soldiers to spend Saturday night of the first weekend leave in a month, in a theatre, watching something by Will Shakespeare. You didn't know what was at stake when the curtain went up—my life practically. Well, what followed is only natural. We all of us, for those brief hours, went into a trance; we were living every emotion in the play. (One was a first Sarge, and my dear Miss Webster, that which moves a first Sergeant is almost miraculous.) . . . Incidentally, going back on the troop train (it's a six hour ride) for the first time in my army career, I saw five soldiers sprawled over the seats, feet in the air, sleeves rolled up, shirts open talking not about the babe they met in the Broadway Brewery, but of all things, a thing called *Othello*.

*M*argaret Webster's *Othello* is regarded as the landmark event that changed American theatre. Paul Robeson first played Othello, with Peggy Ashcroft as Desdemona, in London in 1930, but when they were to tour the United States they discovered that American audiences weren't ready to see a middle-aged black man touching a young white woman, and the American tour was canceled. Robeson's outspokenness, both as socialist and as civil rights advocate, fueled the controversy even further. Finally, in 1942, Webster brought Robeson's *Othello* to the United States, where it played in several cities before opening on Broadway in 1943. It ran for almost three hundred performances, a record at that time for a Shakespeare play in America.

Charles "Roc" Dutton on Ira Aldridge, American Black Theatre, and Othello

If lives have plots, than Charles "Roc" Dutton's has been one of almost Shakespearean magnitude. His training in Shakespeare began with life, not elocution. Born in Baltimore in 1951, he was convicted of manslaughter at the age of seventeen. When he talks about Macbeth's having blood on his hands, he knows whereof he speaks. Soon after being paroled, Dutton was picked up for possession of a deadly weapon, and after assaulting a prison guard, received eight more years. This was the beginning of what Aristotle called a dramatic crisis, the point at which the hero's fortunes take a turn. Placed in solitary confinement, he turned, out of sheer boredom, to an anthology of black playwrights and was struck by the power of drama. Upon his release from solitary, he began a prison theatre workshop at the Maryland Correctional Institution. Then, after being stabbed by another prisoner with a homemade icepick, Dutton devoted himself wholeheartedly to studying drama. In 1976 he simultaneously received his parole and his associate degree, and enrolled in the theatre department at Towson State University. He then went on to Yale Drama School. Today he is regarded as one of America's finest actors, appearing in his own television series, "Roc," films (Mississippi Masala*), and stage (his portrayal of Willie in August Wilson's* The Piano Lesson *earned him a Tony award nomination). In 1986 he played Othello at the Yale Repertory Theatre, and he has conducted master classes on Shakespeare. While at Yale he created a one-man show,* The Prince of Senegal, *about the great neglected nineteenth-century black Shakespearean actor Ira Aldridge.*

NE: *Let's start with Ira Aldridge. How did you become interested in him?*

CD: I didn't know anything about him until I was at Yale Drama School. I knew that Howard University's theatre is called the Ira Aldridge Playhouse, but I thought that he had probably been an instructor or a founder of the Theatre Department. During my first year at Yale I took a theatre history class, and when we got to the last part of the semester the professor talked about the great nineteenth-century Shakespeareans, Macready, Kean, the Booths, and then he suddenly said, "Oh yes, there was this black guy who was doing Shakespeare in Europe at the time. His name was Ira Aldridge." And then he just as abruptly skipped over it. I asked about Aldridge and did some research. There was only one book written about him in English, but I discovered several in Polish, Russian, and German. As I studied, I realized that there was a concerted effort to wipe Ira Aldridge out of theatre history books in the United States.

NE: *He is rarely mentioned, but is this solely due to his race?*

CD: Definitely. It's hard to get an all-black cast of Shakespeare on anybody's stage in America *today,* let alone in 1818. If you go to London, professors can give you a half-hour spiel on Aldridge. If you go to Poland, Russia, France, Germany, you'll find paintings, statues, museums in his honor. In Poland on the anniversary of his death there's a festival. Here is a man who played Othello in over three hundred fifty different productions! *Not* times. But different *productions!* Not to mention how many performances he gave during each run. He played Othello and Lear more times than anybody since Shakespeare began writing. Yet no one hears about him.

NE: *Why did he leave the States?*

CD: You have to remember that Aldridge was born in 1805, at the time of slavery. But to understand why he left the States, you have to know something about American black theatre. The first black theatre was founded in 1818. It was on the northwest corner of Bleecker and Mercer streets in [Greenwich] Village and it was called The African Grove Theatre. It was originally an ice-cream parlor owned by a West Indian pirate by the name of Mr. Brown, and black actors would come in and do excerpts from Shakespeare. The theatre was controversial because blacks could be arrested for doing Shakespeare. Things heated up in 1820, when a production of *Hamlet* starring Edmund Booth was put on at the Park Theatre and Mr. Brown and a black actor named James Hewlett rented a hotel next door and did an all-black production of *Richard III.* It became a hit because it was a curiosity, and the white *Hamlet* got less business than the black *Richard III.*

Certain producers, particularly Mr. Edwin Forrest, were quite annoyed that black actors were doing Shakespeare and getting press out of it. White rowdies were sent to the theatre to watch the production. First fights, then actual race riots took place outside the theatre. The African Grove closed in 1823, when it was burnt down by whites. The troupe basically disbanded, and the genuine black actors who had trained themselves to do verse and classical drama were forced out to make way for the white-nigger minstrels that went on for a hundred twenty-five years. Given that background of racial tension, Aldridge decided to act abroad.

NE: *How was he treated in Europe?*

CD: His career began in 1833 and lasted thirty-three years. He basically became the toast of the European continent. It wasn't all peaches and cream, but he worked—that was the main thing: he was allowed to practice his God-given talent. He never returned to the United States, and died in Poland in 1867 at fifty-nine.

NE: *Did Aldridge wear whiteface when he played white parts?*

CD: Whenever he played Lear, Richard III, Macbeth, or Shylock, he painted his face. But it wasn't the whiteface of a clown. From the photographs we can see that he looks like a white man.

NE: *What sort of actor was he?*

CD: He was the first to break the declamation style of Shakespeare. Stanislavsky studied under Ira Aldridge and used his style as a prototype for the naturalistic method. Before Aldridge, Shakespearean actors had been rhetorical—like this, "O!!! the moon!!" With Aldridge, it was realistic. When the audience saw him dragging Desdemona, they were shocked. Remember, you had a real black man with real black hands around a real white woman's neck.

NE: *The British actress Madge Kendall complained that he practically killed her during the strangulation scene.*

CD: Aldridge had a joke about that. Whenever he was asked about brutalizing Desdemona, he said, "I've played in over three hundred fifty productions of this play, and I've injured only two Desdemonas and murdered only one. With odds like that I don't see why any actress should be wary."

NE: *Is it true that black actors had to wear blackface when they played Othello?*

CD: In America, yes—even if you were black you had to wear blackface because that's what audiences were accustomed to. Not in Europe, though.

NE: *Who was the first black actor to play Shakespeare on the mainstream stage? Paul Robeson?*

CD: Probably Robeson. I believe there might have been some blacks in subservient roles, but Robeson was the first big star. But Aldridge was a hundred years before Robeson!

NE: *What about Othello today? Is it politically correct for a white man to play Othello?*

CD: In London, sure. Not in America. You would be pretty hard pressed to get a white actor. . . . The period of not casting Othello with a white actor occurred during the time of so-called liberalism in America. It's been a while since a white actor played Othello. But if, for example, an artistic director said, "I want Christopher Walken for Othello," needless to say, Christopher would have to put the mud on.

NE: *How do actors and directors feel about blackface today? Everyone was outraged or insulted by Olivier's blackface when he did the part in 1965. A critic at* The New York Times *said he looked like "the end man in a minstrel show."*

CD: I don't know if it was so much the blackface but the manner in which he portrayed Othello. I thought he portrayed him like a monkey—all that eye rolling. It was degrading. That was one time his creativity missed the boat.

NE: *Is Othello a play about race?*

CD: Of course it's about race. Is *The Merchant of Venice* a play about anti-Semitism? I think, however, it has little to do with whether or not you've got a white man standing on a stage with black makeup on—it has more to do with the spirit of the production.

NE: *Did you draw upon your own experiences as a black man when playing Othello?*

CD: No, not at all. The problem with a black actor playing Othello is that since it's one of the few classical roles, at least from a European point of view, he feels that he has to represent the whole race and be dignified and majestic: "This is a classic black figure, I have to be classic and black." But you can't be too self-conscious; you have to play a human being.

NE: *Why isn't Cleopatra considered a black part in the same way Othello is? The text is very explicit on this point: She's definitely not white.*

CD: There we have the question of racism again. It's not as obvious as it is in *Othello*. Whether she was African, Arabian, Turkish, or Greek—whatever—she wasn't European. But how many times does Marc Antony have to say that she's been burnished by the sun? And I don't think he means a damn tan.

NE: *Paul Robeson once said, "If I thought anyone could accept a black Hamlet . . ." Is that still true today? The idea of Hamlet as a sensitive Nordic blonde is so ingrained in audiences, can they accept a black Hamlet?*

CD: It's a tough one. In some of the plays, you have to stick with the cultural sensibilities; Hamlet is one of them—Hamlet the character, I mean.

NE: *But women play Hamlet. Perhaps this is because he is androgynous, rather like Peter Pan.*

CD: Yes, people don't see a black man playing Hamlet because he's so delicate. It's easier to see a black man doing Lear, Macbeth, Richard—the warrior, the big, broad parts. When it's a character who is sophisticated, soft, and introspective, then the part is reserved for the "higher order" in some people's heads. That's fine with me. I don't think you should have a black Iago. You have to be truthful to the play at some point. If you do these things then you have to say to yourself, OK, *why* a black Hamlet?

NE: *Do you think blacks are discriminated against in the parts they are given?*

CD: Black actors are often cast in the evil roles. If you do an Edgar and an Edmund [in *King Lear*] it's done with Edmund as black, Edgar as white. Blacks are Edmunds, blacks are Calibans. So people say, If we have to cast a black, let's make him the evil character.

NE: *What about multiracial casting? Is it bewildering to an audience to see a black Hamlet and a white Gertrude? What about the history plays, in which so much of the plot depends upon understanding the familial relationships? Wouldn't an audience be confused by a black Clarence and a white Richard?*

CD: I was at an artistic seminar on multiracial casting where they talked about its pros and cons, and I don't want to sound derogatory, but I simply said, "All it takes is for an artistic director to have the balls not to judge for the audience. You're not going to get people to feel that it's natural if you only do it [a mixed-cast production] every five, ten years. We are so hypocritical—we stand in a classroom and say, Shakespeare is universal and Shakespeare's for the world, and yet do you see a black man in the major roles? Well, I don't. It's a continuing hypocrisy.

NE: *Do you feel that your background as urban, black, and not classically trained, at least not until you went to Yale, which was rather late in life, has held you back as a Shakespearean? Have you had to approach Shakespeare differently from someone like Gielgud?*

CD: I know god-awful white Shakespearean actors. I've seen the most boring all-white productions I ever want to see. You know, god-awful. Not only American, but British too. But Shakespeare *is* elitist: not everyone can do him. There isn't a great Shakespearean actor who is a bad contemporary actor. The roles call for great physical stamina, high endurance, concentration, insightfulness about life and the world, not just the immediate play—but the world! The great Shakespearean actor is first and foremost blessed with a gift. You can learn it, but you have to be blessed.

Great Shakespearean Moments in American History

The wit that said that Shakespeare was the most widely known American author may have spoken more wisdom than he knew.

—*LOUIS MARDER*

February 17, 1736: *Richard III* is performed at the Dock Street Theatre in Charleston, the first recorded public performance of a Shakespeare play in the New World.

1770: During the American struggle for independence, the Massachusetts *Spy* lampooned the British by parodying Hamlet's famous speech:

> *To be taxt or not be taxt—that is the question*
> *Whether 'tis nobler in our minds to suffer*
> *The sleights and cunning of deceitful statesmen*
> *Or to petition against illegal taxes*
> *And by opposing, end them?*
> *To live, to act, perchance to be all slaves,*
> *Aye, there's the rub.*

1835: During the second Seminole rebellion, the Indians ambushed a group of itinerant Shakespearean players, massacred two of them and made off with the company's costume trunk. For a while a strange, unidentifiable tribe could be seen galloping through the range, clad as ancient Romans, Scotsmen, and Danes. Later when they were finally overtaken, several were found wearing the costumes of Othello, Hamlet, and an assortment of other Shakespearean characters.

1850s: According to Abraham Lincoln's law partner and best friend, William H. Herndon, "When he was young [Lincoln] read the Bible and when of age he read Shakespeare. This latter book was scarcely ever out of his mind and his hands." Guests at the Lincoln household were treated to dinner and Shakespeare recitations. Lincoln, who suffered from severe depression, continually turned to Shakespeare for consolation, wisdom, and strength. In "What Lincoln and Jefferson Read," Douglas L. Wilson wrote, "Lincoln seemed to have assimilated the substance of the plays into his own experience and deepening sense of tragedy."

April 14, 1865: President Lincoln is assassinated by John Wilkes Booth, a member of one of the most famous acting families of the day. His father, Junius Brutus Booth, was named after Brutus, the assassin who killed Julius Caesar. On November 25, 1864, all three Booths had taken part in a benefit performance of *Julius Caesar,* John Wilkes's favorite play, to raise money for a statue of Shakespeare in Central Park in New York. Four months later, at a performance of *Our American Cousin,* John Wilkes, an ardent secessionist, shot and killed President Lincoln. In a final dramatic gesture, he leaped from the presidential box onto the stage screaming "*Sic Semper Tyrannis*" ("Thus Be It Ever to Tyrants," the motto of the state of Virginia).

c. 1975: A new edition of Shakespeare translates Elizabethan English into contemporary American: Thus, "O, what a rogue and peasant slave am I!" is now infinitely more intelligible as "Oh, what a bum and miserable flunky I am!"

1989: "B-2 or not to B-2. That is the question." (Edward Markey, Massachusetts congressman, on the stealth bomber debate.)

King Lear

The theme of King Lear *is the decay and fall of the world.*

—*JAN KOTT*

In the nuclear age, we, like Macbeth, have "supped full with horrors," but nothing prepares us for *King Lear.* The play opens as a fairy tale and ends as a parable of despair. By the last act, the characters we love most are dead, leaving their survivors, and us, stunned.

The plot of *Lear* is mainly derived from the play *King Leir* (c. 1590), but Shakespeare did something unusual with it. All non-Shakespearean versions of the play (and critics have counted over forty) have a happy ending, in which the virtuous Cordelia lives, marries, and thrives. Only in Shakespeare's does she die, hanged in her prison cell, an act that has revolted readers and audiences for centuries. In *Lear,* Shakespeare deliberately challenges the assumptions we hold most dear about justice, the nature of humanity, and the ways of God to man.

Of the two intricately connected plots in *Lear,* the first deals with Lear and his three daughters, the wicked Goneril and Regan and the honest Cordelia; the subplot recounts the story of the Earl of Gloucester and his two sons, the illegitimate Edmund and the legitimate Edgar. Lear believes that the loving Cordelia is unkind, and in a parallel situation, Gloucester believes that the innocent Edgar is a traitor. In *Lear* we enter a mad world where appearances are deceiving, and truth and goodness, as represented by Edgar and Cordelia, are hidden and disguised.

The play begins, as so many Shakespearean plays do, in a disarmingly casual manner. Gloucester, in the middle of a conversation with an acquaintance (who is never seen again), introduces his bastard son, Edmund. Then, without considering Edmund's presence, he boasts about his son's conception: "There was good sport at his making." Gloucester is proud of his sin and pleased with his own virility, but it's precisely lust and pride that lead to his fall: unlawful appetite breeds unholy offspring, and Gloucester's sexual vanity distorts his vision so that he can see a handsome son only as the living proof of his own physical prowess, not as a reminder of his sin. Edmund must have heard his father's crude boast a thousand times, but to an Elizabethan audience, bastardy was no laughing matter: it always signaled something wayward and unnatural. The illegitimate line of a noble family bore a crest with the bar sinister—"sinister" meaning "left" as opposed to right, but also implying what is morally sinister about bastardy, a violation of the sacred marriage vow. In the course of *Lear*, *all* bonds—between father and child, nature and humanity, the gods and man—become loose and unraveled.

In Act I, scene 2, Lear sweeps onstage with a lavish entourage. At eighty, he has capriciously decided to renounce the responsibilities and cares of kingship while retaining its pomp and privileges. He plans to divide his kingdom, give up his castle, and reside with each daughter in turn. He then stages an elaborate contest to award the biggest portion of his kingdom to the daughter who vows the most love for him. The two eldest, Goneril and Regan, don't disappoint him, and Lear smugly takes in their flattery. Now it's Cordelia's turn. She is his favorite, and he has high hopes, but when he turns to her and confidently asks, ". . . what can you say to draw / A third more opulent than your sisters'?" she refuses to cheapen the honesty of her love, answering simply "Nothing," a word that will reverberate throughout a play in which all the main characters are ultimately stripped of status, wealth, property, and identity.

With the division of the kingdom and the banishment of Cordelia, the orderly cosmos reverts to anarchy and misrule. Storms, eclipses, and other strange upheavals of nature indicate a return to the primordial chaos. As Gloucester says: "These late eclipses in the sun and moon portend no good to us. . . . We have seen the best of our time." The social world also turns upside down: daughters rule their fathers, a fool has more wisdom than the king he serves, a bastard becomes legitimate, madmen lead the blind, and truth and virtue are forced underground.

Most important, the king no longer commands, and without authority, nothing checks the rising surge of evil that engulfs everything. Anything can, and does, happen. At first Goneril merely scolds Lear for disrupting her household; then she banishes him from the house itself. And this moral sickness quickly spreads. In what must be the most horrifying scene in dramatic history, Edmund and Goneril, who have now joined forces, triumphantly pluck out Gloucester's eyes in full view of the audience: "Out, vile jelly!" / Where is thy lustre now?"

Through all his suffering, Lear never looks within himself for the cause of his sorrow. He curses his daughters, the gods, the "system"—everyone and everything but his own folly. The center of the play, and Lear's emotional turning point, is the storm on the heath, long identified with *Lear* the same way that Yorick's skull is associated with *Hamlet*. The storm is a mirror of Lear's mind, its chaos and upheaval reflecting his psychic turmoil, rage, and increasing insanity.

Goneril and Regan have cast their father out into the night, and for the first time Lear directly experiences what it's like to be homeless, naked, and cold. Divested of rank, clothing, pomp, family, and his belief in divine justice, the king stands as he came into the world, naked, shivering, and helpless: "we came crying hither. / Thou knowst the first time that we smell the air / We wawl and cry."

Images of nakedness pervade *Lear.* Shakespeare doesn't simply refer to nudity and physical exposure, but to a stripping down to the essential self. Gazing into the eye of the storm, Lear sees into the heart of man: What are we when dispossessed of everything that defines us as human? "Is man no more than this?" he cries, and over and over he asks, Who am I? This is what makes *Lear* so wrenching: not only does it tell a moving story, but it also unflinchingly asks the most profound questions, forcing us to confront matters we'd prefer to ignore.

Against this bestial view of human nature is set another, more optimistic one. Immediately after Lear rails against life and its cruelties, he does something surprising: he places his Fool's comfort before his own. "Come on, my boy. How dost my boy? Art cold?" he asks the shivering creature. The almost casual remark reveals how far Lear has come, for these words, uttered with such startling tenderness, hardly recall the imperious tyrant of Act I. But Lear still has far to go: he must lose the veneer of civilization before he can become truly civil, and he must lose his wits before he gains genuine wisdom. In Act IV, scene 6, he enters "fantastically dressed with wild flowers," and with terrible clarity he sees through man's petty pretenses, his false virtue, his ambition, his vanity, and his indifference to the sufferings of others. At last he realizes that the society he condemns is one he helped to create.

Meanwhile, the French have rallied to Cordelia's aid in her father's cause and are about to land at Dover. In Act IV, scene 1, all the principal characters meet, and the subplot links with the main plot. Abandoned and alone, Gloucester has been wandering aimlessly when he meets up with Edgar, disguised as the madman Tom of Bedlam. This is one of the most disturbing twists in a disturbing play: the father is blind and the son unrecognizable. Dramatically and symbolically, this makes sense, for when Gloucester *could* see, he did not recognize his faithful son. Just as Lear becomes wise when he goes mad, Gloucester finds inner vision with blindness.

As Tom, Edgar pretends to lead his father to the edge of a cliff, where the old man intends to leap to his death. Gloucester jumps a few inches into the air and falls to the ground. Rushing to him, Edgar, now pretending to be a peasant, says he has witnessed the old man's miraculous survival, and he tells the dazed Gloucester, "Think that the clearest gods . . . have preserved thee." Critics complain that the scene is absurd and incongruously comical, but it strikingly emphasizes Shakespeare's point: even as Edgar's lie deters his father from suicide, it tells the audience that the gods are creatures of man's imagination and that believers are blind.

Lear is also led to Dover, to meet Cordelia and her army, but by the time she arrives he is insane and has fallen into a coma. Their reunion, traditionally referred to as a "recognition scene," brings father and daughter together for a moment of excruciating tenderness. It's also a scene of rebirth, for as Lear awakens in Cordelia's arms he regains his senses, her forgiveness giving him new life. The potent monarch who once demanded a lavish entourage would now be content with a prison cell—if it's shared with Cordelia.

No, no, no, no! Come, let's away to prison.
We two alone will sing like birds i'the cage;
When thou dost ask me blessing I'll kneel down
And ask of thee forgiveness; so we'll live,
And pray, and sing, and tell old tales, and laugh
At gilded butterflies, and hear poor rogues
Talk of court news; and we'll talk with them too—
Who loses and who wins, who's in, who's out—
And take upon's the mystery of things
As if we were God's spies; and we'll wear out,
In a walled prison, packs and sects of great ones
That ebb and flow by the moon.

(V.3.8–19)

Lear's dream is idyllic: father and daughter alone in a state of grace, gossiping. Surely Shakespeare must be planning a happy ending. But you can't trust anything in this play—neither the gods nor the playwright. But Edmund, unmoved by what he has just seen, says, "Take them away." The beauty of the reconciliation intensifies the hideous end. The next time we see father and daughter, Lear is carrying her corpse in his arms, and the question he asks is the only one that makes sense in an absurd world: "Why should a dog, a horse, a rat have life, / And thou no breath at all?" Again and again Lear asks, Why? Why is human life as cheap as a beast's? The final irony is that Lear dies happy—not because events turn out well, but because he mistakenly believes that Cordelia is alive:

Do you see this? Look on her! Look, her lips!
Look there! Look there!
He dies

(V.3.308–9)

The only joy in this play is based on an illusion. *Lear* depicts a pitiless world where men look to the heavens but find only a void. Perhaps they have been looking in the wrong place. Abandoned by the gods and betrayed by his own illusions, Lear ultimately finds comfort in Cordelia, Kent, Edgar, Gloucester, and his Fool. There is no divine protection for Cordelia, but her old father, with strength born of rage, kills her executioner. Perhaps this is one of the few messages in a play that doesn't seem to offer any solace: the gods may be indifferent to human suffering, but human beings can redeem one another. At the end, Lear ultimately triumphs over cosmic aloofness and, indeed, creates something out of nothing.

King Lear is a paradox: it appears nihilistic, but it affirms the value of human life. It asks abstract, unanswerable questions, but it addresses real and enduring problems: aging parents, sibling rivalries, the relationship between father and child, the social problem of homelessness, and how easy it is to ignore suffering—when it happens to others.

STAGE HISTORY

Considered depressing and unactable, *King Lear* as Shakespeare wrote it was not performed from the late seventeenth through the mid-nineteenth century. In 1681, an Irish playwright, Nahum Tate, rewrote the play with a happy ending, thus illustrating that Providence smiles on the virtuous. Tate's version, the only one audiences knew for more than one hundred fifty years, was a decorous little tragicomedy with a tidy moral and all the fierce energy of Shakespeare's drama refined and softened. Lear is the wicked old father of fairy tale, not a powerful patriarch; Gloucester's suicide attempt is omitted; the Fool's part is completely cut; and Cordelia survives and marries Edgar. Lear is restored to his throne, and after his retirement Cordelia and Edgar rule happily ever after.

After the mid-nineteenth century, Shakespeare's play was gradually restored, piece by piece. In 1823, Edmund Kean brought back the tragic ending; the Fool was restored in 1838; but it wasn't until the late nineteenth century that directors could bring themselves to reintroduce Gloucester's blinding.

King Lear was banned from the stage from 1788 to 1820, the time of George III's insanity, lest the public make the obvious parallel between Lear's and their own king's condition.

* * *

Written by a Englishman during the reign of James I, *King Lear* takes place in prehistoric Britain. The play's Old Testament ferocity and its story of a patriarch who is abandoned by his children made it a classic of the Yiddish theatre. The Russian director Grigori Kozintsev claimed that his 1971 movie of *Lear* was partly influenced by Yiddish productions.

What to Look for in
<u>King Lear</u>

*A*long with Iago and Richard III, Edmund is one of Shakespeare's most provocative villains. Throughout the play he's despicable, yet as he lies dying, he unexpectedly wins us over with his anxiety to save Cordelia at the last minute. Shakespeare hasn't changed his mind about Edmund; he just reveals a hidden side of his character. The revelation is startling, yet true.

Goneril and Regan are not the indistinguishable villainous sisters of fairy tale; Shakespeare takes special pains to differentiate them. Goneril, the eldest, is weak and mean-spirited. Like a cancerous growth that initially appears benign, her malignancy spreads to everything she touches. At first the audience can be seduced by her cool reasonableness, particularly when she advises Lear to reduce his retinue. After all, the crotchety old man *is* a nuisance: after his retirement he spends his days lying about her castle with one hundred boisterous knights, all of whom demand her attentions. First she patronizes her father, then she unmans him, and finally she destroys him, body and soul. Her initial reasonableness makes her eventual corruption all the more sickening.

Regan is the true sadist, a woman with an appetite for blood who is aroused by wanton cruelty. In the scene in which she plucks out Gloucester's eyes, she is mesmerized by evil, enthusiastically urging the others to more and greater tortures: the ropes that bind him must be pulled tighter; one eye is not enough, she must have both. Then, when the deed is done, she flings the old man out, screeching, "Go thrust him out at gates and let him smell / His way to Dover."

*I*n Act II, scene 4, Goneril has asked Lear to reduce his entourage, the symbol of his former power and authority. Now that he's no longer king, he doesn't require a monarch's privileges. But Lear has based his whole life on the outer manifestations of kingship. He takes the emblems of authority for the thing itself, and without them he feels he is nothing. As he watches his power diminish he becomes frightened, and he pleads with his daughter: "O, reason not the need!"—i.e., Don't base your decision on the grounds of bare necessity. Only beasts live by necessity. If we were to dress solely for comfort, why wear silk? To a certain degree, Lear is absolutely right. Beauty, comfort, even luxury make us civilized; but excessive materialism makes us inhuman and uncivil. Goneril's demand forces Lear to examine his true needs, the selfishness of one character precipitating the enlightenment of another.

*I*n Act V, scene 3, Lear has just entered, carrying his dead daughter in his arms. Shakespeare could have had him say "My daughter is dead" or "Cordelia's dead" or even "My poor fool is dead." But "And my poor fool is hanged!" is inspired. Sometimes the only way to appreciate Shakespeare is by looking at what he *didn't* say. With economic precision, Shakespeare conveys a wealth of meaning. "My" suggests his tender possessiveness; the endearment "fool" hints at all the intimacy that existed between them even before the play begins. These sentiments, juxtaposed against the barbaric image of her hanging, make this simple utterance absolutely heartbreaking.

Comments on Lear

*N*o, Lear is easy. He's like all the rest of us, really: he's just a stupid old fart. He's got a frightful temper. He's completely selfish and utterly inconsiderate. He does not for a moment think of the consequences of what he has said. He is simply bad-tempered arrogance with a crown perched on top. He obviously wasn't spanked by his mother often enough.

—LAURENCE OLIVIER

I was many years ago so shocked by Cordelia's death, that I know not whether I ever endured to read again the last scenes of the play till I undertook to revise them as an editor.

—SAMUEL JOHNSON

*A*ll my life I have held that you can class people according to how they may be imagined behaving to King Lear.

—ISAK DINESEN

*O*ne wicked daughter would have been quite enough, and Edgar is a superfluous character.

—GEORGE ORWELL

*D*oubtless *King Lear* is still recognized as a masterpiece, beside which even *Macbeth* and *Hamlet* seem tame and pedestrian. *King Lear* is compared to Bach's Mass in B Minor, to Beethoven's Fifth and Ninth Symphonies, to Wagner's *Parsifal,* Michelangelo's *Last Judgement,* or Dante's *Purgatory* and *Inferno.* But at the same time *King Lear* gives one the impression of a high mountain that everyone admires, yet no one particularly wishes to climb.

—JAN KOTT

I turned to *Lear* again because of my search for some eternal verities in this pop-culture, celebrity-worship, trash-TV world.

—KEITH LOVE, writer, *Los Angeles Times*

*T*he first breakthrough came in a rehearsal of the heath scenes when Adrian [Noble, the director] asked each of the actors involved to find an animal to play, in order to release the savagery and wildness of the situation. I chose a chimpanzee, chattering and clapping hands, hurling myself around in forward rolls, and found this very liberating for the role. That weekend I hurried to London Zoo to watch the chimps and became even more convinced that they had all the requisite qualities for the Fool—manic comic energy when in action, a disturbing sadness when in repose. A delightful coincidence that day at the zoo was rounding a corner to discover that Michael Gambon was also there presumably also in search of his character, leaning against the plate-glass of the gorilla's cage, man and beast locked in solemn contemplation of one another.

—ANTONY SHER

*T*he last line of the play is unique in Shakespeare. All his other plays suggest an optimistic future; no matter how terrible the events that have passed, there is hope that they will not happen again. In *Lear,* the last line poses a question. Edgar says: "We that are young shall never see so much nor live so long," and no one can give a simple explanation of this. It is loaded with inexplicable hints of tremendous meanings. It forces you to look at a young man, his eye naturally on the future, who has lived through the most horrifying times.

—PETER BROOK

Tony Church
on Playing Lear

*T*ony Church has had a long and various association with King Lear. *From 1962 to 1964 he played Cornwall and was Paul Scofield's understudy in Peter Brook's stage production of the play. He has since gone on to play the title role three times, once in 1974 for the Royal Shakespeare Company in a production at the Other Place directed by Buzz Goodbody, then in 1982 in the Santa Cruz Shakespeare Festival, and finally in 1989 at Nasa State College in Grand Junction, Colorado. He is one of the few actors to play Gloucester (in 1976–77, with the Royal Shakespeare Company) after having played Lear, an experience which he compares to being* *elected president before becoming vice president. "Indeed, I don't think I want to do Gloucester again, whereas with Lear, you want to go on doing him forever," said Church, whose voice can be heard in more than twenty-six Shakespearean audiocassettes.*

NE: *How do you play Lear without having a nervous breakdown?*

TC: You have to suffer with the role—it's part of your machinery as an actor. You have to create a breathing space from which you can run the machine. You have to concentrate on relaxing yourself inside the part so you can enjoy it—otherwise you'll burst. No matter how much you suffer, you must enjoy it. If you don't, you can't play it. At the same time, you can't actually suffer. Something inside you must be in control and yet free to express what you feel. Just being frustrated on stage doesn't communicate itself to the audience.

NE: *Do you play the part as relentlessly as Shakespeare wrote it?*

TC: Oh, absolutely! Lear is first shown to us as an unredeemable monster. His love for Cordelia is possessive; his love for Regan is probably incestuous; he is already in a state of opposition with Goneril. Here is a man who is *encrusted* in the armor of eighty years—most of which has been spent as an absolute dictator. During the first part of the play, he suffers the tortures of the damned because nothing, *nothing,* can get through that. His hysteria is a terrible pressure that can't get out. He breaks down because he doesn't have any more defenses to hold himself up.

The really terrifying scene to play is when he is just about to leave Goneril's house and he says, "I will have such revenges on you both / That all the world shall—I will do such things— / What they are yet I know not; but they shall be / The terrors of the earth." And he can't even say what they are.

NE: *Why is the play so moving?*

TC: It's about being a father, about being a daughter. There's a domestic quality to *Lear.*

NE: *How would you compare Gloucester and Lear?*

TC: Lear and Gloucester are totally different. What happens to Gloucester is visually much worse, so often an audience tends to identify with

Gloucester more. Both men reach an understanding. Gloucester realizes he was betrayed by his son, and he also realizes that suicide is not a way out.

NE: *What about that suicide attempt? It's an odd scene.*

TC: Yes. [After Gloucester jumps] Edgar says, "What, in ill thoughts again? Men must endure / Their going hence even as their coming hither." And the blind old man says the most unbelievably laconic statement: "And that's true *too*." This is his last line. It's the most wonderful last line I know. He doesn't say, "That's true." He sees both sides to the question. He doesn't measure up to the big thing but seeks to compromise.

NE: *Is that why he can't be truly tragic, like Lear?*

TC: No, he can't be. Lear is tragic on many levels. Lear suffers for humanity—and for himself. His suffering continues to the very end.

NE: *But doesn't he die believing that Cordelia lives?*

TC: No, his last words are "Look there! Look there!" We don't know *what* he's talking about. He's already said, "Thou'lt come no more; / Never, never, never, never, never," and there's no way back from that.

Lear's Fool

*L*ear's Fool must be one of the oddest characters ever to make his way onto the Shakespearean stage. There's a curious, otherworldly quality about him, as if he had suddenly dropped into this bleak and cruel landscape, a fantastic figure in motley. Since he's unclassifiable, it's fitting that he's the only Shakespearean fool without a proper name. He's simply "Lear's Fool," a term that has come to express his paradoxical blend of manic wit, shrewd innocence, wicked glee, truthful foolery, and, above all, devotion.

As a court jester, the Fool is on Lear's payroll. His job is to amuse the king and his courtiers. He *can* make audiences laugh (depending on the actor playing him), but he's not lightheartedly funny. His dramatic function isn't to amuse us, but to tell Lear the truth. The king is his jester's pupil:

> LEAR. Dost thou call me fool, boy?
> FOOL. All thy other titles thou hast given away; that thou
>   wast born with.
>
> (I.4.146–48)

Like most court jesters, he is allowed a verbal freedom denied to ordinary folk, but Lear's Fool speaks with a knowing pungency that's uniquely his own. He utters a strange jumble of riddling parables, oracles, paradoxes, and nonsense in an inspired idiom. On the heath he proclaims a terrifying prophetic vision of the world and then cryptically adds, "This prophecy Merlin shall make; for I live before his time." Antony Sher, who played the Fool in Adrian Noble's 1982 Stratford production, remarked: "The thing that made Lear's Fool fascinating to me is that his unintelligible jokes *add* to the nightmare." Instead of providing comic relief, the Fool acts as a one-man chorus who comments on and observes Lear's downfall. At the same time, he also participates in, and is a victim of, the same tragedy as his master.

The Fool Vanishes

One thing that adds to the Fool's mystery is that after playing such an important part, he abruptly vanishes after the storm scene. Lear never even mentions him again. Did Shakespeare simply forget about him? Did Lear? It seems unlikely that after lavishing so much care and attention on the Fool, Shakespeare, or Lear, would abandon him.

One explanation derives from the fact that Robert Armin, the Buster Keaton of the day, played both Cordelia and the Fool. The two are never on stage at the same time. He isn't present when she has her big court scene, and he arrives soon after her banishment. When she returns in Act IV, he has already disappeared. The Fool's last words, "And I'll go to bed at noon," could very well be Armin's apology for leaving the part early so that he could play Cordelia. Significantly, when Cordelia lies dead in her father's arms, Lear cries out, "And my poor fool is hanged!" Why would he say "fool"? It's his daughter he's talking about. "Fool" was a common Elizabethan term of endearment, but in this case it could also be a wry allusion to Armin's dual roles.

As we've noted, there are few stage directions in Shakespeare's plays, so we have no way of knowing exactly what happened on stage. Simply because a character is no longer mentioned in the script doesn't mean he is no longer on stage, just that he doesn't have any lines. Given the Fool's garrulousness, however, it's likely that only death could silence him. Several recent productions have explained his departure by making him a casualty of the storm on the heath—another victim in a play filled with death. "And I'll go to bed at noon" makes a fitting epitaph, suggesting the Fool's untimely end. Thus Lear's cry, "And my poor fool is hanged!" is ambiguous—perhaps he is referring not only to Cordelia but to another wise fool who dared to speak the truth.

The Fool in History

$\mathcal{T}$he image of the court jester invariably calls to mind the traditional figure in motley with a cockscomb cap (so called because it resembles a cock's comb in shape and color) and bells, carrying a baton, or bauble, in his hand. The bauble, the source of much phallic humor, was originally a stick with a pig's bladder tied to the end. For a quick laugh, the fool would go around slapping people with it; hence our word "slapstick." There's no modern equivalent of the court jester or household fool.

The Elizabethans divided fools into two types: natural and artificial. The natural fool was a simpleton, a lunatic, or a freak, usually a dwarf or a eunuch, and was often regarded as a beloved household pet or mascot. Very often he would have been a gift to his master and would be presented to someone else when his owner died or could no longer keep him.

The artificial fool's humor was more intellectual and verbal. Some claimed to possess second sight; others were musicians, poets, storytellers, or riddlers. But even the artificial fool's humor was not always cerebral. His repertory was at times frankly scatological, since any ref-

CLOWNS AND FOOLS

*T*he character designated "Clown" in the cast of characters isn't a Fool. Clowns are often amusingly simple folk (usually country yokels), while a fool or jester is a professional wit whose humor can be erudite, complicated, and at times offensive. More often than not, his jokes are disguised verbal jabs at his betters. A good fool was more like Lenny Bruce, a gadfly who specialized in biting social satire.

erence to excrement guaranteed a laugh. According to Clive James, "Court jesters of old used to wow the monarch and all his retinue by unleashing, as a grandstand finale, a simultaneous leap, whistle and fart." If that didn't work, they would make faces, sing vulgar ballads, trip people, and play practical jokes (a favorite being to stand behind someone and shout "boo").

But whether freak, jester, clown, mascot, or wit, a fool possessed a unique status. A social misfit, he was dependent on society yet exempt from rules and was thus permitted a verbal freedom denied the rest of the court. Since he was treated as if he were a child, his most pointed barbs seemed innocent. As Shakespeare said, "There is no slander in an allowed fool, though he do nothing but rail." Often, when the fool entertained at parties, he was allowed to abuse the guests—within limits. Nonetheless, a shrewd fool soon learned how much his owner would tolerate. Whenever Lear's Fool speaks too freely, his master pointedly reminds him of the whip.

The court fool in England originated in the twelfth century and flourished in the fifteenth and the sixteenth, when he became a prominent figure in contemporary social life, as well as in art and literature. Shakespeare's Touchstone, Feste, and Lear's Fool may have been based on actual persons.

As a recognized member of a household, the fool regularly turns up in family portraits and memoirs. Seated in the background of a drawing of Henry VIII and his family is a serious little figure who seems to have slyly crept into the picture without anyone's being aware of it. It is Will Somers, Henry's favorite fool.

The Tudor account book is filled with references to expenditures for clothing and other luxuries for "Patch," "Phip," "Mr. Martin," and "Mr. John." Some fools, like team mascots, were dressed in the livery of the household and on ceremonial occasions would appear in outfits matching those of their masters.

Henry VIII and his daughter Queen Elizabeth had two of the greatest jesters for their amusement. Will Somers, Henry VIII's fool, was gifted at rhymes and riddles, and would freely improvise with his master; Henry would start a rhyme that Will would then try to cap. Will's biographer records that one day Henry, Cardinal Wolsey, and the fool were driving by the house where the king kept his mistress, whereupon Henry began the following rhyme:

> *Within yon tower*
> *There is a flower*
> *That hath my heart.*

We'll never know Will's retort, because at this point his biographer modestly breaks off, remarking that in these "pure days" he couldn't possibly print the reply. Will's nemesis, Cardinal Wolsey, couldn't resist rejoining with:

> *A rod in school*
> *And a whip for the fool*
> *Are always in season.*

To which Will swiftly returned:

> *A halter and a rope*
> *For him that would be Pope*
> *Against all right and reason.*

The royal fool's primary function was to lighten the burdens of kingship. Queen Elizabeth, known for her moodiness, had for her fool Richard Tarleton, one of the biggest talents in the country, and probably the model for Hamlet's Yorick. According to his biographer John Fuller, Tarleton, like a Hollywood star, was "discovered": he was in the field tending his father's pigs

when a servant of Robert Earl of Leicester passed by, he was so highly pleased by Tarleton's *happy unhappy* answers, that he brought him to court where he became the most famous jester to Queen Elizabeth. . . . When Queen Elizabeth was serious, I dare not say sullen, and out of good humour, he could *undumpish* her at his pleasure. Her highest favourites in some cases would go to Tarleton before they would go to the Queen, and he was their usher to preface their advantageous access to her. In a word, he told the Queen most of her faults more than her chaplains, and cured her melancholy better than all her physicians.

Archy Armstrong, fool to James I, was the Mort Sahl of his day. A satiric railer, he had an opinion on everything and would even meddle in affairs of state. One day the king was overheard to complain that his hunting horse remained scrawny no matter how much he fed it. Archy replied:

"If that be all, take no care: I'll teach your Majestie a way to raise his fleshe presently; and if he be not as fat as ever he wallow, you shall ride me." "I pr'y thee, foole, how?" sayd the King. "Why do but make him a Bishoppe . . ." [said Archy].

Queen Mary had the only female fool on record. Known simply as Jane the Fool, she appears regularly in the Tudor account books as a recipient of valentines, kirtles, and an inordinate number of shoes: in one year she was granted thirty-six pair. According to the writer Denise Selleck, Jane, like her male colleagues, had her head shaved at least twice a month, and on top of her bald head she wore a "strange tight-fitting cap."

In life, the royal fool was clothed, fed, humored, and loved. In death, he was buried with touching solemnity. Will Somers, perhaps the most beloved fool of all, received this poignant epitaph:

> *He that beneath this Tombstone lies*
> *Some called Fool, some held him wise*
>
> . . . .
>
> *But whether he was Fool or knave*
> *He now lies sleeping in his grave.*

"The Wren Goes To't"

The comedies treat sexual desire as a natural and joyous part of human existence; in the tragedies and the problem plays, it reduces men to beasts. As Lear rages in the storm, he sees life as one gigantic orgy: "The wren goes to't, and the small gilded fly / Does lecher in my sight." Othello mutters about goats and monkeys, animals regarded by the Elizabethans as prone to lechery. Particularly in *Lear,* bestial imagery suggests that beneath civilized behavior lurks an animal driven by appetites. Four hundred years later, Freud would concur, naming this beast the "id."

The tragedies reveal a male imagination besieged by images of diseased sexuality; Hamlet is haunted by his mother's "enseamèd bed." "Enseamèd" meant filthy, but it punningly suggests that Gertrude's marital bed is smeared with semen. In his sickened state, Othello imagines that every woman lies to, and with, every man. Worst of all is Lear's blistering screed against female sexual hypocrisy. The actor Tony Church says, "There's not much in dramatic literature that equals the horror of this speech—if you read exactly what it says."

> Behold yond simpering dame [Regan]
> Whose face between her forks presages snow,
> That minces virtue and does shake the head
> To hear of pleasure's name—
> The fitchew nor the soiled horse goes to't
> With a more riotous appetite.
> Down from the waist they are centaurs,
> Though women all above;
> But to the girdle do the gods inherit,

Beneath is all the fiends'—
There's hell, there's darkness, there is the sulphurous pit—
burning, scalding, stench, consumption! Fie, fie, fie! Pah,
pah! Give me an ounce of civet; good apothecary, sweeten
my imagination. There's money for thee.

(IV.vi.118–32)

("Forks" refers to legs, though some squeamish editors annotate it as "a type of
hair comb"; a fitchew is a polecat; "hell" is slang for the female genitals; "civet"
refers to a perfume made from the civet discharge, today known as musk.)

Shakespeare began his career writing about lovely young women who possess beauty, wit, and pluck. During his middle period his women can be terrifying viragos, faithless and cruel; and during his final stage, his women are daughters, innocent and true. The unprecedented number of strong women in Shakespeare between 1600 and 1609 (Gertrude, Goneril, Regan, Lady Macbeth, Cleopatra, and Volumnia) leads scholars to speculate that these roles were inspired by a specific adult actor who was adept at handling the complexity of these parts. His departure, probably after *Coriolanus,* forced Shakespeare to turn again to ingénues, which were typically played by young boys.

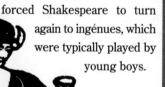

Lear asserts that women—those bright and beautiful creatures of the early comedies—are hybrid beasts ("centaurs"). Above the waist they all seem divine, but their maidenly skirts hide putrefying genitalia that stink like a sulphurous pit. Lust leads to man's undoing, for it is this "dark and vicious place" that costs Gloucester his eyes.

Church notes that there's nothing in the play to support Lear's intense sexual nausea, and that the outburst could only arise from some unbridled idea within Shakespeare's psyche, perhaps from the experience that inspired the Dark Lady sonnets. Although the terrible intensity of this speech suggests that it comes close to Shakespeare's own experience, it nevertheless also corresponds to Lear's belief that all life can be reduced to bestial desire. According to this perspective, women *are* nothing more than sulphurous pits, gaping pudenda. This image, redolent of the stench of the inferno, relates to the numerous references to birth as a horrifying ordeal. In Lear's mind, infants don't arrive into a safe world from a warm womb, but screaming from one hell into another.

*T*his is something Lear blurts out when he feels himself infantilized and unmanned. There is a pervasive anxiety throughout the sixteenth century about women on the throne all over Europe, so there's a whole language of misogyny—which is often put into the mouths of characters. I don't think this means that Lear in his off-hours or in his study holds this view in general. And certainly not Shakespeare.

—MARJORIE GARBER

*H*ere's somebody who could talk about sexual relations that are so weird. And most plays never acknowledge that! *All's Well* is just as weird as you can get, and *The Winter's Tale* too. All of them have these elaborate sexual metaphors and they have an understanding of the way men and women really treat each other. They are amazingly honest.

—PETER SELLARS

Robert Brustein

*D*rama *critic of* The New Republic, *director of the Loeb Drama Center, and artistic director of the American Repertory Theatre at Harvard University, Robert Brustein is involved in every aspect of theatre, which he believes is "our last chance to see animate human beings engaged in a collective creative act." Incisive, acerbic, and outspoken, he both enrages and delights theatregoers in his productions and his columns. He rarely follows the prudent course (take his sci-fi Macbeth), and even his enemies are forced to concede that he's never boring.*

NE: *Why are there so many boring Shakespeare productions?*

RB: Nine times out of ten the problem with bad Shakespeare is that the play is not freshly seen. Instead of going back to the text of the play, directors and set designers go back to previous productions. What we get then are imitations of imitations.

NE: *What about* Hamlet? *Can we ever come to that play fresh?*

RB: It's not easy. Well . . . Ingmar Bergman did it—maybe because he was directing in another language. His interpretation was completely original—not a single cliché in the whole play. He was never pious or sentimental about Hamlet, whom he saw as rather brutal and overbearing. He brought a completely new perspective to Ophelia, who after her death was a ghostly witness to the crudity and barbarism of the Danish court. He had Claudius and Gertrude copulating on stage in front of the courtiers. He revealed a court that had become totally debased and corrupt—sexually, morally, politically. I am certain Bergman reached this interpretation simply by looking at the text as if he had never seen it before.

NE: *Do you try to do this with your own interpretations? You wrote that you weren't pleased with your own* Macbeth [*1970–71 Yale Repertory Theatre season*]. *Why?*

RB: Well, I *thought* I had a marvelous idea with *Macbeth*. I had been reading science fiction, and I came up with this notion of the Weird Sisters, who are referred to as "not like the inhabitants of the earth and yet are on it." I thought to myself, What if they *weren't* inhabitants of the earth but aliens who came down to advance humankind an evolutionary step forward, as in Arthur C. Clarke's *Childhood's End* or the movie *2001*? One of the ways they would do this would be by changing the regal line of Scotland. The set was fashioned like the dolmens in Stonehenge, and the witches were projections onto the dolmens, which, in effect, were spaceships. When they left Earth all that was left behind were the dolmens. That's the origin of Stonehenge in my fanciful interpretation. I didn't have to add a single line. I think it would have worked, but I didn't have the technology to do it at that time, and as a result it was rather crudely executed. I also did something else that didn't work: I set the play during a primitive age when men ate raw meat and wore animal skins—an idea that didn't connect very well with Shakespeare's extremely sophisticated language.

NE: *When did you realize it wasn't going to work?*

RB: In rehearsal. I realized that I had imposed a concept that chopped the play up so it could fit into the metaphorical bed. But I should also say it was a very successful production—we were sold out every night. But the critics weren't too enthusiastic.

NE: *Obviously you must be sympathetic to all those wildly ingenious interpretations of Shakespeare.*

RB: I think there are two different ways to approach the classics. One way I call "simile"; the other, "metaphor." The simile approach looks at a play and says, Well, this play is *like* that action or that setting. For instance, a director says, *Much Ado about Nothing* reminds me of the Napoleonic Wars or Spanish Texas, so I'll set it there and then. So a simile production is when you do an exact translation from one period or setting into another. That's less interesting to me than a metaphorical production, which finds an essential image or passage around which the play is built and then, like all poetry, lets that image resound throughout the play without precisely saying, It's *like* this.

The Ingmar Bergman production of *Hamlet* was essentially metaphorical. It wasn't set in any particular time or place—except at the very end it turned into a simile with the entrance of Fortinbras, who was dressed like a South American dictator. He shot everybody in the court, dragged their corpses out, including the bodies that had been strewn there from previous carnage, and threw them all in a pit. Then, with the line "Go, bid the soldiers shoot," the soldiers aimed their machine guns at the ceiling and just rat-a-tatted with a deafening roar. Shock!

NE: *Finally, can you sum up what makes Shakespeare so great?*

RB: No one ever created such actions, characters, and truths with such exquisite grace and profundity.

Macbeth

I don't see why the Penguin-books people had to get out Shakespeare's plays in the same size and everything as the detective stories. . . . Anyway, I got real comfy in bed that night and all ready to read a good mystery story and here I had The Tragedy of Macbeth—*a book for high-school students. Like* Ivanhoe *or* Lorna Doone.

—*From JAMES THURBER's story "The Macbeth Murder Mystery"*

Macbeth is visually dark, a Shakespearean *film noir.* There's only one moment of sunlight, just before Duncan's murder. The rest of the play takes place in shadows, in rain, in storms, at twilight, or in the middle of the night. Because the play is so short, it's dense with the intensity of a fever dream, filled with prophecies, ghosts, daggers hovering in midair, shrieks in the night pitched ever more shrill by a deepening paranoia and dread. Although the story of Macbeth *is* as exciting as a murder mystery, it's the play's atmosphere, not its plot, that's the thing. For gloomy intensity, there's nothing like it in all of Shakespeare.

The play opens on a "blasted heath," where the air is so filthy and foggy (like the smoky streets of Los Angeles in a classic *film noir*) that one can barely see. Visual obscurity here suggests moral ambiguity, the boundaries between good and evil incomprehensibly blurred. *Macbeth* depicts a disorienting world where "Fair is foul, and foul is fair." Upon entering this blasted heath, we, along with Macbeth, leave moral guideposts behind us.

Here the three Weird Sisters, like mysterious strangers lurking in a dark alley, wait to give the hero a tip about a future event. For at this point, Macbeth *is* still a hero, fresh from the battlefield where his valor led to victory. As he passes, the Witches greet him with a repetition of three pronouncements (three being a magical number). The first Witch presents him with a known truth:

All hail, Macbeth! Hail to thee, Thane of Glamis!

The next, with a possibility that will become true:

All hail, Macbeth! Hail to thee, Thane of Cawdor!

And the last, with a statement that's seemingly beyond his grasp:

All hail, Macbeth, that shalt be king hereafter!

Thus, by degrees, they lead him from the actual to the probable and then, finally, to the seemingly impossible. Upon hearing the final pronouncement, Macbeth's hair becomes "unfix[ed]" and "[his] seated heart knock[s] at [his] ribs."

The central question of the play is whether the Witch's final statement is a warning, a temptation, or a prophecy. The mystery is not, as the woman in Thurber's story thought, a whodunit, but a whocausedit? What role do the Weird Sisters play in Macbeth's fate? "*Wyrd*" meant "fate" in Anglo-Saxon. But the word, as the critic Marvin Rosenburg points out, also suggests "weyward," or "wayward," the Witches being projections of Macbeth's wayward imagination. Do they determine his fate or merely suggest what his ambition craves? Shakespeare thus asks, Are our lives determined by fate or by free will?

The prophecy arouses complex emotions in Lady Macbeth. She is frequently called ambitious, but her aspirations are fired by an intense sexual current. She's concerned not with Macbeth as her husband but with her husband as king. She is compelled by male power, and by appealing to her husband's manhood, she seduces and humiliates him into doing a deed that at first he only contemplates:

> MACBETH. I dare do all that may become a man;
>   Who dares do more is none.
> LADY. What beast wasn't then
>   That made you break this enterprise to me?
>   When you durst do it, then you were a man;
>   And to be more than what you were, you would
>   Be so much more the man.
>
> (I.7.46–51)

By murdering Duncan, Macbeth violates and disrupts divine, human, and natural laws: he has murdered his king, to whom he owes complete loyalty; his kinsman, whom he should love; and his guest, who deserves his hospitality and protection. And he has killed an innocent man while he lies asleep and defenseless. Most important, Duncan is a wise and a good ruler. Unlike Bolingbroke in *Richard II,* Macbeth has no political or moral excuse for his deed. All of nature revolts against Duncan's murder. By killing the king, who presides over earthly order, Macbeth sets off a chain reaction that unleashes anarchy in heaven and on earth: the eve of Duncan's murder is "unruly" (i.e., unruled); a violent storm suddenly picks up; the earth shakes as if with a fever; Duncan's horses turn wild and eat each other; and prophetic shrieks fill the night air.

After Duncan's murder, Shakespeare creates one of the most harrowing scenes imaginable. Husband and wife, now accomplices, speak in a terse, conspiratorial whisper, the atmosphere one of suppressed hysteria. If they weren't whispering, they'd be screaming.

> MACBETH. I have done the deed. Didst thou not hear a
>   noise?
> LADY. I heard the owl-scream and the cricket's cry.
>   Did not you speak?
> MACBETH.   When?
> LADY.   Now.
> MACBETH.   As I descended?
> LADY. Ay.
>
> (II.2.14–16)

Their nerves are so raw, every noise seems like an explosion. Staring at his bloody hands, Macbeth at last recognizes that the murder is no longer an abstract idea but an accomplished fact. "To know my deed 'twere best not know myself." This one act has transformed him, irrevocably, from Macbeth into an assassin, strange to himself. But Lady Macbeth dismisses such talk as childish: "A little water clears us of this deed." Yet Macbeth soon becomes accustomed to his new identity. He has killed to get the throne, and his reign becomes one long bloodbath in a futile attempt to maintain it.

As in most *film noir,* the distinction between criminal and hero is vague. For a while, Macbeth still has a conscience. He broods on the deed; he can't sleep; Banquo's ghost appears to him; and he's filled with dread at what he has become. A decent man imprisoned in a murderer's body, he can only stand back and watch as the killer continues to strike. The play's real terror comes not from Macbeth's deeds but from how they transform and corrupt him. Shakespeare was one of the first writers to create both criminal and hero in the same person. He penetrates into what Joseph Conrad would later call the "heart of darkness"—the potential for evil within every civilized human being. If the honorable Macbeth could kill his king, then anything is possible—on heaven, on earth, and within the heart of man.

Macbeth briefly enjoys a sense of security as the stereotypical hardboiled villain—after all, he is now king, the Witches have assured him of his continued success, and his only threat comes from two seemingly unnatural occurrences: from a man not "of woman born" and when Birnam Wood marches to Dunsinane. In his eagerness to feel secure, Macbeth forgets that the Witch-

GUILT OR INDIGESTION?

*I*n an article on the Scottish national dish, haggis, the *Newsweek* writer Mark Starr wrote, "A number of Shakespearean revisionists now believe that Macbeth spied the ghost of Banquo at the banquet not out of guilt, but as a result of having just dined on haggis." Starr helpfully provides the recipe: "Sheep's lungs, heart and liver, mixed with suet, oats and seasonings—all boiled in the animal's stomach."

es are crafty equivocators who play with words, making truth seem like fiction and fiction, truth.

Even as Macduff and the English forces gather around him, Macbeth struggles to maintain his sense of invulnerability. But as events start closing in and he becomes increasingly isolated, his beliefs topple, one by one, as he sees through the illusion of worldly power. Kingship, power, his wife, existence itself are meaningless. Macbeth is one of the first existentialist antiheros. Inured to horror, he is exhausted, bored, and cruel. After basing his existence on portents and prophecies, he now looks at life and sees that tomorrow is just as meaningless as today:

*L*ouis Marder cites a German production of the play in which in each act, the walls of the stage increasingly close in on Macbeth.

> Tomorrow, and tomorrow, and tomorrow,
> Creeps in this petty pace from day to day
> To the last syllable of recorded time;
> And all our yesterdays have lighted fools
> The way to dusty death. Out, out, brief candle!
> Life's but a walking shadow, a poor player
> That struts and frets his hour upon the stage
> And then is heard no more. It is a tale
> Told by an idiot, full of sound and fury,
> Signifying nothing.
>
> (V.5.19–28)

As he wades through evil, Macbeth moves further and further away from all natural human impulses and sensations. The murder that first bound him to his wife has now driven them apart. Once, Lady Macbeth believed that "a little water" could wash her of the deed; now she compulsively washes her hands, unable to rid herself of guilt. Horrified by her capacity for sin, she relives the crime over and over again. Upon learning that Lady Macbeth, the sole prop of his life, has committed suicide, Macbeth says, "She should have died hereafter."

The story of a bad man who commits a crime is not a tragedy but a straightforward tale of evil. *Macbeth,* however, is about a good man who becomes evil, and that *is* his tragedy. At the end, numb to all feeling, he distantly remembers what he once was and what it was like to be human:

I have almost forgot the taste of fears.
The time has been my senses would have cooled
To hear a night-shriek, and my fell of hair
Would at a dismal treatise rouse and stir
As life were in't. I have supped full with horrors:
Direness, familiar to my slaughterous thoughts,
Cannot once start me.

(V.5.9–15)

It is his capacity for self-scrutiny that makes Macbeth a worthy tragic subject. He never lies to himself about the nature of his deed, never rationalizes to justify his actions. Aware that he is doomed, he pursues his damnation headlong to his own destruction.

The Porter Scene

*N*o one has written a more thrilling theatrical moment than the knocking in *Macbeth* (although many people can scarcely remember who came through the door).

—JOHN MORTIMER

> PORTER. Knock, knock! Who's there in the other devil's name? Faith, here's an equivocator that could swear in both the scales against either scale, who committed treason enough for God's sake, yet could not equivocate to heaven. O, come in, equivocator.

Macbeth's drunken Porter believes he is the gatekeeper to hell and welcomes all "equivocators" to the castle. "Equivocator" had an explosive meaning for the Elizabethans, specifically alluding to the Gunpowder Plot, a conspiracy to blow up the houses of Parliament and kill

James I in an attempt to put a Catholic monarch on the throne. When the Jesuits Henry Garnet and Guy Fawkes were interrogated at their trial in March 1606, they invoked the Doctrine of Equivocation, which permitted a Catholic to commit perjury in a morally acceptable cause. Shakespeare associated Garnet and his fellow conspirators with the diabolical trio in *Macbeth*. Like them, Garnet ingeniously played with the double meanings of words, uttering statements in which truth and lies were ingeniously mixed. As the Porter said, the "equivocator" could "swear in both the scales against either scale." The Witches tell Macbeth he can't be harmed by anyone "of woman born," a statement that in a *sense* is true; Macduff was ripped from his mother's womb in a cesarean birth. Finally, when Macbeth discovers how the trees have "marched" to Dunsinane, he cries, "I . . . begin / To doubt the equivocation of the fiend, / That lies like truth."

Although few remember Henry Garnet, Guy Fawkes's downfall is still celebrated with bonfires every November 5, the day the Gunpowder Plot was detected.

*T*o mankind in general Macbeth and Lady Macbeth stand out as the supreme type of all that a host and hostess should not be.

—MAX BEERBOHM

*M*acbeth is a tale told by a genius, full of soundness and fury, signifying many things.

—JAMES THURBER

I thought of a kind of sitcom approach to *Macbeth*. The king is Macbeth's guest. Macbeth is a middle-level executive. The boss is coming to dinner. And if he likes his reception, the host will get a promotion. But in this case the boss is the king; in this case, the boss is his kinsman; in this case, the middle-level executive will murder his boss. Well, if you think of it, the amount of magnification is the ultimate: an ordinary human situation that can be treated as simply as the boss coming to dinner.

—SAM SCHOENBAUM

The Curse of "The Scottish Play"

*Macbeth is an unholy riddle we
still hesitate to name for the fear
of retribution.*

—*MICHAEL PENNINGTON*

Macbeth is to the theatrical world what King Tut's tomb is to archaeologists. No other play has had more bad luck associated with it: coronaries, car accidents, mysterious ailments, botched lines, and sword wounds. The theatrical superstition is not taken lightly: even to pronounce the play's title is considered bad dressing-room form. Its very name is a curse, and actors will use any euphemism rather than actually say the "M" word. It's also considered as the height of bad dressing-room form to quote from the play under any circumstances. For hundreds of years it's been delicately referred to as "The Scottish Play" or simply *"That* Play."

How did the superstition originate? Is it because of the sinister atmosphere that shrouds the play with its cackling Witches, shrieking night birds, and damp, swirling fogs? Or perhaps it's because unpleasant events seem to occur whenever it is performed.

❖ During the play's very first performance, on August 7, 1606, Hal Berridge, the boy who played Lady Macbeth, died backstage.

❖ In 1849, after years of intense animosity, the rivalry between the American actor Edwin Forrest and the British actor John Macready culminated in a riot in which thirty-one people were killed. It took place in front of the theatre where Macready was appearing in *Macbeth*.

❖ In one memorable week at the Old Vic in 1934, the play went through four different Macbeths. Michael Kim came down with laryngitis; Alastair Sim caught a chill; and Marius Goring was fired. John Laurie survived to finish the run.

❖ The 1937 Laurence Olivier–Judith Anderson production at the Old Vic must have been the unluckiest ever. Just before the scheduled opening night Lilian Baylis's favorite dog, Snoo, died. (Miss Baylis was the founder of the Old Vic.) The next day, Miss Baylis herself succumbed after learning that the opening night was to be postponed. According to Olivier's biographer, Donald Spoto, the director "barely escaped death in a taxi accident; Olivier was nearly brained by a falling stage sandbag; the scenery did not fit the stage; and [composer] Darius Milhaud was not happy with his musical score and kept tearing up pages of his composition." Moreover, Olivier, with characteristic gusto, accidentally wounded the various Macduffs in the final battle scene.

❖ The Scottish Play seems to have given Miss Baylis a particularly hard time: when *Macbeth* opened in 1954 her portrait fell off the wall and smashed into pieces.

❖ In 1938 the Stratford Festival opened with a production of *Macbeth*. During that season an old man had both his legs broken when he was hit by his own car in the parking lot; Lady Macbeth ran her car into a store window; and Macduff fell off his horse and had to be replaced by an understudy for several days.

❖ Not even animals are immune: In Orson Welles and John Houseman's all-black "Voodoo *Macbeth*," five live black goats were sacrificed late one night by Abdul, a genuine witch doctor, who was part of the cast.

❖ A warning to critics who pan *Macbeth:* After the first night's performance of "Voodoo *Macbeth,*" Percy Hammond, the conservative drama critic of the New York *Herald Tribune,* wrote a scathing review criticizing the New Deal and the government's endowment for the arts, calling the production "an exhibition of deluxe boondoggling." Shortly after the review appeared, John Houseman was visited by the group of African drummers who appeared in the play, along with Abdul. According to Houseman's account in his autobiography, *Unfinished Business,* they wanted to know if the review was evil and if it was the work of an enemy: "He is a bad man?" Houseman concurred: "A bad man."

The next day Welles and Houseman were greeted by the theatre manager with some unsettling news: the theatre's basement had been filled all night with "unusual drumming and with chants more weird and horrible than anything that had been heard upon the stage." Welles and Houseman "looked at each other for an instant, then quickly away again, for in the afternoon paper . . . was a brief item announcing the sudden illness of the well-known critic Percy Hammond . . . [who] died some days later—of pneumonia, it was said."

Dame Judith Anderson

*S*he played three Shakespeare roles: Gertrude (to Gielgud's Hamlet), Lady Macbeth (with Olivier in 1937 at the Old Vic, with Maurice Evans in 1941, and on "The Hallmark Hall of Fame" in 1954) and finally, at age seventy-two, she played Hamlet at Carnegie Hall. But it's as Lady Macbeth that she's best remembered, her wonderfully fierce glare and piercing eyes having become synonymous with the role. Her terrifying portrayal of Lady Macbeth led one critic to say, "She almost makes me afraid of the part." Some sixty years after her original performance, her voice still had the imperious ring of Macbeth's royal lady. Dame Judith died on January 3, 1992, at the age of ninety-three.

NE: *What about Lady Macbeth?*

JA: Ah, well, there you've got somebody. Lady Macbeth was pure and clean, she knew every inch of her husband. There's that wonderful speech. What does she say now? "Thou woulds't be great, / Art not without ambition, but without / The illness should attend it. . . . wouldst not play false, / And yet wouldst wrongly win." She has a complete and total picture of Macbeth—but not of herself. She made excuses for not doing the murder even when she had the opportunity: "Had he not resembled / My father as he slept, I had done't." Well, that's not true at all. She says, "Give me the daggers," but the second the blood touches her hand, she cannot get it out of her system. It's in her mouth, in her eyes, her ears, her whole being.

NE: *Is she simply cruel?*

JA: No, just madly, passionately in love with her husband—and ambitious! I don't think she saw anything wrong with that. That was what she wanted, and that's what she should be. She was obsessed with power, both for herself and for her husband. She was an extremely passionate woman.

NE: *What was it like to play Lady Macbeth?*

JA: Wonderful.

NE: *Is that your favorite role?*

JA: No, no, not that. She was perfect; it was a small part. I heard one actress say she didn't want that role because it was too small. But Lady Macbeth has great arias. I played *Macbeth* in London, which was a very unhappy experience.

NE: *Why?*

JA: The director [Michel Saint-Denis] *talked* a wonderful *Macbeth,* but the longer the rehearsals got, the more it fell through his fingers.

NE: *What happened?*

JA: But everything went wrong! Lilian Baylis's dog died, which was a tragedy. Then *she* died. Then the sets couldn't be brought into the theatre. They were so big, they had to be taken back and cut down. Everything was overdone. The trains to our costumes were practically in our dressing rooms. [Donald Spoto, Olivier's biographer, records Vivien Leigh's reaction to this overblown production: "You hear Macbeth's first line, then Larry's make-up comes on, then Banquo comes on, then Larry comes on."]

NE: *Is that the "curse of* Macbeth*"?*

JA: Oh, no! The curse of *Macbeth* is worse than *that.*

NE: *What about the* Macbeth *with Maurice Evans? Do you play Lady Macbeth differently with each actor?*

JA: Well, you have to, really. I don't particularly wish to talk about the Evans production, because I didn't agree with him on a lot of things. And he couldn't seem to feel the passion between the two at all. Don't ask me why, but he couldn't. But I mustn't talk like that. He wasn't manly enough.

NE: *The critics said he was physically too small for the role.*

JA: Oh, not only that way. His emotions. I've seen some of Maurice's performances that were brilliant, but they weren't noted for their masculinity.

NE: *What makes that play so great?*

JA: Because it is.

NE: *You've even played the part of Hamlet. What is his so-called mystery?*

JA: Well . . . no, I couldn't say. I'd say he was not totally masculine, missing the . . . what do you call it?

NE: *Macho?*

JA: Yes, he was highly sensitive.

NE: *But not effeminate?*

JA: He had his little moments in school, but I suppose a lot of boys do. He loved Ophelia as best he could, but there was something lacking.

NE: *What?*

JA: I think that in his school days he had a little affair with Horatio. Horatio was a tender person and was obviously impressed by Hamlet's princely background. It's so obvious, particularly when Hamlet says, "I could accuse me of such things that it were better my mother had not borne me." He's not a murderer or a cheat or a thief, and he's a very tender person. And then he died in Horatio's arms. But I never heard anyone make that suggestion.

NE: *Why doesn't he kill Claudius right away?*

JA: Because he can't. He hasn't got that in his system. He's too sensitive.

NE: *Why is he finally able to do it?*

JA: Well, he's up against a brick wall. Claudius has killed his mother and poisoned the rapiers. He's about to die, and it's his last chance.

NE: *Do you think he wants to die?*

JA: Well, he has no choice.

NE: *What was it like to play Hamlet? Was the difference in sex an obstacle?*

JA: It's exhausting. I played Hamlet because it's the greatest play I know. Though Bernhardt played Hamlet, Mrs. Siddons played Hamlet, a female Hamlet isn't accepted. But I never felt I was competing with Olivier or Gielgud. I just wanted kids to know of Shakespeare's genius, and how beautiful and understandable he is.

NE: *How can teachers and actors convey how wonderful Shakespeare is to children?*

JA: You've got to love beauty, you've got to love the best.

NE: *How did you play Gertrude to Gielgud's Hamlet?*

JA: As well as I could! I just saw Gertrude as a weak person, and not a highly exciting woman. Not overly brilliant. A dutiful wife. I don't think she thought there was anything frightfully wrong about betraying her dead husband. I don't believe she knew anything about her husband's murder.

NE: *Who is your favorite Hamlet?*

JA: Gielgud was a great Hamlet, the greatest I've seen.

NE: *Do you like the Olivier movie version of* Hamlet?

JA: No. Movies are entirely different from theatre. You can't do anything in movies. You can't make an angry gesture, because it's overdone. When you raise your eyebrows you raise them a quarter of an inch; on stage you raise them three feet. You have to adjust everything—a gesture, a grimace. I saw the *Henry V* with Branagh the other day, and his closeups were unattractive because you could see his tonsils. With the anguish and the anger and the opening of his mouth, you could see his tongue. But I liked the movie better than Olivier's *Henry.* Larry's was pretty and clean and neat, and the tents were all ironed. It wasn't war. Branagh's war was too much war, I thought. But one has to judge them side by side, and Branagh's was truer than Larry's.

NE: *Was there a particular moment in your life when you were suddenly seized by Shakespeare's genius?*

JA: Don't talk to me about when I was young. I was a fiend from hell.

International Shakespeare

*B*en Jonson wrote of Shakespeare, "He was not of an age, but for all time." What he didn't say was that Shakespeare was of all places. To those who believe that the soul of Shakespeare resides in his language, Shakespeare in translation seems blasphemous. Yet the cliché about the universal appeal of the Bard takes on new life when you realize that this Elizabethan playwright, dead for almost five hundred years, is still performed more than any other dramatist, in practically every country and language in the world. Terry Priston of the *Los Angeles Times* writes: "Itinerant productions of *Julius Caesar* are performed before throngs of up to 10,000 people; the comedies have been performed in African huts; and the Compañía de Teatro en Vecindades enact Shakespeare in the barrios of Mexico City." According to Felicia Londré, professor of theatre at the University of Missouri, "There are often six or seven Shakespeare productions running in Bucharest at any given time."

Some non–English speakers regard Shakespeare with the fierce loyalty reserved for their own literary titans. Known as *Unser Shakespeare*—"Our Shakespeare"—in Germany, he is performed there, according to Priston, ten times more than in any English-speaking country; and as Boris Pasternak's translation of *King Lear* and the music of Tchaikovsky, Prokofiev, and Shostakovich attest, Shakespeare resonates within the Russian sensibility as well.

If it's difficult for us to comprehend the Elizabethan concept of justice, consider how difficult it must be for someone from a non-Western country to transcend the barriers of history, language, and culture to comprehend exactly what Shakespeare meant by such an abstract concept as justice in, say, *Measure for Measure*. Thus, a non-

Western *Measure* necessarily differs from a Western one, because law and punishment naturally suggest something very different to Asians than they do to us. The drama critic John Elsom also points out that images we take for granted, such as those concerning topography and climate, may sound absurd to a non-Westerner. For instance, the metaphors in the well-known speech "Now is the winter of our discontent / Made glorious summer by this sun of York" simply don't make sense to an Arab, whose winter is "closer to the British spring, for it brings rain, whereas summer is the time of drought and death." In an interview the Japanese pianist Mitsuko Uchida said that the only Shakespeare plays the Japanese do well are *King Lear* and *Macbeth*, the former because it is about the relationship between parent and child, the latter because it is about a woman's covert manipulation.

There are basically two kinds of foreign Shakespeare productions. The more orthodox adopts a literal translation of the text and adheres to the doublet-and-hose tradition. Thus, a Japanese actor plays Hamlet, and the only difference between this production and a British one is that "To be, or not to be" is in Japanese instead of in English. (When English-speaking actors appear with a foreign company, they speak in English while the rest of the cast continues in their native language, thus creating a linguistic mélange that makes

In David Lodge's novel *Small World,* one character translates the titles of Shakespeare's plays from Japanese back into English:

Strange Affair of the Flesh and the Bosom
(*The Merchant of Venice*)

Lust and Dreams of the Transitory World
(*Romeo and Juliet*)

Swords of Freedom
(*Julius Caesar*)

A Sad Case of Early Retirement
(*King Lear*)

The Oar Well Accustomed to the Water
(*All's Well That Ends Well*)

Courtesy Point Tokyo Co. Ltd.

Not all Shakespeare is done by the Royal Shakespeare Company or other English-speaking companies. Set in sixteenth-century Japan, the Toho Company's *Macbeth,* directed by Ninagawa, was described by the drama critic Michael Billington in the *Guardian* as the most "achingly beautiful" he had ever seen. Apparently the production was an intriguing blend of East and West: the actors used a direct translation from Shakespeare's text, the only change being that Ireland was referred to as "Western Country" and England as "Southern Country." The production was extremely Asian in its stylized loveliness: cherry blossoms, symbolic of love and death, drifted to the ground continuously throughout the play, and characters wore traditional Samurai costumes. Surrounding the stage and enclosing the action was a huge Buddhist altar of the type found in many Japanese homes.

for some intriguing performances.) But as the power of British imperialism waned, non-English directors began to consider how they might adapt Shakespeare to fit their own cultural beliefs. During the latter half of this century, directors such as the Japanese Kurosawa and the Russian Kozintsev turned to Shakespeare as a means of exploring their own cultural preoccupations.

Very often it's the non-English directors who come up with the most innovative and beautiful interpretations of Shakespeare. A South African director retells *Othello* as if it were the tale of Beauty and the Beast and King Kong. Ariane Mnouchkine of Le Théâtre du Soleil uses large Oriental-style puppets, her Shakespeare productions a strange mix of traditional Balinese, Japanese, Persian, and Chinese theatre. By presenting Shakespeare in a new and unfamiliar way, she revives *Othello*'s original power to evoke pity and terror. Unfortunately, many English directors rely on Shakespeare's language to do all the work; hence, all those boring Shakespeare-by-rote productions that put audiences to sleep. Because non-English, and particularly non-Western, directors lack the encrusted reverence toward Shakespeare inculcated in English-speaking schools, they are liberated from predigested images and poses. They frequently transform the familiar and banal into something rich and strange.

A Shakespearean critic recounts the tale of an American tourist who upon seeing *Measure for Measure* in Beijing returned to the States in raptures about the performance. Exclaiming on its beauty and clarity, he at last burst out, "Shakespeare should always be done in the original Chinese!"

───────

There is a typical Hungarian story, about the very well-known Hungarian theatre director, Arthur Bardos, who left Hungary in 1949 to direct *Hamlet* in England; and he was asked by the BBC what it was like to do so. Mr Bardos answered: "Of course, it is a great honour and a challenge, but to tell you the truth, it's strange to hear the text in English because I am used to the original version, translated by Janos Arany."

—ANNE FÖLDES,
Hungarian theatre critic

Subversive Shakespeare

Coriolanus explores the danger of tyranny—whether by the ruling class or by the masses, depending on how you look at it; *Julius Caesar* is about the death of a dictator; in *Macbeth,* a loyal subject murders his king; *Measure for Measure* deals with corruption in high places; even the seemingly innocent *A Midsummer Night's Dream* can be interpreted as a nightmare about tyranny and spying. A director can always find a political or social subtext in a Shakespeare play. When Shakespeare is banned by a repressive regime, he becomes a vital symbol of defiance and freedom. Stalin banned *Hamlet,* a play dear to the Russian spirit; after his death, it was triumphantly performed in practically every theatre in the country. Just the name "Hamlet" signified the victory of the individual over the masses.

Dissident directors often use Shakespeare as a way to smuggle subversive messages to their countrymen, awakening them to the significance of political and social events happening around them. In a 1989 London seminar entitled "Is Shakespeare Still Too English?" Toby Robertson admitted that he chose to direct *Measure for Measure* in China for "one particular reason. The trial of the Gang of Four was looming all over China, and nobody knew what was going to happen. There is one line in [the play], 'The law hath not been dead, though it hath slept,' and I believe that this production was being used as a restatement of the value of the law. In one way, it had a propaganda purpose."

Professor Londré notes, "What the public wanted was for theatres to say what couldn't be said in the media. A 1933–34 production of *Coriolanus* at the Comédie-Française aroused political passions that fomented disturbances in the theatre, shook the Third Republic, and helped precipitate the fall of the Leftist Daladier government. Some accused the theatre administration of making Shakespeare the ally of Léon Daudet and Charles Maurras, who ran the right-wing newspaper *Action Française.*" Other examples cited by Professor Londré include a French post–World War II production of *King Lear* in which Gloucester's torture suggested an interrogation of Gestapo officers, and a 1950 *Othello* at the Comédie-Française in which Iago's insinuations to Othello anticipated modern brainwashing techniques. André Gide began his translation of *Hamlet* in 1922 and then abandoned it, claiming that the task was impossible, but he resumed and completed it in 1942, while

France was under German occupation. Today, Gide's *Hamlet* is regarded by critics as an angry gesture of resistance: through Hamlet, the translator tries to "catch the conscience" of his countrymen. More recently, a German production of *Measure for Measure,* produced after the collapse of the Berlin Wall, was the last time East Germans had to depend on words written more than four hundred years ago in a foreign land to relate what newspapers were not allowed to print. Professor Londré notes that in this particular production, a despised dictatorship forced its subjects to perform meaningless acts to prove their fidelity, and it concluded with the destruction of a huge castle wall.

Although many non-German writers were banned under Hitler, the German people, unable to part with *"Unser Shakespeare,"* used him as propaganda to further the aims of the Third Reich, thus proving once again that Shakespeare, like the Bible, can be adapted to all purposes. Asserting that the Shakespearean spirit was essentially Nordic, the Ministry of Propaganda stated that Shakespeare's plays "demonstrate the German spirit, German scholarship, German thoroughness, and the German capability of recognizing and supporting great geniuses of other nations."

According to an official decree, Shakespeare was to be regarded as a German author. In one instance, according to Professor Londré, the Shakespearean heroine's perspicacity in choosing a mate, and the procreative sonnets (1–17) advising the young man to marry and reproduce, were cited to support the Reich's advice to young fräuleins to breed good Nordic stock.

Antony and Cleopatra

Antony and Cleopatra is five acts of hyperbole. As one of Shakespeare's last tragedies before he turned to the "brave new world" of the romances, it captures a decadent, fin de siècle sensibility. Everything in the play, from character to setting, is overripe to bursting. It's the most voluptuous play Shakespeare ever wrote—perhaps the most voluptuous ever written. Since the role of Cleopatra was originally played by a boy, the dramatist couldn't rely on physical intimacy to convey eroticism, so he poured all the play's sexuality into luscious imagery that "beggars the imagination."

In a key passage, Antony compares himself to clouds as they float, shift, dissolve, and gather themselves into new shapes: "That which is now a horse, even with a thought / The rack dislimns, and makes it indistinct / As water is in water." ("Rack" refers to the drift of clouds.) This is the essence of the play itself: moods, settings, scenes, incidents, and characters are in a constant state of flux. Take the play's first scene. Two Roman bystanders, Demetrius and Philo, await the approach of Antony and Cleopatra, who, like aging Hollywood legends, are about to make their grand entrance. Of course, the two nobodies must disparage them.

Flourish. Enter Antony, Cleopatra, her ladies Charmian and Iras, the train, with eunuchs fanning her

PHILO. Look where they come.
　　　　Take but good note, and you shall see in him

The triple pillar of the world transformed
Into a strumpet's fool.

(I.1.10–13)

From the Roman perspective, the Queen of the Nile is a whore, the ruler of the world her doting fool. But as soon as we see the couple and hear their ravishing poetry, Philo's opinion shrinks into insignificance, and we, too, at least momentarily, become fans.

> CLEOPATRA. If it be love indeed, tell me how much.
> ANTONY. There's beggary in the love that can be reck-
>   oned.
> CLEOPATRA. I'll set a bourne how far to be beloved.
> ANTONY. Then must thou needs find out new heaven,
>   new earth.

(I.1.14–17)

("Bourne" means "limit.")

In the very next line, there's an intrusion: a messenger from Antony's headquarters in Rome arrives, quickly shattering the amorous mood, and at once the play's tone becomes practical and businesslike. Antony's wife, Fulvia, has died, and he is needed back in Rome. Though Cleopatra manipulates and cajoles in an attempt to get him to stay, Antony is now a Roman tribune and not a mere gigolo. Within the space of one short scene we are presented with conflicting impressions and perspectives that Shakespeare takes little pains to reconcile.

The first word spoken by Cleopatra is equivocal. She says, "*If* it be love. . . ." The word is crucial. Throughout the play, this maddening woman keeps us—and Antony—guessing. Does she genuinely love him, or is she a sexual sorceress who takes perverse joy in enslaving men? Is she dallying with Antony until another great ruler comes along? Perhaps it's difficult to classify love in this play because we tend to define it according to the Western ideal of Romeo and Juliet. What draws these two together is deeper than romance and comes from a fatal and irresistible chemistry that transcends worldly affairs, time, and space.

Antony, too, wears many faces. One of the "triple pillar[s] of the world," is he the world's greatest lover or the world's biggest fool? He's caught between two identities, past and present: the shrewd military strategist who once commanded armies and conquered realms, and the voluptuary who renounces world power for passion. His conflict is implied by the play's diverse settings: Cleopatra's Egypt, an irresponsible holiday realm of feminine mystery and a threat to masculine authority, and the austere, sexless Rome where his co-rulers reside. To adore romance above all else and yet know that it's utterly worthless—this is Antony's strange conflict. His indecisiveness is dramatically mirrored in the dizzying speed with which the scenes shift from Rome to Egypt and back again. (There are forty-two brief scenes in *Antony and Cleopatra,* more than in any other Shakespeare play.) And it's his indecisiveness that spells his downfall. When Antony carelessly agrees to marry Caesar's sister, Octavia, as a way of solidifying a new world alliance, the act has tragic implications. Even so, it leads to one of the funniest scenes in this mercurial play. After bullying the terrified messenger who has just brought her the news, Cleopatra, with typical contrariness, first theatrically swoons (she is the type of person who faints by carefully lowering herself onto a couch) and then pragmatically demands to know all the details about Antony's new wife:

> CLEOPATRA. I faint. O, Iras, Charmian! 'Tis no matter.
> Go to the fellow, good Alexis; bid him
> Report the features of Octavia, her years,
> Her inclination. Let him not leave out
> The colour of her hair.
>
> (II.5.110–14)

"Bring me word how tall she is," she cries as she is led out, prostrate. In Cleopatra, Shakespeare has created a woman of tragic grandeur who also happens to be funny.

Naturally, the dwarfish Octavia can't compete with the magnificent Cleopatra, and Antony abandons his Roman wife for his Egyptian mistress, thus setting off a full-scale war, which the middle-aged hero is ill-equipped to fight. For a while, it seems as if Antony's old prowess is returning. After winning one minor battle, he talks like an aging film star who, having landed one minor part, is suddenly buoyed with plans for a comeback.

> My nightingale,
> We have beat them to their beds. What, girl! Though grey

Do something mingle with our younger brown, yet ha' we
A brain that nourishes our nerves, and can
Get goal for goal of youth.

(IV.8.18–22)

Fighting a dying cause against time and mortality, Antony must give way to the paltry yet efficient Caesar.

Unique among the tragedies, *Antony and Cleopatra* is not simply about the fall of the great, but the fall of greatness. The past tense is used in *Antony and Cleopatra* more than in any other Shakespeare play: "My salad days, / When I was green in judgement," Cleopatra says. Later, she says, "Eternity was in our lips and eyes, / Bliss in our brows' bent." Enobarbus, recalling the first time Antony saw Cleopatra, says, "The barge she sat in. . . ." Antony says, ". . . for when my hours / were nice and lucky, men did ransom lives / of me for jests. . . ." Cleopatra's days are filled with remembrance of decadent pleasures past with Antony. She describes how she once put her "tires and mantles on him, whilst / I wore his sword Philippian" (that is, he wore her feminine headgear while she swaggered about with his sword, actions that suggest their decadence), and the time she drank him under the table during one of their endless nights of debauchery.

The play's keynote is struck in Act I, scene 1, when Cleopatra publicly demands a reckoning of how much she is loved, and Antony replies that love that can be measured is contemptible. She yearns for infinity and immortality, but her means of gratifying her longings are finite and petty, and a queen with "immortal longings" is reduced to playing billiards with her eunuch. Cleopatra is like some Norma Desmond of the Nile. Time is her enemy, and without Antony she doesn't know how to fill it. Alone, with only her servants, she calls for a potion to "sleep out this great gap of time" while her lover is away.

To the very end, Cleopatra remains an obscure, sultry siren, tragic heroine, pragmatic politician, and magnificent queen: Shakespeare leaves us with so many conflicting impressions that we never feel we truly understand her. When Antony dies, she cries out, "And there is nothing left remarkable / Beneath the visiting moon." Is Cleopatra mourning Antony or the fact that, in a life devoted to the extraordinary, there is nothing left to live for? Though she indirectly causes Antony's suicide, she obviously has no intention of killing herself over him. Unlike in a tragedy of love, the two do not expire together. Antony dies at the end of Act IV, while Cleopatra, the more businesslike of the two, sensibly waits to see if she can strike a bargain with her lover's conqueror. She kills herself only when she realizes that she is doomed to become Caesar's trophy, and the play ends with her death. Cleopatra can survive without Antony, but she can't survive the loss of her pride. The thought of being paraded through the streets for gawking, sweaty plebeians violates her sense of majesty. In her world, appearance is all, and losing face means the loss of life. Yet she never forgets Antony. In one of her final moments she cries out, "Husband, I come." Cleopatra is a stunning creature of caprice and "infinite variety." She loves Antony, she betrays him, she is a survivor, and, though fickle in everything else, she remains resolute in her decision to die like a queen.

Her body, that mortal clay beneath the moon, slowly dissolves: "I am fire and air; my baser elements / I give to baser life." According to Elizabethan cosmography, everything beneath the moon was mortal and subject to decay. At last these earthbound lovers have thrust off the constraints of the terrestrial sphere and have joined the extraordinary realm above the moon.

What to Look for in Antony and Cleopatra

Although Antony at times appears ludicrous, he's never pitiable. While he is battling his enemies at sea, Cleopatra capriciously takes it into her head to sail by him in her own little boat—like a mistress unexpectedly popping up at her lover's office. Upon her appearance, however, he disgraces himself by turning tail, abandoning his army, and following her. Later, he bungles his own suicide attempt, only to die in her arms after being hoisted up to her monument in some ridiculous contraption. But Shakespeare keeps him from becoming pathetic by contrasting him with Caesar's studied bloodlessness. Antony has a casual elegance and, unlike his rival, is generous and likable.

*C*leopatra is a male fantasy, both terrifying and glorious, engulfing men yet unattainable. She's every man's ideal, because she never lapses into domestic predictability: "Age cannot wither her, nor custom stale / Her infinite variety." She always keeps Antony guessing: look at the following passage between Charmian, Cleopatra's handmaid, and Cleopatra, as the two women debate the best way to keep a man. With few alterations in vocabulary, it could easily be a debate excerpted from a story in a modern woman's magazine.

> CLEOPATRA. (*to Alexas*)
> See where he is, who's with him, what he does.
> I did not send you. If you find him sad,
> Say I am dancing; if in mirth, report
> That I am sudden sick. Quick, and return.
> CHARMIAN. Madam, methinks, if you did love him dearly,
> You do not hold the method to enforce
> The like from him.
> CLEOPATRA. What should I do I do not?
> CHARMIAN. In each thing give him way. Cross him in
> nothing.
> CLEOPATRA. Thou teachest like a fool: the way to lose
> him.
>
> (I.3.2–10)

*A*s Antony's right-hand man, Enobarbus is a stolid, brisk, and practical soldier whose wry observations serve as a counterpoint to Antony and Cleopatra's rhetorical excess. As Antony throws himself into life with abandon, Enobarbus, his foil, cynically observes. Despite his disapproval of Antony's behavior, he remains loyal almost to the end. His is a minor tragedy that mirrors that of his superior's; in abandoning Antony, he forsakes his own ideals, losing his honor, and himself.

Act IV, scene 3, is very brief and unearthly. As the music of hautboys (an Elizabethan oboe) rises from the earth, Hercules, Antony's tutelary god, at last abandons his favorite son. The uncanny airs emanating from another world reveal that there is a realm of godlike beauty beyond this mortal one.

In Act II, scene 2, Shakespeare brilliantly puts one of the most famous descriptions of female beauty in all Western literature into the mouth of the unromantic Enobarbus, thereby making Cleopatra's allure all the more convincing. If she can inspire *him* to poetic heights, then she must be spectacular. The matter-of-fact opening, "I will tell you," does little to prepare us for the sumptuous description that follows:

> The barge she sat in, like a burnished throne,
> Burned on the water. The poop was beaten gold;
> Purple the sails, and so perfumèd that
> The winds were lovesick with them. The oars were silver,
> Which to the tune of the flutes kept stroke and made
> The water which they beat to follow faster,
> As amorous of their strokes. For her own person,
> It beggared all description. She did lie
> In her pavilion, cloth-of-gold of tissue,
> O'erpicturing that Venus where we see
> The fancy outwork nature. On each side her
> Stood pretty dimpled boys, like smiling cupids,
> With divers-coloured fans, whose wind did seem
> To glow the delicate cheeks which they did cool,
> And what they undid did.
>
> (196–210)

Comments on
<u>Antony and Cleopatra</u>

I don't want to play Cleopatra! I never know whose camp I'm in when I'm reading her. She tangles me. I want to be clean and clear and know who I am and where I am when I play a part.

—JUDITH ANDERSON

*A*ntony has become a Cleopatra-addict, for whom sixteenth-century audiences felt the same mixture of attraction and repulsion as modern man does for wealthy drug abusers. In the end both lovers extend "the world's best-ever holiday romance" into the only world where adolescence is perpetual death.

—JOHN RAY

A queen is *never* a whore! Even if she is, she's never a whore.

—JAN KOTT

*M*ost people say their favorite Shakespeare play is *Hamlet,* some say *King Lear.* I sympathize. But my own favorite is . . . God help me, *Antony and Cleopatra.* And to my mind, one of the greatest moments in drama is the one in which Cleopatra asks the asp to bite her. She's dying, yet the serpent is her baby, so the image is maternal; she's Cleopatra, so it's sexy. She's a great queen, so it's regal. All at once! At once! Sexy, maternal, and queenly. It's just like Shakespeare to work on all those levels!

—SAM SCHOENBAUM

*T*o me, Cleopatra has always been a most interesting problem. Is *Antony and Cleopatra* a great love story? I do not think so.

—AGATHA CHRISTIE

I never really thought a lot about Antony—as a person, that is. I mean, really, he's an absolute twerp, isn't he?

—LAURENCE OLIVIER

THE TRAGICOMIC

*F*antastical, superficial, artificial, improbable, impressionistic, inferior, miraculous, boring—or the best: no one can agree on the merits of Shakespeare's romances. The eminently reasonable Dr. Johnson dismissed them as foolish, and they are. But, in the words of the playwright Dennis Potter, they are "sweetly foolish."

*R*OMANCES

With *Pericles, Cymbeline, The Winter's Tale,* and *The Tempest* we enter Shakespeare's final period; from *Pericles,* which is loosely plotted, to *The Tempest,* which is one of his most tightly structured plays, the middle-aged dramatist realizes the final vision of his art. All the great Shakespearean themes come together at the end: theatrical illusion and its relation to life, the conflict between appearance and reality, the discovery of the self, the capacity of art to transform terror into beauty, and the power of love to heal.

At their most superficial, the romances are spectacular shows filled with special effects (one reason why they are now coming back into vogue), and Shakespeare, capitalizing on the contemporary taste for such spectacle, proves himself the Elizabethan equivalent of a Steven Spielberg. In these last plays he sets his imagination free. Filled with such marvels as a statue coming to life, an enchanted shipwreck, and a sprite who flies through air and earth, they contain the most elaborate stage directions of all Shakespearean plays—an indication that the dramatist was becoming increasingly interested in stagecraft (some of the more famous directions suggest the plays' extravagant effects: "*Exit Antigonus, Pursued by a Bear*" and "*Thunder and lightning. Enter Ariel, like a harpy; claps his wings upon the table; and with a quaint device the banquet vanishes.*"

But it isn't the supernatural events that make the romances miraculous; it's that they appeared at all. It might seem that after writing the tragedies, Shakespeare might have reached an artistic impasse. How could he find meaning beyond such negation and despair? But the romances, like an unexpected thaw, melt the wintry vision of the tragedies with images of rebirth and reconciliation. Out of evil and torment spring extraordinary plays where wrongs are righted and warring families are reconciled. The romances are tragedies played in reverse. *The Winter's Tale* opens with a husband's jealousy and a dead wife, and it ends with their reunion, as if Shakespeare had decided to write an *Othello* in which Desdemona wakes up unharmed. In *Pericles* and *The Winter's Tale,* fathers and daughters find each other again, as if Shakespeare were trying to undo the horror of Cordelia's death. In *The Tempest,* one brother tries to murder another, and a son finds his "dead" father alive—essentially *Hamlet* in reverse. The romances are obsessively concerned with domestic reconciliations. The comedies depict the "Green World" of youth; the tragedies are about the problems of maturity. But Shakespeare's last plays bring the generations together in a final vision of harmony.

The world of the romance is not perfect. Terrible events—death, incest, attempted murder, and betrayal—cause suffering that can never be undone. The wrongs of the past are not forgotten, but they *are* forgiven. In *The Winter's Tale,* Leontes must mourn for sixteen years before his wife and daughter are returned to him—years that will never be restored. Nevertheless, the children of the older generation marry, and the play concludes with a glimpse into the future. In the final plays, the word "regenerated" takes on a double meaning. In comedy, the future is wide open; in tragedy, the past is irrevocable; but in the romances, "What's past is prologue."

Not to be dismissed as escapist fantasies, these plays reassure us on a deep, almost subconscious level that whatever is precious can never be completely lost. The dead come back to life, abandoned children are found, and in returning, they are altered, transformed by suffering, magic, and love. Through magic, endings are turned into beginnings; the enchantment of the romances is not mere hocus-pocus, but the inexplicable alchemy of art and love. Thus Ariel's mysteriously suggestive song in *The Tempest* alludes to the power of art to transform even death into something "rich and strange":

> Full fathom five thy father lies;
>   Of his bones are coral made;
> Those are pearls that were his eyes;
>   Nothing of him that doth fade,
> But doth suffer a sea-change
> Into something rich and strange.

(I.2.397–402)

The Tempest

The Tempest begins in the middle of a shipwreck. Certain of death, men scream out against the roar of waves crashing, while overhead, lightning streaks the sky. This is one of the most gripping opening scenes Shakespeare ever wrote, as if more than ever he wanted to draw his audience into the dramatic action one last time. By the end of the scene, it seems the men have drowned, and the audience feels as if they, too, have been through an ordeal. Yet with its extravagant effects, the scene, unlike Shakespeare's usual muted beginnings, calls attention to itself as theatre. We are drawn into the tumult while at the same time we marvel at the stagecraft needed to create the illusion.

These two perspectives—one engaged, one distant—are mirrored in the next scene: from on shore, Miranda watches the shipwreck, and although her father allays her fears, assuring her that "there's no harm done," she weeps for the drowning men. Prospero serenely observes the disaster (which he calls a "spectacle"), his perspective one of god-like detachment, secure in the knowledge that the men are safe. Suddenly we realize, as we have suspected all along, that we've been duped; what seemed so realistic and thrilling turns out to be an illusion of an illusion, Prospero's magic, analogous to theatrical sleight of hand. Both magician and playwright seem to manipulate nature, bringing forth objects out of "thin air," making us believe in a reality without substance. Throughout The Tempest Shakespeare continually reminds us that we are watching transient shadows:

> Our revels now are ended. These our actors,
> As I foretold you, were all spirits, and
> Are melted into air, into thin air;

And, like the baseless fabric of this vision,
The cloud-capped tow'rs, the gorgeous palaces,
The solemn temples, the great globe itself,
Yea, all which it inherit, shall dissolve,
And, like this insubstantial pageant faded,
Leave not a rack behind. We are such stuff
As dreams are made on; and our little life
Is rounded with a sleep.

(IV.1.148–58)

When he speaks these words, Prospero has just presented a betrothal masque for Ferdinand and Miranda, and the spirit-actors, their revels having ended, immediately vanish. We watch Miranda and Ferdinand, unwitting actors in Prospero's plot, watch actors in a play-within-a-play. The distinction between art and life blurs further when we realize that the "great globe" refers to the literal theatre in which the actors played their parts. Life, like drama, is as evanescent as a dream, a passing show in the midst of oblivion. Although Prospero's statement recalls the weary detachment of Macbeth's vision of life as a "poor player" or Jaques's "all the world's a stage," it also suggests an awareness that life is more precious for its transience. Shakespeare is simultaneously preoccupied with his art and the reality that his art must depict. Several levels of theatricality operate within the play: *The Tempest* itself, Prospero's plot in which a deserted island suggests an empty stage (an analogy further strengthened by the fact that Shakespeare's theatre was without walls), and a wedding masque, all concluding with an epilogue in which the actor playing Prospero steps forth, revealing that he is only an ordinary man playing a part. With his words, the carefully constructed illusion dissolves.

Critics sometimes divide an artist's career into three phases, and the distinction, while simplistic, is helpful. In the first, his work is unselfconscious, exuberant; in the middle, he exhibits mature prowess and control; and, last stage of all, he is nostalgic, self-conscious, and so completely the master of his material that he playfully revives old themes and ideas in a new and intriguing way. Many of Shakespeare's works reveal an intense awareness of their own artifice, none more so than *The Tempest,* his last, most retrospective play. Shakespeare isn't simply rehashing old material; he is mixing themes together with such odd source materials as Montaigne's essay "On Cannibals," Ovid's *Metamorphoses,* travel literature, accounts of shipwrecks, and pamphlets about the New World—all creating a drama both nostalgic and innovative.

As in *King Lear,* the play begins with a storm, which marks the beginning of moral regeneration. The shipwreck itself looks back to both a comedy and a tragedy: *Twelfth Night,* in which another supposedly drowned character is restored to life; and *Macbeth,* in which another ship is magically "tempest-tossed." The marriage masque and the warring dukes recall *As You Like It;* and in its treatment of illusion and reality, *The Tempest* is a rewrite of *A Midsummer Night's Dream,* with Prospero taking the place of Oberon, and Ariel of Puck.

The Tempest opens with Prospero's plot to restore himself as the rightful Duke of Milan, to punish his brother and arrange a marriage between Miranda and Ferdinand that will solidify the alliance between the two duchies. The sea storm, part of Prospero's plan to bring his evil brother Antonio to the island, also casts ashore the counsellor, Gonzalo; Alonso, Duke of Naples; his son Ferdinand; and the clowns Trinculo and Stephano. The ship is a microcosm of the world, with the castaways the group upon which Prospero practices his "art." Ariel, Prospero's stage manager, must keep a watchful eye on the crew, for when left on their own, Antonio and Sebastian plot to murder Gonzalo and Alonso, and Trinculo and Stephano join forces with Caliban to murder Prospero. An Elizabethan *Lord of the Flies, The Tempest* reveals that beyond civilization's constraining influence, human nature is a "thing of darkness." Still, despite these conspiracies and threats, we remain distanced from the dramatic action, secure in the knowledge that Prospero is in complete control and that no one is truly in danger.

But even playwrights and magicians have anxieties. Prospero worries endlessly that he won't be able to punish his brother, get his dukedom back, and cause Miranda and Ferdinand to fall in love within his allotted time span. Throughout the play we are reminded of the amount of time the men have been on the island. The shipwreck begins between two and three o'clock; at the end, when they all go in to dinner, it's about six o'clock. Not an arbitrary number: a performance at the Globe ran three hours, and Shakespeare's own power lasted for only that length of time. Mimetic and real time schemes coincide; the two plots, Prospero's and Shakespeare's, end at the same time. Just before his time runs out, Prospero suddenly realizes that he's left Stephano, Trinculo, and Caliban stuck in a swamp and must bring them back before the play ends.

It's easy to get caught up in the play's self-conscious artistry and forget its larger, more penetrating vision. *The Tempest* is more than magic and trickery. Prospero's spell works a change in the human heart, and *The Tempest* is ultimately about virtue, forgiveness, and love—human feelings, not godlike detachment. The transformations of art are entertaining, but metamorphosis within the self is more deeply satisfying. The "sea-sorrow" that the characters undergo ultimately leads to a "sea change." As soon as Alonso repents of his treachery, his son is immediately restored; the faithful Gonzalo embraces Prospero; Ariel is set free; Miranda and Ferdinand create a new alliance out of their fathers' enmity. Even the brutish Caliban says, "I'll be wise hereafter,/And seek for grace" (V.1.295–96). The play, which begins with disorder in the heavens, ends with a new order on earth.

Only Antonio remains unrepentant, and Prospero, who has scarcely been able to contain his rage throughout the play, abandons his revenge and forgives his brother, setting his own "nobler reason 'gainst [his] fury": "The rarer action is/In virtue than in vengeance" (V.1.26.27–28). As a civilized man, Prospero realizes that true civility—and civilization—depend on graciousness.

> For you, most wicked sir, whom to call brother
> Would even infect my mouth, I do forgive
> Thy rankest fault—all of them. . . .
>
> (V.1.130–32)

Antonio says nothing to this, his only other comment in the play being a nasty comment about Caliban. Thus we are reminded that although we may be transformed through suffering and love, some parts of human nature remain obdurate.

But to Miranda, who has known only her father, Caliban, and Ariel, humanity seems wondrous:

> How many goodly creatures are there here!
> How beauteous mankind is! O brave new world,
> That has such people in't!
>
> (V.1.183–85)

To which her father gently replies: "'Tis new to thee." Although Miranda is deluded, there is no bitterness in Prospero's remark. He tempers the joy of a first vision of the world with the compassionate understanding that each age must rediscover the world (and its evil) afresh.

In regaining his usurped dukedom in Milan, Prospero returns to Caliban the island he took from *him*. But before Prospero departs, he must claim his monster and free his sprite. Turning to Caliban, he says, "... this thing of darkness/I acknowledge mine" (V.1.275–76). Renouncing his godlike powers, Prospero must acknowledge himself as a man, and therefore he now can look upon Caliban, the uncivilized brute within us all, as a part of himself. His release of Ariel suggests that the imagination must remain unfettered, not chained to human desire.

Shakespeare ends *The Tempest* by asserting that human beings can't live solely in art—Prospero and Miranda belong in the ordinary world of time and mortality, where he will rule and she will marry and have children. Yet even as he endorses mortal life, the dramatist questions the nature of this "real" world. Prospero's plot concludes at six o'clock, with all the characters returning to his house for dinner, just at the time that Shakespeare's spectators would probably return from the Globe to *their* houses and sit down to *their* dinners. Illusion and reality merge as the actor playing Prospero steps forth with a plea to the audience:

> I must be here confined by you,
> Or sent to Naples. Let me not,
> Since I have my dukedom got
> And pardoned the deceiver, dwell
> In this bare island by your spell;
> But release me from my bands
> With the help of your good hands.
>
> (Epilogue, 4–10)

Just as Prospero set his spirit-actor, Ariel, free, we are asked to liberate this actor that he, too, may return home. Like the audience, like Prospero and Miranda, he will return to the real world, but he will only be exchanging one dream for another.

Caliban

Critics have recently taken a revisionist approach to *The Tempest,* seeing Caliban, not Prospero, as the play's real hero. If the play is interpreted as an indictment of colonialism, Prospero is the arrogant European adventurer who seizes another's land, imposing his culture and language on the natives who trust him. In this view, Prospero is not a wise ruler but a white dictator who tyrannizes his daughter, Caliban, and Ariel, and thus does to others what was done to him in Milan. Similar to the Native Americans, Caliban originally shows the new settlers where to collect berries and water—in short, he shows them how to survive in the new land. Only later does he plot the white man's destruction, not because he is innately evil but because he is enslaved on the land that is rightfully his own. Almost the first words Caliban speaks in the play claim his hereditary right to the island and his grievance against the man who has stolen it: "This island's mine, by Sycorax my mother,/Which thou tak'st from me" (I.2.332–33).

Shakespeare is typically ambiguous with regard to Caliban's character. Called a monster by the Europeans (who are too drunk to observe him), he is blessed with the loveliest and most tender lines in the play—lines that express his deep joy in the island that's no longer his:

> Be not afeared: the isle is full of noises,
> Sounds and sweet airs that give delight and hurt not.
> Sometimes a thousand twangling instruments
> Will hum about mine ears; and sometime voices
> That, if I then had waked after long sleep,
> Will make me sleep again; and then, in dreaming,
> The clouds methought would open and show riches
> Ready to drop upon me, that, when I waked,
> I cried to dream again.

(III.2.132–44)

It's also intriguing that this illiterate brute utters verse when alone and prose when with Europeans.

Until recently Caliban had traditionally been played as either a fish, a lizard, an ape, a frog, or a monster with scales and fins—never a man. In 1978 David Suchet changed all that. Having been offered the role in the 1978–79 production of the Royal Shakespeare Company, Suchet, tired of the Caliban-as-monster portrayals, began to examine the text carefully, as well as accounts of discoveries in the New World published during Shakespeare's lifetime. The evidence for regarding Caliban as a beast is the drunken Trinculo's comment, "A fish: he smells like a fish . . . A strange fish . . . his fins like arms!" (II.2.25–34). Suchet writes: "Shakespeare did *not* write 'arms like fins.' And I started to read the speech again and it became so clear to me, that Shakespeare was not describing a fish-like man but a human being whose appearance, let alone his smell, was strange to Trinculo." Noting that native Africans and Americans had been often char-acterized by Europeans as monsters, Suchet con-cluded that in creating Caliban, Shakespeare was meticulously describing the popular misconception of an African or American native, not an actual monster at all. Since the play has always been been presented from Prospero's European perspective, audiences tend to sympathize with the learned magician, particularly when he exiles Caliban after the latter attempts to rape Miranda—an act that has always been an obstacle to identi-fying with Caliban. Suchet, however, sees the attempted rape as Caliban's natural desire to people his island with his own kind. In Act I, scene 2, he recalls his attempt and with surprising wit laughs, "O ho, O ho! Would't had been done!/Thou didst prevent me; I had peopled else/This isle with Calibans." Caliban's tragedy consists not only in the loss of his home but in his need for a master—whether the foolish Trinculo or the wise Prospero doesn't seem to matter. With *The Tempest,* Shakespeare gives us a strikingly accurate glimpse into the future of English imperialism, which was then in its early stages. As Joseph Conrad's *Heart of Darkness* and Rudyard Kipling's *The Man Who Would Be King* point out, greedy Europeans are only too eager to supply natives with gods.

It would be too facile to interpret *The Tempest* simply as a condemnation of colonialism. The play presents the problem from both perspectives—that of the colonists, who like Prospero were themselves exiles in search of a home; and that of the natives, like Caliban, exiled in their own country. Suchet's performance demonstrated that, as in the case of Shylock, Shakespeare reveals the humanity within the alien, showing us, if we let him, how to be humane. In "Mixed Blood: Columbus's Legacy," Richard Rodriguez writes: "European vocabularies do not have a silence rich enough to describe the force within Indian contemplation. Only Shakespeare, of all Europeans, understood that Indians have eyes. . . . Shakespeare saw Caliban eyeing his master's books, well, why not his master as well?"

A Retrospective Look: "Our Revels Now Are Ended"

Shakespeare's career has a pleasing shapeliness that attracts biographical interpretation, and nineteenth-century scholars were especially fond of tracing Shakespeare's life through his plays. Ignoring the histories, they saw his career as beginning with the comedies, optimistic romances filled with the buoyant spirits of youth. Next, the problem plays, hinting at an impending spiritual crisis. Finally, the tragedies, a period beginning with Hamlet's melancholy and gradually deepening into the harsh ugliness of Timon. If Shakespeare's career had ended after *Timon,* critics would have said that he had died while his powers were failing, a bitter old man. But the period of inward calm that follows, reflected in the tranquil joyousness of the romances, belies this view. *The Tempest* is Shakespeare's requiem to the stage. As Prospero breaks his staff, flings his books into the sea, and leaves his enchanted isle for Milan, so Shakespeare abandons his charmed stage and returns to ordinary life in Stratford. But Shakespeare, like so many celebrities today, apparently felt compelled to return for yet another farewell. Two years later he is back in London, collaborating with John Fletcher on *The Two Noble Kinsmen, Henry VIII,* and the lost play *Cardenio,* his last recorded ventures in the theatre. The rest, however, was not silence, but centuries of noisy adulation. With the possible exception of Jesus, Shakespeare has inspired more foolishness and brilliance than any other human being.

James Joyce has his hero Stephen Dedalus supply Shakespeare with a fitting epitaph: "He returns after a life of absence to that spot of earth where he was born, where he has always been, man and boy, a silent witness and there, his journey of life ended, he plants his mulberrytree in the earth. Then dies. The motion is ended."

THE SPIN-OFFS

Shakespeare and Music

*I*s it as good as the book? is usually the question people ask whenever a work of fiction is made into a movie. The same question is often just as pertinent to Shakespeare and music. Shakespearean music isn't a soundtrack to a play; it doesn't literally transcribe dramatic episodes into music. Ideally, it is a wordless evocation of the play—its mood and its poetry. Quite simply, Shakespearean music is any form of music that derives from anything Shakespearean, whether an image or an entire play. Shakespeare has been the inspiration for every possible musical genre, both in Western and non-Western countries: operas, tone poems, songs, incidental music, show tunes, symphonies, and film scores. (*The Boys from Syracuse* is a musical takeoff on *The Comedy of Errors* that many believe is superior to its source, and *Kiss Me Kate,* with its famous song "Brush Up Your Shakespeare," is based on *The Taming of the Shrew.*) A *Shakespeare Music Catalogue,* a five-volume work compiled by Bryan N. S. Gooch and David Thatcher, lists more than 21,000 musical compositions inspired by Shakespeare's plays and poetry, with *Hamlet* music alone accounting for 1,405 of the entries.

Shakespearean Musical Highlights

❖ Since it's based on a character rather than a play, Verdi's opera *Falstaff* (1893) is a slightly different case from his *Otello* (1887).

Loosely derived from *The Merry Wives of Windsor*, *Falstaff* is one of those rare cases in which the adaptation is equal to the original.

❖ Prokofiev's ballet *Romeo and Juliet* must be one of the greatest pieces of musical theatre ever written. Its rapidly shifting moods range from the playful to the erotic to the brutal. "The Mask at the Capulets" expresses all the strangeness of new love, along with an increasing sense of ominousness. Prokofiev has distilled the play's emotion and crystallized it into music. Since its first performance in 1940, the music—most often heard in three popular suites—has taken on a life of its own, independent of the ballet and the play.

❖ Benjamin Britten is a wonderful composer, but he lacks the genius that would make him equal to his text. His opera *A Midsummer Night's Dream* (1960) is close to its source, and Britten uses music to elucidate the play rather than to create, as Verdi does at his best, an entirely original work.

❖ Mendelssohn's *A Midsummer Night's Dream* (1843), incidental music that accompanies the play, is probably the best-known Shakespearean music ever written—everyone knows the Wedding March. The overture, with its excited buzz of woodwinds and strings, suggests the humming anticipation of the fairy kingdom, immediately luring the listener into a magical realm. Listening to it, you're transported into a childhood you never had, except in memories and dreams.

❖ Tchaikovsky's *Romeo and Juliet* (1869, revised 1870, 1880), a tone poem (or, in the composer's words, an "overture-fantasia"), is probably the most famous love music ever written by a classical composer.

❖ Edward Elgar's symphonic study *Falstaff* (1913) is psychological analysis translated into music. The fat knight's essence—his self-importance, his swagger, his sadness, and his gluttonous appetite for life—are poured into rich Edwardian music that grumbles, dances, and roars with laughter. Recurring motifs and themes match Falstaffian episodes, such as the Boars Head scenes and the Gad's Hill robbery.

❖ Ralph Vaughan Williams, like Shakespeare, possessed a profound love of all things English. This sensibility emerges in his settings of Shakespeare's songs, and particularly in the secular cantata *Serenade to Music* (1938), the homage to music from the last act of *The Merchant of Venice.*

❖ David Diamond's incidental music to *Romeo and Juliet* (1947). Diamond is a contemporary composer who could be considered as a latter-day Tchaikovsky. Though not as grand or as schmaltzy, he writes in the same romantic vein. Diamond has also composed a song cycle from the Sonnets called *We Two.*

❖ Don't forget Shostakovich's film scores to Grigori Kozintsev's *King Lear* and *Hamlet,* as well as Patrick Doyle's score to the 1989 *Henry V,* both available on cassette and compact disc.

❖ There's a terrific film version of Zeffirelli's lavish production of Verdi's *Otello,* filmed on location and at the Scala opera house. Conducted by Loren Maazel, it stars Plácido Domingo as Otello, Katia Ricciarelli as Desdemona, and Justino Díaz as Iago. It is available on video.

Shakespeare and Opera

Shakespeare was thirty-three in 1597, when the first opera was performed in Italy, and it's not likely he could have heard one. Still, many of the plays are ideal for opera: they are epic in scope and demand extraordinary physical capabilities on the part of the actor; and the plots, with their roller-coaster extremes, make tremendous appeals to the emotions of the spectator. On a practical level, they are filled with soliloquies and dialogues that can be transformed into arias and duets. In short, Shakespearean drama is both operatic in style and a gold mine for composers looking for operatic subjects. Twenty-three out of Shakespeare's thirty-seven plays have been made into operas, and all but six of these more than once. According to one count, there are thirty operatic versions of *The Tempest* alone, and Mozart made notes for one just before he died. One of the best Shakespearean operas—some say *the* best—is Verdi's *Otello* (1887). Through a form of artistic cross-pollination, one genius has fused with another through the centuries and created a new masterpiece. The play's extravagant gestures, intense theatricality, and electrifying emotions make it seem more operatic than dramatic. As George Bernard Shaw pointed out, "*Othello* is a play written by Shakespeare in the style of Italian opera."

Verdi expressed musically what Shakespeare expressed through language. Otello's frenzy is translated musically through growling trumpets, screaming flutes, and pounding timpani, just as Othello's is expressed linguistically through broken sentences and chaotic syntax. One of the set pieces of the opera is Iago's "Credo" (at one point, Verdi considered calling the opera *Iago*), in which the demon asserts his belief in "a cruel god" and the fundamental evil of human nature.

Othello's operatic end is as breathtaking as it is in the play. Just before Othello kisses Desdemona for the last time, Verdi returns to the love duet of Act I, a reminder of the idyllic past that has degenerated into chaos. Othello dies with the knowledge that he has destroyed what he loved best on earth. Such a piece could only have been written by a composer with a strong affinity to Shakespeare. When the seventy-three-year-old Verdi set the last notes of Boito's extraordinary libretto, he sent his collaborator a short note expressing his sentiments: "All hail to us . . . (and to Him!)."

Music: "Moody Food"

With their penchant for startling yet simple imagery, Shakespeare's lyrics anticipate those of the young Paul McCartney: in Shakespeare's songs, the eyes of a drowned man are transformed into pearls; golden youth return to dust, a sprite blissfully lies in a cowslip; yellow sands beckon the dancer as "wild waves whist." Often written for prepubescent boys, Elizabethan airs have a sweet, unearthly quality, evoking a mood of ineffable sadness. The moodiness of *Twelfth Night,* the mystery of *The Tempest,* and the wondrous magic of *Cymbeline* are in part created by their songs. Unlike the songs of a musical, which spring with predictable regularity out of a specific dramatic situation, Shakespeare's airs, ballads, flourishes, and snatches are interludes—fleeting distillations of a play's atmosphere.

Shakespeare's Greatest Hits

"When daisies pied and violets blue" (Love's Labour's Lost, V.2.883)

"Tell me where is fancy bred?" (The Merchant of Venice, III.2.63)

"Under the greenwood tree" (As You Like It, II.5.1)

"Blow, blow, thou winter wind" (As You Like It, II.7.175)

"It was a lover and his lass" (As You Like It, V.3.15)

"O mistress mine! Where are you roaming?" (Twelfth Night, II.3.37)

"Come away, come away, death" (Twelfth Night, II.4.50)

"For the rain it raineth every day" (Twelfth Night, V.1.386)

"The Willow Song" (Othello, IV.3.38)

"Fear no more the heat o' th' sun" (Cymbeline, IV.2.258)

"Hark, hark the lark" (Cymbeline, II.3.20)

"When daffodils begin to peer" (The Winter's Tale, IV.3.1)

"Come unto these yellow sands" (The Tempest, I.2.375)

"Full fathom five thy father lies" (The Tempest, I.2.397)

"Where the bee sucks, there suck I" (The Tempest, V.1.88)

Set to music by Elizabethan as well as by modern composers, Shakespeare's songs are widely available on compact disc and tapes. Some recordings use period instruments, such as lute and sackbutt, in an attempt to reproduce the sound Shakespeare's audience might have heard. Some modern composers have also set Shakespeare's lyrics to music. For instance, Aaron Copland's arrangement for "Tell me where is fancy bred?" with its insistent "Reply, reply," is unforgettable.

Great Moments
in Bardolatry

Mulberry Trees and
Other Assorted Relics

*I*n 1756, the Reverend Francis Gastrell moved to New Place, the enormous house Shakespeare bought for his retirement. The irritable cleric was disgusted to find his property besieged by tourists who, at all hours, could be found roaming the lawn, scraping off pieces of bark from a mulberry tree, and carving their initials into it. According to legend, this was the hallowed tree that Shakespeare himself planted and sat under on hot summer days. But Gastrell was not a romantic, and, besides, he thought the tree caused dampness in the house. In a fury, he had the tree chopped down—a sacrilege that made him the Judas of Shakespeareana. According to one eyewitness, "Excited by the discovery of his profanation, [there was a] general fury against the perpetrator, and the enraged populace surrounded the premises and vowed vengeance." The locals rallied together and broke all of Gastrell's windows.

Gastrell's neighbor, the enterprising and aptly named Thomas Sharp, bought a good portion of the tree's wood, and like the goose that laid the golden egg, it miraculously brought forth a steady supply of riches. For forty years the prolific timber provided literary pilgrims and tourists with a seemingly inexhaustible supply of mementos in the form of toothpick holders, tobacco stoppers, goblets, tea chests, chairs, salt shakers, boxes, and canes. At one auction, a toothpick case and a goblet made from the tree sold for six pounds more than a Holbein and a Van Dyke.

Even in the twentieth century, the tree continued to fascinate Shakespeare lovers. In 1922, Ernest Law published *Shakespeare's Garden,* which contained a chapter entitled "The Position of the Mulberry Tree."

In the early days of Shakespeare worship, anything to do with the playwright, no matter how trivial or spurious, became a valuable commodity. John Jordon, a wheelwright and self-proclaimed tourist guide, was not to be outdone. In 1762, he began manufacturing articles from a crabapple tree, claiming that it was under this very tree that the Bard, along with his crony Ben Jonson, lapsed into a stupor after an extended drinking binge.

The First Jubilee

*I*n 1769, with the Shakespeare Jubilee, Shakespeare became a full-fledged culture hero. Hailed as the bicentenary of the poet's birth, it actually took place five years too late, and not in April, his birth month, but in September. Directed by the actor David Garrick, the self-proclaimed "Jubilee's Steward," the fete was a fiasco from beginning to end. Stratfordians were bemused by the event, many of them never having read the plays. One local called it the "resurrection of Shakespeare," and, as Sam Schoenbaum points out, "Uncomprehending townsmen confused the forthcoming Jubilee with the Jew bill that had aroused political passions fifteen years earlier."

Preparations were chaotic: the special lamps arrived shattered; annoyed at the furor, the locals refused to lend the carpenters their tools. The amphitheatre, where the numerous guests were to dine on a 327-pound turtle, dance at a Shakespeare costume ball, and watch performances of the plays, was barely completed on time.

But at last, on September 6, at 5:00 a.m., the Jubilee began with the firing of cannons, followed by bells, choristers, and musicians. ("This is a day, a holiday! a holiday! Drive spleen and rancor far away!") For the next three days the air was flooded with song, including the alliterative "The Will of all Wills Was a Warwickshire Will" and the chummy "Avonian Willy, Bard Divine," both sung with tiresome regularity by singers bearing wooden cups made from the Mulberry Tree, which inspired its own composition:

> Behold this fair goblet was carved from the tree
> Which O my sweet Shakespeare was planted by thee.
> As a relic I kiss it, and bow at the shrine,
> What comes from thy hand must be even divine.
> All shall yield to the Mulberry Tree
> Bend to thee,
> Blest Mulberry.
> Matchless was he
> Who planted thee
> And thou, like him, immortal be. . . .

There were eight more stanzas of this, the last concluding with the by-now familiar "All shall yield to the Mulberry Tree. . . ." (Shakespeare's birthday has inspired an endless stream of bad lyrics; one, a poem written for the tercentenary in 1864, began with the phrase "Come let us Tercentenerate.")

The day ended with a glorious ball at the Rotunda. The author of *The Great Shakespeare Jubilee,* Christian Deelman, writes, "At this point the many existing accounts of the Jubilee diverge. Nearly all the later ones determined to make the first day seem as splendid as possible, describe in amazing detail a wonderful firework display that never took place."

The next day, September 7, the weather turned against the Bard, and three days of torrential rain ensued. The Avon rose until the streets of Stratford were streaming with water, and the deluge was so terrific that participants declared it the wrath of God directed against the idolatrous proceedings. The special parade and the ceremonial "Crowning of the Bard" were promptly canceled. Garrick was frightened he would be forced to cancel his recitation of the ode he had composed for the occasion, and which he hoped would be the triumph of the Jubilee. In a last-minute effort to save the ode, he decided to recite it in the Rotunda. Thus it was that two thousand guests crammed into a building built to hold half that many. As they sat among the puddles and the rising floods listening to a Mrs. Baddeley sing "Thou Soft Flowing Avon,"

Garrick, the consummate actor, dramatically flung open the doors of the Rotunda to reveal the "soft flowing" river, now dangerously swollen. With a theatrical flourish he slipped on a pair of gloves presumably worn by Shakespeare himself, and as the crowd enthusiastically applauded, several benches collapsed, dumping hundreds of people unceremoniously on the ground.

On the third day, with the flimsy Rotunda still knee-deep in water, the communal dinner that was to cap the festivities was canceled. Many guests left early, sick of the rain, the noise, the crowds, and the Bard. The Jubilee itself may have been a flop, but it marked the unofficial beginning of the Shakespeare industry. Long after the actual event was forgotten, Jubilee gift books and souvenirs remained popular items.

Shakespearean Hobbyhorses

*N*o matter what their other hobbyhorses or professions may be, bardolaters will find some way of combining it with their love of Shakespeare. The Shakespeare bibliography is filled with startling titles, such as the novelist Robertson Davies's favorite, *Shakespeare's Knowledge of Chest Diseases*. There are also books on Shakespeare as lawyer, medical man, angler, botanist, sportsman, astrologer, ornithologist, and naturalist.

Gardeners plant "Shakespeare gardens," restricted to those flowers and vegetables mentioned by Shakespeare. Inexplicably, it seems that the most zealous Shakespeareans are lawyers and bird watchers. Excluding professional critics, more lawyers write about Shakespeare, particularly about the authorship question, than members of any other profession, and there are even Shakespearean societies composed solely of attorneys.

In 1890, bird lovers tried to combine their two passions—with disastrous results. Taking their cue from the starling in *Henry IV* that Hot-

*A*pril 1936:

PLEASE SEND EARTH SHAKESPEARE'S
GARDEN WATER RIVER AVON FOR
DEDICATION SHAKESPEARE THEATRE
DALLAS TEXAS JULY 1.

*D*ecoded, this cable was a request for water from the Avon River and soil from Shakespeare's Garden at the Birthplace, both necessary for the formal dedication of a replica of the Globe Playhouse in Dallas. As soon as they received the wire, the directors of the Stratford-upon-Avon Festival Society went into action. Soon afterward, a party of local dignitaries and actors met with the American vice consul at the garden, where dirt was placed reverently into a box fashioned from charred wood salvaged from the remains of the Shakespeare Memorial Theatre, which had burned down in 1926. At the river, Mr. Fordham Flower, one of the descendants of the theatre's original benefactors, and the vice consul took a raft out to the middle of the river and filled a cup bearing Shakespeare's coat of arms with water. Dirt and water were borne to the Cunard Lines, which carried the relics, free, to New York. From there they traveled to Dallas, where the new theatre was consecrated with all solemnity.

spur wanted to teach to "speak nothing but 'Mortimer,' " a group of well-meaning British bird lovers decided to import to America all the birds mentioned by Shakespeare. They brought twenty English starlings to New York and let them loose in Central Park; the birds took to the New World with alacrity, reproducing at an astonishing rate. The English starling has since become a veritable pest, preying on flowers and fruits—including those in Shakespeare gardens.

Stratford-upon-Avon and the Shakespeare Industry

*Stratford is Mecca and the Wailing
Wall rolled into one.*

—*AN AMERICAN TOURIST*

*T*here are two sides to Stratford. On the one hand, it's Shakespeareland, where the Bard is a profitable logo. But it's also a lovely village, a moving testimony to the endurance of Shakespeare, where visitors can genuinely feel his presence. The scholarly Shakespeare Centre houses one of the finest collections of Shakespeareana in the world, as well as the Shakespeare Memorial Theatre, the home of the Royal Shakespeare Company. Nearby are the ubiquitous souvenir stands selling Bard playing cards, tea towels, spoons, T-shirts, and mugs.

Just as the pious rail against what they see as the materialism of the Church, so critics decry the Shakespeare industry, the flagrant traffic in souvenirs and knickknacks and the selling of the Bard as if he were a Disney character. Shakespeare himself probably would not have objected. He wrote for the masses—precisely the people who visit Stratford on holiday; and he was never averse to exploiting popular taste.

Detractors claim that Shakespeare probably wasn't even born in the house that's so lovingly preserved and displayed to visitors as "the

*T*ourists at Stratford-upon-Avon.

🦢

Birthplace." But Stratford is not a land of make-believe; it's a place where probabilities are presented as facts. Using authentic Tudor furniture and household goods, the Birthplace trustees scrupulously maintain historic verisimilitude, and although the furnishings of the Shakespeare bedroom may not be those the infant Bard first smiled upon, they very well may have been.

A Brief History of Stratford

*I*n the eighteenth century, the rise of Shakespeare's reputation and the unprecedented growth of tourism as an industry combined to make Stratford a major attraction. In a religious age, people satisfied their wanderlust by embarking on pilgrimages and purchasing saintly relics; in a more secular one, they take vacations and buy souvenirs. For votaries of Shakespeare, the five houses that make up the Birthplace estate are like the stations of the cross, the Shakespearean knickknacks near-sacred relics, and the complete works, on sale everywhere, the Holy Writ.

With the advent of the railway in the nineteenth century, the Victorians traveled with their characteristic gusto. Earnest and middle-class, their tours usually included places that offered opportunities for self-improvement. Stratford, birthplace of the hallowed Bard, became a favorite holiday spot, and it was during the age of Victoria that the sentimentalization of Stratford-upon-Avon and its own "Sweet Swan" finally became embalmed into myth.

For those Americans for whom Shakespeare is synonymous with England and high culture, a trip to England is not complete without a stopover in Stratford. Picture-postcard perfect, the charming town with its thatched-roof cottages and silvery Avon preserves everything Anglophilic Americans love about England.

QUERY TO A RESIDENT OF STRATFORD-UPON-AVON

——⇒◆⇐——

NE: *Do you think all these visitors have actually read Shakespeare?*

A:. No, I don't.

NE: *Then why are they here?*

A.: They think he's England.

The Rise of Stratford: a Time Line

1793–1820: The Shakespeare Birthplace is part butcher shop, part tavern, called the Swan and Maidenhead. (A local wit once remarked that the pub sign was the only maidenhead left in Stratford.) The tavern attracts worshipful visitors eager to sleep in Shakespeare's room (a fact that led the bardolatry expert Ivor Brown to note that only here could one get "Bed, Board and Bard under one roof").

A widow by the name of Mrs. Hornby operates the butcher shop, where, along with a cut of beef, one can purchase a chip of the celebrated Shakespeare Chair. Amazingly, no matter how many pieces are sold, the chair, like the Mulberry Tree, never seems to diminish in size. When the widow who owns the building, one Mrs. Court, decides that she, too, would like to cash in on the Bard business, she promptly evicts Mrs. Hornby and sets up trade for herself, upon which the Widow Hornby packs up her relics and opens a shop across the street, triggering what many dub the "Widows' War of Stratford." According to one contemporary account, the widows "parted on envious terms; they were constantly to be seen at each others' doors abusing each other and their respective visitors, and frequently with so much acerbity as to disgust and even deter the latter from entering either dwelling."

A final note: according to Ivor Brown and George Fearon, before the Widow Court moved to the Swan and Maidenhead, the following notice was seen in the window:

WILLIAM SHAKESPEARE

WAS BORN

IN THIS HOUSE.

N.B. A horse and taxed cart to be let.

1843: Shakespeare's Birthplace is offered for sale. A rumor spreads that the American showman P. T. Barnum is interested in buying up the whole lot and transporting it to America. The British, fearful of crass American ingenuity, purchase the site by public subscription, and for the first time trustees scrupulously manage the estate, buy period furnishings, and restore the house. The Birthplace becomes a museum, and mulberry trees, crabapple boughs, courting chairs, and assorted relics are banned.

1847–1930: The Shakespeare Birthplace Trust acquires the five properties that make up the estate: the Birthplace, Mary Arden's house, New Place (rebuilt), Anne Hathaway's Cottage, and Nash's House (a museum and the former house of Thomas Nash, Shakespeare's granddaughter's first husband). Visitors pay one admission fee to view them all.

1879: The Shakespeare Memorial Theatre is built.

1925: George Bernard Shaw calls the theatre "a Victorian atrocity" and an unsightly edifice, and demands that it be pulled down immediately and a new one erected in its place.

1927: The Shakespeare Memorial Theatre burns down. George Bernard Shaw sends a congratulatory telegram to the governors. The relics trade enjoys a brief revival: cigarette boxes made from charred remains of the theatre are offered for sale.

1986: Stratford is reduced to exhibiting itself as a phenomenon in its own right. Tourists are variously disappointed and amused to find a display entitled "Famous Americans Who Have Visited Stratford."

The Cynic's View of Stratford

*I*n a riverside park at Stratford stands a statuary group: in the centre a large pedestal surmounted by the figure of Shakespeare, sitting like patience on a monument, smiling at the bus station. He is surrounded by creatures of his imagination: Lady Macbeth, Falstaff, Prince Hal, and of course Hamlet, staring philosophically at the obligatory skull.

—GRAHAM HOLDERNESS

*W*e have ourselves noticed in Stratford's parish church, after the announcement by some unscrupulous guide that Shakespeare was here as a choir-boy, and had sat in a certain stall, the thrill of excitement which animated the bosoms, even the entire frames, of a conducted party of young American womanhood. . . . these blessed women were on the actual spot, and here had the opportunity to "contact"—as they themselves would have said—Shakespeare's reputed seat. "Contact" it they most eagerly did, each placing her rump for one glorious moment on the sacred oak and evidently deriving—such was the air of rapture on each face—a sense of inspiration, of instant and loving community with genius, *a posteriori.*

—IVOR BROWN and GEORGE FEARON

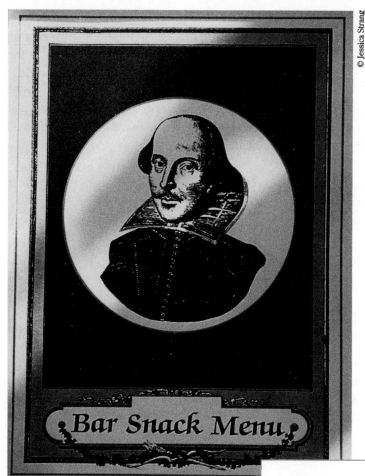

© Jessica Strang

Bar Snack Menu

A Shakespearean menu.

*T*he Shakespeare presence is most immediately noticeable in Stratford by the number of quotations which append all forms of commercial life. Shakespeare the Copywriter. . . . Every hotel worth its accountant will greet you at each turn with such selections: "A good traveller is something at the latter end of a dinner"; every dining room with "Sir, to your pleasure humbly I subscribe." You tuck into your Falstaff Game Pie, Hamlet Omelette, and Agincourt French Fries followed by Macduff plum duff, Othello piña colada and King Lear café au lait.

—*TIME OUT* MAGAZINE

*T*he Birthplace is where the visitor picks up the first threads of Shakespeare's biography. But he hears few facts. There's no record, for instance, that Shakespeare was born in this house. Instead the visitor hears what may have happened . . . and is given a choice of possibilities. . . . The tour is so skillful, a visitor may not notice that nothing here can actually be traced to Shakespeare himself.

—PBS, *Frontline,* "The Shakespeare Mystery," April 18, 1989

I feel that our fetish [with Shakespeare] is safe for three centuries yet. The bust too—there in the Stratford Church. The precious bust, the calm bust, the serene bust, the emotionless bust, with the dandy mustache and the putty face, unseamed of care—the face which looked passionlessly down upon the awed pilgrims for a hundred and fifty years and will still look down upon the awed pilgrims three hundred more, with the deep, deep, deep, subtle, subtle, subtle, expression of a bladder.

—MARK TWAIN

The Romantic's View of Stratford

*T*his, the 9th May, was our last day and fine. So we saw Warwickshire . . . at its best: thick green leaves, stubby yellow stone houses and a fine sprinkling of Elizabethan cottages. All this led very harmoniously to Stratford-on-Avon; and all crabbers be damned—it is a fine, unselfconscious town, mixed, with 18th Century and the rest all standing cheek by jowl. All the flowers were out in Shakespeare's garden. "That was where his study windows looked out when he wrote *The Tempest,*" said the man. And perhaps it was true. Anyhow it was a great big house, looking straight at the large windows and the grey stone of the school chapel, and when the clock struck, that was the sound Shakespeare heard. I cannot without more labour than my roadrunning mind can compass describe the queer impression of sunny impersonality. Yes, everything seemed to say, this was Shakespeare's, had he sat and walked; but you won't find him, not exactly in the flesh. He is serenely absent—present; both at once; radiating round one; yes; in the flowers, in the old hall, in the garden; but never to be pinned down.

—VIRGINIA WOOLF, *A Writer's Diary*

Whenever I come up here [Stratford-upon-Avon] for a season I like to go into Trinity Church usually when there's no one else about and stand in front of his tomb. Just stay there for a while. You know, in astonishment.

—SEBASTIAN SHAW

The Ireland Affair

*B*orn in 1721, William Ireland spent his childhood playing among the great Shakespearean relics of the day. His father, Samuel, an avid collector, counted among his possessions the celebrated Courting Chair and an assortment of knickknacks made from the wood of the famed Mulberry Tree. To Samuel Ireland, the Bard was only slightly lower than the angels, and he would often announce that he would give half his library for Shakespeare's signature. Little did he suspect how his dream would be realized.

Young William was something of a disappointment to his father, a fact that Samuel did not refrain from pointing out. One day, after a pilgrimage to Alexander Pope's villa, Ireland Senior turned to his son and said, "I fear you will never shine such a star in the hemisphere of literary fame." William, however, was determined to prove his father wrong.

When the unpromising youth grew into mediocre manhood, he took a position as a clerk in a conveyancer's office. Given access to ancient deeds and titles, he spent his days poring through official records in search of the literary grail: Shakespeare's autograph. When his search failed, William began creating his own Shakespearean documents, an activity which he took to with unprecedented skill and energy. He started off humbly with a simple signature on a legal deed. To explain the lucky find to his father, William invented a tale of a young aristocrat who, impressed with the clerk's enterprise, invited him to visit his estate to examine his collection of antiquities and documents. William demurred, but finally, after much cajoling, appeared at the ancestral doorstep. It was here, in a massive old chest, that he made his first discovery. The mysterious aristocrat's name? Ah, William was honor-bound to secrecy. Father and son were ecstatic: Ireland Senior craved Shakespearean documents; Ireland Junior, approval. William became unstoppable.

Soon his father began making specific requests. A poem? No problem. William just happened to find "Willy's" courting poem to Anne Hathaway:

> *Is there inne heavenne aught more rare*
> *Thann thou sweete Nymphe of Avon fayre?*
> *Is there onne Earthe a Mann more trewe*
> *Thanne Willy Shakspeare is toe you?*

The trunk's contents proved inexhaustible: poems, prayers, private letters, and, best of all, a lost tragedy were suddenly brought to light.

Shakespeare's "lost masterpiece," *Vortigern,* no doubt inspired by a portrait of Vortigern, a fifth-century king of the Britons, hanging in Samuel Ireland's study, led to complex negotiations among various London theatres, which angled furiously to produce it. Plans were stalled, however, when Richard Sheridan, the dramatist and proprietor of the Drury Lane, actually read *Vortigern* and was forced delicately to concede that "Shakespeare must have been very young when he wrote the play."

Opening night April 2, 1796, was a disaster. (John Kemble, the manager at the Drury Lane, slyly scheduled opening night for April Fool's Day, but the plot was thwarted.) One actor became entangled in the curtain, and a group of skeptics in the back row made a pact to jeer when the leading man said a particular word, so flustering him that he kept repeating the word over and over again, much to the delight of the audience, which broke into uncontrollable laughter every ten minutes. The performance—and *Vortigern*'s run—ended in pandemonium.

Meanwhile, Londoners and antiquarians still flocked to the Ireland home for a glimpse of the sacred relics. Upon seeing them, the ever-credulous James Boswell fell to his knees and feverishly cried, "I now kiss the invaluable relics of our bard, and thanks to God I have lived to see them!" (He died three months later.)

The imaginary aristocrat, now dubbed "Mr. H.," began writing long letters to Samuel in praise of William, comparing him to the matchless Bard himself ("Your *son* is brother in Genius to Shakespeare . . ."), and displaying a penmanship very much like that of the object of his accolades. But William surpassed his father's wildest fantasy when he discovered a late version of Shakespeare's will, which testified that because an Ireland ancestor had once saved Shakespeare's life, the family could now consider themselves the dramatist's sole heirs—meaning that William's forgeries could now safely remain in the family.

Even William was astonished by his father's credulity. His poetry was terrible, his spelling imaginative, and his dates wildly inaccurate. He dated a letter concerning the Globe theatre in 1589, ten years before it was built. Yet no one, not even the leading Shakespearean experts of the day, detected the numerous errors. It took the levelheaded—and outraged—Shakespearean scholar and editor Edmund Malone to expose the hoax. As Malone prepared his exposé, and word got around that the relics were fakes, London wits amused themselves by parodying the forger's work. For example, Shakespeare to his grocer:

Thee cheesesse you sentte meee werree tooee sweattie, and tooe rankee inn faluvorre, butte thee redde herringges werre addmirabblee. 1687 [seventy-one years after Shakespeare's death].

A little over two years after the first forgery, in March 1796, Malone published his indictment and William confessed to everything. Surprisingly, his father staunchly maintained William's innocence. He simply didn't believe his son was clever enough to have pulled it off.

"Shall I Die?" (By All Means!)

*I*n November 1985, Gary Taylor discovered the literary grail: a poem written by Shakespeare—the first such find since the seventeenth century. Unfortunately, the poem is terrible. The first stanza reads:

> *Shall I die? Shall I fly?*
> *Lover's baits and deceits,*
> *Shall I fend: Shall I send?*
> *Shall I shew, and not rue my proceeding?*
> *In all duty her beauty*
> *Binds me her servant for ever.*
> *If she scorn, I mourn,*
> *I retire to despair, joying never.*

Nine more stanzas continue in this vein. As Taylor said at the time, "It's not *Hamlet.*"

The unnamed poem, now called "Shall I Die?," was found in a manuscript folio at the Bodleian Library at Oxford University, where it had been lying in relative neglect since 1756. Although the poem was attributed to Shakespeare, it had been examined only twice in 239 years, in 1895 and again in 1965. Then, in 1985, Taylor noticed it and brought it to the world's attention. By the next day it was on the front page of *The New York Times*.

Although some scholars praised the poem's "internal rhyme" and its "ironies and multiple meanings," the consensus was that "Shall I Die?" was a dud. The headlines it inspired were almost as bad as the poem itself: "Too Bard to Be True," said the *Economist*, "Labored Love Found," read the editorial in *The New York Times*. Would-be poets could take comfort in the knowledge that even Shakespeare nodded.

In April 1990, computer researchers at the Claremont Colleges, California, subjected "Shall I Die?" to extensive stylistic analysis. The results cast doubt on the poem's authenticity. Nevertheless, "Shall I Die?" is included in the *Oxford Shakespeare*—of which Taylor is co-editor.

Five years later, Taylor had this to say about his experience:

I still get criticism for that poem. The furor in the media is just another example of the sort of idolatry that surrounds Shakespeare. People were enraged that someone could say that Shakespeare wrote a bad poem. But the evidence is just as good as it is for the Sonnets. If you dig around in the complete works of any major author you're going to find little tidbits that don't announce themselves as masterpieces. It's not a fantastically great poem, but that's irrelevant as to whether or not it should be included in collections of Shakespeare's works.

If a scholar is going to find a lost poem, he must find one that's an obvious masterpiece, so that even if the evidence for attributing it to Shakespeare isn't very good, people will want Shakespeare to have written it because it conforms to their conception of "The Bard." My advice: if you're going to find a Shakespeare poem, find a good one.

Literary sleuths needn't despair. There still might be plenty of Shakespeare manuscripts buried in records offices and library vaults. In an interview with *The Washington Post* in November 1985, the Shakespearean expert Sam Schoenbaum said, "A past that has been buried for several hundred years will still yield its secrets for those who will burrow in it and look for them, and God knows what will be found in the future."

Attention, Shakespeare Shoppers!

❖ In the 1970s an enterprising pharmaceutical manufacturer hit upon a way of combining Shakespeare with the marketing of new drugs. Along with samples of tranquilizers, the firm included a brochure that analyzed the personality disorders of such confused types as Ophelia, Lady Macbeth, and Hamlet. (The brochure also included recorded discussions of Falstaff's "alcohol problem" and Ophelia's "personality disorder.") It described Ophelia's condition thus: "With her first serious suitor, Hamlet, she was overwhelmed by problems that caused her to speak and walk about like one gone mad." A modern Ophelia could have been helped by psychotherapy and drugs. Obviously the drug company wanted to keep Shakespeareans informed of their research, for they sent the critic Frank Kermode their supplement. Writing in the *Daily Telegraph,* Kermode wryly noted that Ophelia probably went mad because her "suitor was violently rude to her and stabbed her father to death."

❖ Shakespeare's characters, notes Kermode, usually dwell on forbidden topics: Hamlet obsesses about incest, Ophelia broods on "country matters," Lady Macbeth is morbidly concerned with guilt, while her husband suffers from bad dreams. If the drug company had its way, all these characters would be on tranquilizers, and, as Kermode points out, Shakespeare needn't have bothered to write the plays.

✤ Shakespearean golfers can enjoy a round at the Club Shakespeare Atlanta, a 640-acre golf course where the holes are named for Shakespearean plays. "There's drama, melodrama, pathos, and all that good stuff," said Jack Berry, the club's manager.

✤ On Valentine's Day you can send your beloved a "Bard-a-Gram": an actor who bears a striking resemblance to the Droeshout Engraving appears at your doorstep, in full Elizabethan regalia, and, in the words of an advertisement, "performs" love poetry.

✤ The same actor also serves as the model for the image featured on British check-guarantee cards, dubbed "Bard Cards." Shakespeare's head was chosen as a logo because it was felt that his serious, unsmiling face symbolized financial prudence and stability. Of course, few are aware that in 1599 Shakespeare was found delinquent by the local tax board.

✤ A Mrs. C. Waldron from Australia wrote to the London *Observer* upon receiving an advertising leaflet entitled "Shakespeare and Management," which modestly proclaimed itself the "most innovative management book of the year." Once again, Lady Macbeth's words are wrenched out of context—unless, of course, the consulting firm is exhorting its salesmen to become assassins. This time, "Screw your courage to the sticking place, and we'll not fail" is adopted as a "motivational slogan." The authors of the leaflet translate it to mean: "Never be deterred by the possibility of failure! Nothing goes well all the time." They apparently forgot that nothing went well at *any* time after Macbeth followed his wife's own advice.

✤ Those who wish to purchase a document with Shakespeare's signature may do so if they have at least five million dollars, the figure estimated by handwriting expert Charles Hamilton. There are six authenticated Shakespearean autographs, but there are more than fifty Shakespearean documents with the Bard's name on them. Hamilton believes that some of these signatures may be authentic. The last document sold with Shakespeare's signature went in 1844, for the current equivalent of about $180.

✤ Three of the signatures appear on Shakespeare's will; the others are on assorted legal documents. The sixth was found in our own century—in 1909—by the enterprising Missouri-born Charles Wallace, in the public record office in London. Along with his wife, Hulda, Wallace is credited with finding over twenty-six Shakespearean documents, more than anyone else since the death of the poet. Wallace was not so much devoted scholar as dogged sleuth, and his uncanny knack for unearthing documents was the envy of distinguished British scholars. The Wallaces' genius for discovery was not confined to matters Shakespearean: in 1922 they struck oil in Texas and retired from Shakespeare-sleuthing, as millionaires.

A Select Filmography

Shakespeare and the Silents

*F*rom 1899 to 1927, more than four hundred Shakespearean silent films were made, including seventeen *Hamlet*s, ten *Julius Caesar*s, eight *Macbeth*s, ten *Merchant of Venice*s, sixteen *Othello*s, and twenty *Romeo and Juliet*s. Shakespeare's plays were a logical choice in the days of silent film, because a director could assume that his audience was familiar with the basic plots and thus dispense with extraneous details and titles. A good Shakespeare silent film could cram hours of plot into minutes of eloquent images. All the actor playing Hamlet had to do was hold up a skull, and the audience could immediately fill in the rest.

For a more detailed listing, as well as information about availability, see Kenneth S. Rothwell and Annabelle Henkin Melzer's exhaustive *Shakespeare on Screen.*

1899, *King John*
Great Britain; directed by Sir Herbert Beerbohm Tree; Tree as King John; Julia Nielson as Constance; Lewis Waller as Faulconbridge; 4 mins.

The first Shakespearean movie ever made—an odd choice, considering that *King John* is rarely performed even as a *play.* Shot on the London Embankment, this film depicts Sir Herbert Beerbohm Tree as King John signing the Magna Carta at Runnymede, a scene not included in Shakespeare's play. In *Shakespeare on Screen,* the authors note that

Tree was "the first director to attempt to impose his own signature as *auteur* on a Shakespeare film."

1900, *Hamlet*
France; Sarah Bernhardt as Hamlet; 5 mins.

Bernhardt was a vigorous fifty-five when she filmed the final duel scene between Hamlet and Laertes. Rothwell notes that when it was first shown, at the 1900 Paris Exhibition, sounds of dueling were created by having assistants clack kitchen knives behind the screen. It is doubtful that the film still exists.

1913, *Hamlet*
Great Britain; Sir Johnston Forbes-Robertson as Hamlet; 22 mins.

"Hamlet scurrying across a Dorset beach" is how the critic John Trewin described the film. It's the only footage that reveals the grand manner of this nineteenth-century Shakespearean actor and is the subject of a well-known essay by Shaw. Those who have seen it comment that although Forbes-Robertson was sixty when he made the film, he still makes you believe he is the young Danish prince.

1913, *A Midsummer Night's Dream*
Germany; directed by Hans Neumann; Werner Krauss as Bottom; 50 mins.

This film is notable for having inspired one of the first censorship ratings: "Forbidden for Juveniles." Puck and Oberon are transformed into sexy femmes fatales, with Oberon being played by an exotic Russian ballerina named Tamra. Robert Hamilton Ball, the expert on Shakespearean silent films, describes Puck's tongue as "loll[ing] from a lascivious mouth."

1916, *King Lear*
USA; Frederick B. Warde as Lear; 43 mins. Available on video.

According to Rothwell, this film reveals "an acting style from a lost world. Warde was a ham; he's absolutely glorious here. He was one of those nineteenth-century Shakespeareans who could play every role with ease." The film triumphed over the technical difficulties of the day with an incredible battle scene filmed in New Rochelle, New York.

1920, *Hamlet;* the Drama of Vengeance

Germany; directed by Svend Gade; Asta Nielsen as Hamlet; Eduard von Winterstein as Claudius; Mathilde Brandt as Gertrude; Lilly Jacobssen as Ophelia; Heinz Stieda as Horatio; 78 mins.

Asta Nielsen plays a Danish princess who, for political reasons, has been raised as a boy. But this *Hamlet* is neither a joke nor a spoof: Gade was convinced that Hamlet's secret gender was the enigma behind the play. Hamlet's gender is the motive behind "his" seemingly incomprehensible abuse of Ophelia and his excessive attachment to Horatio, who supplies the love interest. Regarded by critics as the finest *Hamlet* of the silent era, it's also one of the first Shakespearean films to depart from the established text and reinterpret the play. Film scholars regard this *Hamlet* as the cinema's equivalent of German Expressionistic painting and a precursor of the *Hamlet*s of Olivier (1948) and Tony Richardson (1966).

1922, *Othello*

Germany; directed by Dimitri Buchowetzki; Emil Jannings as Othello; Werner Krauss as Iago; 93 mins. Available on video.

An avant-garde film of the German Expressionist school.

The Modern Age—Sound Films

*I*ncluding silent films, spoofs, burlesques, offshoots, videos, television performances, filmed ballets, opera and stage productions, documentaries about the staging of plays, and modern adaptations of Shakespeare's plots, there are roughly fifteen hundred Shakespearean films. But that figure drops to thirty-three if you count only straight English-language versions of the plays—that is, those which adhere to the original text. Strictly speaking, there is no such thing as pure Shakespeare on film—all Shakespearean movies are necessarily adaptations, since in translating one medium into another the director reshapes the material to the demands of the camera. What works on stage is not always effective on screen.

1929/1966, *The Taming of the Shrew*
USA; directed by Sam Taylor; Mary Pickford as Kate; Douglas Fairbanks as Petruchio; 68 mins.

Today this film is primarily known for its notorious screen credit "By William Shakespeare, with additional dialogue by Sam Taylor." (Rothwell and Melzer provide a different version, in *Shakespeare on Screen,* in which the credit reads "With additional dialogue by William Shakespeare"—a droll touch unappreciated by serious-minded critics.) Apparently, the producer Laurence Irving tried to dissuade Taylor from sharing screen billing with the Bard, but Taylor insisted: "Well, I did the stuff, didn't I?" Later, Irving overheard one salesman say to another: "Sure, we're making *The Taming of the Shrew,* but we're turning it into a *cah-medy.*" Like Taylor and Burton thirty-seven years later, Pickford and Fairbanks play their roles with extraordinary vigor; in one scene they go at each other with whips. This is an extremely condensed version of the play, running only 68 minutes. It was rereleased in 1966 with a soundtrack and music.

1935, *A Midsummer Night's Dream*
USA; directed by Max Reinhardt and William Dieterle; Ian Hunter as Theseus; Veree Teasdale as Hippolyta; Victor Jory as Oberon; Anita Louise as Titania; Mickey Rooney as Puck; Olivia de Havilland as Hermia; Jean Muir as Helena; Ross Alexander as Demetrius; Dick Powell as Lysander; James Cagney as Bottom; Hugh Herbert as Snout; Joe E. Brown as Flute; 132 mins. Available on video.

Shakespeare as a Warner Bros. extravaganza: an orgy of Mendelssohn, tulle, and gossamer. The Athenian forest is Oz with fairies instead of Munchkins. Rather than a unified drama, Reinhardt's *Dream* is a confusing floor show. Although Shakespeare presents multiple plots, he at least manages to make them all cohere. The different groups of characters seem to have wandered in from other sets on the Warner Bros. lot: the lovers are coeds from a 1930s college movie, the artisans slapstick

With head bandaged and whip in hand, Douglas Fairbanks takes a break from swashbuckling his way through *The Taming of the Shrew* (1929).

vaudevillians, and the fairies from a musical spectacular. Worse, none of the principals knows what to do with Shakespearean verse. De Havilland has an unfortunate tendency to wail and whine, while Rooney's Puck is a manic Huck Finn with a laugh that's both boyish and sinister, *and* unbelievably irritating. The movie's divergent moods suggest that its two directors couldn't decide whether it was an exploration into the subconscious or a sentimental Victorian valentine: high art or Hollywood?

1936, *Romeo and Juliet*

USA; directed by George Cukor; Norma Shearer as Juliet; Leslie Howard as Romeo; John Barrymore as Mercutio; Basil Rathbone as Tybalt; Edna May Oliver as Nurse; 126 mins. Available on video and occasionally shown on television and in revival houses.

A very decorative and decorous picture, in which the thirty-five-year-old Norma Shearer plays the thirteen-year-old virgin, with the forty-year-old Leslie Howard as her sixteen-year-old Romeo. One wonders if Howard is playing Romeo, or if Romeo is just another passionless Howardian hero. His Romeo is Ashley Wilkes in tights. Howard was third choice for the role; Clark Gable, aged thirty-four, was first, and the twenty-eight-year-old Olivier second. (Curiously, Olivier, who went on to make the greatest Shakespeare films of all time, rejected the offer, saying that Shakespeare wasn't conducive to film.) Barrymore, however, is at his best as the mercurial Mercutio.

1936, *As You Like It*

Great Britain; directed by Paul Czinner; Laurence Olivier as Orlando; Elisabeth Bergner as Rosalind; Henry Ainley as the exiled Duke; 97 mins. Available on video and occasionally shown on television.

Olivier makes a handsome Orlando in his Shakespearean film debut, but everything else about this movie, especially Bergner (the director's wife), is dreadful. The critic John Trewin sums it up best: "What do I remember? . . . a flock of sheep, another flock of sheep."

1944, *Henry V*

Great Britain; directed by Laurence Olivier; Olivier as Henry V; Freda Jackson as Mistress Quickly; Nicholas Hannan as Exeter; Esmond Knight as Fluellen; Felix Aylmer as the Archbishop of Canterbury; Robert Helpman as the Bishop of Ely; Robert Newton as Pistol; Frederick Cooper as Nym; Roy Emerson as Bardolph; Max Adrian as the Dauphin; music by William Walton; 137 mins. Widely available on video.

Olivier designed this film for people who believed that "Shakespeare was not for the likes of them," and it remains one of the most likable

Shakespearean movies ever made. It has a robust "we can lick 'em" swagger—not surprising, since it was made at the request of Winston Churchill in an effort to boost war morale in 1943. All the guts and glory, myths, and clichés about patriotism come vividly to life. The English are portrayed as manly, stouthearted, and true, the French (read Nazi) as dandified and ridiculous.

Henry V was filmed just before D-Day, when horses and equipment were scarce. But Olivier turns this into an advantage. He wanted not a naturalistic portrayal of war but an idealized image of how a medieval battle appears in our mind's eye. The colors of the battlefield are brighter and more vivid than in a dream, and the arrows of the spirited yeomen soar with balletic precision.

Olivier takes his cue from the Prologue, in which the Chorus invokes a "Muse of fire" that will transform the "wooden O"—the bare stage—into the battlefield of Agincourt: "Can this cockpit hold the vasty fields of France?" The Chorus's question is answered as Walton's magnificent score swells in the background. *Henry V* begins with a panoramic view of London—its sky a rarefied blue, the Thames silvery pure—which narrows down to the Globe playhouse, where a performance is about to begin. All the picturesque color of Elizabethan life is here: the orange sellers, the bustling groundlings, and the bumbling actors. This is the age not as it was in history but as it exists in our fantasies.

The film opens with Olivier as Richard Burbage, the actor who originally played Henry V. His smile is fixed, his acting style wooden; he speaks in the faltering yet declamatory manner of the self-conscious actor. But as the play-within-the-movie progresses, something extraordinary happens. Our involvement deepens and the Muse of fire quickens, the Globe becomes the globe itself: the stage disappears, the setting grows increasingly naturalistic, and the actor *playing* Henry *becomes* Henry. And to show that our imagination needn't be confined to reality, the film bursts through the constraints of realism, ending with a brilliant tableau set at the French court, a dream kingdom straight out of an illuminated manuscript. At the end, the scene returns to the Globe, suggesting that our imaginations must inevitably return to earth.

1948, *Hamlet*

Great Britain; directed by Laurence Olivier; Olivier as Hamlet; Eileen Herlie as Gertrude; Basil Sydney as Claudius; Felix Aylmer as Polonius; Jean Simmons as Ophelia; Norman Wooland as Horatio; Terence Morgan as Laertes; music by William Walton; 152 mins. Available on video.

This is a movie about which this viewer can't make up her mind. At one viewing, it seems very good; at another, it seems terrible. And Olivier can't seem to decide what sort of Hamlet he wants to portray. Despite all those publicity shots of a languid Olivier as a Nordic blond, he is surprisingly athletic and vigorous, particularly in the spectacular final dueling scene (a ten-minute sequence that took fourteen days to shoot). But for all his wit and intellect, Olivier's *Hamlet,* as the movie's portentous—and reductive—opening statement declares, is still about "a man who cannot make up his mind." And, despite Olivier's much-vaunted athleticism, the movie is surprisingly static. Olivier seems to associate Hamlet's melancholy with fatigue, and in the "To be, or not to be" scene, which *should* be the movie's high point, he sounds as if he has already decided *not* to be. The critic Robert Brustein wrote: "Olivier's idea of introspection was to hood his eyes, dentalize his consonants, and let the camera circle his head like a sparrow looking for a place to deposit its droppings."

The movie has certainly had its share of complaints. For one thing, Olivier presents a severely cut version of the play. Gone are Fortinbras and Rosencrantz and Guildenstern. The absence of this famous duo, the Tweedledum and Tweedledee of Shakespeare, leaves a void in the play that to those who know it well is unforgivable. Detractors also dismiss the movie's heavy-handed psychoanalytic overtones. Having just finished reading Ernest Jones's *What Happens in Hamlet,* Olivier was seized with the then-novel idea that the son's lust for the forbidden mother was the key that unlocked the Hamlet enigma.

Still, the black-and-white film is visually stunning, the stark emptiness of the sets highlighting Hamlet's intense isolation. Practically every scene takes place within the castle walls, and the camera lens becomes Hamlet's perspective as the viewer is led through long, empty corridors. In what Olivier would call "the longest-distance love scene on record," Hamlet glimpses Ophelia 150 feet away, a faroff vision of lost joy. At times, however, the movie seems overly mannered and self-conscious, and the director's hovering presence, like that of the Ghost, is palpably felt in almost every scene.

1948, *Macbeth*

USA; directed by Orson Welles; Welles as Macbeth and Narrator; Jeanette Nolan as Lady Macbeth; Edgar Barrier as Banquo; Dan O'Herlihy as Macduff; Roddy McDowall as Malcolm; Keene Curtis as Lennox. Welles made two versions: the original runs 105 minutes; the revised, 86.

Macbeth for those in a hurry. The play is one of Shakespeare's shortest, yet Welles still pares the action to the bone. Everything happens at lightning speed; unfortunately, Macbeth's transformation from thane to thug happens too quickly to be convincing. As usual, Welles was working on the brink of financial and emotional disaster, and it shows. But the opening Witches sequence, shot in clouds of mist, is effectively chilling: one of the Weird Sisters slowly forms a grotesque clay figure of Macbeth upon which she then viciously plunks a golden crown. This one gesture changes the play from the tragedy of a man torn by inner impulses to the story of a man trapped by external forces. Macbeth's transformation becomes too facile, and the movie lacks a sense of his inner torment and his deepening sense of doom.

Admittedly, *Macbeth* is supposed to be dismal, but Welles's version is relentless, his sets drab and colorless. When Duncan, upon visiting the Macbeths, remarks, "This Castle has a pleasant seat," we can only stare at the screen in amazement. Are we missing something? The film is also audibly confusing, the Scottish brogue that Welles insisted his actors use (he thought it made their voices deeper) distracting.

Jeanette Nolan, a radio actress, is incapable of creating the gestures and movements that would individualize her character. Her Lady Macbeth is the generic power-mad woman. Moreover, as a couple, Welles and Nolan are entirely unconvincing, and they lack the erotic intensity that would explain their *folie à deux*. Perhaps Welles's first choice, Tallulah Bankhead, or even his second, Agnes Moorehead, would have provided the allure to convince us that a man would kill his king for the woman he loved.

Finally, Welles just doesn't look right for the part. According to the actor, the problem might be his nose: "For all normal uses, my nose is quite pleasant. . . . It stopped growing, however, when I was about ten years old. Thus, it is violently unsuitable for roles such as Lear, Macbeth, and Othello."

1952 (completed), 1955 (released), 1992 (re-released), *The Tragedy of Othello, the Moor of Venice*

Morocco/Italy; directed by Orson Welles; Welles as Othello and Narrator; Michael MacLiammòir as Iago; Suzanne Cloutier as Desdemona; 91 mins.

In contrast to his *Macbeth,* which was filmed in twenty-three days, Welles's *Othello* took four years to make—and it is a much better movie. Welles freely adapts from the Shakespearean original: the movie opens with Desdemona and Othello's funeral procession as Welles's sonorous voice narrates from Cinthio's *Hecatommithi,* Shakespeare's Italian source for the play. The movie is thus framed like a romantic tale: "There was once in Venice a Moor, Othello. . . ."

Ever under financial and emotional duress, Welles brilliantly improvised to fit necessity; and one of the most effective scenes, Iago's murder of Roderigo, was filmed in a Turkish steam bath because the actors' costumes weren't delivered on time.

1953, *Julius Caesar*

Great Britain; directed by Joseph L. Mankiewicz; Marlon Brando as Mark Antony; James Mason as Brutus; Louis Calhern as Caesar; Edmund O'Brien as Casca; John Gielgud as Cassius; Greer Garson as Calpurnia; Deborah Kerr as Portia; 90 mins. Available on video.

The presence of Gielgud and Brando merges England and Hollywood and their respective acting styles. As the Shakespearean film expert Roger Manville points out, "Brando shouted his lines in spurts of eloquence without regard to rhythm. But at the same time the more traditional Shakespeare style was allowed to be present in the masterly delivery of John Gielgud as Cassius."

Inspired by Orson Welles's 1936 Mercury Theatre production, the director, Mankiewicz, and producer, John Houseman, wanted the black-and-white film to allude to the events of fascist Germany. Mankiewicz sets up a parallel between the Nazi followers and the Roman plebeians.

The crowd's frighteningly uniform response to Antony's funeral oration in the forum was supposed to sound like *"Sieg Heil."* According to Manville, the mob's roars were recorded at a baseball game. Still, the film is as static as the play. Peggy O'Brien of the Folger Shakespeare Library said, "First you have a bunch of men sitting around talking about what they are going to do, and then you have a bunch of men sitting around talking about what they did."

1954, *Romeo and Juliet*
Great Britain/Italy; directed by Renato Castellani; Laurence Harvey as Romeo; Susan Shentall as Juliet; Flora Robson as Nurse; Mervyn Johns as Friar Lawrence; Sebastian Cabot as Father Capulet; Aldo Zollo as Mercutio; John Gielgud as Prologue and Epilogue; 138 mins. Available on video.

Don't bother. See the Cukor or the Zeffirelli.

1955, *Richard III*
Great Britain; directed by Laurence Olivier; Olivier as Richard III; Cedric Hardwicke as King Edward IV; Claire Bloom as Lady Anne; John Gielgud as Clarence; Ralph Richardson as Buckingham; music by William Walton; 138 mins. Available on video.

For newcomers to Shakespeare, this is the place to begin. The language is accessible; the acting could scarcely be better. It's said that all subsequent portrayals of Richard are based on this version and that Olivier was the first to exploit the villain's comic potential. At times he virtually flirts with the camera, which seems to prance along with him as he minces through the castle in pursuit of his victims. And though Richard is droll—almost camp—he is also chilling. Just after he's crowned, all feigned modesty is whisked aside, and he quickly slides down a bell rope to the ground; then, like a bat on wing, with a swoop of his black cloak, he forces a stunned Buckingham to kneel before him. Olivier is typically superb at quick changes in atmosphere and mood. As he lets the two doomed princes ride on his humpback, he is jolly Uncle Richard. But, all in a flash, avuncularity vanishes, and for a moment we catch a heart-stopping glimpse of the unsmiling murderer beneath the mask.

1957, *Throne of Blood (The Castle of the Spider's Web)*

Japan; directed by Akira Kurosawa; Toshiro Mifune as Taketoi Washizu (Macbeth); Isuzu Yamada as Asaji (Lady Macbeth); Minoru Chiaki as Hoshiaki Miki (Banquo); 105 mins. Available on video.

Peter Hall and Peter Brook claim that this is the finest Shakespearean film ever made, but for the newcomer it might prove intimidating. The English Shakespeare is hard enough, but a Japanese version seems daunting. Some people find the exotic location, the unfamiliar costumes, and the subtitles a barrier to understanding, and at times the film seems interminable.

First, don't expect traditional Shakespeare. *Throne of Blood* is not *Macbeth* with Oriental actors, but an entirely new drama inspired by Shakespeare's plot. Not one word of Shakespeare's text is used. Kurosawa is particularly drawn to Noh drama, which depends upon stylized, mimelike gestures to convey meaning. To inspire the cast, Kurosawa made masks for each actor representing his or her character, and the facial expressions of the actors throughout the film possess a masklike immobility—taut, stark, and strangely inhuman. Asaji's almost expressionless face, whitened by makeup, suggests the bleached countenance of Death itself.

1964, *Hamlet*

USSR; directed by Grigori Kozintsev; script by Kozintsev based on a translation by Boris Pasternak; Innokenti Smoktunovsky as Hamlet; Anastasia Vertinskaya as Ophelia; V. Erenberg as Horatio; Yuri Tolubeyev as Polonius; Michail Nazwanov as Claudius; Elza Radzin-Szolkonis as Gertrude; music by Dimitri Shostakovich. 148 mins. Available for rental through Corinth Films, 34 Gansevoort Street, New York, NY 10014; 800-221-4720.

Kozintsev's films are hard to come by, but if you ever get the chance to see one, consider yourself lucky. Both his *Lear* and his *Hamlet* were translated by Boris Pasternak and are set to scores by Dimitri Shostakovich. Kozintsev's aim was to translate Shakespeare's verbal poetry into visual imagery that is so strong, subtitles are all but unnecessary. The movie begins not with the sentry scene but, as Kozintsev noted in his diary, with images of stone, iron, fire, and sea. The opening shot shows Elsinore with waves crashing against massive castle walls. Accompanied by Shostakovich's romantic score, Hamlet is seen from a distance riding toward the castle to attend his father's funeral. As Bernice Kliman points out in her study *Hamlet: Film, Television and Audio Performance,* "the last slow shot of the drawbridge and the moat enclosing Hamlet effectively image Denmark as a prison. . . . To complete this image of Denmark Kozintsev has Hamlet, after his death, carried to freedom, beyond the drawbridge."

Kozintsev and Pasternak refuse to see Hamlet as the traditional vacillating weakling; Smoktunovsky is a mature man and a hero. (His "To be, or not to be" conveys more passionate intelligence in Russian than Olivier's does in Shakespeare's English.) The movie ends with a voice reciting Sonnet 74, because, as Kozintsev explained, he believed that *Hamlet* expressed the "force of noble aspirations."

1966, *The Taming of the Shrew*
USA/Italy; directed by Franco Zeffirelli; Richard Burton as Petruchio; Elizabeth Taylor as Kate; Michael York as Lucentio; Michael Hordern as Baptista; Cyril Cusack as Grumio; 122 mins. Available on video.

This belongs to the bodice-ripping school of Shakespeare. Burton seems blasé, but Taylor is in top form: shouting, throwing objects, snarling, she mocks her own off-screen image with gusto. The legendary screen lovers play out their own splashy love affair in period costumes, and we're never allowed to forget that we're watching a movie with two famous film stars (just as in the original play we are never allowed to forget that Kate and Petruchio are playing a part).

Despite its raucous energy, Zeffirelli's *Taming* is tame, a noncontroversial "sex romp" with lots of broken crockery and high-spirited taming (for example, Burton chases Taylor across the roof and they land in a feather bed). It's obvious that Kate and Petruchio are attracted to each other from the start, so there's no hint of the underlying cruelty that makes the play so controversial today. Zeffirelli's Shakespeare films lack intellectual bite, but they're flamboyant spectacles that make few demands on the viewer. In his appeal to public taste, he probably comes closest to Shakespeare's own intention.

1967, *Chimes at Midnight*

Spain/Switzerland; directed by Orson Welles; Welles as Falstaff; Margaret Rutherford as Mistress Quickly; Jeanne Moreau as Doll Tearsheet; Fernando Rey as Worcester; John Gielgud as Henry IV; Ralph Richardson as Narrator; 119 mins.

Chimes at Midnight is a combination of four plays: *Henry IV, Part 1* and *Part 2; Henry V;* and *The Merry Wives of Windsor.* Along with Charles Foster Kane, Falstaff is the part Welles was born to play. Instead of focusing on the rise and succession of Prince Hal, Welles concentrates on the defeat and death of Falstaff. In places it's laugh-out-loud funny: the Gad's Hill robbery scene, where a white-robed Welles, like an obese Druid (his ample girth was padded further for the role), cavorts nimbly through the forest at midnight, is pure magic. But the movie is, according to Welles, a dark comedy, the story of the "betrayal of a friendship," and its tone is elegiac and troubling.

This was Welles's favorite part, and it's not hard to imagine that he saw himself as a Falstaffian figure: a fat spendthrift who frittered away money and genius and who was ultimately neglected and betrayed.

1968, *Romeo and Juliet*

Great Britain/Italy; directed by Franco Zeffirelli; Olivia Hussey as Juliet; Leonard Whiting as Romeo; John McEnery as Mercutio; Pat Heywood as Nurse; Michael York as Tybalt; Milo O'Shea as Friar Laurence; Laurence Olivier as Prologue and Epilogue; 139 mins. Available on video.

Although critics complained that the two young stars couldn't speak Shakespearean verse, the chemistry between the fifteen-year-old Hussey and the seventeen-year-old Whiting captures the essence of Shakespeare's play, which is about youth, desire, and death. Indeed, it was teenagers, not Shakespeare lovers, who made this the most financially successful Shakespearean film ever made. Hussey and Whiting act their parts with an awkward grace, and Hussey has the serene innocence of Botticelli's Flora. The lavishly beautiful sets turn this film into a Renaissance painting, and it's so sensuous, you can almost smell the fruit in the Veronese marketplace.

1968, *A Midsummer Night's Dream*

Great Britain; directed by Peter Hall; Ian Richardson as Oberon; Judi Dench as Titania; Ian Holm as Puck; Paul Rogers as Bottom; David Warner as Lysander; Michael Jayston as Demetrius; Diana Rigg as Helena; Helen Mirren as Hermia; 124 mins. Available on video.

Peter Hall's "mod" *A Midsummer Night's Dream* was hailed as groundbreaking when it came out in 1968. Determined to make Shakespeare relevant, he gave the play the forced casualness characteristic of the period. Puck's potion is more like an LSD trip than a magic elixir, and the actors adopt the obligatory "natural look" of the sixties. Indeed, they seem as if they would be more at home on Carnaby Street than in an Athenian forest. The heroines, sporting Elizabethan miniskirts, peer out from behind lanky hair; the heroes, wearing Nehru jackets over their doublets, look like ungainly adolescents in Beatle wigs. Judi Dench plays Titania nude with green body paint, and Oberon is sexually menacing in the manner of a rock star.

While Hall desperately tries to escape Reinhardt's nineteenth-century romanticism, the movie suffers from sixties earnestness. Unflattering closeups of the young lovers reveal their smudged faces, camera shots are disjointed, and at times the complexions of Oberon and Titania take on hues never found in nature. Hall wants us to enter an opium dream where anything can happen, and he emphasizes the play's intense eroticism, particularly the bestiality between the newly transformed Bottom and Titania. The underlying message here is not Shakespeare's but the dictum of the sixties, "Do your own thing."

1969, *Hamlet*

Great Britain; directed by Tony Richardson; Nicol Williamson as Hamlet; Marianne Faithfull as Ophelia; Judy Parfitt as Gertrude; Anthony Hopkins as Claudius; Gordon Jackson as Horatio; Michael Pennington as Laertes; 117 mins. Available on video.

Along with Peter Hall's *Dream,* Richardson's *Hamlet* represents a new, experimental attitude toward Shakespeare characteristic of directors during the 1960s and 1970s. This *Hamlet* is about the generation gap: how the older generation continually betrays the trust of the younger. Williamson's Hamlet is a high-strung graduate student who, upon arriving home, suddenly sees through the rank hypocrisy of his parents' generation. He *knows* that the Establishment in Denmark is rotten. In this morally pretentious production, Claudius and Gertrude are portrayed as bourgeois sensualists who lie in bed gorging on delicacies. The relationship between Laertes and Ophelia is frankly incestuous, showing how the sexual corruption of the court has infected even the innocent.

1970 (U.S. release), *King Lear*

USSR; directed by Grigori Kozintsev; script by Kozintsev based on a translation by Boris Pasternak; Yuri Yarvet as Lear; Elza Radzin as Goneril; Galina Volchek as Regan; Valentina Shandrikova as Cordelia; Oleg Dal as Fool; Karl Sebris as Gloucester; Vladimir Emelianov as Kent; Regimentas Adomaitis as Edmund; Leonard Marzin as Edgar; music by Dimitri Shostakovich; 140 mins. Available for rental from Corinth Films, 34 Gansevoort Street, New York, NY 10014; 800-221-4720.

Kozintsev's *King Lear* is not only triumphant filmmaking; it stretches our understanding about what it means to be human. The Russian critic Alexander Anikst points out that unlike so many other *Lear*s, this production does not adopt any doctrinal viewpoint; neither existentialist, experimental, nor Marxist, it simply and eloquently recounts Shakespeare's tragedy about the human condition.

Yuri Yarvet is an Estonian actor who learned Pasternak's Russian translation phonetically for the role. Unlike Scofield's Lear in Peter Brook's 1971 film, Yarvet's is a scrawny child-man, a crank, and a tyrant. The film is a response to the cruelty of Brook's *Lear,* which Kozintsev had seen on the London stage, and the Russian director emphasizes everything Brook omits, creating a film about the redemptive power of love and endurance. Kozintsev's *Lear* is filled with extraordinary images, the most memorable being that of Cordelia's corpse hanging from a castle wall. Yet even here, amid carnage and desolation, Kozintsev insists upon humanity's almost miraculous capacity for survival. The movie ends with the Fool, who *does* survive, playing the flute while peasants begin clearing away the wreckage of war.

*P*aul Scofield as Lear in Brook's 1971 movie version.

☙

1971, *King Lear*

Great Britain; directed by Peter Brook; Paul Scofield as Lear; Irene Worth as Goneril; Susan Engel as Regan; Anne-lise Gabold as Cordelia; Patrick Magee as Cornwall; Cyril Cusack as Albany; Tom Fleming as Kent; Alan Webb as Gloucester; Robert Lloyd as Edgar; Ian Hogg as Edmund; Jack MacGowran as Fool; Barry Stanton as Oswald; 137 mins. Available on video.

In the eighteenth century, Nahum Tate rewrote *King Lear* to make it less depressing; in the twentieth, Peter Brook adapted it to make it more so. A *King Lear* for our time, this version omits any expressions of sympathy, redemption, and justice. The scene in which Regan's servants bathe Gloucester's eye sockets with egg whites is retained visually but not verbally. Brook's Edmund, unlike Shakespeare's, dies unrepentant. This *Lear* is Shakespeare translated into Beckett: King

In contrast to Brook's *Lear,* Kozintsev's emphasizes the redemptive power of suffering.

❧

The Museum of Modern Art/Film Stills Archive

and Fool wait for a salvation that never arrives. Filmed in Lapland, the movie depicts a wide expanse of monochromatic blankness, a world in which we are all strangers and outcasts, wandering in the night.

The bleakness of the landscape contrasts with stunning, surrealistic film techniques, which are used to show the dizzying heights imagined by the blind Gloucester or Lear's hallucinatory escape into madness. Brook has a genius for capturing the human face *in extremis*.

1971, *Macbeth*

Great Britain; directed by Roman Polanski; Jon Finch as Macbeth; Francesca Annis as Lady Macbeth; Terence Baylor as Macduff; script by Kenneth Tynan and Polanski; 140 mins. Available on video.

"I am in blood / Stepped in so far, that, should I wade no more, / Returning were as tedious as go o'er." Macbeth is just the vehicle for Polanski's taste for gratuitous violence. It's bloody and it's about a repressive regime, much like the one he suffered under as a child in Poland. Produced in conjunction with Playboy Pictures and Kenneth Tynan, it was hailed as "the Nude *Macbeth*" when it first appeared.

Finch and Annis make an attractive couple, not the usual middle-aged tyrant and his harpy wife ("They're Young, They're in Love, They're the Macbeths," read the headline in *The New York Times* review). As Tynan, the film's literary director, remarked, "It makes no sense to have Macbeth and Lady Macbeth performed by 60-year-old menopausals. It's too late for them to be ambitious." In fact, these Macbeths could be the upwardly mobile couple next door scheming to scale the corporate ladder. Lady Macbeth's beauty convinces us that she could seduce a man to kill a king, and from one scene to the next, Finch's face hardens, tracing his transformation from hero to Hitler.

Polanski's *Macbeth* reveals politics and power as a meaningless game. The team itself doesn't matter—players move from one side to the other with ease. Ross consoles Lady Macduff, but then shortly returns with hired killers to murder and rape the members of her household. That done, he defects to the other side and soothes the victim's husband.

The director can't resist a chilling non-Shakespearean touch at the end. Just after Macbeth's head has been hoisted on a pole, the tyranny of his reign at last over, the scene shifts to Duncan's other son, Malcolm, as he "accidentally" comes upon the three Weird Sisters. . . .

1972, *Antony and Cleopatra*

Great Britain/Spain; directed by Charlton Heston; Heston as Antony; Hildegard Neil as Cleopatra; Eric Porter as Enobarbus; 160 mins. Available on video.

A bland and disheartening production that is full of histrionics but very little feeling. Heston is clearly out of his league with Antony, one of Shakespeare's most ambiguous characters. Heston probably thought the role of Antony was made for him—another battered warrior; Ben-Hur with a midlife crisis. If you don't know Shakespeare's play, the movie is mediocre. If you do, it's terrible.

1984, *King Lear*

Great Britain; made for Granada Television; directed by Michael Elliot; Laurence Olivier as King Lear; Leo McKern as Gloucester; Diana Rigg as Regan; Dorothy Tutin as Goneril; Anna Calder-Marshall as Cordelia; John Hurt as Fool; Colin Blakely as Kent; Robert Lindsay as Edmund; David Threlfall as Edgar; 158 mins. Available on video.

Olivier's *Lear* is more about domestic upheaval than cosmic disintegration, and the relationship between father and daughter makes this interpretation very moving. This king, unlike the traditional, more formal Lears, saunters into the room of state arm-in-arm with Cordelia, joking and laughing. Her terse rejoinder to his demand that she exhibit her love is seen by him as the ultimate betrayal, and even when he banishes her, Olivier reveals that his rage is mingled with love. This is not a stern and terrible tyrant, but a petulant old man.

As usual, Olivier quickly establishes character through gesture and costume. Lear's vanity is evoked by fastidiously precise gestures, perfectly coiffed hair, and well-tailored attire. His increasingly disheveled appearance reveals his growing indifference to material concerns and his deepening sense of powerlessness. The final scene is searing: no longer king, but a frail old man, he carries his daughter's corpse in his arms, tears scalding his cheeks as he weeps for his folly. When he sees the rope-burns on his daughter's neck, he goes mad with rage and dies.

It's hard to tell whether you're moved by Lear or by the seventy-five-year-old Olivier. Reportedly the entire crew wept after the final scene. Lear is one of the most taxing roles ever written, and Olivier, who knew he was dying, must have pushed himself to the limit in this, his last Shakespearean role.

1985, *Ran*

Japan; directed by Akira Kurosawa; Tatsuya Nakadai as Hidetora (Lear); Akira Terao as Taro; Jinpachi Nezu as Jiro; Daisuke Ryu as Saburo; Mieko Harada as Lady Kaede; 160 mins. Available on video.

Ran means "chaos" in Japanese, and Kurosawa's film, like Shakespeare's *Lear*, is about cosmic, social, and political anarchy. A slow-motion epic set in sixteenth-century Samurai Japan, *Ran* begins with a sweeping panorama that reveals the extent of Hidetora's empire. The high-pitched Oriental flute renders the landscape portentous and inscrutable, and the viewer is thrown at once into an alien culture in which everything is remote and mesmerizing.

Goneril, Regan, and Cordelia have become three sons, Taro, Jiro, and Saburo. The movie begins with the Lear figure, Hidetora, giving away his kingdom to his eldest son, Taro. The brutal civil war that ensues is the result not only of Hidetora's division of the kingdom but of the cruelties he has perpetrated throughout his reign. Brother fights brother, and both turn against their father in primordial anarchy, an Armageddon between the forces of good and evil. Choreographed meticulously to uncanny Oriental music, the battle sequences turn brutality into a bloody ballet. *Ran* is not simply about an old man lost in the night: the fate of the moral world hangs in the balance.

Kurosawa's meticulousness and fidelity to period detail are legendary. In *Ran* he insisted on having genuine sixteenth-century Japanese medicines in the cabinets, although they were never opened to the audience's view.

1989, *Henry V*

Great Britain; directed by Kenneth Branagh; Branagh as Henry; Derek Jacobi as Chorus; Judi Dench as Mistress Quickly; Ian Holm as Fluellen; Paul Scofield as the Dauphin; 138 mins. Available on video.

This film and Olivier's 1944 version dramatically illustrate how a Shakespeare play can inspire two completely different interpretations. Like Olivier, Branagh wanted audiences to discover that Shakespeare can be accessible and "real," but unlike his predecessor, he wasn't concerned with medieval pomp and pageantry. Branagh's Agincourt is a picture of real war, with all its filth and gore, not the stylized choreographical precision of Olivier's battle.

What Jan Kott said of Hamlet is also true of Henry: he is a "sponge" that can absorb the cultural ideals of any age. In an interview after the movie was released, Branagh said, "It cannot be a simplistic interpretation. He [Henry] is complex. I want people to come away and think 'Christ, who was he?' "—a view that seems much closer to Shakespeare's contradictory portrait of Henry than Olivier's. "Olivier's *Henry* was about a decisive and resolved king in a shining armoured image," said Branagh. "My film is about a less certain journey toward maturity. This *Henry* is about a young monarch burdened with guilt because his father unlawfully seized the crown."

Branagh's appearance is deceptive. While he looks like a stocky adolescent, he speaks in the weary voice of a man who has seen—and lived through—everything. He abhors the barbarism and futility of war and yet he gives a heart-stirring Saint Crispin's day speech, in which every word rings true. Branagh's Henry shrewdly knows that he needs to inspire his men at the final hour, so the speech is part theatrics, part propaganda; still, he means every word of it.

One of *Henry V*'s most thrilling moments takes place, not on the battlefields of France, but in a film studio. The movie begins with the Chorus (superbly played by Derek Jacobi) initiating the action with the flick of a light switch and illuminating an empty set with cinematic paraphernalia and discarded medieval props strewn about. Then, as the music's pace quickens, he hastens to a massive door, and, dramatically flinging it open, magically thrusts us into medieval England. If in Shakespeare's age all the world was a stage, in our own electronic era the world has become a movie set.

1990, *Hamlet*
USA; directed by Franco Zeffirelli; Mel Gibson as Hamlet; Alan Bates as Claudius; Glenn Close as Gertrude; Ian Holm as Polonius; Helena Bonham-Carter as Ophelia; Paul Scofield as the Ghost; 135 mins. Available on video.

This is basically Mel Gibson's *Hamlet*—it's not *Hamlet* the psychodrama, but a revenge movie that happens to be set in Denmark with a hero named Hamlet. The scene on the parapets of Elsinore between the Ghost and Hamlet reveals what we tend to forget: Shakespeare, no less than Hitchcock, is a master of suspense. Here, the story is all. Even though we've seen the play a hundred times, we still wait anxiously for the Ghost to appear. And his triple intonations—"List, list, O, list!" and "O, horrible! O, horrible! Most horrible!"—still have the power to send chills down your spine.

As usual, the love interest is not between Hamlet and Ophelia but between mother and son. This film's closet scene, which is unusually erotic and romantic, must be one of the most torrid ever performed. Close makes an intriguingly innocent Gertrude. She seems even more naive than Ophelia, and unlike the typical portrayal of the lusty, middle-aged queen in décolletage, she is girlish in her newfound love for Claudius, which appears quite genuine and not at all calculated. Her remarriage is hasty and foolish, proving she's just as reckless as her son.

You should have no trouble understanding this *Hamlet*, and it's a good place for those uncomfortable with Shakespeare to begin. Zeffirelli's first priority is to tell an engrossing story, not to give a faithful rendering of the text, and to that end, he freely cuts and adds scenes and speeches. The movie opens with old King Hamlet's funeral, which, though not included in the play, provides background information to anyone unfamiliar with the plot.

If Olivier's Hamlet is athletic and languid, Kozintsev's a mature scholar, and Williamson's a nervous intellectual, Gibson's is purely visceral. It doesn't sound at all literary when this Hamlet says, "Now could I drink hot blood."

Spoofs, Offshoots, Parodies, and Adaptations

*T*hey say that behind every movie there lurks a Shakespeare play. Some, like *Harry and Tonto, Godfather III,* and *The Dresser,* overtly draw upon Shakespearean plots and motifs. Others include Shakespearean interludes: in *The Goodbye Girl,* Richard Dreyfuss does a hilarious imitation of a gay *Richard III,* and in *Morning Glory,* Katharine Hepburn recites "To be, or not to be." More recently, *Star Trek VI: The Undiscovered Country* contains Shakespearean allusions, including the subtitle, which is from *Hamlet,* Act III, scene 1. Then there are offshoots, or spinoffs, such as Paul Mazursky's *Tempest;* the cult sci-fi movie *Forbidden Planet,* also based on *The Tempest;* and *Joe Macbeth,* which loosely translate a Shakespearean plot into a radically different setting. Shakespeare even makes his way onto the small screen: in 1986, viewers may have been startled to turn on "Moonlighting" to find Maddie and David transformed into Kate and Petruchio in Shakespeare's battle of the sexes, *The Taming of the Shrew.* Scriptwriters generously gave credit to "William Budd Shakespeare" for supplying the concept.

The sheer range and abundance of Shakespearean adaptations on stage, television, and screen make you realize that Shakespeare, like his own Falstaff, is not only brilliant in himself, but inspires brilliance in others.

1942, *To Be or Not to Be*
In this American black comedy set in occupied Poland, the oddly matched Jack Benny and Carole Lombard play Joseph Tura (the "world's greatest Shakespearean actor") and his wife, Maria, the Polish

"Oh, Yorick . . ."
(Jack Benny)

version of the Lunts. Furious at the Nazis for invading Poland and thus ruining his career, Tura takes revenge by turning his troupe into spies and his dramatic gifts into espionage. The funniest part of the movie is Benny's classic glare when he spies a member of the audience (Robert Stack) sneaking out in the middle of what he considers his greatest scene. Directed by Ernst Lubitsch. Using the same title, Mel Brooks remade the film in 1983 with himself and Anne Bancroft playing Joseph and Maria Tura.

1947, *A Double Life*
Written by Ruth Gordon and Garson Kanin, *A Double Life* stars Ronald Colman as Anthony John, an actor who tries to boost his flagging career by playing serious roles. Having landed Othello, he confuses the on-stage part with his reality. Also starring Shelley Winters, the movie won Colman an Academy Award for Best Actor. Interspersed throughout this film are scenes from *Othello* itself, and critics point out that it contains some of the finest Shakespearean acting on film. The play-within-a-play device in which the private lives of actors mirror their on-stage roles is genuinely Shakespearean in its self-conscious theatricality.

1953, *Kiss Me Kate*
Best known for its music by Cole Porter (including the famous "Brush Up Your Shakespeare"), this breezy, lovely movie is based on Porter's musical, which, in turn, was based on *The Taming of the Shrew.* The backstage warfare of a theatrical couple (Kathryn Grayson and Howard Keel) parallels their onstage roles as Kate and Petruchio.

1955, *Joe Macbeth*
A *film noir* updated *Macbeth* with the thane as a mobster whose wife nags him to the top. This Duncan, "the Duke," is a Mafia chieftain who is not so much assassinated as "rubbed out." Paul Douglas and Ruth Roman star as Joe and Lilli Macbeth.

1956, *Forbidden Planet*
This sci-fi epic combines typically fifties' preoccupations with Freud, robots, and space travel with a Shakespearean plot. Prospero's desert-

ed island has become the planet Altair-4—not surprising, considering that outer space was to the fifties what the sea was to the Elizabethans: uncharted territory, vast and unconquered. "We are such stuff as dreams are made on," says Shakespeare's Prospero; Prospero can control his imagination, but dreams in *Forbidden Planet* are uncontrollable "Monsters from the Id" that emanate from a mad scientist's unconscious desire to kill his daughter's boyfriend. Walter Pidgeon stars as Dr. Morbius, with Anne Francis as a nubile teenager, scantily clad in futuristic space gear.

1961, *West Side Story*

Set on the Upper West Side of New York with a fire escape replacing the familiar balcony, *West Side Story* captures all the heated urgency of Shakespeare's tragedy of love *Romeo and Juliet*. Separated by rival street gangs instead of feuding families, Tony (Richard Beymer) and Maria (Natalie Wood) are modern versions of Shakespeare's misunderstood teenagers. Juliet's yearning "Come, night! come, Romeo!" speech is translated musically into the ardent lyricism of "Tonight." With music by Leonard Bernstein and choreography by Jerome Robbins, the movie is an American classic. The impact of *West Side Story* was so explosive that, as Rothwell notes, Zeffirelli's famous *Romeo and Juliet* was just as inspired by the modern musical as by the Shakespeare play.

1963, *The Bad Sleep Well*

Kurosawa's first and least known Shakespeare adaptation is loosely based on *Hamlet* and is set in a modern corporation. The Hamlet figure is a businessman who marries the boss's daughter in a plan to take revenge on the executives who drove his father to suicide. With Toshiro Mifune, Tokashi Kato, Mosayuki Mori, and Tokashi Shimura.

1965, *Shakespeare Wallah*

This Anglo-Indian movie was the first successful product of the Ismail Merchant–James Ivory team. The title's juxtaposition of Hindi and English is misleading, for this elegiac movie is, to use E. M. Forster's word, about the failure of East and West to "connect." The film is about Shakespearean actors who "stayed on" after the British voluntarily left India in 1947. Once celebrated, they now play to dwindling and indifferent audiences who are interested only in their native arts and cinema. On a general level, the film is about the conflict between high art and popular entertainment. More specifically, it's about Anglo-Indian relations; Shakespeare, the icon of British culture and imperialism, is now just another British import—like cricket, only not as popular. The Bard has become irrelevant and superfluous, outlasting his usefulness, like the British who remain behind. The film, as its title suggests, is about the attempt to graft one culture onto another, but the failure to do so suggests one culture's inability to understand the other. Encased within the movie's larger concerns is a love story between a young British actress (Felicity Kendal) and an upper-caste boy (Shashi Kapoor), who, like Romeo and Juliet, and their respective nations, are destined to remain apart.

1973, *Theatre of Blood*

Famous Shakespearean actors (Diana Rigg, Michael Hordern, Milo O'Shea, and Coral Browne) assemble for this wonderfully self-conscious travesty that sends up both Shakespeare and horror movies. Edwin Trueheart (Vincent Price) plays an aging Shakespearean thespian who, with his daughter Edwina (Rigg), seeks to avenge himself on every critic who has ever panned him, using methods described in Shakespeare's plays.

1973, *Catch My Soul: Santa Fe Satan*

Directed by Patrick McGoohan, *Catch My Soul* is a rock-opera adaptation of *Othello,* along the lines of *Godspell* and *Jesus Christ Superstar,* set in a cult commune in the New Mexico desert. Richie Havens plays a hippie Othello, with Season Hubley as Desdemona in granny glasses. Iago (Launce le Gault) is the Santa Fe Satan of the movie's subtitle. According to Rothwell and Melzer, *Catch My Soul* closely follows the original play, leaving much of its poetry intact. The hip Othello recites the famous "Put out the light" speech as he strangles his wife, only in this adaptation it's accompanied by the throbbing strains of electronic rock.

1982, *A Midsummer Night's Sex Comedy*

Set in 1900, this pastoral comedy with Mia Farrow, José Ferrer, Mary Steenburgen, and Julie Hagarty is Woody Allen's homage to Ingmar

Bergman and Shakespeare. Allen combines his own sexual lunacy with Shakespeare's fantastical vision of love and yearning. Three couples wander through the forest one moonlit night, and their pairings and confusions ultimately lead them back to their true desire—and themselves.

1982, *Tempest*

Bored and disillusioned with urban life, a New York architect, Philip (John Cassavetes), flees to a deserted Greek island with his teenage daughter, Miranda (Molly Ringwald). On the way, he meets up with Aretha (Susan Sarandon), a free-spirited drifter who plays the sprite Ariel to Philip's Prospero. Raul Julia is the earthy Kalibanos, who in one memorable line tries to seduce Ringwald with the tempting offer: "I got TV in my cave! Sony Trinitron!" At the end, Philip, like Prospero, returns to reality in Manhattan/Milan. The movie ends with his giving Aretha her freedom, his reunion with his wife, Antonia (Gena Rowlands), and the reconciliation characteristic of Shakespeare's final romance.

1983, *The Dresser*

A *King Lear* of the dressing room, from Ronald Harwood's play. Albert Finney plays the aging Shakespearean actor-manager deferentially known only as "Sir"; Tom Courtenay is Norman, his loyal dresser and "fool." An itinerant Shakespearean tragedian of the old school, Sir plays Othello one night, Lear the next—a state of affairs that only increases his befuddlement. In the movie's most poignant and funniest scene, the confused tragedian, left alone to dress for Lear, is found by Norman happily applying blackface. Sir possesses all the tragic dimensions of fallen royalty, and as Shakespeare's tragedy is about the madness and death of a king, *The Dresser* is about the decline and fall of a great actor when he no longer knows his lines—or, like Lear, who he is.

1987, *King Lear*

The cast is as incongruous as the movie. Directed by Jean-Luc Godard, with Peter Sellars as William Shakespeare Junior the Fifth; Norman Mailer as himself (Godard's first choice was Richard Nixon); Woody Allen as Mr. Alien, a film editor; Molly Ringwald as Cordelia; Burgess

Meredith as Don Learo, and Godard himself as the Professor. The venture, which reportedly began as a publicity stunt with Godard signing the contract on a napkin at the Cannes Film Festival, ended in disaster. Boasting that he never read the original *Lear* (which hardly seems credible, since he uses lines from the text), Godard creates a meta-Lear for the postmodern generation, with Cordelia dictating Learo's experiences to Shakespeare Junior. Writing in the *Times Literary Supplement,* David Nokes commented, "Not the least of the privations of a nuclear winter would be the threat that its culture would be comprised of films like this."

1990, *Men of Respect*

The blasted heath becomes gangland Bronx, the three Weird Sisters a gypsy family in a tenement. This transcription is unintentionally laughable in its literalness: Macbeth is Mike Battaglia (John Turturro), Banquo is Bankie Como (Dennis Farina), and Macduff (Peter Boyle) is Matt Duffy. Just before Macbeth is about to blow away a bunch of mobsters, he screams out, "Not o' women born, are ya?" Mrs. Battaglia, described by the *Hollywood Reporter* as a "pushy broad," prods her husband to kill the Padrone, played by Rod Steiger.

Shakespeare and Television

*I*n an old *Twilight Zone* episode, Shakespeare returns to the twentieth century and becomes a television writer. This idea is closer to truth than fantasy, for the Elizabethan popular theatre was in many respects similar to television today. Like television, Elizabethan playhouses offered fare that was mixed in quality: one day *Hamlet;* the next, a slapstick farce in a jog-trot rhythm by Anonymous. Moreover, both encompass the widest possible audience, composed of regular viewers ranging from the illiterate to the sophisticated. From what we know about Shakespeare, he wrote for the masses, and so he would have been comfortable with the prodigious output required for television production. The dramatist, unlike the poet, couldn't sit waiting for inspiration from a reluctant Muse. At the peak of his career, Shakespeare wrote at least two to three plays a year, certainly the equivalent of a television season.

At the beginning of a new genre, whether film, television, or compact discs, practitioners tend to turn to the classics. Innovation seems to breed a desire to return to the past, as if pioneers wanted to start a new tradition by drawing on an old one. Shakespearean productions were a staple of television's early years. In 1937 Shakespeare debuted on television with a BBC production of *Henry V,* an abridged adaptation transmitted to the few Londoners lucky enough to own home receivers. In the United States, according to *Shakespeare on Screen*, the first televised Shakespeare production was a live broadcast of a performance of Verdi's *Otello* at the Met in 1948.

During the Golden Age of television, from 1950 to 1965, U.S. producers were confident of a market for classical drama and quality performances. Those were the days of *Philco Television Playhouse, Kraft Television Theatre, Studio One,* and *Hallmark Hall of Fame.* From 1953

*T*he frequency of advertising on commercial TV can have a shattering effect on viewers who are expected to move from Lear railing against society to a distressed man in pajamas complaining of acid indigestion. John J. O'Connor, TV critic of *The New York Times,* put it best in a review praising Trevor Nunn and Jon Scoffield's *Antony and Cleopatra,* which aired in January 1975:

> At the end of the play, the split-second cut from the dead Queen of Egypt in robes of state to a middle-aged man in pyjamas announcing "That's my last cough" would have been incredible, except by then, after three hours of similarly ludicrous hijinks, not even a plug for an asp antidote would have been surprising.

*R*oyal jealousy; accused queen dies; schoolboy prince felled by psychosomatic illness; princess abandoned in diapers as chief of mission is eaten in animal encounter. But younger generation heals all wounds as king repents and maternal statue walks off pedestal.

—SHELDON ZITNER,
the plot of *The Winter's Tale*
in the style of a *TV Guide*
capsule summary

to 1960, the Hallmark Card Company sponsored some of the finest Shakespeare on television, including George Schaefer's 1954 *Macbeth,* with Maurice Evans and Judith Anderson, and the splendid 1960 *The Tempest,* with Evans as Prospero, a radiant Lee Remick as Miranda, Roddy McDowall as Ariel, and an earthy Richard Burton as Caliban.

Tom Shales, television critic of *The Washington Post,* recalls, "When I was a kid I saw Hallmark's *Richard II* and it made a fabulous impression on me." But except for star showcases such as Kevin Kline's Hamlet on PBS and Mel Gibson's on film, today's young viewers will remember little of the Bard from television. As television programming becomes more rigid and scheduling tighter, any deviations from the half-hour or hour time slot are usually reserved for sports events and Oscars, certainly not Shakespeare, whose unwieldy plots are difficult to fit between a sitcom and the nightly news.

"There's never going to be much Shakespeare on television, I'm afraid," says Shales. "Straight Shakespeare won't play for a mass audience. Television has weaned audiences away from Shakespeare's plays onto more utilitarian forms, topical dramas and documentaries. We want modern kings and queens."

The BBC
Time/Life Series

After this, and the Henry VI*s, we've
only got twelve more plays to go.*

—*BBC OFFICIAL,*
at a press showing of one of the
plays in the Shakespeare series

*I*n 1978 the BBC and Time/Life Inc. made television history by announcing their grand scheme to televise all thirty-six Folio plays in six years. Their mission: to deliver Shakespeare to a mass market—those who might not attend a stage performance but wouldn't mind flipping the knob on their TV sets. If viewers won't come to Shakespeare, why not bring Shakespeare to them?

Seven years after the last play aired in the United States, critics still debate the artistic merit of the series as well as the broader question of whether a Shakespeare play can become a TV script. In retrospect, *The Shakespeare Plays* was (and still is) a mixed blessing. The series brought Shakespeare to millions of people who wouldn't know Titus from Timon, and for some, it must have been a revelation that Shakespeare wrote plays to be seen, not texts to be read. On the other hand, the project's sense of its own importance, coupled with the BBC's acute awareness that it was presenting Shakespeare to people who were unfamiliar with him, placed a hefty burden on directors who must have felt that the future of Shakespeare's reputation began and ended with their own particular effort. Thus, many of the productions patronized the viewer with their bland characterizations and simplistic, if earnest, interpretations. The overall dullness of most of the productions—with some crucial exceptions—only reinforced the public's impression that Shakespeare was, is, and always will be a bore, whether on television or off.

Because the interpretations were essentially aimed at and marketed to educational institutions, the BBC stressed that they were to be "definitive"—a meaningless concept when dealing with the vagaries and multiplicity of choices within a text. In fact, the desire to respect the text, while allowing for some necessary editorial cuts, led to pedantic productions without subtlety and verve. To ensure uniformity of presentation, the BBC, to use the critic J. C. Bulman's term, adopted a "house style" that would cover all the plays, from the early comic farces to the late tragedies. Moreover, the productions had to be no-nonsense Shakespeare, that is, no Juliets on mini-bikes or Lears in Masaratis: "The brief was no monkey-tricks, and I think monkey-tricks are at least fifty percent of what interesting direction is about," said Jonathan Miller, who took over from Cedric Messina as producer of the series.

*M*ost colleges and public libraries own the complete series, so the plays are easily come by. You may also want to try a video store, since some carry them.

Except for two of the plays (*Henry VIII* and *As You Like It*), all were to be filmed in the studio, not on location. (The performers, mostly stage veterans, accustomed to the responsive presence of a live audience, must have felt disheartened, as if playing to an empty house—which, in fact, they were.) The plays also had to be set during the period Shakespeare intended, such as ancient Rome or Greece, or else during Elizabethan England. As Bulman points out, the plays were presented from the Elizabethan perspective "in matters moral, political, religious, and aesthetic." If a director wanted to deviate from an orthodox interpretation, he or she had to do so within the context of the play, not with gimmicks or the hindsight of a modern perspective. Thus Jack

Gold's *The Merchant of Venice* subtly suggested Antonio's lonely passion for Bassanio, which is only suggested in Shakespeare's play. His melancholy pinched face lights up in hopeful eagerness whenever Bassanio appears, and at the end, when the many newlyweds go off to bed, he remains solitary, shrouded in darkness.

Yet, as several critics noted, after two decades of reckless Shakespearean novelties, the BBC's conservatism could be refreshing. For instance, unafraid of charges of sexism, *The Taming of the Shrew,* with John Cleese as Petruchio (inspired choice!), presented the play from the orthodox Elizabethan perspective: as a straightforward argument for the male position in the social hierarchy, an interpretation that, if uninspiring, was neither cruel nor smug.

Most inflammatory of all, however, was the British Equity's refusal to hire American actors, a surprising move considering the nationality of their co-sponsors, Time/Life. Once again, British and American tensions over each nationality's ability to "do" Shakespeare flared. Led by Joseph Papp, U.S. actors staged a letter-writing campaign against the veto, but to no avail: all the accents heard on the series were pure BBC.

Despite the absence of American voices, the casting could scarcely have been better: Derek Jacobi as Hamlet, Claire Bloom as Gertrude, John Cleese as Petruchio (who, surprisingly, underplayed the comic aspects of the play), and Anthony Quayle as Falstaff, to name a few. The critic Susan Willis points out that few Americans could have been aware of the BBC's inventive casting, which consisted of familiar but non-Shakespearean stars. The kick British viewers got out of seeing their sitcom favorites incongruously popping up in a Shakespeare play (as if Ed Asner were to suddenly appear as the Porter in *Macbeth*) was a pleasure denied American audiences.

All in all, *The Shakespeare Plays* series was a success in that it introduced viewers to such obscure plays as *Henry VI, Part I, Part II,* and *Part III, Henry VIII, Coriolanus, All's Well that Ends Well,* and *Measure for Measure*—all of which, unexpectedly, offered the most intelligent, well-thought-out interpretations of the lot. The general consensus seemed to be that the more esoteric the play, the better the production—perhaps because directors didn't feel obliged to comply with audience expectations and the viewer didn't know what to expect.

The series, which began in England in March 1978 with *Romeo and Juliet* (considered the worst), ended in May 1984 with *Love's Labour's Lost* (one of the best). The long-range effects of the series probably surpassed even the BBC's grandiose goals: *The Shakespeare Plays* transformed the manner in which Shakespeare is taught in high schools and colleges. Now on videocassettes, the series is a staple of almost every college's media center and will probably be imprinted on future generations as definitive. In years to come, when today's adolescents think about Othello—if they ever do—they'll visualize him with Anthony Hopkins's face.

Highlights of the Series

✤ One of the few plays to break with the BBC policy, *Love's Labour's Lost* is set in an age other than that of Elizabeth. Director Elijah Moshinsky apparently decided that the play's witty elegance was more suited to the eighteenth century, the age of Watteau and Fragonard than that of Elizabethan England, which tends to remind one of wool. Although many of the play's jokes are confined to a particular period, and are thus unintelligible, the production manages to suggest humor without confusing the audience with superfluous verbiage. With Jennie Agutter as Rosaline, British comedienne Maureen Lipman as the Princess, and David Warner as Armado.

✤ Directed by Don Taylor, the usually vapid *The Two Gentlemen of Verona,* with its improbable and distasteful denouement, is transformed into a Renaissance confection. A treat of a production, it is more courtly masque than drama: it has fat-cheeked putti, flowing fountains, stylized love debates, golden-haired maidens, and blind winged Cupids. The production is so artificial that, paradoxically, you believe in its truth.

✤ When viewed as a historical miniseries instead of primitive Shakespeare, the rarely seen *Henvy VI* trilogy makes for exciting fare. Critic and novelist Peter Ackroyd wrote: "It extracted enjoyment from a play which otherwise would have been sheer torture to watch."

✤ Anthony Quayle as Falstaff is a rotund delight in *Henry IV, Part I* and *Part II,* and Tim Piggott-Smith (*Masterpiece Theatre* aficionados will remember him from the celebrated series *Jewel in the Crown*) makes a wonderfully impulsive Hotspur.

❖ *The Winter's Tale* is one of the most moving plays in the series. Its final moments, when the inert statue tentatively steps off its pedestal and comes to life, reawakens, no matter how many times the viewer has seen it, the original sense of wonderment and joy. The austere yet surrealistic sets complement this beguiling play.

❖ Rosemary Leach as Emilia in *Othello* plays the part with a homely good nature, and yet at the end, when she confronts her husband and her own unconscious complicity, she takes on a tragic dimension worthy of Desdemona's.

❖ Moshinsky's *All's Well That Ends Well* is an intelligent and sophisticated production aimed at the literate viewer. Celia Johnson makes an excellent Countess of Rossillion. As usual Moshinsky's sets are painterly, and this one resembles the subtle lights and serene textures of an interior by Vermeer. The quiet set blends with a play that appeals to the mind rather than the emotions.

❖ One of the more intriguing questions about the series was the manner in which *The Merchant of Venice* would be presented. Its producer, Jonathan Miller, its director, Jack Gold, and the actors who played Shylock and Jessica, Warren Mitchell and Leslie Udwin, are all Jewish. Critics wondered how the Semitic moneylender would be portrayed: sentimental victim, jokey Jew, or crafty villain. Mitchell did a superb job of combining all these elements, displaying the complexity of Shylock's character.

The Flops

❖ Replacing accuracy with dramatic sense, director Alvin Rakoff cast a fourteen-year-old as his tragic heroine in *Romeo and Juliet*. This choice was based on the patronizing assumption that viewers couldn't respond to tragedy unless they saw a real child committing suicide. The unfortunate actress looked perfect but couldn't act. "She does have limitations—which you're bound to have at that age—but at least she is fourteen," admitted Rakoff, as quoted by J. C. Bulman.

❖ As critic and professor H. R. Coursen noted in his review of *Antony and Cleopatra:* "Faced with this production, we as teachers can only exclaim, 'Believe it or not, this is a great play!' "

❖ *The Tempest:* What should astonish is merely boring—the most leaden play in the series.

Sources

Select Bibliography

*T*here are no footnotes in *The Friendly Shakespeare* because, useful as they can be, they seemed out of place in a book that is meant to be read for pleasure. I have acknowledged my debt to others in the text, but I have especially benefited from the works of S. Schoenbaum, whose *Shakespeare's Lives* provided much of the information in my chapter on Baconian ciphers, and it's a mine of information about Shakespeare-inspired lunacies. The credits and information about availability for films are from Kenneth S. Rothwell and Annabelle Henkin Melzer's *Shakespeare on Screen*. In compiling this select bibliography, I have included my major sources as well as suggestions for further reading.

One final word about literary criticism: critical analysis can complement reading or seeing a play, but remember that critics write for each other, and to the nonspecialist their works may seem airless, unintelligible, and occasionally ludicrous in the way they strain at arcane meanings in the text. Note, too, that all the major editions of the individual plays usually have excellent introductions. The works cited below are among the most accessible.

Barber, C. L. *Shakespeare's Festive Comedy: A Study of Dramatic Form in Relation to Social Custom.* Princeton: Princeton University Press, 1959, 1972.

Barton, John. *Playing Shakespeare.* London: Methuen, 1984.

Boyce, Charles. *Shakespeare: A to Z: The Essential Reference to His Plays, His Poems, His Life and Times, and More.* New York: Facts on File, 1990.

Bradbrook, Muriel. *The Growth and Structure of Elizabethan Comedy.* London: Peregrine Books, 1963.

Bradley, A. C. *Shakespearean Tragedy.* New York: St. Martin's, 1985.

Brook, Peter. *The Empty Space.* Harmondsworth: Penguin, 1972.

Brown, John Russell. *Shakespeare's Dramatic Style.* London: Heinemann, 1970.

Brown, Ivor, and George Fearon. *Amazing Monument: A Short History of the Shakespeare Industry.* London: Heinemann, 1939.

Bulman, J. C., and H. R. Coursen. *Shakespeare on Television: An Anthology of Essays and Reviews.* Hanover, N.H., and London: University Press of New England, 1988.

Burgess, Anthony. *Nothing Like the Sun: A Story of Shakespeare's Love Life.* New York: W. W. Norton, 1964.

Deelman, Christian. *The Great Shakespeare Jubilee.* London: Michael Joseph, 1964.

Elsom, John, ed. *Is Shakespeare Still Our Contemporary?* London: Routledge, 1989.

Fraser, Russell. *Young Shakespeare.* New York: Columbia University Press, 1988.

Foster, Donald W. *"Master W.H. R.I.P."* Publications of the Modern Language Association of America, January 1987, pp. 42–54.

Fowler, Gene. *Good Night, Sweet Prince.* New York: Viking, 1944.

Goddard, Harold C. *The Meaning of Shakespeare.* Chicago: University of Chicago Press, 1973.

Grebanier, Bernard. *The Great Shakespeare Forgery: The Audacious Career of William Henry Ireland.* New York: W. W. Norton, 1965.

Hankey, Julie. *Othello: Plays in Performance.* Bristol Classical Press, 1987.

Gurr, Andrew, *Playgoing in Shakespeare's London.* Cambridge, England: Cambridge University Press, 1987.

———. *The Shakespearean Stage 1574–1642.* 3rd ed. Cambridge, England: Cambridge University Press, 1992.

Gurr, Andrew, and John Orrell. *Rebuilding Shakespeare's Globe.* New York, Routledge, 1989.

Harbage, Alfred. *Shakespeare's Audience.* New York: Columbia University Press, 1941.

Hill, Errol. *Shakespeare in Sable: A History of Black Shakespearean Actors.* Amherst: University of Massachusetts Press, 1986.

Holderness, Graham, ed. *The Shakespeare Myth.* Manchester, England: Manchester University Press, 1988.

Honigmann, E. A. J. *Myriad-Minded Shakespeare: Essays, Chiefly on the Tragedies and Problem Comedies.* New York: St. Martin's, 1989.

Jackson, Russell, and Robert Smallwood, eds. *Players of Shakespeare: Essays in Shakespearean Performance by Players with the Royal Shakespeare Company.* 2 vols. Cambridge, England: Cambridge University Press, 1986, 1988.

Jorgens, Jack J. *Shakespeare on Film.* Bloomington: Indiana University Press, 1977.

Kliman, Bernice W. *Hamlet: Film, Television and Audio Performance.* Rutherford, N.J.: Fairleigh Dickinson University Press, 1988.

Knight, G. Wilson. *The Wheel of Fire.* Rev. ed. London: Methuen, 1940.

———. *The Imperial Theme.* London: Methuen, 1954.

Kott, Jan. *Shakespeare Our Contemporary.* New York: W. W. Norton, 1974.

Greene, Gayle, Ruth Carolyn Lenz Swift, and Carol Thomas Neeley, eds. *The Woman's Part: Feminist Criticism of Shakespeare.* Urbana: University of Illinois Press, 1980.

Greg, W. W. *The Editorial Problem in Shakespeare: A Survey of the Foundations of the Text.* Oxford: Clarendon Press, 1951.

Londré, Felicia Hardison. "A Great Feast of Languages: In This Wide and Universal Theatre." Keynote Address given at symposium "Shakespeare in the Non-English-Speaking World." Shakespeare Globe Centre, Los Angeles, April 20, 1991.

Marder, Louis. *His Exits and His Entrances: The Story of Shakespeare's Reputation.* Philadelphia: Lippincott, 1963.

Mortimer, John. *William Shakespeare: The Untold Story.* New York: Delacorte, 1978.

Ogburn, Charlton. *The Mysterious William Shakespeare: The Myth and the Reality.* New York: Dodd, Mead, 1984; rev. ed., E.P.M. Publications, McLean, Virginia, forthcoming.

Olivier, Laurence. *On Acting.* New York: Simon & Schuster, 1982.

———. *Confessions of an Actor.* New York: Simon & Schuster, 1986.

Partridge, Eric. *Shakespeare's Bawdy.* New York: Routledge, 1991.

Penguin Critical Studies. Brief guides to individual plays that provide scene-by-scene analysis and final summary.

Ribner, Irving. *The English History Play in the Age of Shakespeare.* New York: Barnes and Noble, 1957; Princeton: Princeton University Press, 1965.

Rothwell, Kenneth S., and Annabelle Henkin Melzer. *Shakespeare on Screen: An International Filmography and Videography.* New York: Neal Schuman Publishers, 1990.

Rubinstein, Frankie. *A Dictionary of Shakespeare's Sexual Puns and Their Significance.* Basingstoke, England: Macmillan, 1989.

Saccio, Peter. *Shakespeare's English Kings.* New York and Oxford: Oxford University Press, 1977, 1981.

Sales, Roger, ed. *Perspectives on Shakespeare.* 2 vols. London: British Broadcasting Corporation, 1984, 1985.

Schoenbaum, Marilyn, ed. *A Shakespeare Merriment: An Anthology of Shakespearean Humor.* New York and London: Garland Publishing, 1988.

Schoenbaum, S. *William Shakespeare: A Compact Documentary Life.* Oxford: Oxford University Press, 1977.

———. *Shakespeare's Lives.* Oxford: Clarendon Press, 1971; rev. ed., 1991.

Sher, Antony. *Year of the King: An Actor's Diary and Sketchbook.* Proscenium Publishers, 1987.

Spencer, Theodore. *Shakespeare and the Nature of Man.* 2nd ed. New York: Macmillan, 1961.

Taylor, Gary. *Reinventing Shakespeare: A Cultural History, from the Restoration to the Present.* New York: Weidenfeld and Nicolson, 1989.

Tillyard, E. M. W. *The Elizabethan World Picture.* New York: Macmillan, 1944.

Weimann, Robert. *Shakespeare and the Popular Tradition in the Theater: Studies in the Social Dimension of Dramatic Form and Function.* Baltimore: Johns Hopkins University Press, 1978.

Wells, Stanley, ed. *Nineteenth-Century Shakespeare Burlesques.* 5 vols. London: Diploma Press, 1977–78.

———. *Shakespeare: An Illustrated Dictionary.* Oxford: Oxford University Press, 1986.

Wilson, Edwin, ed. *Shaw on Shakespeare.* New York: Dutton, 1961.

PERIODICALS AND NEWSLETTERS

Shakespeare on Film Newsletter. Department of English, Nassau Community College, Garden City, New York. (Incorporated by *Shakespeare Bulletin,* Department of English, Lafayette College, Easton, Pennsylvania 18042).

The Shakespeare Newsletter. Issued by Department of English, University of Illinois at Chicago Circle.

Shakespeare Quarterly. Official publication of the Shakespeare Association of America. Washington: Folger Shakespeare Library.

Shakespeare Survey: An Annual Survey of Shakespearean Study and Production. Cambridge: Cambridge University Press; New York: Macmillan.

Personal Interviews

Anderson, Dame Judith: May 12, 1990; May 14, 1990

Ashcroft, Peggy: November 22, 1990

Branagh, Kenneth: July 31, 1991

Brustein, Robert: February 23, 1990

Church, Tony: December 3, 1990

Dutton, Charles: February 17, 1992

Garber, Marjorie: February 16, 1991

Gurr, Andrew: September 26, 1990; November 16, 1991; June 26, 1992

Hamilton, Charles: July 2, 1992

Kott, Jan: March 30, 1990

Lange, Ted: May 24, 1992

Love, Keith: Letter to author, January 31, 1990

Marder, Louis: September 22, 1990

Marowitz, Charles: December 21, 1989

Melchior, Ib: January 16, 1990

O'Brien, Peggy: January 9, 1990

Ogburn, Charlton: February 11, 1990

Pringle, Roger: October 20, 1990; December 12, 1990; Letter to author, December 13, 1990

Rothwell, Kenneth S.: February 11, 1991

Schoenbaum, Sam: December 17, 1989

Sellars, Peter: March 15, 1990

Shales, Tom: February 24, 1992

Suchet, David: July 27, 1991

Sweet, George Elliott: April, 5, 1990

Taylor, Gary: December 13, 1989; December 15, 1989

Thomas, John: February 4, 1991

Tolaydo, Michael: January 14, 1990

Waller, John: August 26, 1990

Wanamaker, Sam: June 5, 1990

Wells, Stanley: February 12, 1991

Index